CONSEQUENCES OF CAPITALISM

CONSEQUENCES OF CAPITALISM

Manufacturing Discontent and Resistance

Noam Chomsky and Marv Waterstone

Haymarket Books
Chicago, IL

Published in 2021 by
Haymarket Books
P.O. Box 180165
Chicago, IL 60618
773-583-7884
www.haymarketbooks.org
info@haymarketbooks.org

ISBN: 978-1-64259-263-4

Distributed to the trade in the US through Consortium Book Sales and Distribution (www.cbsd.com) and internationally through Ingram Publisher Services International (www.ingramcontent.com).

This book was published with the generous support of Lannan Foun-dation and Wallace Action Fund.

Special discounts are available for bulk purchases by organizations and institutions. Please call 773-583-7884 or email info@haymarketbooks.org for more information.

Cover photograph, *Occupied Freeway (BLM Series)*, Oakland, CA, Summer 2020, © Jorge Gonzalez. Cover design by Rachel Cohen.

Printed in the United States.

Library of Congress Cataloging-in-Publication data is available.

2 4 6 8 10 9 7 5 3

CONTENTS

PREFACE

R ampant, seemingly endless wars, both hot and cold. Widespread and wide-ranging environmental catastrophe. Unparalleled levels of global wealth and income inequality. And, in response to these and other symptoms of system breakdown, increasingly repressive and authoritarian regimes, playing upon virulently divisive rhetoric. Conditions that characterize everyday life for billions on the planet at this moment. This book is based on a course that we have co-taught at the University of Arizona over the past three years that has attempted to connect this set of existential conditions to their underlying, systemic causes. The course has also endeavored to make these connections in ways that point to coalitional politics and efficacious actions.

The principal aims of the course, and now of this book, are to think about the predominant way society is organized socially, politically, economically, culturally, and then to make the theoretical, historical, and practical connections between that way of organizing society and the kinds of consequential outcomes that are produced by doing so. And secondly, by demonstrating the systemic structural underpinnings of these seemingly disconnected issues, we hope to provide a set of rationales for political cohesion and coalition among the numerous and diverse groups that are working toward economic, social, political, and environmental justice. Particularly as presented by the major mechanisms that shape widely shared worldviews, these phenomena almost always appear, on the surface, as though they are completely unrelated to each other. This predominant characterization is true even for practitioners and activists, and therefore rarely elicits the kinds of political cohesion and coalition that are necessary for effective, coherent, and progressive responses.

Clearly, a great deal has changed on the US and international political stage since we first offered the course in 2017, but our goal, over the past three years, has been to try to emphasize the continuities in the issues that are of concern to us. That is, while we are interested in reflecting on changing conditions, we are principally focused on contextualizing such change within a broad sweep of historical, political, economic, and social phenomena. We want to make these changes explicable and highlight their inherent connections, rather than simply leave them, as often is done, as unrelated and distinct events. We endeavor to illuminate some of the new forms and emphases these issues have taken over the past several years, but again in a manner that demonstrates their linkages and grounding in long-standing systemic and institutional frameworks.

We begin, both in the course and in this book, by asking a very basic question: How do we know what we think we know about the world? In this initial inquiry, we take up a set of questions that examine the ways in which people come to understand how the world works. This set of processes, usefully understood as the production, reinforcement, and changing of common sense, is a constant project. Those who are advantaged by the status quo are continually at work to make us understand that the way things are is the way things should be. And thus, the ways in which we understand the world are very much connected to the ways in which we interact with the world. We are also intent on elucidating the complex linkages between common sense and power. Here we take up the Gramscian notions of hegemony, the definition and role of intellectuals, and the ways in which the economy (broadly understood) and other dimensions of society interact to produce the varied experiences of everyday life for different classes and categories of people.

In the second chapter, we undertake an examination of what we think about as the predominant, current common sense in much (though not all) of the world. If, as we contend, common sense is a very useful notion for understanding how we think and understand the world, what is the current common sense? We, along with other analysts, call the prevailing common sense *capitalist realism*. We interpret this term to be not merely descriptive of the dominant political economic framework, but also to highlight proponents' additional assertion that there is really no meaningful alternative to organizing society along the lines of late-stage industrial state capitalism. Clearly, much of society, certainly US society but many other societies as well, is organized along these lines. This is the basic framework within which we will attempt to understand the resultant issues and consequences. Again, there have been substantial changes within and among the variants of late-stage capitalism over the past several years, and our assessment situates these changes within appropriate continuities and contexts.

In the third chapter, we begin to examine some of the more consequential effects that have resulted (as would be expected, we argue) from organizing societies along the lines of a capitalist realist political economy. We begin with the multipronged relationships between capitalism and the various historical and contemporary mechanisms that capitalists (and their vital partners within state systems) have used to spread this form of political economy around the globe. These processes have been known most commonly as colonialism or imperialism (in either their historical or neo- forms), and have often been accompanied by the often-necessarily related processes of militarism. In this chapter, we will think very carefully about how capital, when uninhibited by constraints against mobility, goes around the globe looking for the conditions that will maximize surplus value and profit. Historically (and contemporaneously as well), these have often included cheaper labor or resources, and/or more lucrative markets. More recently, alluring conditions have also included more desirable regulatory (e.g., environmental or labor), monetary, or fiscal environments to maximize profit accumulation. These adventures, quite often necessitating incursions on the prerogatives and sovereignties of others, have produced a long and bloody history and present, and a likely calamitous future.

In chapter 4, we move on to examine the most significant effects of the relationship between a capitalist political economy and the environment, which, we would argue, now constitute a second set of existential crises. While there are certainly variants of the abstract capitalist model, one persistent and typical tendency is to assess the planet as either storehouse (of needed resource inputs, including energy resources) and/or sink (for waste products of all kinds, due in large measure to a continually sought novelty, and the concomitant obsolescence of the old). As a consequence of this orientation, nature, as both inherent worth and utilitarian guarantor of sustainable life, must be subjected to the ruthless calculus of costs and benefits. In such evaluations anything that fails to maximize profits or minimize losses must be discounted, ideally to a value of zero. In combination with an intensifying focus on shorter and shorter time frames for a maximum return on investment, a competition-driven imperative to externalize all costs that do not contribute to the bottom line has produced the by-now exhaustive litany of environmental woes, including the climate catastrophe that now threatens life on the planet as we have known it.

In the subsequent chapter (chapter 5), we begin to examine the more mundane, everyday violence of capitalism in its present neoliberal, globalized, and financialized form. Though not necessarily as dramatic in some ways as militarism or environmental catastrophe, these quotidian issues are emblematic of the kinds of impacts that are being produced for billions of people in their everyday lives on the ground around the world. Beginning largely in the late 1970s and flourishing in the early 1980s (though the original ideas actually date back much further), especially in the US and UK, neoliberalism has been an ongoing project of elites to claw back the few gains made by other classes in the immediate aftermath of the Second World War. The central tenets include the elimination (or preferably the privatization) of government services of all kinds, an all-out assault on the ability of labor to organize, the massive deregulation of every segment of the economy, and the absolute faith in market-based principles to adjudicate all elements of social, political, cultural, and economic life. The results have been staggering levels of wealth and income inequality, the disappearance or significant shredding of even the most grudging social safety net provisions, the loss of the "commons" in virtually all sectors, and the truncation (ideally to zero) of public expectations for anything that might be provided by something called "society."

These then are three broad categories of consequences that we take up below: militarism (and threats of war and "terrorism"), environmental catastrophe, and the seemingly more mundane suite of neoliberal effects. But these phenomena produce reactions. Once these effects are out in the world, we need to think about the way in which social movements cohere around them, and demands for progressive change are asserted. But at the same time, we want to think about the ways in which elites (who are advantaged by maintaining or reinforcing the status quo) respond to those reactions. These are the matters that we take up in chapter six. Over the past several years (as in the many decades before), we have seen an enormous panoply of social movements for social, political, and economic justice: anti-austerity movements, environmental activism, human rights promotion (including expansions of the definition of "human" and the list of rights themselves), criminal justice reform, poverty elimination/reduction, and many others. One disheartening continuity has been the successful ability of elites to keep these movements separated from, and often, in fact, antagonistic to each other. One of our key objectives here is to demonstrate the fundamental linkages among these seemingly disparate issues, in order to provide the rationale and impetus for coalition and unity.

In the face of rising resistance, elites have been able to exploit present discontent in order to pit elements of society against each other. We also take up this side of the question in chapter six. Often this set of strategies is delivered in the guise of so-called populism (or nationalism, or patriotism, or nativism, etc.), in which blame for present conditions is placed on the most vulnerable segments of populations (immigrants, non-dominant communities, the old, the young, the differently abled, "deviants" from sexual or other norms), who are then relentlessly scapegoated for the sake of the "virtuous" and deserving elements of society. This has (at least) the twofold effect of vesting additional power in the hands of authoritarian "populists" who will protect the worthy from the unworthy, and of diverting attention and blame away from those in the society who really make the decisions that produce the unwanted consequences.

In the final chapter, we examine some concrete elements involved in working toward progressive change, as well as some of the obstacles that constrain those efforts. It is crucial to bear in mind, as we try to convey to students in our courses, that these issues and problems do have solutions. There are people working on answers and implementing them. Their work demonstrates that useful change can be accomplished, but also that there are barriers, almost always quite significant barriers. Many of these obstacles are institutional and built into the systems of power. As an important part of any remedial work, we have to try to understand these barriers, and configure ways to overcome them. Despite such impediments, however, strenuous attempts at remedies cannot be avoided.

That, then, is the arc of the book. We begin by examining how we think we understand the world: thinking about how the world is principally organized, at least for the purposes we want to talk about; some of the most crucial consequences of that organization; and then thinking about the ways in which movements organize around those kinds of impacts. Each chapter is composed of (rather lightly and somewhat amended) edited versions of the lectures we have given over the past three years, but relying principally on those we delivered in the spring of 2019. Reflecting their differing, though linked, intentions, the two parts of each chapter are quite distinctive stylistically. In the first part of each chapter (based on Waterstone's lectures), we endeavor to elaborate a theoretical, conceptual, and historical overview of the particular topic. The more formal style, therefore, generally elaborates this analytic and deliberately abstract emphasis. In the second part of each chapter (based on Chomsky's lectures), we present a set of quite concrete historical and contemporaneous illustrations to drive home the more abstract points. Here, the tone and style, driven by the grounded empirical nature of the material, take on a more narrative and conversational tenor. Though in the course these two components have actually comprised separate lectures, in our delivery of them, we have been able to point out their most important linkages quite explicitly. Based upon extensive feedback, for the more than one thousand students who have taken the course over the past three years, this combination and integration of content and style has proven to be both provocative and productive. At every opportunity, here, as we hope to broaden the circulation of these ideas beyond the classroom, we will repeat that approach of drawing out the connections between the two complementary parts of each chapter.

One final word about organization and content. In order to substantiate and reinforce the points about the necessity and possibility of progressive change, and to help relieve some of the doom and gloom of the lectures, in the most recent version of the course, we included twice-weekly visits (with two exceptions, when we only had one visitor in a particular week) from activists and practitioners working on the issues under discussion during that week. Some of these were local guests who visited the class in person; others were virtual visitors who came in electronically from around the country. As part of a section for each chapter on further resources (located all together at the end of the book), which will include all of the required and suggested readings for each chapter as well as a few key, additional references, we will also present a very brief overview of the presentation by each of our visitors, as well as links to their organizations. Again our sense, from student feedback, is that these visits accomplished our intended purpose of providing class participants with hope that change is possible, and with some entrée into that sphere of activity.

The younger generation in our courses, and those reading this book, are facing problems that have never arisen in human history, in all of history. Will the species survive? Will organized human life survive? Those questions cannot be avoided. There is no way to sit on the sidelines. If one takes that option, it is essentially making a choice for the worst. This book is our attempt to articulate what more efficacious actions might look like and how they might be undertaken.

Chapter 1

COMMON SENSE, THE TAKEN-FOR-GRANTED, AND POWER

Waterstone Lecture, January 15, 2019

How do we know what we think we know about the world? How do we navigate through our day-to-day lives, and how do we negotiate novel situations? In this first chapter, we are interested in taking up questions about the mechanisms involved in producing, reinforcing, and sometimes changing the interpretive processes through which people come to conclusions (sometimes correct, but often incorrect or inaccurate) about: (1) how the world *does* operate in specific circumstances; and (2) how the world *might* or *should* operate. While we begin this discussion at a somewhat abstract and general level, we are concerned throughout with thinking about such matters within the contexts that are of foremost interest to us; that is, in public social, political, and economic contexts rather than in predominantly private spheres of thought and activity. As a beginning shorthand, we will term what many people in a particular time and place believe *common sense*.

THE NOTION OF COMMON SENSE

"Central to the notion of common sense is that its truths need no sophistication to grasp, and no proof to accept. Their truth is agreed to by the whole social body, and immediately apparent to anyone of normal intelligence." This definition, from Kate Crehan's book (2016), includes a number of very slippery concepts, things that we should be very troubled by whenever we see them, things like "the whole social body," "anyone of normal intelligence," and things or ideas that we accept simply on their face without proof. All of those things should be alerts to us. But they are elements clearly of what we think we understand about the notion of common sense. In fact, that's part of how common sense works, through these kinds of unexamined, taken-for-granted mechanisms.

There are several different senses of common sense. The first one from Aristotle is that common sense is actually a sixth sense that organizes the other five senses and allows us to understand the world. In other words, we experience all kinds of sensory input, whether it's through hearing or through sight, smell, touch, or taste, but there is a sixth sense, which, according to Aristotle, allows us to integrate all of that and make things that come into our brain meaningful. That's one notion of common sense, a kind of mechanistic notion.

Second is what people in a particular time and place know about the world and how it works. Scale actually matters here; that is the closer you are, the more proximity you have to others, the more common is your common sense (at least as posited in this sort of framing), and the more distinguished from distant others. This notion is where we get a phrase like, "Well, it's only common sense. Of course that's how things operate." That's another sort of notion of common sense.

A third one is one that actually puts a normative valence on some common sense and gives it a kind of positive inflection. This notion of common sense makes it the equivalent of good sense. This variant is sometimes characterized as street smarts versus book smarts. You know what your gut tells you. We have many people who operate in society that way. This is where a phrase like "Use your common sense" is employed. In other words, "You know how the world works, right, so use your good sense."

Now let's turn to a formulation that characterizes all of this a little bit differently: British sociologist and social theorist Anthony Giddens and his notion of practical consciousness (1984). This is related to common sense. The first two of the framings of common sense just described (the Aristotelian notion and the notion of what everybody sort of knows about how the world works) are related to what Giddens thinks of as practical consciousness, which he describes as an accumulation of learned behavior for navigating the situations that confront us in our everyday lives. He calls it practical consciousness, and he distinguishes it from what he defines as discursive consciousness (1984).

When utilizing discursive consciousness, one must have an internal conversation that tells you how to operate in the world. You have to think about things very carefully. Practical consciousness doesn't work that way. You actually sort of know, under many circumstances, how to behave, what to expect, what will happen in the world if you behave a particular way, which is why last year I opened by yelling at people because it's not what we think we understand about a situation like this. It's not part of the decorum. It's unexpected.

But practical consciousness is rarely raised to this kind of discursive internal conversation level. This is essential. The fact that we don't have to think about every single thing we do and how we operate in the world is a very good thing. Otherwise, we would essentially be paralyzed. If we had to relearn every instance in which we operate in the world every day, we would in fact be constrained from behaving at all. So it's a good thing that much of what we do in our interactions is routinized in this way; that is, that it is, in fact, a practical rather than a discursive consciousness.

There are some circumstances where we become aware that we are operating in a rule-bound way. One of those circumstances is when we are in novel situations. For example, when we travel and come into settings where we don't know the rules. A couple of things happen then. If you've had this experience, you know this is the case. One thing, you have to think a bit about how to behave, what's the proper behavior, what will keep you in a safe zone rather than encountering things that become un-comfortable. So that's one of the things that happen: you begin to think about how things work in unfamiliar settings. If they work differently than how they work where you usually operate, well, you might wonder how will I find out how things work? That's one thing that happens.

The second thing that happens if we're at least conscious of that process, is that we begin to understand that much of behavior is in fact rule-bound. It's rule-governed, even if in most situations we don't have to think about those rules, or even the fact that there are rules.

This is a very important kind of step, to think about the fact that much of behavior is rule-bound, and this is what Giddens is thinking about when he says that practical consciousness works for most everyday situations, but there are circumstances in which we begin to become aware that we have internalized a whole number of rule-governed be-haviors (1984). In fact, to use a phrase that I want to emphasize, we take things for granted.

A second circumstance in which we might move from practical to discursive consciousness is when we are operating in situations where we think we know the rules, but something unexpected happens. Either something unpredictable occurs, or we don't like the consequences. But again, this kind of situation produces in us this notion that life is rather rule-bound and that we need to understand how things work.

One important question that Giddens asks about all of this, and that we'll come back and think about, is where do all these rules come from? How do these rules of behavior come into play? I'll come back to this in a little bit more detail in a minute, but just for the moment, let me intro-duce this very unfortunate word that Giddens coined. This is a process that he calls structuration (1984).

What he means by that is that people through their practices make and reinforce the rules, but then forget about the fact that they are people-made rules. The rules begin to take on a character that looks like they simply oper-ate independently of society. That issue where we forget that we are the rule makers is what makes the status quo so persistent to some degree. Again, we come to take the rules of everyday life for granted. This is how things work;

this is how things should work. It's just common sense. I'll come back and talk about that. I also want to make clear, at this point, that not everyone is in an equal position in making these rules and making them stick, and we'll come back and think about that.

Where does our common sense come from? How do we learn these rules? One quote from Kate Crehan again: "In a sense, we all have our own particular stock of common sense. Much of this will be shared by others in our immediate environment [that is this proximity issue], diverging as those others become more distant. So we're acculturated into understanding these rules" (2016).

The earliest influences clearly, and this will be fairly prosaic, are our parents and immediate family. There is some notion that some of this learning actually occurs in the womb, but not going to get into that at the moment. After our immediate family, our extended family, our friends, the educational system, including religious education if that's part of our background, the media, very broadly defined, the culture apparatuses, the kinds of things that get our attention, and then our own accumulated experience.

I just want to note here a little caution, which again I'll say a bit more about in a bit. Our own accumulated experience becomes increasingly solidified over time. That is, we start to think we know how the world works, and things that accord with that evolving viewpoint we take in much more easily than things that seem to contradict how we think the world works. This evolution is a kind of ongoing process to the extent that we need to understand further and further how the world works.

It's also important here to distinguish between what's possible to know and understand firsthand from information that must be delivered second-, third-, fourth-hand by a various media; that is, mediated information, which is more and more the case. I mean, we know less and less about the world firsthand than we do through other sources of information.

It is also critical to point out that nothing enters our brains or minds unfiltered. Going back to the idea from Aristotle, the first definition of common sense (i.e., the extra sense that allows us to make meaningful what other senses tell us about the world) sidesteps the very important question of how this additional sense is itself built. What I'm suggesting is that part of our acculturation, part of the way we develop a sense of the common sense, is to develop a set of filters that tells us what's important, what's not important, how we should interpret what we get as stimuli. Some of that can be right, some of it can be wrong.

So the issue of taken-for-grantedness, and reinforcement of common sense, is a very important phenomenon. This is, in fact, what I just described, that is that we begin to filter those things that don't really accord with how we think the world works, and we reject those things that really are contradictory. This is especially the case, I would suggest, and is becoming increasingly the case, through what we think about as either this bubble or silo effect. This is where we're channeled in many of our media interactions, particularly into things that we seem to have already accepted.

So anytime you see a prompt, "If you liked this, you will love that," know that this tactic works according to algorithms that produce this channeling effect. This is happening in all kinds of ways on social media and even in the mainstream media. People are CNN people, or they're MSNBC people, or they are Fox News people. So there's a tendency to sort of silo ourselves or put ourselves in these bubbles, and that's becoming increasingly the case.

Now, an important question: Are we thinking about common sense (singular) or are we thinking about common senses (plural)? All too often, one rational being's obvious fact is another's questionable or flat-out wrong assertion. There is more than one common sense, and even seemingly incontrovertible facts have a way of shifting over time. Even for ourselves, something that we may have believed at one point in time, if we are open-minded, we might believe something quite different at a later date. But quite clearly, there are different common senses operating simultaneously. These are the sources of controversy and argumentation.

The notion of the single common sense, "[w]hich all men have in common in any given civilization is quite foreign to the spirit of the [Gramsci prison] notebooks. For Gramsci as for Marx, any given civilization is so fractured by inequality that understanding it requires us to begin with that inequality. Those most elementary things which are the first to be forgot, the fact that there really do exist rulers and ruled, leaders and led. Common sense in all its multitudinous confusion is the product of a fractured world" (Crehan 2016).

Yes, there are multiple common senses operating at any particular time and place. There are always competing common senses at play, which tells us several things. Immediately, it tells us that common sense is unstable. It changes over time. It changes from place to place, from one group, for example a social class, from one setting to another, and so on. This also tells us that common sense is both malleable and subject to manipulation. It's not a stable thing. Common sense can shift.

Let's begin to tie those notions of what common sense is about to political action. Ultimately, as Kate Crehan argues, "what interests Gramsci is the knowledge that mobilizes political movements capable of bringing about radical transformations" (2016). This is what Gramsci was interested in. One of his central questions was trying to understand how the Italian people came to accept Mussolini and fascism. So he was very interested in coming to grips with that kind of question.

The most important knowledge would seem to be precisely knowledge that when embodied in self-aware collectivities has the potential to act in the world. For Gramsci, the primary such collectivities as a good Marxist were class, classes. He was interested in class struggle.

The webs of intelligibility in which our socialization wraps us from the day of our birth are a reality from which we all begin. We are all to some degree creatures of popular opinion, and yet of certain historical moments, there is radical social transformation. When and why does this happen? Running through the Gramsci notebooks is the question, what is the relationship between popular opinion, another phrasing of common sense, and social transformation? How are these things tied together, if they are tied together at all? This was a central question for Gramsci and one that Marx really did not take up to any significant degree. So Gramsci is thought of in many ways as a cultural theorist of Marxism.

"Despite all his criticisms" of common sense—and Gramsci was quite critical of it; he thinks of it as a kind of hodgepodge, and he thinks of it as very unsophisticated in many ways—"Gramsci's attitude wasn't wholly negative. Embedded within the chaotic confusion of common sense, that is both home and prison, he identifies what he terms *buon senso* [good sense]" (Crehan, 2016). That is, we feel comfortable in our notion of common sense, but we're also bounded by it. That's home and prison in this case. And there's a kernel of good sense in common sense.

The phrase "being philosophical about it," in addition to calling for patience or resignation, can also be seen, and it was for Gramsci, as an invitation for people to reflect and to realize fully that whatever happens is basically rational and must be confronted as such. This is the way in which good sense can be extracted out of common sense, but it's a process. It's a process that Gramsci says has to be extracted, made coherent by intellectuals, that this is the role of intellectuals for Gramsci.

But he has a very ecumenical notion of intellectuals. Anyone, in Gramsci's view, given the opportunity, could be an intellectual, that is, a person who could reflect on the conditions of their own material existence and think about why that existence has the characteristics that it does. So for Gramsci, anyone could be an intellectual.

The role of intellectuals is to extract the good sense out of the hodgepodge of common sense. Gramsci thinks about intellectuals as falling roughly into two categories. Organic intellectuals are those that remain connected to their class and further class interests. Now by saying that, that doesn't necessarily mean of one sort of political stripe or another. Adam Smith, the classical economist, I would argue, is an organic intellectual for his class, the bourgeois class.

Traditional intellectuals, as Gramsci describes them, are people who are interested in being apologists or explainers or supporters of the status quo. The traditional intellectuals are also what Marx would have called the vulgar economists, with whom he was engaged in conversation and contention. So the role of intellectuals is to extract the kernels of good sense out of common sense.

Okay. Now, let me turn from the abstract for a minute and think about a concrete example of something that we think about as common sense, which we will come back to in certain ways through other parts of the course. So as common sense, the American dream. If I say that phrase, do you get a picture in your mind immediately? What does it look like?

The American dream, here it is: In America (and this is not just confined to America of course), if you work hard, play by the rules, you will succeed. Work hard, play by the rules, you will succeed. That's part of the dream. Typically, it also includes a metric for what constitutes success. It almost invariably takes a commodified form, success. Since that's the kind of reward a capitalist system can and must deliver.

For example, a recurrent formulation is a home of one's own. Now, I don't want to go very far into a discussion of why this particular measure of success, that is, a home of one's own in the suburbs and so forth, was the preferred form of connoting and illustrating the American dream. But it had a great deal to do with the rise of mass consumption. The phrase itself, the American dream, was coined in the '30s basically in the heart of the Depression. Much of this framing was pointed at the need to keep the economy rumbling at a great pace when World War II ended. So one of the ways in which industry could keep going was to promulgate not collective consumption, but individual consumption. So everybody had to have their own house. And, consequently, everybody had to have their own Kelvinator, their own appliances. You couldn't share these things in common. That wasn't enough market. So the American dream takes a particular, that is, a commodified, form.

The American dream, as common sense, also has some taken-for-granted presumptions underlying it. The first is that America is a meritocracy. That is, a system in which people's success in life depends on their talents, abilities, and efforts. This is one of the presumptions underlying the notion that if you work hard, play by the rules, you will succeed. There's an ethos of individual achievement. You get this on your own—the self-made man, the self-made woman.

This translates into a number of other societies. Some of you may remember the iron lady, Margaret Thatcher. One of her many, many quotable quotes was "There is no such thing as society," spoken as she was dismantling British society at the time. There is no such thing as society. There are only individual men and women, and then it's kind of, after that, and their families, okay, if you can keep them together under those circumstances.

Another tacit presumption is that the rules are fair and are known or knowable to all, that is, that we operate on a level playing field. If these presumptions are violated, then the formulation of the American dream is very much in jeopardy. But if we presume that these things are the case, then we might be persuaded that the American dream is in fact a viable conception of society.

But I'm going to suggest . . . I'm not going to suggest. I'm just going to say, there's an obverse meaning to take away from the common sense understanding of how our society operates. That obverse meaning is this: In America, if you don't succeed, you are either not working hard enough, or you are not playing by the rules, or both. So if you don't succeed, and this is the obverse of thinking about the American dream as it's laid out, essentially, your failure is your own fault. This is another corollary of the individualized notion of how society works. All the opportunities are there. If you fail, it is your fault. There is nothing structural or systemic or unfair getting in your way, either historically, contemporaneously, or into the future.

Let's think about these presumptions and the obverse for a minute. How can you work hard if there are no jobs for you? Which is increasingly the prospect, as we think about the export of jobs that has occurred; as we think about automation taking jobs away; as we think about productivity going up but the demand for labor going down. One of the problems might be, "Well, I'd like to work hard, I just can't find work." Or what if your job pays so poorly that despite working very hard, and sometimes at more than one job at a time, you still can't make ends meet? So the pay structure doesn't allow success, despite hard work.

Anybody who's interested in this kind of thing, I'd recommend any of the works by Barbara Ehrenreich, either *Nickel and Dimed* or some of her more recent works, in which she talks about the fact that many people are working really, really hard and simply can't get by. What if the rules are rigged against you in some way and are unfair?

I know we are in a post-racial society, but I suspect there are still a few impediments. We are also now in the feminist utopia. So fifty-nine cents on the dollar should go just as far as a dollar on the dollar, right? Or what if there are unwritten or unspoken rules that discriminate against some people? Or what if there are early impediments to equal educational opportunities or family connections or other factors that make the playing field anything but level, which, as I suggested, should be the hallmark of a meritocracy?

An interesting study was done by the Center for Budget Priorities called *Born on Third Base*. This is an analysis of people who are on the Fortune 400. This is not the Fortune 500, which charts companies, but the Fortune 400, which lists the richest individuals in the world. This study does an assessment of how those people started out. Third base means you've inherited at least $50 million. So our current president wouldn't qualify at least in his first six years of life. But then they go all the way down to first base, which is still pretty substantial. A first-base person would be someone like Bill Gates, who's one of the poster children for the self-made person. He had the opportunity to go to Harvard and by his own admission was not a self-made person, and has really been helped by society a great deal, including all the infrastructure paid for by public R&D upon which the computer industry itself was built.

But in any event, they go through this list, and it turns out that only 35 percent of people on the Fortune 400 were born anywhere but first base (itself a space with substantial material advantages). Most people don't even know there's a ball field, okay, let alone come anywhere close to be on-deck circle or anything else like that. But these early advantages or impediments, either to educational opportunities or family connections, may have something to do with your success, no matter how hard you work, or how much you play by the rules.

So the American dream is like that. But if we let the common sense notion of the American dream stand just for a moment, here are a couple questions that we should ask of any taken-for-granted elements of the political, social, and economic status quo. The first is who benefits from this view of society? That is, if we believe the American dream, that to succeed, people must work hard, must play by certain rules that are written not by them, but with which they must comply. If we believe that, who benefits from that kind of orientation to society and who loses? We should always be thinking about who are the winners and the losers here.

It also suggests some questions about the political, social, and economic implications of such an understanding. For example, what does it mean about the role of government? If everything is by your own bootstraps, does government have any role in helping people out? Or what about civil society? Does anything require the intervention of civil society? Or should we just let the tender mercies of the market tell us how things ought to operate? But taking the American dream in its typical formulation has very serious implications for what we think about the role of any of these institutions. So we need to think carefully about that. And it's one of the reasons we can see assaults on things like welfare, unless it's called a subsidy, assaults on entitlement programs, so-called, even though we've paid for them.

But if your belief is that people just make it or don't make it simply on their own by their own dint of activity and effort, then there really is no role for society. People simply make it or they don't make it. But as I say, thinking about this has some implications for that.

If you have a high tolerance for obscenity, I would urge you to find this on YouTube. The late George Carlin. I'd urge you to take a look at "The American Dream. You Have to Be Asleep to Believe It."

All right. Now let's turn to the relationship between common sense and power. Here's a quote from the late cultural theorist Stuart Hall. It's a little bit long but it's worth going through:

> Why then is common sense so important? Because it is a terrain of conceptions and categories on which the practical consciousness of the masses of the people is actually formed. It is the already formed and taken for granted terrain on which more coherent ideologies and philosophies must contend for mastery, the ground which new con-

ceptions of the world must take into account, contest and transform if they were to shape the conceptions of the world of the masses and in that way become historically effective. (Hall 1986)

Basically, what Hall is talking about here is that we have embedded within us very heavily cemented notions of how the world works. If we want to change people's minds and think about the world operating differently, we have to contend with those deeply embedded and vitally held conceptions of how the world operates. He uses this language quite deliberately. We have to contend. This is a struggle.

So "popular beliefs, the culture of a people," Gramsci argues, "are not matters, are not arenas that can be left to look after themselves. They are themselves material forces. Common sense is a field of struggle and contestation" (Hall 1986). That is, for Hall, this is an arena for very fierce battles. The reason for this, of course, is that to have one's view of how the world operates become predominant is a very potent form of political power. If you can convince people that your sense of how the world ought to operate *is* the way it ought to operate, this is an extremely powerful political tool.

This form of power is also related to Gramsci's important concept of hegemony. One definition of hegemony, and there are other definitions, I mean, we have some definitions of hegemony in common parlance, like the US is the world's only hegemon, which is a debatable point no matter what, but that's not exactly the meaning I'm using here. Hegemony, as I'm using the term here, is governance with the consent of the governed.

The alternative form of governance is coercion. Now think about it, if you're an elite and you want to govern people, which of these forms is preferable? Well, of the two, hegemony is much more desirable for the governors since governance with consent does not produce opposition and resistance by definition. If people are consenting to be governed, why would they object? Why would they resist?

It should also be noted, though, that these two forms are never mutually exclusive, but rather they exist on a continuum, since governance structures invariably reserve to themselves the exclusive and legitimate use of coercion when necessary or when consent fails. These forms are related to each other. But given the option, governors would prefer the hegemonic form rather than the coercive form, which does produce resistance.

But why do people consent to be governed? This is the way in which we're going to now begin to tie this back to questions of common sense and so forth. It's a question of legitimacy. The ruled must believe that the rulers are operating in their interest. This is the basis upon which people cede consent or give consent to be governed. They think the governors, their rulers, are operating in their interest. So they accord those rulers legitimation. In fact, the failure of this form of governance is often referred to or often is contained in a legitimation crisis, that is, when legitimacy begins to fail.

How is this belief developed, that governors act in the interest of the governed? By the rulers promulgating and constantly reinforcing a particular common sense about the world, not only is the way they are operating the way the world is, but it's the way the world should be. I just want to emphasize that this is a constant project. Rulers have to constantly promulgate and reinforce this idea that they are operating in the public good on behalf of the governed. It is a constant project.

In the second half of this chapter, we present a number of cases, both from recent history and from contemporary situations that illustrate the ends of this continuum. We make the point that for societies that purport to be democratic, consent, based upon a constantly reinforced common sensical understanding of the legitimacy of the rulers, is not only the most desirable form of governance, but is necessary to maintain the veneer (whether thick or thin) of democracy itself. For more dictatorial or despotic regimes, even the pretense of consent is less necessary, at least for a time.

By definition, everything in opposition to that common sense becomes quite literally unthinkable and becomes—and I use this term advisedly—nonsense. It is not sensical to object to the governors, if they're acting in your interest. This is the fundamental idea that underpins the way in which this form of governance works. And many, many philosophers have articulated it, but it is that the governors are acting in the interests of those who are being governed, and therefore have legitimate control over the reins of governance.

Again from Kate Crehan's book, "the narratives that become hegemonic are those that reflect the world as seen from the vantage point of the rulers rather than the ruled typically" (2016). We'll come back to this. Again from Stuart Hall: "First, hegemony is a very particular historically specific and temporary moment in the life of a society. It's rare for this degree of unity to be achieved, enabling a society to set itself a quite new historical agenda under the leadership of a specific formation or constellation of social forces [with a critical part here]. Such periods of settlement are unlikely to persist forever." There's nothing automatic about them. They have to be actively constructed and positively maintained. Otherwise, such hegemonies risk falling apart.

We can see this when we see schisms even within the ruling class, and there are many times when that occurs, and those may be moments of interesting opportunity. But hegemony is unstable and begins to break down when rulers lose their legitimacy. This can happen when the ruled no longer believe, for a whole variety of possible reasons, that governance is in their interest. This is what I refer to as a legitimation crisis. It's at that point that governance structures even lose the ability to wield coercion uncontested.

Gramsci makes a very clear argument that before coercion can be legitimately utilized, governance structures have to have won a war of position, that is, they already have to be seen as legitimate before they can legitimately wield even coercive forms of government. So when this begins to break down, and you can begin to think about all kinds of reasons why people would start to lose faith that their leaders are, in fact, acting in their interests. We're at a particularly fraught moment right now [winter 2018–2019], I would say. I mean, I don't know how many of you were thinking of not coming tonight in sympathy with the government shutdown. I thought about it momentarily, but I decided I'd come in and do this.

But in any event, there are moments clearly when the seeming solidity of the governance structures are revealed to be rather fragile. And when they are, this is a moment when people begin to call into question all kinds of things about the way in which their society operates.

So legitimation crises are extremely troubling moments for governance structures and for elites. As Hall is arguing here, this is invariably the case. And people who want radical change need to be prepared for those moments.

Also from Creehan's book: "For there to be fundamental social change therefore, there needs to be cultural transformation. That is to say a new common sense, and with it a new culture that enables subalterns, that is those who are ruled or governed, to imagine another reality" (2016). Part of the potency of common sense, and this is why I used the alternative word "nonsense" a moment ago, part of the potency of the common sense, is to rule out our thinking any differently about the world. That is, to subjugate our own mental capacity to imagine the world otherwise.

It's why I used that phrase, which I took from Mark Fisher (2009), which he took from an unnamed and unclaimed source about capitalist realism. It is now easier to imagine the end of the world than to imagine the end of capitalism. That's an emblematic form of this kind of notion of the constraints on our own imagination. We know we're hurdling over several different cliffs, as Noam talked about last Thursday, and yet we can't seem to imagine our way out of this form that is so genocidal, suicidal, planet-cidal, right?

As Crehan is arguing, based on Gramsci, we need to be able to formulate a new common sense to combat the existing one and open up the possibilities of different imaginaries. "The value of Gramsci's concept of common sense is that it offers us a way of thinking about the texture of everyday life that encompasses its givenness [that is, the way in which we're thrown into it at birth]—how it both constitutes our subjectivity, the way we think about ourselves, and confronts us as an external and solid reality" (2016). This is back to Giddens's notion of structuration (1984).

The way the world works doesn't seem to have been created by us. It simply seems to confront us as a kind of materiality that we have no say in changing. This is what we really need to be combating. "But that also acknowledges its contradictions, fluidity and flexibility. For all its apparent solidity, it [that is, common sense] is continually being modified by how actual people in actual places live it" (Giddens 1984). So it's important, it's vitally important, to understand the sort of fluid nature of common sense, that it is not solid in the way that it's constantly being told to us.

In a work by Edward Bernays there is, in fact, a conversation about how all of this actually works. This is Edward Bernays: "Propaganda is the executive arm of the invisible government" (1928). So Bernays, interesting character, he was twice, and in two different ways, a nephew of Sigmund Freud and fancied himself a kind of amateur psychologist of the popular mind. Very early on, he was the self-described father of public relations. He invented the form, according to himself. He was involved in a whole number of early activities, some of which we'll talk about a bit later. He was involved in the Creel Commission, which was organized with Walter Lippmann and others to motivate a very reluctant US public into supporting the US entry into World War I under Woodrow Wilson. We return to this effort in a bit more detail below.

So he was involved in a number of those kinds of things. One of his most famous and long-standing sets of efforts had to do with tobacco. He really was very, very influential in getting people to smoke. Later in life, in an autobiographical kind of mea culpa, he regretted that activity. But one of the things that he did (and this is just by way of illustration of the sort of mental attitude he had about public opinion), one of the last impediments to the market for cigarettes was getting women to smoke, and particularly getting women to smoke in public.

So one of the large grandstand events that Bernays organized was a liberty march in the Macy's Thanksgiving Day parade in New York. He hired about thirty debutantes. I don't know if that word draws any resonance. These were young women of society who were going to be introduced to society. He had them march in the parade, each of them holding aloft a little torch of freedom. That little torch of freedom was a Lucky Strike cigarette. This was the kind of thing he was engaged in.

But here are some of his views: "The conscious and intelligent manipulation of the organized habits and opinions of the masses is an important element in democratic society. Those who manipulate this unseen mechanism of society constitute an invisible government, which is the true ruling power of our country." Some people might now call that the deep state. I wouldn't, but some people might. "We are governed, our minds are molded, our tastes formed, our ideas suggested largely by men we have never heard of" (1928). He is referring to himself and other people who are behind the scenes manipulating public opinion, which is another phrase for common sense.

"In almost every act of our daily lives, whether in the sphere of politics or business, in our social conduct or ethical thinking, we are dominated by the relatively small number of persons . . . who understand the mental processes and social patterns of the masses. It is they who pull the wires which control the public mind" (1928).

Now for Bernays, this was a very good thing. I mean, in his mind, this was a good thing, and this is the reason for it: "Truth is mighty and must prevail. And if anybody, and any body of men believe that they have discovered a valuable truth, it is not merely their privilege, but their duty to disseminate that truth. If they realize, as they quickly must, that this spreading of truth can be done upon a large scale and effectively only by organized effort, they will make use of the press and the platform as the best means to give it wide circulation" (1928). So he was engaged, remember, in the onset of public relations and mass marketing. So he's starting to use these levers that had become recently available for disseminating these truths.

"Propaganda becomes vicious and reprehensible only when its authors consciously and deliberately disseminate what they know to be lies, or when they aim at effects which they know to be prejudicial to the common good" (1928). But of course the common good is defined by these people, so it's almost invariable that they will not be defined as the common good. But the danger is there, and he's warning people about it.

"The imaginatively managed event can compete successfully with other events for attention. Newsworthy events involving people usually do not happen by accident, they are planned deliberately to accomplish a purpose to influence our ideas and actions" (1928). And many of the things that Bernays was engaged in were these kinds of grandstanding, large-scale public events. So as I say, he sort of describes himself as the father of public relations. This is part of the mechanism that he used. We return to Bernays in the second part of the chapter in order to connect some of his work in "public relations" to projections of US political and military power.

All right. Let's bring this a little bit up-to-date. This is in a piece by Chris Hedges called "The Permanent Lie," and it will now start to resonate in slightly different ways with the contemporary moment. "The most ominous danger we face comes from the marginalization and destruction of institutions, including the courts, academia, legislative bodies, cultural organizations and the press that once ensured that civil discourse was rooted in reality and fact, helped us distinguish lies from truth, and facilitated justice" (2017).

"The permanent lie is not circumscribed by reality. It is perpetuated even in the face of overwhelming evidence that discredits it. It is irrational. Those who speak in the language of truth and fact are attacked as liars, traitors and purveyors of fake news" (Hedges 2017). So this is what Hedges is concerned about happening at the moment. Then he quotes Hannah Arendt from her book *The Origins of Totalitarianism*: "The result of a consistent and total substitution of lies with factual truth is not that the lie will now be accepted as truth and truth be defamed as a lie, but that the sense by which we take our bearings in the real world—and the category of truth versus falsehood is among the mental means to this end—is being destroyed" (quoted in Hedges 2017).

So it's not that a particular lie is believed, or that a particular truth is devalued, but the mechanisms that we have for discerning one from the other are themselves under assault. This is what Arendt was concerned about and what Hedges now sees coming back around.

The press and the media more generally are often described as the enemy of the people, which has some very long . . . There's a long history of such attacks as part of authoritarian regimes, which we'll discuss further a little bit later on. Assaults on journalism and journalists. So the pieces that are in today's readings describe a very significant uptick in the sort of ways in which journalism, journalists, and facticity and evidence are really being very much undermined by activities.

Finally, Edward Bernays again. "Freedom of speech and its demo-cratic corollary, a free press have *tacitly* expanded our Bill of Rights to include the *right of persuasion*" (1947). Again, he's justifying this activity of his. "This development was an *inevitable* result of the expansion of the media of free speech and persuasion. All these media provide open doors to the public mind." So he's saying that this is just . . . it's a kind of technological determinism. Once you have the platform there, of course people are going to use it for these purposes. "*Anyone* of us through these media may influence the attitudes and actions of our fellow citizens." I've added those emphases just so you'll know which words are again a little bit suspect and slippery.

So we've already established the fact that common sense is mal-leable. Now we have to look at the very uneven power landscape on which such contests, over the common sense, are waged. This discus-sion will focus mostly on the US media landscape, but the basic points apply quite well to many other media environments (with some excep-tions for state-owned media, for better or worse). It's clear from the Bernays piece that even at that time, 1947, particular actors in society are in much more advantageous positions to influence public opinion than others, another name for common sense. What's happened since that time?

This a quote from Katherine Graham, the former publisher, during the Watergate episode, of the *Washington Post*: "News is what someone wants suppressed; everything else is just advertising." What's happened since that time? Mass media, and I'll talk about social media in a minute. At the moment, and this is always in a little bit of flux and a little bit confusing, six corporations control 90 percent of what we read, watch, or listen to. Six corporations. It's a little bit mystifying for me to put it that way. When I say six corporations, it makes it sound as though there's no-body there really making decisions, but in fact corporations don't decide, people in them decide things. We'll talk about the ways in which these corporations decide things in a minute.

In 1983, 90 percent of what Americans saw, watched, heard, and so forth, was controlled by fifty corporations. By this point in 2012, six corporations. And the number six is a little bit misleading, because all of the cross-linkages among these companies make it even fewer than the apparent six in some ways. There are all kinds of joint ownership operations, and all kinds of cooperative agreements, so that any particular cultural or media entity or product has very few hands on it.

Another way to look at it, same six corporations. If you follow the business news, you will see mergers being suggested all the time even among these six corporations of various sorts. Some have gone through in the last couple of years; some have been thwarted. I would also suggest, and we'll talk about this when we talk about neoliberal financialized, globalized capitalism, this is not unique to the media industry. That this kind of merger, this kind of consolidation of ownership is now system-wide. And there are lots of very good reasons why this makes sense to the corporations themselves.

So these six corporations, and more precisely, the key decision makers within them, set the boundaries on acceptable debate on what's socially, politically, economically possible. They make their decisions on those things based on profit maximization, both short and long term. If you think they're making their decisions on anything else, you are mistaken. I'll just put that out as a very bald assertion, okay? But, as we discuss in the second half of the chapter, even these kinds of decisions are bounded by the prevailing common sense, in terms of what is permissible, in any particular time and place, to say, or even to think.

Now, I'm hedging on that a little bit by saying short and long term. Short-term, they want to maximize profits in the immediate sense for their investors, who are always looking for the next best thing. And with electronic financial trading now, that means in basically nanoseconds. So big funds jump from investment to investment on the marginal returns that they think they will get in the next not quarter, but maybe quarter of a minute. So they make their decisions based on that.

But these decision makers also make their decisions as being part of the governance structure, the hegemonic governance structure, on what will maintain their legitimacy. So they think about that a little bit. But when they have to make a trade-off between short and long term, they decide short term, otherwise the CEO and the board of directors are out fairly quickly.

All right. They make their decisions that way. Let me just go back for this for one second, and ask you to think a little bit about what the media's products are, which I put out as a question before. Are they selling an entertainment thing? Are they selling news? Are they selling information? No. They're selling you. They're selling you to advertisers. You are their product. There's no question about that.

So when they make a decision about what to put in the newspaper, or what to put on television, or what to put on any other platforms, or put into movies or whatever, they're making decisions on how they will garner the most of you. That's the basis for the decision. Don't be deceived by the fact that they make claims about being representatives of the First Amendment, and their duty to the public, I mean which is partly . . . okay, it's not really even partly true, except for performing a legitimation function. Virtually entirely, they make their decisions based on what will sell the most.

Do the media companies engage in censorship? Yes. They certainly do. At a minimum, they engage in censorship of this kind, of selection bias. So how many of you know the motto of the *New York Times*?

Crowd: All the news . . .

Female: That's fit to print.

"All the news that's fit to print," right, which in fact should be modified to "all the news that fits, it prints." And how much news fits? It depends on the advertising space that's taken up in the paper. What's left over is the news hole, which is how it's described, and maybe has a kind of negative connotation.

The news hole grows or shrinks depending on how much advertising space is taken up. So at a minimum, they engage in a selection bias. Of all the things that happen in the world on any particular day, they have to make judgments about what to either print or to broadcast or to put on the air, and so forth. How do they do that? They do it by determining which things out of the panoply that's available are likely to attract the most eyes, the most readers, the most viewers. That's how they do it.

It's one of the reasons why if you flip around, and you can try this at home, from channel to channel on the network news, not only will you see the same stories out of the thousands and thousands of things that happen in the world that day, but you'll see them basically in the same order with the same presentation. It's not because the editors are sitting in a room colluding, I know that's a very bad word, with each other, but they are in fact using the same kind of lens to think about that panoply of events, which things are likely to produce the most number of viewers or readers or whatever.

Now, do you remember this: 658? Any idea what this is? I haven't given you any hints whatsoever. But now, I'm going to give you a hint, a big hint. What if I said 658 days?

Female: Till the next elections.

There are 658 days to the next national election. The reason I'm asking about this at this point is I want you now to think about as you look at media, what they cover over the next 658 days, and the way they cover it. There are many, many issues that could be covered. How can we possibly at this point, 658 days out, be thinking about the relative merits of Joe Biden versus Julian Castro versus Elizabeth Warren? Yet, if you look at the news hole on NBC, MSNBC, CNN the horse race is already well underway.

Now, that means of course that there are opportunity costs. The more that the horse race is covered, the less actual issues and policies will be covered, not to mention stories outside of the endless election cycle. Again, think about, as we proceed through the course and as we proceed over the next interminable number of months to the election, how much time and energy is devoted, and not to the issues that the candidates are raising, but simply to their relative strengths and weaknesses vis-à-vis their electability: the personalities, the horse race, not the issues and so forth. Just think about that. Now you can use this and stump your friends, but remember to change it every day by one day.

I'm coming to the very end. Up to this point, I've been talking about mass media, and mostly in the US context. Now I want to turn to the internet and social media. They have tremendous democratizing potential. They also raise very serious issues about privacy and surveillance, as many of you know. This has been in the headlines. These kinds of media impose censorship of a different kind. So much information that truth and credibility are very difficult to determine. How do we know what we see on the internet is real? Where's the validation? Where's the corroboration?

These social media are subject to increasingly stringent gatekeeping by internet service providers. And this raises the very serious issue of net neutrality. Right now, things are relatively unimpeded. You can access any website and download information. What ISPs would like to do is be an intermediary between you and that content. They will make determinations on speed and accessibility, again based on profit maximization for themselves, since many of the companies who are involved in this are also content providers. They want to charge differential rates for different sites and different content and so forth. That's a very different view of how the internet would operate than the way it operates currently.

Now we're back to the starting point regarding filters that we use to make sense of the world. Because we take certain things about the world for granted when we encounter new data, we accept it or reject it based in large part on whether it corresponds with or contradicts what we think we already know. This is what I had said earlier. This is being increasingly reinforced by the so-called bubble or silo effect in which computer algorithms channel our online behavior so that we rarely encounter views with which we disagree.

Unless we train ourselves to be open-minded and skeptical, which is actually what critical thinking and learning are all about, we continue to accept the status quo even when we are disadvantaged by it. We are also diminished in our capacity to imagine alternatives to the taken-for-granted status quo, and we come to accept its inevitability.

Being open to new views is a very difficult and destabilizing proposition, since we have a stake, a very potent stake in thinking we know how the world operates. That practical consciousness that I described at the beginning is extremely useful for us. We have to have it. So we abandon it very, very reluctantly, and we abandon it in large measure depending on what's at stake. But it's necessary to break down the taken-for-granted common senses that are not in our interest, and that's partly what this course is about. We're going to think about what is the prevailing common sense in the next chapter and then begin to think about what are the consequences of accepting that as inevitable.

Chomsky Lecture, January 17, 2019

The main topic that we're discussing this week is Gramsci's concept of hegemonic common sense, and how it plays out in practice. The assigned reading for today was chosen in part because it provides many striking illustrations of the effective imposition of hegemonic common sense. But also, in part, because it quotes an early and perceptive commentary on this concept, in the mid-eighteenth century, by Scottish philosopher David Hume, one of the great figures of the Enlightenment and a founder of classical liberalism. The quote is from a study of his called "Of the First Principles of Government"—a very important work on democratic theory. In the background is the first modern democratic revolution, in England in the preceding century.

In the opening paragraph, Hume gives a brief exposition of something like the Gramscian concept. Hume writes that he found nothing more surprising "than to see the easiness with which the many are governed by the few; and to observe the implicit submission with which men resign their own sentiments and passions to those of their rulers. When we enquire by what means this wonder is brought about, we shall find, that as Force is always on the side of the governed, the governors have nothing to support them but opinion. 'Tis therefore, on opinion only that government is founded; and this maxim extends to the most despotic and most military governments, as well as to the most free and most popular."

Words worth pondering.

The maxim applies with far more force to governments that are free and popular—governments like ours—than to despotic and military governments. These can freely resort to violence, which often suffices, whatever public opinion may be—at least as long as those who exercise the violence, the security forces, remain loyal.

I discuss Hume's essay in my book *Deterring Democracy*. The book opens with Hume's remarks on consent and goes on to discuss the exercise of violence in despotic and military governments. For quite substantial reasons to which I'll return, it concentrates on the US-supported military dictatorships in Central America in the 1980s, which carried out a brutal war against their populations. Hundreds of thousands were killed; huge numbers hideously tortured and mutilated. The countries were ruined. The trauma persists.

The book was published thirty years ago, so the examples might seem no longer pertinent. But that's a mistake. In fact, they're quite relevant today. They provide a crucial background for front-page news as Trump demands a "beautiful wall" to protect us from the invasion of rapists, murders, Islamic terrorists, and the like. The reality of the invasion is very vivid in our immediate experience here in Tucson, not far from the harsh desert where miserable people fleeing from our destruction of their countries are dying in the searing heat—and sometimes being given some succor by the heroic activists of No More Deaths. All happening right here. Many are fleeing from the horrors of the 1980s and the brutal legacy that they left, others from more recent US crimes to which we'll return.

As many of you know, there's an ongoing trial of volunteers from No More Deaths at the federal court in Tucson—in one case, a felony charge that could bring twenty years in prison. The trials are for such crimes as leaving food and water in the desert for desperate people who are fleeing the results of our crimes.*

---

* As an important update, as of November of 2019, one member of the group, Dr. Scott Warren, was acquitted of the only felony charges levied against No More Deaths volunteers.

In the past, No More Deaths had a tacit agreement with the border patrols, which allowed them to carry out their humanitarian work with a certain degree of impunity, but that's changed. Enforcement has sharply increased under the Trump administration's hardline immigration stance. Hence the trials, and also a lot of sadistic acts, like border patrols destroying food and water so that people will die of thirst and starve when they wander in the desert. Sometimes helicopters hover over groups of refugees and scatter them into the desert so that they'll get lost and be more likely to die in agony and join the many corpses that are constantly being found.

We cannot emphasize too often that these rapists, criminals, and Islamic terrorists are fleeing from the wreckage of US crimes in Central America, some of which are discussed in today's reading. Now, these days, that reading should probably have trigger warnings. For example, Father Santiago's vivid description of the hideous scene he witnessed with his own eyes, just an instance of what was happening throughout the region (Chomsky 1991).

In the last year or two, the flight of refugees is mostly from Honduras. There's a caravan being formed right now in Honduras. You've probably read about it. There's a reason why the refugee flow is now coming from Honduras. In 2009, a mildly reformist government came into office in Honduras, breaking with a brutal history of terror and repression. The president, Mel Zelaya, proposed some measures to overcome the horrors of the traditional Honduran system, in which the US had been directly involved, particularly during Reagan's wars in the eighties, when Honduras was turned into a base for US-run terrorist operations in the region.

Zelaya's efforts didn't last long. He was thrown out by a military coup, which was condemned throughout the hemisphere, throughout the world. With an exception. The Obama-Clinton administration refused to call it a military coup because if they had, US law would have required that they stop sending arms to the military junta that had restored a brutal dictatorship. Washington would not agree to that, so it endorsed the coup regime under the ludicrous pretense that it was restoring democracy.

The military dictatorship ran what they called "an election," which was mostly ridiculed and dismissed. Again, with one notable exception. The Obama-Clinton administration praised it as an encouraging step toward democracy, so we could continue to support this promising new regime as it instituted a reign of terror.

Honduras, which was always dangerous enough, became maybe the homicide capital of the world. There were huge atrocities, and soon people were fleeing in desperation. Honduras was the source of the plurality of the refugees fleeing from Central America in the last few years, and that's where the caravans are starting from. The US role in the flight of refugees is not secret. It's all public. You can easily find out about it—except on the front pages of newspapers, where it should be highlighted.

Throughout the hideous decade of the 1980s, there was never any secret about what was happening. It was reported extensively by church sources and all the major human rights and aid groups, by solidarity organizations, and by the thousands of Americans who flocked to Central America to help the victims—something entirely new in the gruesome history of imperialism, and a tribute to important strains of American society and culture. Like No More Deaths today, right here in Tucson.

The earlier role of the US in Central America, Latin America altogether, is terrible enough. We'll come back to that later. But the crimes escalated sharply under Reagan in the 1980s. The terrible decade opened with the assassination of Archbishop Oscar Romero, recently designated as a saint. He was known as the "voice for the voiceless." He was a simple man, of remarkable integrity and courage, who understood well that the course he was following would probably lead to martyrdom. He was assassinated while reading mass, by close US allies, as was known at once and reported by US ambassador to El Salvador Robert White—who was withdrawn, because he was considered a little too open about what was happening. The voice for the voiceless was stilled by the assassins shortly after sending a letter to President Carter urging him to withhold military aid from the governing junta, which, he warned, will use it to "sharpen injustice and repression against the people's organizations [struggling] for respect for their most basic human rights." Exactly as happened.

Right after the assassination, the Reagan administration came into office, and sharply escalated the war. Archbishop Romero's successor, Bishop Arturo Rivera y Damas, described the US-backed crimes as "a war of extermination and genocide against a defenseless civilian population." That was El Salvador. They were sort of lucky. It was still worse in Guatemala in those years.

In both countries, the crimes go back much earlier. In Guatemala they intensified after the overthrow of a popular democratic government by a CIA coup in 1954. That initiated decades of state terror and repression, raised to new horrors under Reagan. What was taking place in Guatemala in the eighties was so horrendous that Congress intervened and imposed constraints on the US supply of weapons to the mass murderers who were running the country. Undeterred, Reagan created an international terror network to replace direct US participation in the slaughter.

There are others who create international terrorist networks, highly publicized and bitterly condemned for their crimes. They hire killers, like the infamous Carlos the Jackal. The US is a much bigger player, so we hire terrorist states, not just individual killers. They're much more effective. The primary component of Reagan's terror network was the Argentine neo-Nazi regime that was the worst of all the Latin American monsters of those years. The competition for that honor is pretty fierce, but they were the winners.

They were also the favorite of Henry Kissinger, Ronald Reagan, and their associates. So it's natural that they should be picked to direct the slaughter and torture in Guatemala when Washington had to pull out directly. But that didn't last long; the Argentine military dictatorship was overthrown. A democratic regime was slowly introduced, so Argentine neo-Nazi killers were no longer available for service in Guatemala. Washington's international terror network had to turn to others: Taiwanese mercenaries, but primarily, Israel, which provided direct support and weapons for horrifying crimes, using its considerable expertise in repression and violence. To this day, the Guatemalan military, which continues its rampages, is supplied with Israeli weapons, standard issue for their forces.

In the early eighties, the atrocities amounted to virtual genocide in the Mayan highlands of Guatemala under a killer later sentenced for genocide. While it was underway, he was lauded by Reagan as a fine man, "totally dedicated to democracy" and given a "bum rap" by human rights organizations. People are still fleeing from that bitter legacy.

The decade of the eighties began with the assassination of the archbishop and closed in 1989, symbolically, with the assassination of six leading Latin American intellectuals, Jesuit priests, in their rooms at the Jesuit university of San Salvador. The assassins also murdered their housekeeper and her daughter to make sure there would be no witnesses. This was right at the time of the fall of the Berlin Wall and the celebration of the liberation of Soviet satellites. The murderers were from a US-trained brigade, the Atlacatl Brigade, known as El Salvador's finest, which had already compiled a horrible record of murders and atrocities.

We can find out more about this from the foreign press. Several years ago (November 21, 2009), a major Spanish journal, *El Mundo*, published facsimiles of official documents showing that the assassination was undertaken on the direct orders of the Salvadoran High Command, which was, of course, always in close contact with the US Embassy. As far as I can determine, the media here never published that crucial information, but you can find it. I published it, the only reference here to my knowledge. The Free Press has other priorities.

A good bit has been learned about the wars in El Salvador and Guatemala since *Deterring Democracy* was published thirty years ago. As the wars wound down, Truth Commissions were established in both countries. Their research revealed that the overwhelming majority of the crimes were carried out by the security forces that were armed, trained, directed by the Reagan administration. I'll come back to all of that and its backgrounds, particularly since the Kennedy years. This is bipartisan. It's highly instructive.

There has never been a Truth Commission here. That's unthinkable, a violation of common sense.

Truth Commissions often have a considerable impact, in Argentina, to take one case. So does their absence. The most important country in

Latin America, Brazil, did not have one. They had a brutal military dictatorship, but there was no reckoning. Actually, the Catholic Church did publish an inquiry, but there was no real Truth Commission. The effects are in the headlines right now. In Brazil, something similar to military dictatorship is taking shape. It's tolerated, even supported, in part because people don't even remember the military dictatorship and its many crimes. Younger people may not even know about it. The new Bolsonaro administration even denies that there was a military dictatorship. Rather, the military coup and the brutal National Security State it imposed were a rescue operation, saving the country from a (mythical) communist plot to destroy Brazilian democracy.

Bolsonaro himself—a Trump favorite, not surprisingly—does criticize the military dictatorship. It was too soft. It should have killed thirty thousand people, as in neighboring Argentina. This softness in Brazil goes far back. He also criticizes the nineteenth-century Brazilian military, which did not duplicate what its counterpart was doing in the US, virtually exterminating the indigenous population. Therefore, Brazil is stuck with these Indians who, Bolsonaro has made clear, must be driven from their reservations in the Amazon—for their own good—while the great tropical forest is handed over to agribusiness and mining, and foreign investors, to exploit and destroy. Incidentally, a serious contribution to the dire threat of global environmental catastrophe.

Going back to the failure to establish a Truth Commission in Brazil, and the consequences of failure to remember even the very recent past, we might recall a comment of Gore Vidal's, who once described the United States as the "United States of Amnesia." It's a useful trait. But Vidal was unfair. It's not only the United States. It's every other great power as well. Britain, for example, is just barely beginning today to face some of the horrible atrocities carried out under British rule since the seventeenth century. Better than most. It is useful to have a state of amnesia. It contributes to imposing the required hegemonic common sense.

Let's go back to David Hume. He was concerned primarily with the more free and popular governments. That's the most interesting case. Especially his own country, Britain, which was unusually free and popular by the standards of the day. But Hume was surely aware of the limits of that freedom. They were discussed quite eloquently by his close friend, Adam Smith, who along with Hume was a leading Enlightenment figure and a founder of classical liberalism.

Smith, of course, is greatly revered as the founder of modern economics. But he also had a good deal to say about political systems in his classic work *The Wealth of Nations*, published in 1776, a date that means something here, too. Smith writes that in England, the "merchants and manufacturers [are the] principal architects" of government policy, which they design to ensure that their own interests "are most peculiarly attended to," however "grievous" the effect on others, including the people of England, but especially those who suffer under "the savage injustice of the Europeans" in their colonies.

British India was the main target of his charges. But more generally, he wrote, "the masters of mankind," the merchants and manufacturers of England, pursue their "vile maxim: all for ourselves and nothing for anyone else."

Smith's vile maxim should be familiar to us. It has considerable resonance today. We'll look into its theoretical background next week. But as you should be aware, the vile maxim has become a leading idea of what's called "libertarianism" in the United States. It was popularized by Ayn Rand. Greed is great, all for ourselves, nothing for anyone else. She was the guru of prominent figures, among them Alan Greenspan, the much-admired chair of the Federal Reserve for many years. Another acolyte is Paul Ryan, former Speaker of the House, the main intellectual architect of the domestic programs of the Trump administration—which are, in fact, motivated by the vile maxim. We'll come back to some of them.

One of the leading intellectuals of the libertarian movement, Nobel laureate in economics James Buchanan, outlined the guiding principle lucidly. In his major work *Limits of Liberty*, he pointed out that the ideal society should accord with fundamental human nature, which makes good sense. And then went on, reasonably, to ask the next question: What is fundamental human nature? He had a very simple answer:

"In a strictly personalized sense, any person's ideal situation is one that allows him full freedom of action and inhibits the behavior of others so as to force adherence to his own desires. That is to say, each person seeks mastery over a world of slaves."

That's libertarianism, the ultimate in liberty. And it's your fondest dream, in case you hadn't noticed, fundamental human nature. That's the vile maxim in modern terms. Actually, it's a thought that Adam Smith would have regarded as pathological, as would David Hume or John Stuart Mill or Thomas Paine or Abraham Lincoln or anyone at all close to the classical liberal tradition.

It's an interesting indication of things that have been happening here—of how remote classical liberalism is from the moral basis of what's called libertarianism in the United States. Something else to think about.

Well, let's go back to the main theme. Hume's insight, developed by Gramsci, explains why elites are so dedicated to indoctrination and thought control. You have to make sure to "engineer consent" as Edward Bernays explained in work that Marv talked about in our last meeting (Bernays 1947). They're pretty frank about it, which is useful, because then we can find out what they have in mind. I'll keep to the left-liberal end of the spectrum, which is in many ways the most revealing because it sets the limits on what's admissible. It says you can go this far, not a millimeter farther. Therefore, it's always quite interesting to look at the liberal extreme of opinion. So let's do so.

Bernays is an important figure, a founder of the huge public relations industry, which spends hundreds of millions of dollars a year to engineer consent. Bernays was a Wilson-Roosevelt-Kennedy liberal. As Marv mentioned, one of his first great successes, which propelled him to fame and fortune, was getting women to smoke. The lethal effects of that were well known but effectively suppressed for a long time. We'll come back to that.

Another notable achievement of Bernays's liberal record was in the early 1950s when he was employed by the United Fruit Company, which virtually owned Guatemala, in fact much of Central America. In the early '50s they were threatened by a new reformist democracy in Guatemala, which overthrew the dictatorship and intended to take unused lands owned by the fruit company and distribute them to poor peasants, along with other reforms.

Bernays was hired to do something about that. He developed a very successful propaganda campaign to engineer consent among the American public for a military coup, the 1953 military coup, which ended these heresies and protected the power of the Fruit Company under the new military dictatorship. The theme of his campaign was, of course, a Soviet base not far from our borders, a communist threat, which was derisory, but worked. The military dictatorship was firmly established. That led to decades of terror and destruction, ending any threat of democracy and social reform, escalating in the Reagan years as I mentioned. And still a major factor in the flood of refugees fleeing here to the border.

Edward Bernays is actually a liberal hero. That's particularly true in Cambridge, Massachusetts, where I spent most of my life. The heartland of American liberalism. He's honored because one of his achievements was to carry out a pro bono propaganda campaign to stop a real atrocity that was going to happen in Cambridge. There's a highway that goes by the river, Memorial Drive. Valeria and I lived there for a while. It has lovely old sycamore trees along the Drive. A very pleasant place, we can testify to that. The city was thinking of widening the highway and cutting down the sycamores. Bernays intervened and organized a campaign that got the city to back off. So the sycamores are still there. And that apparently effaces the rest of the record, as far as liberal opinion is concerned.

Bernays explained his principles in 1947, in the *Annals of the American Academy of Political and Social Science*.

He informed the world of science that

> leaders, with the aid of technicians in the field who have specialized in utilizing the channels of communication, have been able to accomplish purposefully and scientifically what we have termed 'the engineering of consent.' This phrase quite simply means the use of an engineering approach—that is, action based on thorough knowledge of the situation and on the application of scientific principles and tried practices to the task of getting people to support ideas and programs. . . . The engineering of consent is the very essence of the democratic process,

the freedom to persuade and suggest. . . . A leader frequently cannot wait for the people to arrive at even general understanding . . . democratic leaders must play their part in . . . engineering consent to socially constructive goals and values. . . . The responsible leader, to accomplish social objectives, must therefore be constantly aware of the possibilities of subversion. He must apply his energies to mastering the operational know-how of consent engineering, and to out-maneuvering his opponents in the public interest (Bernays, 1947).

Bernays's conception was given scientific endorsement in 1971 by B. F. Skinner, the leading figure in the behaviorist movement that became highly influential in the post–World War II period. As Skinner put it in his book *Beyond Freedom and Dignity*, keeping to careful scientific concepts, "Ethical control may survive in small groups, but the control of the population as a whole must be delegated to specialists—to police, priests, owners, teachers, therapists, and so on, with their specialized reinforcers and their codified contingencies." The "responsible leaders," dedicated to the public interest.

Since democratic leaders can't wait for the people to arrive at even general understanding and have to engineer consent to socially constructive goals and values, some obvious questions arise. Who makes the decisions about these goals and values? What factors enter into the decisions of "democratic leaders"? How is their "responsibility" and dedication to the public interest established? Bernays avoids the questions, but when we look into them we find that very much as in Adam Smith's day, the decision makers are primarily the "masters of mankind," who have far higher priorities than "the public interest," much as Smith described. They are the ones with the power to exercise the freedom to persuade and suggest, the essence of the democratic process—power that is not exactly equally distributed. And they are the ones who judge what is socially constructive. These days, it's not just Smith's merchants and manufacturers. Nowadays, it's huge conglomerates, multinational corporations, and financial institutions and other centers of economic power.

It's important to bear in mind how deeply rooted these ideas are among the intellectual classes, across the spectrum. I'll still keep to the liberal extreme of the spectrum. One important example is perhaps the most prominent and respected public intellectual of the twentieth century, Walter Lippmann, also a Wilson-Roosevelt-Kennedy liberal, like Bernays. Wilson, like Bernays, had been a member of the Creel Commission, which Marv mentioned in our last session, the commission that Woodrow Wilson set up to try to convince the American population to join the First World War. Wilson was elected in 1916 on the slogan "Peace without victory." But he quickly changed that to "Victory without peace."

There was then a problem of getting a pacifist population to become raving anti-German hysterics. It was achieved. So, for example, the Boston Symphony Orchestra couldn't play Beethoven, and similar things were happening around the country. It was achieved very quickly by a grand propaganda campaign, and it greatly impressed the people who were involved, including Lippmann and Bernays. As Lippmann wrote afterward, this achievement shows that what he called "manufacture of consent," Bernays's engineering of consent, is a "new art" in the practice of democracy.

Lippmann was a major figure in many domains, including political theory. The main collection of his political essays is called "political philosophy for liberal democracy." In these essays he explains that the "public must be put in its place" so that "the intelligent minorities" may live free of "the trampling and roar of the bewildered herd," the public. Members of the bewildered herd are supposed to be "spectators of action," not "participants." They do have a function, however. Their function is to show up periodically to push a button to vote for a selected member of the leadership class. Then they are to go away and leave us alone. That's progressive democratic theory.

I won't talk about the harsher versions.

Another influential liberal figure, Harold Lasswell, one of the main founders of modern political science, also had something to say about these matters. In the *Encyclopedia of the Social Sciences*, he explained that we should not be deluded by "democratic dogmatisms about men being the best judges of their own interests." They're not. We are.

Continuing, "The modern propagandist, like the modern psychologist, recognizes that men are often poor judges of their own interests, flitting from one alternative to the next without solid reason or clinging timorously to the fragments of some mossy rock of ages. . . . The older democratic doctrines allowed the nominal leader to escape his task of leadership by some procedural rigmarole: a 'general will' was supposed to be 'out there,' and the leader's duty was to watch carefully for it to manifest itself through the machinery of balloting and legislative discussion." But we must put such nonsense behind us in the modern age of scientific psychology and political science. "With respect to those adjustments which do require mass action the task of the propagandist is that of inventing goal symbols which serve the double function of facilitating adoption and adaptation. The symbols must induce acceptance spontaneously and elicit those changes in conduct necessary to bring about permanent adaptation. The propagandist as one who creates symbols which are not only popular but which bring about positive realignments of behavior is no phrasemonger but a promoter of overt acts."

Note the free use of the term "propagandist," as with Bernays. This was in the '30s. In those days, the term did not have the negative connotations it has since assumed (in English; other languages still use the term neutrally).

Putting aside the pseudo-scientific gobbledygook, we're back to the same principles. In a democratic society, we, the intelligent minority, have the duty of directing the "ignorant and stupid" masses to what we decide are proper goals, using whatever deception is required. All for their own good.

These points were elaborated by Reinhold Niebuhr, a highly respected liberal political analyst and theologian, often described as "the theologian of the (liberal) establishment." He explained that because of "the stupidity of the average man," enlightened leaders have to construct "necessary illusions" and "emotionally potent simplifications" to ensure that the best interests of the general public are served by the "responsible intellectuals." From a different perspective, the responsible intellectuals are what Gramsci called "experts in legitimation," whose task is to somehow legitimate what's happening.

Henry Kissinger, who was a master in the art, explained it a little differently. Paraphrasing one of his insights, the "expert" is someone who can "articulate the consensus of the powerful," and thus, by implication, can manage their affairs for them.

Not everyone qualifies as an expert or responsible intellectual. There are also "the wild men in the wings"—the phrase used in a major article in the major establishment journal *Foreign Affairs* in 1968 by Kennedy–Johnson national security advisor McGeorge Bundy, former Harvard dean, later head of the Ford Foundation. He was referring to people who are so remote from reality that they don't just question the government's tactics but even raise questions about motives. Specifically, he had in mind critics of the Indochina wars that he had been conducting. Plainly total insanity. Insanity that is incidentally well documented in the *Pentagon Papers* released by Dan Ellsberg shortly after Bundy wrote. It contains ample material on motives, sometimes quite explicit and not too attractive, to put it mildly. And not just confirming but substantially extending the lunacy of the wild men.

Well, every society has its wild men in the wings. In the old Soviet Union, the wild men in the wings, from the point of view of the rulers, were the dissidents. They were harshly treated in the Soviet Union but of course greatly honored here. We all know their names. When we come back home, the values are reversed. The dissidents are wild men, condemned or more often simply ignored. Who, for example, even knows the names of the leading Latin American intellectuals assassinated in 1989 by the elite forces that we armed and trained? Anybody here know their names? Or even that it happened?

There's a long list of others—often suffering the "martyrdom, which, in an infinite variety of shapes, awaits those who have the heart and will and conscience to fight a battle with the world," to quote Nathaniel Hawthorne's *House of the Seven Gables*.

We don't have time to go through the history, which is a revealing one. But in brief, the pattern goes way back to the earliest recorded history. So go back to classical Greece and ask who had to drink the hemlock and commit suicide. It was the guy who was corrupting the youth of Athens by asking too many questions, Socrates. Roughly at the same time, if you look at the biblical record, there were people who are called prophets, a misleading translation of an obscure Hebrew word. They were what we might call dissidents. They were criticizing the evil acts of the kings, giving geopolitical analysis, warning of what was going to happen as a result of these terrible policies, calling for mercy for widows and orphans, clearly wild men in the wings. They were not welcomed. They were treated harshly—imprisoned, driven into the desert, condemned as haters of Israel, in this case, the prophet Elijah. That's the origin of the phrase "Jewish self-hatred" used today to condemn Jewish critics of Israeli policy by prominent Israeli political figures like Abba Eban and, commonly, by defenders of these policies here.

Centuries later, the prophets were honored. But not at the time. At the time, the people who were honored were the flatterers at the Court, those who were later called false prophets. The experts in legitimation. And so it goes right through history. An interesting story.

Take Gramsci. When he was condemned to prison by the Mussolini dictatorship, the prosecutor said that we must stop this brain from functioning for twenty years. Now that was fascism. We are a little harsher. Romero and the Jesuit intellectuals—and a long list of other religious martyrs—simply had their brains blown out and were silenced forever, not just for twenty years.

And you have to make sure that they're unknown forever. It's very interesting to see how this works in detail. So let's go back to Boston, the most liberal city in the country. In 1990, shortly after the assassination of the Jesuit intellectuals, the American Psychological Association had its conference in Boston. There was a series of panels. I was participating in one, which was devoted to the work of one of the murdered Jesuit intellectuals, a prominent social psychologist. The conference was covered by the *Boston Globe*, at the time I think the most liberal newspaper in the country, which had excellent Latin America coverage, probably the best in the country.

The *Globe* covered the conference, but not this section. Instead the journal preferred a paper on male facial expressions that are attractive to women. That was much more important. You have to have your priorities straight. It's necessary to cultivate the right kind of intellectuals.

I don't mean to blame the reporter, who had probably never heard of the massacre of the Jesuit intellectuals a few months earlier.

Well, I'll leave to your imagination what the reaction would be if things like this were going on in the old Soviet Union under the Kremlin dictatorship.

The essential point was made by the acute and often bitter critic H. L. Mencken, referring to an Irish American writer who was in and out of jail on trivial charges: "If [he] were a Russian, read in translation, all the professors would be hymning him."

All too accurate.

Actually, George Orwell had some interesting things to say about this. You've all read *Animal Farm* in school, I'm sure. But it's pretty unlikely that you've read Orwell's preface to *Animal Farm*, which was not published. It was discovered many years later in his collected papers. It sometimes appears in contemporary editions, but was probably missing from the book you read.

You'll recall that *Animal Farm* is a satirical critique of Bolshevik Russia, the totalitarian enemy. But the preface, directed to the people of free England, says that they shouldn't feel too self-righteous about it. England too has literary censorship, of a kind appropriate to free societies in thrall to hegemonic common sense. "The sinister fact about literary censorship in England," Orwell wrote, "is that it is largely voluntary. Unpopular ideas can be silenced, and inconvenient facts kept dark, without any need for any official ban." He did not explore the reasons in any depth, merely noting the control of the press by "wealthy men who have every motive to be dishonest on certain important topics," reinforced by the "general tacit agreement that 'it wouldn't do' to mention that particular fact." As a result, "Anyone who challenges the prevailing orthodoxy finds himself silenced with surprising effectiveness." Relegated to the category of wild men in the wings, if noticed at all.

An essential mechanism of censorship, in Orwell's view, is a good education. If you've gone to the best schools, you have instilled into you the understanding that there are certain things it wouldn't do to say, or, we may add, even to think. It all becomes part of your being. And if you're a good student and have properly absorbed the lessons, you can become a responsible intellectual.

That's the unpublished preface to *Animal Farm*. But what are the kinds of things it wouldn't do to say? Or to think? I've just given a number of examples. US crimes in Latin America, for example, and also the very interesting comparison of Latin America, US domains, with Russian domains in Eastern Europe. There are some quotes in the reading.

Latin American intellectuals recognized that Eastern Europeans are "in a way, luckier than Central Americans," one wrote—the publisher of a journal that was blown up by US-backed state terrorists, arousing no interest in the United States. "While the Moscow-imposed government in Prague would degrade and humiliate reformers," he continued, "the Washington-made government in Guatemala would kill them. It still does, in a virtual genocide that has taken more than 150,000 victims . . . [in what Amnesty International calls] a 'government program of political murder.' . . . One is tempted to believe that some people in the White House worship Aztec gods . . . with the offering of Central American blood." The White House installed and supported forces in Central America that "can easily compete against Nicolae Ceausescu's Securitate for the World Cruelty Prize," referring to the most bloodthirsty of the East European dictators (and, incidentally, a US favorite because he was somewhat independent of the Kremlin).

That happens to be a rather typical voice of victims. But they are not alone. It's also the assessment of Western scholarship. The standard scholarly source on post-war political history is the multivolume *Cambridge History of the Cold War*. The chapter on Latin America was written by John Coatsworth, a respected Latin American expert, former Dean of Columbia University's School of International and Public Affairs. He writes that from 1960—remember the date—from 1960 to "the Soviet collapse in 1990, the numbers of political prisoners, torture victims, and executions of nonviolent political dissenters in Latin America vastly exceeded those in the Soviet Union and East European satellites."

Again, you might ask yourselves how many of the Eastern Europeans you've heard of? And how many of the Latin Americans? An interesting study, never undertaken as far as I know. I mentioned that you should think about 1960. I'll come back to the reasons, if not today, later.

Well, let's turn to some further examples of what it wouldn't do to say today. So take the *New York Times*, a couple of days ago, a front-page story. It's about how National Security Advisor John Bolton asked the Pentagon to draw up plans for an attack on Iran. Bolton is already on record in an article in the *New York Times* calling for immediate bombardment of Iran. That's one story.

Another story is about the gentleman recently appointed attorney general, William Barr, who holds that the president has "unfettered power to start a major land war on his own, not only without Congressional permission but even if Congress voted against it" (Savage 2019).

The unsophisticated might think that Barr's pronouncement violates Article I of the Constitution, which vests the power to declare war in the Congress—a crucial break from common practice of the day that assigned this role to the monarch. This revolutionary innovation was motivated by the opposition of the Founders to unconstrained centralized power and their concern that such serious decisions should be based on the considered judgment of Congress. But Barr is too good a lawyer to violate the Constitution so blatantly. He therefore talks about launching a war, not declaring it. He is thus violating the clear intent of the Founders, but not their actual words.

Adopting the role of wild man, let's ask what is missing in these two front-page stories, because it wouldn't do to say.

One of the things that remains unsaid is that there is indeed a document called the US Constitution, which we're supposed to revere. It's precious, particularly among "conservatives" like Barr, who worship it. We can put aside the chicanery of violating Article I, and take a look at Article VI. There we discover that "all treaties made, or which shall be made, under the authority of the United States, shall be the supreme law of the land; and the judges in every state shall be bound thereby."

Presumably the chief executive too (though Barr and Trump might disagree).

So let's take a look at treaties that have been made under the authority of the United States.

The most important since World War II is the UN Charter, established on US initiative, the foundation of modern international law. So let's take a look at that, in particular Article 2(4). Here we discover that "the threat or use of force" is banned in international affairs. Not just the use, but even the threat. There are some exceptions, but they are transparently irrelevant here.

In passing, we should recall that there is a category of professionals, called "international law scholars," who can learnedly explain that words don't mean what we say. But we wild men are simpleminded folk who don't appreciate these subtleties, so let's accept the plain meaning of the text.

Among the things it wouldn't do to say is that the leading figures of the administration are violating the US Constitution, the supreme law of the land. Does anybody care? Apparently not. It seems to be of no concern to responsible intellectuals.

In extenuation, it is only fair to observe that Barr is not entirely breaking new ground. Though his contempt for the Constitution in these remarks is extreme, it is normal for political leaders to violate the Constitution by threatening force. It has been normal for years, for example, for the president and others to say that all options are open against Iran. "All options" means all options, up to nuclear attack.

More generally, all of this is pretty standard. So take the invasion of Iraq, 2003, a textbook example of aggression without credible pretext. It's criticized. By President Obama, for example, who is greatly respected for having criticized it as a strategic blunder. Did we praise Russian generals when they criticized the invasion of Afghanistan as a strategic blunder? Or Nazi war criminals who criticized Hitler's two-front war as a strategic blunder, because they should have knocked out England first? I don't recall any such thing. Is there a difference in this case? If so, what is it—apart from us versus them? Worth thinking about.

Obama's criticism of the Iraq war is as far as you can go. Try to find somebody who said that it wasn't a mere blunder, it was the supreme international crime. That's the judgment of Nuremberg where Nazi war criminals were condemned. Many of them hanged. It described aggression—and again, the Iraq invasion is a textbook example—as "the supreme international crime differing only from other war crimes in that it contains within itself the accumulated evil of the whole": in the case of Iraq, the accumulated evil is a long list, all the way to ISIS and beyond.

The US prosecutor at Nuremberg, Robert Jackson, gave an interesting talk to the Tribunal. He said that we are handing the defendants "a poisoned chalice," and if we sip from it—if we are guilty of similar crimes—we have to suffer the same fate. Otherwise, we should concede that the judicial proceeding is a farce, victor's justice. Well, you can draw your own conclusions. But these are all things that it wouldn't do to say or to think about—under the reign of hegemonic common sense.

Let's take a look at the worst international crime since the Second World War, the US invasion of Vietnam, then all of Indochina, leaving many millions of corpses and three countries in ruins. Sometimes the assault was undertaken with explicit directives reaching to such levels of criminality that they defy words, such as the infamous orders that Kissinger obediently transmitted to the US Air Force calling for "a massive bombing campaign in Cambodia. Anything that flies on anything that moves" (Becker)—a call for genocide that is hard to duplicate in the historical record. Orders that were carried out, providing a major stimulus for the creation of the Khmer Rouge, as revealed by scholarship (Ben Kiernan and others) but hardly penetrates to common sense.

The wars ended in 1975, and of course everyone of any significance had to write a comment about it. There were basically two groups. The hawks said that if we'd fought harder, we could have won. Maybe we were stabbed in the back by antiwar protesters. The second group was the doves. At the extreme critical end in the mainstream, perhaps, was Anthony Lewis of the *New York Times*. Again, it's always useful to look at the establishment Left, marking the limits of what it is OK to say.

Lewis wrote in *New York Times* (May 1, 1975) that the war began with "blundering efforts to do good." How do we know that? Because it's an axiom, a necessary truth. If the United States did it, it was an effort to do good. You don't need any evidence for that. That's hegemonic common sense. Why "blundering efforts"? Because it didn't work.

So the war began with blundering efforts to do good, "but by 1969 it was clear to most of the world—and most Americans—that the intervention had been a disastrous mistake. . . . The argument [against the war] was that the United States had misunderstood the cultural and political forces at work in Indochina—that it was in a position where it could not impose a solution except at a price too costly to itself."

That's the extreme left criticism expressible in the mainstream.

There was another view expressed at the same time: that the war was "fundamentally wrong and immoral . . . not a mistake" (Rielly 1987). But that's of course the kind of anti-American hysteria you expect from the wild men in the wings, so it was quite reasonable to deny it expression.

Except that the wild men in the wings in this case were the large majority of the population.

There are regular studies of US public opinion on international affairs. The major monitor of public opinion on such matters is the respected Chicago Council of International Relations. They had polls in 1975, and, of course, among the questions posed were questions about attitudes toward the war in Vietnam. There were various options available. One of the options was that the war was "not a mistake," it was "fundamentally wrong and immoral." That option was selected by 70 percent of the population. The "wings" must be pretty broad to cover all of these wild men. One can sympathize with the contempt of the liberal intellectual elite for "the stupidity of the average man," who doesn't even realize what it wouldn't do to say.

That question continued to be asked in the polls for many years, with about the same result. Roughly two-thirds or more said the war was fundamentally wrong and immoral, not a mistake. You would be hard put to find one comment by left-liberal intellectuals who made it into the mainstream who could express the views of the population.

There is, of course, a lingering question. What did people mean by this?

That question was finally raised by the academic director of the studies, political scientist John Rielly. He wrote that the responses show a "preference to avoid undertaking major burdens in foreign interventions." Possibly. Or possibly they show that the public thought that the war was fundamentally wrong and immoral, not a mistake. It wouldn't have been hard to determine the answer, but apparently the inquiry was never undertaken. Perhaps it was considered superfluous since the right conclusion is so obvious.

All of this raises quite interesting questions about the hold that hegemonic common sense exercises over the responsible men as compared with the stupid and ignorant masses. Quite interesting questions. It wouldn't be too surprising to discover that the experts in legitimation are more deeply indoctrinated than those who are not subjected constantly to streams of propaganda and are not its purveyors. There is some evidence to this effect on a number of issues, but it's never been investigated systematically, as far as I know.

Since I still have a few more minutes, I'd like to say a few words about how the issues we are discussing arose in the first modern democratic revolution in seventeenth-century England, along with the problem of "putting the public in their place"—Lippmann's problem three centuries later. That's the immediate background for Hume's observations on engineering consent.

The mid-seventeenth-century conflict is usually presented as a war between king and Parliament, the latter representing the rising merchant and manufacturing classes. The final "glorious revolution" established the primacy of Parliament. And also registered victories for the rising bourgeoisie. One not inconsiderable achievement was to break the royal monopoly on the highly lucrative slave trade. The merchants were able to gain a large share of this enterprise, a substantial part of the basis for British prosperity.

But there also were wild men in the wings—much of the general public. They were not silent. Their pamphlets and speakers favored universal education, guaranteed health care, and democratization of the law. They developed a kind of liberation theology, which, as one critic ominously observed, preached "seditious doctrine to the people" and aimed "to raise the rascal multitude . . . against all men of best quality in the kingdom, to draw them into associations and combinations with one another . . . against all lords, gentry, ministers, lawyers, rich and peaceable men." Particularly frightening were the itinerant workers and preachers calling for freedom and democracy, the agitators stirring up the rascal multitude, and the authors and printers distributing pamphlets questioning authority and its mysteries. Elite opinion warned that the radical democrats had "cast all the mysteries and secrets of government . . . before the vulgar (like pearls before swine)," and have "made the people thereby so curious and so arrogant that they will never find humility enough to submit to a civil rule." It is dangerous, another commentator ominously observed, to "have a people know their own strength"—to learn that power is "in the hands of the governed," in Hume's words.

The rabble did not want to be ruled by king or Parliament, but "by countrymen like ourselves, that know our wants." Their pamphlets explained further that "it will never be a good world while knights and gentlemen make us laws, that are chosen for fear and do but oppress us, and do not know the people's sores."

These ideas naturally appalled the men of best quality. They were willing to grant the people rights, but within limits. After the democrats had been defeated, John Locke commented that "day-labourers and tradesmen, the spinsters and dairymaids" must be told what to believe; "the greatest part cannot know and therefore they must believe."

The second modern democratic revolution, the American Revolution, launched a century later, exposed somewhat similar conflicts, which entered crucially into the framing of the Constitution. It's a very important topic, with many crucial lessons and consequences. Too late to talk about it now. We'll return to it.

Chapter 2

THE CURRENT COMMON SENSE: CAPITALIST REALISM

Waterstone Lecture, January 22, 2019

W elcome to the second week of What Is Politics? Tonight, I have a small task. I'm going to summarize Marx's *Capital*, Volume 1, which will help refresh your memory of your K–12 Marxism classes, just in case you've forgotten a few things. Remember, this is only Volume 1 of three volumes of *Capital*, and I'll try to get through all those, plus a few of Marx's other works. Tonight's topic: capital and capitalist realism, which is the title of Mark Fisher's book *Capitalist Realism*. This phrase, which I've used before, I think captures in an interesting way this notion of capitalist realism, which is Fisher's term for a capitalist common sense. That is, "it's now easier to imagine the end of the world than to imagine the end of capitalism."

This is appropriate, I think, the day after MLK Day, as Martin Luther King Jr. said, "I'm convinced that if we are to get on the right side of the world revolution, the nation must undergo a radical revolution of values. We must rapidly begin to shift from a thing-oriented society to a person-oriented society. . . . When machines and computers, profit models and property rights are considered more important than people, the giant triplets of racism, materialism, and militarism are incapable of being conquered." The context in which Martin Luther King made this comment was a pivotal point in his own career. This is his "Beyond Vietnam" speech, after which virtually all of his former allies turned against him. He was isolated after giving this speech. The beginning of the speech basically is, one cannot remain silent. He says this in the title of this talk, "A Time to Break Silence," which he did.

This is when he made a very public transition from simply, not simply, but from exclusively working on civil rights, to working on issues of poverty and societal change. Over the next several weeks, we are going to take a look at the relationship between a political economic system, that is late-stage industrial capitalism, and some of its weightiest consequences. The relationship between capitalism as a political economic system, and militarism, between capitalism and environmental catastrophe, and between capitalism and the effects produced from its globalized financialized form. But before we examine those connections, we have to have a clear understanding of what capitalism is (and must be) as a way to organize the political economy of society.

In the presentation that I'm going to give this evening, I'm talking about capitalism in a kind of idealized sense, in the best sense in which it presents itself. This is not necessarily the form that it takes in everyday life. This approach is meant to give you a sense of the essential features of a capitalist system. Features without which it is not capitalism, and the reasons why it is then tied to these other consequences, in fundamental and rather necessary ways. That's the purpose of the conversation this evening.

Let's begin to think about how the system works. I want to start with the notion of production, which is the most basic human interaction with nature. It combines human labor, sometimes historically using animal labor and tools, combines that labor with elements of nature to satisfy human needs and wants, which themselves are quite variable categories, of course. What, beyond very basic physiological requirements, defines needs, and what marks the point when we move from needs into wants. This is a very slippery category, one that is quite explicitly exploited by the advertising and marketing fields, whose entire job is to convert wants into needs.

Resources derive from the neutral stuff of nature. In this case, "neutral" simply refers to unappraised. That is, the neutral stuff of nature only becomes a resource when it's recognized by society, or by individuals, or by small groups as being useful. This recognition depends on the state of knowledge, the state of capability, and whether the materials are accessible. This is clearly then changeable over time, and from place to place, and from culture to culture. Usability and accessibility depend on the state of technology, economic conditions, and so forth.

Something that is a resource at one place or time may not be a resource at another place or time, and vice versa. Something that is not recognized as a resource in one moment may become recognizable and accessible as a resource under other circumstances. The idea of resources are not that they exist, but that they become. The original notion of production, historically, anthropologically, was for use only. That is, the interaction between people and the physical world produced goods that were useful. Most production was by families or small groups.

The means of production, that is the raw materials, and tools, and labor, are at this point held in the same hands. The people who are doing the producing are the people who control both the means of production, and labor. Eventually over time, there is a division of labor, and some specialization. This leads to a surplus, in some circumstances, of particular goods. That is, some production goes beyond immediate needs. So that not everything that's produced is immediately consumed. This is connected to this idea of specialization and division of labor.

This allows then for the trade of that surplus. We are moving from this individuated production for immediate consumption needs, to a system in which there is some surplus, and this fosters the ability to engage in trade. The first kind of trade is barter, that is, one useful thing for another. Usually occurs under face-to-face circumstances, no separation in time and space. The people who are engaged in barter know each other, they interact, this is one commodity or one good for another: C ←→ C.

I put that notation there because I'm going to use it again in a couple of minutes. The idea of one good for another. At first, exchange is incidental to production for use. That is, exchange is not the primary intention of production; it's incidental. One question that immediately arises in even barter situations is what is the rate of exchange, how to know how much of one thing to trade for another. How do we equilibrate those things? Whether it's bread for shoes, shoes for wine, and so on.

One measure is the necessary labor time that goes into the production of the good. This is a very rudimentary kind of labor theory of value. That is, what the good is worth is how much time it takes to produce it. That could include the acquisition of the raw materials that are necessary and so forth. It is clearly not perfect, since one producer may be much more or less efficient than another with whom he or she is trading goods. But, it produces a rough equivalence, that is, we know how many pairs of shoes to trade for how much grain for example, or how much bread. This is one basis for thinking about how we make that equivalence.

In *Capital*, Volume 1, Marx begins with the concept of the commodity. It's the first chapter in the book. It's a very interesting story about how he gets to that. In a previous work called the *Grundrisse*, which is an outline of his major work on capital, or political economy, he ends the *Grundrisse* with a little tiny note on the notion of the commodity. He has a little note to himself at the end of this; it is less than a one-page comment that says, "This to be moved forward." Then he begins *Capital* by speaking about the commodity, which he thinks about as the most basic element of capital.

The commodity includes two components: use value; that is, the commodity has to be useful for someone for something. Under capital, however, a commodity also has to have this other essential element, which is exchange value. That is, it has to be capable, in addition to it being useful, of carrying something that the society values. We'll talk about what that is in just a minute. The commodity must have these two elements to be useful in a capitalist sense. To perform its function as I say, it has to include both elements.

These elements are reciprocal and antithetical to each other. That is, to operate as a capitalist bearer of value, in an exchange, one has to give up the use value to get the exchange value, and vice versa. That is, if you come to a market with a pair of shoes, but you can't give up the pair of shoes, because you need them, you can't put them into the exchange and get the exchange value. Vice versa, if you come to the exchange with money (which we'll discuss in a moment), you must give up that money to get the use value. These things are embodied in the commodity, but as I say, they are held in an interesting kind of antithetical tension with each other. You must give up one to get the other.

Another word that Marx uses for this is that the commodity must be alienable for you. You must be able to give it up in order to get back what you think it is worth. So let's talk about another issue that becomes very necessary in this sort of formulation. This arises when the division of labor, that is, specialization of tasks, and exchange become more generalized. That is, when they are not simply incidental to production as a little bit of surplus, but when this becomes a dominant part of the pattern of society. When specialization and exchange become generalized, there is a need for something called a universal equivalent.

Under such circumstances, a universal equivalent is a particular commodity in terms of which all other commodities can be valued. It gets very awkward if you have a lot of goods being exchanged, to think about simply talking about the amount of labor time, or average labor time that went into them. Rather than being able to talk in those terms, we need something called a universal equivalent. That universal equivalent we call money. Performing as the universal equivalent is one of the functions, one of the several functions, that money performs, but I'm going to stay just with this one for tonight.

Anything can serve as money. Historically, many things have served as money over time. You know the word *salary*. Comes from the word *salt*, and salt at one point was a form of money. For reasons historical, other reasons, reasons of portability, durability, consistent quality, things like gold and silver, and sometimes copper and other precious metals, have served most typically over time as money. The important point to note here is that money performs this function of a universal equivalent. The value of every other commodity can see itself in money.

Let's start now by thinking about how this works. This is the most basic form of commodity exchange: C ←→ M ←→ C

C, commodity; M, money; C, another commodity. This is selling in order to buy. You come to market with a commodity, say you have a surplus of shoes, but you don't specialize in making bread, you come to market, you sell the shoes, you get money, you use the money to buy bread.

Exchange, rather than use, starts to become the rationale for production. Early in the production cycle, remember, use is the predominant rationale for production. Once we are in this kind of setting, where exchange and specialization have taken over, production for exchange predominates. The item must still have a use value for someone; otherwise, there is no sale. So, one has to keep in mind the usability of the item, even though it's not use for oneself that is the primary rationale for production.

The arrows are bidirectional, because every purchase is always simultaneously a sale, if it's going to happen as a transaction. Once money is in the picture, as opposed to barter, many things change in this kind of setting. The most important of which (and we'll talk about this in a couple of different contexts in a minute) is that there is now a very significant power asymmetry at work. That is, the owner of a commodity must find a buyer for that specific commodity. The owner of money can buy anything that's on offer, or buy nothing at all. You can see that the relationship between the commodity owner and the money owner here is a very interesting and hierarchical one. That is, the owner of money has a significant advantage over the owner of the commodity.

I now want to expand this notion and think about capitalism as a mode of production, rather than just simple exchange. Here we have a formula that we are going to look at a number of times and in slightly different settings each time: M ←→ C ←→ C' ←→ M'.

I want to go over the basics of it. We start with M, which is money, C, which are input commodities, C primed is the output of one cycle of production, and M primed is more money. Start with M, one end, you end up with M primed, you hope, at the other end, and something happens in between.

This, unlike simple exchange, is buying in order to sell, rather than selling in order to buy. This is buying in order to sell. In this model, what capitalists buy is inputs or the means of production, that is, raw materials, plant and equipment, things of that sort, and labor power. So, the M at the beginning is used to buy C, which are, as I say, means of production, and labor power. Those get thrown into the production cycle, produces additional C primed output at the end of one cycle. Then, eventually, hopefully, more money.

In the capitalist mode of production, the means of production are in private hands. This is an essential feature of a capitalist mode of production. So the decisions about what to produce, how to produce it, what to do with the profits, if any, are also in private hands. We simply take these things for granted, this is how the system works. The only thing workers have to sell is their labor power. Let me repeat that, the only thing workers have to sell is their labor power.

I put a note in here, not their *labor*, and I'll make that distinction clear in just a little bit. The only thing workers have to sell is their *labor power*. So, here is an interesting thing. In the labor market, as in other commodity exchanges, there is a tremendous power asymmetry, just like in any other exchange. The owner of the commodity labor power, that is the worker, must find a willing buyer for his or her specific labor. The owner of money, that is, the capitalist, can buy whatever is on offer, or buy nothing at all.

This is something useful to think about when we reflect on Milton Friedman's piece on this issue of economic freedom, in which the participants enter into this agreement willingly, voluntarily, and on equal footing. This is clearly not the case. The worker coming into this exchange must find a buyer for his or her particular labor skills, abilities, capabilities, and so forth. The person coming in with money can either buy those or buy somebody else's, or not buy anything at all.

This immediately jeopardizes Friedman's position on this notion of economic freedom. I'll examine that in a little bit further detail in a minute. I want to turn now to another related topic. This is the idea of *primitive accumulation*. It's going to help us answer a few questions that spring to mind when thinking about these fundamental elements of a capitalist mode of production. The first question is, why are the means of production in the private hands of the few? If an essential feature of capitalism is that the means of production are in private hands, and I didn't say of the few, but we can infer that easily, why is that the case?

Second, how is it that the capitalists find people ready and willing to sell their labor power, and that's all that they have to sell? How is that the case? Let's turn to Karl Marx:

> Here is the myth first of all. This primitive accumulation plays in polit-
> ical economy about the same part as original sin in theology. Its origin
> is supposed to be explained when it is told as an anecdote of the past.
> In times long gone by there were two sorts of people; one, the diligent,
> intelligent, and above all frugal elite. The other lazy rascals, spending
> their substance more in riotous living. Thus it came to pass that the
> former sort accumulated wealth, and the latter sort had at last nothing
> to sell, except their own skins. That's really what happened. From this
> original sin dates the poverty of the great majority, that despite all its
> labor has up to now nothing to sell but itself, and the wealth of the few
> that increases constantly although they have long ceased to work. Such
> childishness is every day preached to us in the defense of property.
> (*Capital*, vol. 1, 873–74)

This is the myth. Does it continue? Do we still have this myth? Here we go. Some of you may recognize senator Charles Grassley. Last year he said, "I think not having the state tax recognizes the people that are investing." He told the *Des Moines Register*, "As opposed to those that are just spending every darn penny they have. Whether it's on booze, women or movies" (December 3, 2017).

Basically the ideas, the myth, have pretty much stayed with us, not disappeared. Again from Marx:

> In actual history, it is a notorious fact that conquest, enslavement, rob-
> bery, murder, in short, force, play the greatest part. The process there-
> fore that clears the way for the capitalist system can be none other than
> the process which takes away from the laborer the possession of his

means of production. A process that transforms on the one hand the social means of subsistence in production in the capital. The other, the immediate producers into wage laborers. If you take away from people their ability to provide for themselves, which was done by violent means, you leave them in a state where all they can sell is their labor. The so called primitive accumulation therefore is nothing else in the historical process of divorcing the producer, that is the worker, from the means of production. (*Capital*, vol. 1, 874–75)

It appears as primitive as Marx says, because it forms, as he argued, the prehistory of capital, and the mode of production corresponding to capital. We are going to complicate that in a minute.

Again, think about this in terms of Friedman's notion of economic freedom. That is, the idea that people simply present themselves as workers, rather than the fact that there's been a very deliberate and ongoing set of activities to separate workers from the means of producing for themselves. So it's a very different picture than is painted. In actuality, primitive accumulation is ongoing. It is not simply a relic of the past. We'll talk about the ways in which this continues to occur.

David Harvey has coined a phrase, calling it "accumulation through dispossession." This can take a whole variety of forms, which we'll talk about in more detail in a couple of weeks, but things like privatization of formerly public goods and services. The theft of intellectual property. The enclosures that are effectuated by things like patents and copyrights. Those are all forms of primitive accumulation, or accumulation through dispossession, and they are ongoing. They are not a relic of the past by any means.

One other crucial element, this is an especially important component of the ways in which people are separated from means of subsistence and production for themselves. This idea of

communal property, always distinct from the state property [which Marx just dealt with in another book], it was an old Teutonic institution, which lived on under cover of feudalism. We have seen how the forcible usurpation of this generally accompanied by the turning of arable land into pastoral land. That is, there were common spaces that were available to people to grow food, to graze their own animals and so forth. People were violently thrown off of that land, so as to not be able to produce for themselves. It begins at the end of the 15th and extends into the 16th century, but at that time the process was carried on by means of individual acts of violence, against which legislation for 150 years fought in vain. Didn't fight that hard, but it tried to prevent these usurpations. The advance made by the 18th century shows itself in this, that the law itself becomes now the instrument of the theft of the people's land. Although, the large farmers make use of their little independent methods as well. The parliamentary form of the robbery is that of the acts of closure of the commons, in other words, decrees by which the landlords grant themselves the people's land, this private property, decrees of expropriation of the people. (*Capital*, vol. 1, 885–86)

Again, every little opportunity that people might have had to produce for themselves is very systematically foreclosed. I mean, the term *enclosure* is exactly right. That these things were taken away as public resources to be utilized by the people, and made into private property.

And finally,

it is not enough that the conditions of labor [that is, the means of production] are concentrated in the mass in the shape of capital at the one pole of society, while at the other are grouped masses of men who have nothing to sell but their labor power. Neither is it enough that they are compelled to sell it voluntarily. Advance of capitalist production develops a working class, which by education, tradition, habit, looks upon the conditions of that mode of production as self-evident laws of nature. The organization of the capitalist process of production once fully developed breaks down all resistance. (*Capital* vol. 1, 899)

This is clearly the production of the common sense around capitalism. It's not enough that this has happened, but over time, people begin to think of it as natural, inevitable, and unavoidable. This is just how things work. Note also that what Marx is talking about here is extreme concentration of wealth at one pole, the few capitalists, and the separation of that wealth from the other pole, the masses of people. Undoubtedly, a number of you saw the latest Oxfam report, where twenty-six individuals now own as much wealth as 3.8 billion people on the planet.

There is something possibly wrong with that. I don't know any of the twenty-six personally, but I'm sure that they could give up a little bit. Even the role of money in politics is also a significant implication for democracy, which we are going to talk about. Here you can compare the papers by Milton Friedman and Robin Hahnel. Wealthy elites are able to control the government structures in their favor to enhance their own interest, and further this inequality.

Just to bring this up to date a little bit, as Mark Fisher puts it in his book *Capitalist Realism*, over the past thirty years (and we are going to talk about this in some detail in a couple of weeks), capitalist realism, which is his term for the prevailing common sense, has successfully installed a business ontology, in which it is simply obvious that everything in society should be run as a business. That's what he means by business ontology. The state of the world is a business world. He points out, and this ties back to last week's conversation on common sense, emancipatory politics must always destroy the appearance of a so-called natural order.

It must reveal what is presented as necessary and inevitable, to be a mere contingency. That is, the common sense of what we think about the capitalist world has to be demonstrated to be contingent, not necessary and inevitable. Then, on the other hand, it must make what was previously deemed to be impossible, seem attainable. He puts out a number of examples in the following paragraph to this quote, where he talks about things that just a few years ago seemed impossible, like the privatization of goods and services and so on: in that twenty- to thirty-year period, privatization did become possible.

Then anything contrary to the way things are now looks completely unattainable, even though a few years ago they seemed to be well within grasp. Again, this is the utility of thinking about things from this point of view of a malleable common sense. That is, that things can change if imaginaries are unleashed.

A couple of others before we get back to the system of how it works. This is again from Marx:

> The discovery of gold and silver in America, the extirpation, enslavement, and entombment in the mines of the aboriginal population, the

beginning of the conquest, and looting of the East Indies, the turning of Africa into a warren for the commercial hunting of black skins, are all things which characterize the dawn of the era of capitalist production. These idyllic proceedings are the chief moments of primitive accumulation. The different moments of primitive accumulation distribute themselves now more or less in chronological order, particularly over Spain, Portugal, Holland, France, and England. In England at the end of the 17th century, they arrived at a systematical combination embracing the colonies, the national debt, the modern mode of taxation, and the protection of system. The concentrated and organized force of society to hasten, hot-house fashion, the process of transformation, of the feudal mode of production into the capitalist mode, and to shorten the transition. Force is the midwife of every old society pregnant with a new one. It is itself, that is force, is an economic power. (*Capital*, vol. 1, 915–16)

Again, he's making the point that these forms of primitive accumulation are essential forms for capital to have gone through in order to get to where it gets to. These methods depend in part on group force, for example the colonial system, but they all employ, and this is something quite important, the power of the state: this, for Marx, is one of the few statements that he makes about the role of the state. He had a planned volume on the role of the state in capitalist society, but never got to it.

Now let's turn to the formula, talking about accumulation: M ←→ C ←→ C' ←→ M'.

M, money, C, input commodities, one cycle; M prime, more money. What happens in this process to allow M to become M prime, which is the whole point? You wouldn't go through all of this if you ended up at the end with the same money as you started out with at the beginning. M just came out as M. The whole point is to get from M to M prime.

To understand this, we have to examine this peculiar commodity of labor power. As an analysis of how more money emerges from the production process than goes in, Marx first rules out any possibilities of cheating or unfairness. In his analysis of the capitalist system, Marx is in a conversation with, and often in argumentation with, the economists, and political economists who came before them, principally the classical political economists. People like David Ricardo, Adam Smith, and a number of others.

He wanted to make his analysis within their frame of rules, which presents capital in its best light. So that if in fact he shows it not to produce the advantages that they claim, he will have done it on their terms. One of the things he does is to rule out things like cheating, like buying low and selling high, which is a sort of principal character of mercantilism. The reason he rules this out is, he says, that on balance in society, this doesn't produce any additional surplus value or wealth. It simply redistributes what value or wealth already exists. That it all averages out; if you cheat somebody, you may have gotten something, but they lost something. It's a kind of zero-sum thing. He rules that out. Everything in the process as Marx analyzes it trades at its true value.

The means of production cannot be the source of the additional value. Remember, he's trying to figure out in his process how we get from M to M prime. One of the things that capitalists do is buy means of production. He says, those cannot be the source of additional value. The reasons are this. They either transfer part of their value to the new products, or, for example, you depreciate machinery over time. You can calculate how much of the value goes into a production in each cycle of production. Or the means of production actually end up incorporated into the new product itself, but there is no new value there. So, if you make something, if you make bread out of wheat, it becomes incorporated in the bread, but there is no new value there. It's necessary for the capitalists to find on the market the commodity that produces more value than it itself costs. That's the trick.

This unique commodity is labor power, and is the only element in the process that produces surplus value, which is the source of profit. It's a unique commodity in that regard. How does this work? Fortunately, there is a simple answer. I hate to be bearer of bad news, but this is how it works: exploitation of the worker. How does this operate?

To understand this process, we have to begin by understanding wages, particularly the notion of a prevailing average wage. Such a prevailing average wage can fluctuate around a mean, depending on supply and demand for labor, but is set by how much it takes to enable the worker to reproduce him- or herself on a daily basis. That is at a minimum to feed, clothe, shelter him- or herself, so as to be able to return to work the next day. This is how the wage is set.

This prevailing average wage that is the price of the reproduction of labor is dependent on the cost of a so-called basket of commodities, that constitute a set of reasonable expectations of compensation in a given society, at a given time and place. Marx very problematically used the nation-state as the scale for this. There could be enormous fluctuations within that. You think about what it takes to feed, clothe, shelter, and so forth, a person at a particular time in place. This is sort of the average wage, and it's this basket of commodities. Quite clearly, this average wage varies over time, and from place to place. What is a reasonable set of expectations in the US in 2019 is clearly different than it was in 1950 or 1970, or what it might be at present in Bangladesh or Germany. Just as a side note, average wages in 2019 in the US are about where they were in 1970. We'll come back to that in a couple of weeks.

What is reasonable in one time and place is clearly different than it might be in another time and place, but the mechanism for determining the prevailing average wage remains the same. That is, you determine a wage by calculating the cost of a basket of commodities. What varies from time to time and from place to place is what goes into the basket.

Now that we know how a prevailing average wage is calculated, we can translate this into our understanding of how M' is derived from M in the production process. We begin by asking what does the capitalist buy when he or she buys the commodity of labor power? What is the capitalist actually purchasing? It is the worker's ability to labor. The capitalist gets to decide how that ability will be put to use. This is the difference between buying labor power, and buying labor. If you buy labor, it's already embodied in a good or service. If you buy labor, the worker has already determined how to expend that labor power. If you buy labor power, you, as the capitalist, get to determine how that will be directed and used. The capitalist buys the worker's ability to labor.

Does the capitalist buy the worker's entire life? Certainly not. That would be slavery, which is too expensive for capitalists, because they have to then pay for the upkeep, much better to rent the wage slave, than to purchase the actual slave. The capitalist buys the worker's capacity to work for a specified period, which is the working day. The length of the working day, I should note, has been a long-standing site of enormous class struggle. At the time Marx was writing *Capital*, an average working day could be sixteen, could be eighteen hours, or even longer. The fight, historically, for what we now typically think about as the eight-hour day, or the forty-hour week, was a long, long struggle. But back to the process, basically what the capitalist is buying is the worker's capacity to work, but for a specified period of his working day.

From the capitalist's point of view, this working day is, of whatever length it turns out to be, divided into two parts. This is from the capitalist's point of view, although the capitalist doesn't think about it this way, either. I'll say something about that in a second. Part of the day is what's called the necessary labor part of the day. That's the part of the working day in which the worker reproduces his or her own cost, and for which he or she is paid through the wage.

The basket of commodities that constitutes the prevailing average wage has a value. A worker has to work so long in a day to produce that value in goods and services. That's the necessary part of the working day. If that part of the working day coincided with the entire workday, there would be no surplus whatsoever. That's clear. If the working day was sixteen hours, but it took sixteen hours to produce the value of that basket of commodities, there is no surplus.

The other part of the working day, called the surplus labor part of the day, is the part in which the worker continues to produce goods or services, but for which she or he is not paid. This is the process that produces surplus value, and it's the source of all of the capitalist's profits. The working day, let's say it now consists of eight hours, but if the worker reproduces him or herself in anything less than that time, then everything above that is surplus. The capitalist has not paid for it, and so this is the source of surplus value and profit. All of this works behind the backs of both capitalist and workers. Nobody sees the working day in this way.

We have this mythology, a fair day's work for a fair day's wages. In fact, that's not how the working day works at all. If it were, capitalism would grind to a halt instantly. The time that it takes to reproduce the worker is always something less than the time that the worker works. It's clearly in the capitalist interest to reduce the necessary labor part of the day, that is, the time that the worker is paying for him or herself, as much as possible, and to increase the surplus labor time part of the day as much as possible. If you could go from the necessary working day being three-quarters of the day to one-quarter, you've increased the surplus by that much.

Marx identified two ways in which this could happen. One was called absolute surplus value. That is, you could do this by increasing the length of the working day. Let's say it takes four hours to reproduce the worker, and the workday is only six hours. Well, if you increase the length of the working day to eight or twelve hours, and all else remains equal, that is, it takes the same amount of time to reproduce the worker, you've increased the surplus time. This ability to increase the length of the working day has both biological limits (that is, you can only work for so long before productivity begins to decline precipitously), and now has, in many places, legal limits. Not every place. There are a lot of places where there are no prohibitions on the length of the working day. At some point the biological constraints do begin to play a factor. You can't do this continuously.

And so another way to increase the surplus part of the day is what Marx called relative surplus value, and this you can do by increasing the intensity of the labor process. Through things like reorganizing the labor process, so there is more cooperation, more efficiency, your throughput becomes quicker, you can speed up the line in a manufacturing setting. At the turn of the last century, there were all these time and motion studies that were trying to actually anatomize each work process to make it as efficient as possible. All those are things that you can do to increase the intensity of the work process, and, importantly, for which the capitalist pays nothing. So again, this is another way to increase the surplus part of the day.

Let's return to this formula one more time: M $\longleftrightarrow$ C $\longleftrightarrow$ C' $\longleftrightarrow$ M'.

We now know where M prime comes from. It comes from exploitation of the worker. If at the end of each cycle the capitalist simply spends the surplus, that is, the M prime, on his or her own consumption, or simply hoards it, sticks it in an offshore account, or something like that, and spends it all up, this is called "simple reproduction," and does nothing to add to economic growth. It's a very uninteresting part of all of this. If, on the other hand, part of the surplus is thrown back into the production process for another cycle of production, by buying more means of production, and/or buying more labor power, this is called "expanded reproduction," and this is what leads to economic growth.

Engaging in this process means that some decisions have to be made. In expanded reproduction, at the beginning of each cycle, the capitalist must decide how much to reinvest, and interestingly, how to divide that reinvestment between labor power (i.e., living labor), called variable capital, and means of production, which are called constant capital or dead labor. The reason they are called that—if you think about tools, and equipment, and raw material—they have labor embodied in them, but they don't have living labor in them. You take a machine, it has labor in it, but that labor has already been expensed. It's called constant capital or dead labor.

At the beginning of each new cycle of production, then, capitalists divide their reinvestment between means of production and labor power. There is a decision to make, how much to reinvest, and how to divide that reinvestment between these two components of capital investment. These decisions are based at least in part, and often in large part, on how the production process is being modified by the capitalist's competitors. Capitalists do not operate in a void typically. That is, they are in a segment of capital, or in a segment of the market, where they have competition.

The decisions that other competitors are making compel capitalists to keep up in one way or another. Under the compulsion of this constant competition, capitalists constantly revolutionize the production process to stay one jump ahead, and thereby maintain, and maximize, their own profits. Others must then either follow them, innovate on their own, or go under. This is why Marx thought of capitalism in very admiring terms in many ways as this revolutionary system. That is, if all of this kind of constant innovation could be turned to other ends, and not simply profit maximization for the few, this had some real promise. Marx was quite admiring of this potential.

The only escape for individual capitalists from this constant competition is monopoly. Over time, this is a trend in capitalism: the big eat the small. When we look at media consolidation, or we look at consolidation in other sectors, this is the driver. The only way in which capitalists can escape this constant competition is by developing a monopoly control over their market segment. This is why they strive for mergers and acquisitions to rule out their competition. It means they can get off of this sort of revolutionizing treadmill.

For a variety of reasons, mostly having to do with the need to control the vagaries of living labor, capitalists tend, over time, to increase the amount they invest in constant rather than variable capital. That is, they tend to put more money into the means of production than into labor. A lot of this has to do, as I say, with a living labor force being somewhat problematic.

One common form of this phenomenon that we see all the time now is automation; that is, replacing living labor with dead labor (machines). This has several important effects. Some of which are social, some of which are economic. Skill is invested in the machines, and the workers become deskilled machine minders. This is a very useful thing for capitalists. It doesn't mean that as you automate there might not be the production of some new jobs that have real value, but in a much more generalized sense, workers are deskilled. They then become quite easily replaceable by other workers.

For example, over the history of technology, in industrial technology, we see women replacing men, children replacing adults. As the necessary strength for a skill gets invested in the machine, or the necessary artisanal skills get put into the machine, you can get much less skilled workers to do the same sort of thing. This has an enormous disciplining effect on existing workers. That is, if you know, not only that there are a number of people waiting to take your job, but that they don't really have to know much, this makes you rather docile in the workplace. Over time, the same amount, or even an increase in production, takes fewer and fewer workers. We are seeing this now. We'll talk about this again in a couple of weeks.

This may also add to a reserve of unemployed labor, or underemployed labor, which is another disciplining effect. We have a very low official unemployment rate in the US now, about 4 percent, or even less.* Many people, though, have either given up looking for work, or are vastly underemployed. We've got to keep in mind that the true unemployment rate is very different than that. Even people who are employed, many of them are not employed in jobs that pay enough to actually subsist. Having that reserve army out there is again another disciplining effect.

This process of investment in constant versus variable capital, that is, in means of production versus living labor, produces two major problems for capital. We are seeing these now. The first problem, since living labor is the only source of surplus value, shifting from living to dead labor may contribute to a falling rate of profit. There are ways in which capital can ameliorate this, but each of these has a cost as well. I'm just going to mention these now, and then come back to what they produced at the end of the 1960s into the 1970s, in a couple of weeks. A falling rate of profit can be ameliorated by a rising rate of exploitation, that is, you can work the existing workforce harder. However, as I said, that has limits, both biological and legal.

If the constant capital that you are investing in itself becomes less expensive, this can also ameliorate a falling rate of profit. You can depress wages below their value, which is a form of cheating, and again won't last very long if there is any competition, and if there is a greater demand for labor power than there is supply. You can increase the industrial reserve army thereby putting more pressure on existing workers to work and perform harder. All those are ways that you could ameliorate this problem. The problem stems from the fact that you've driven out the investment in living labor, which, as I say, is the only source of surplus value and profit.

---

* As of June 2020, the unemployment rate was at approximately 11 percent, a decline from an earlier peak of 14 percent due to the Covid-19 pandemic. (See Afterword for additional analysis.)

There is another problem as well. Again, from replacing living labor with dead labor; that is, investing in constant versus variable capital. Let's return one last time to this formula: M $\longleftrightarrow$ C $\longleftrightarrow$ C' $\longleftrightarrow$ M'.

Now we know how C prime, that is, the surplus product, is produced through the exploitation of the worker. We know that C prime commodity contains both use value and an increased exchange value. That's essential. That's important. For the capitalist to realize that value, however, that is, to actually get the profit, the commodity has to be sold; we have to move from C' to M'.

A capitalist can go through this entire production process, but if s/he doesn't sell the product, s/he can't get the profit. How is this tied to this notion of reducing investment in living labor? For the sale to occur there must be effective demand, which means a buyer with both the desire to buy the commodity and the means to buy it. You can certainly create the demand through advertising, and so forth, but if you've now got people who are either unemployed, underemployed, or underpaid, you don't have the second component of this, the capacity to buy the product.

If each capitalist acting in his or her own self-interest continually lowers his or her own labor cost, for example, through automation, or through lowering wages, or exporting jobs elsewhere, the aggregate effect is to reduce overall effective demand. That's in essence a huge part of what we've been experiencing since the crash of 2008, and is a problem that is sometimes called overproduction, and sometimes called under-consumption. They are not quite the same thing, but I'm not going to go into the differences here. Essentially, it's a capitalist crisis, where you have goods and services going unsold, because there is not enough effective demand to purchase them.

This, then, brings us very briefly to the role of the state in capitalism. We've already seen that the state plays a role in securing the conditions necessary for capitalism to flourish. Things like military conquests, and imperialism and colonialism, through the legal system that gets set up, things like the enclosure movements, protection of private properties, security of contracts, those sorts of things, through the provision of needed infrastructure, which we haven't talked about yet, but all of these capitalist enterprises rely upon an environment in which they can actually operate. Roads, communication systems, research and development.

All of these sorts of things are typically provided by the state, but also the role of the state in a capitalist system is to protect capitalism from capitalists. Left to their own devices, and I just showed you an example of this, the aggregate effect of each one acting in his or her own self-interest could lead to a systemic kind of catastrophe. Just think about FDR's New Deal, which was, in fact, in large part a measure to save capitalism from capitalists. The 2008/2009 bank bailout is another example, as is the minimum wage. Anybody who is against the minimum wage doesn't understand how capitalism works.

Now, I want to make some ties between this political economic system, and the kind of consequences, necessary consequences, we are going to look at in the next couple of weeks. The first one is the set of relationships between capitalism and militarism. Some of the underlying motives, the need for access to labor supplies and markets, as well as access to means of production, both positive and negative resources. That is, things that go into production as well as places to dump the waste, and so forth. That's what I mean by positive and negative resources. Historically, such militarism has taken very different forms: imperialism, colonialism, neocolonialism, neo-imperialism.

There are also numerous connections, as we've seen, to primitive accumulation and accumulation through dispossession, and militarism and force continue to undergird those kinds of activities. Also, militarism is a source of profits in and of itself. The military industrial complex is extremely lucrative, and now I would add in security-industrial complex, and the surveillance-industrial complex. Any number of other things you might want to use to modify that.

It is also important to keep in mind the multiple connections between militarism abroad and militarism at home. These connections are underlain by an evolving of pervasive common sense, which is a fear of dangerous others. This is a common sense that must be constantly reinforced. A part of this element of common sense has to do with the legitimacy of the state. Given a globalized economic system, individual nation-states can't guarantee the economic security of their own citizens in many cases. The decisions that need to be made about the economy are not made by states. And therefore, a new basis of legitimacy (i.e., rather than economic security) had to be found. This now depends on protection from these dangerous others. Targeting of these people is often used to divide the working class against themselves. We see this in the rise of nationalism, populism, so-called, and so forth.

These dangerous others include foreign enemies. This role used to be filled by communists, but this was very difficult to sustain since the fall of the Berlin Wall and the collapse of the former Soviet Union. Communism has, therefore, become much less of an issue, so we've had to switch to a different enemy: the global terrorist, along with immigrants and refugees. We are also constantly reminded to be very afraid of domestic enemies: women, people of color, the young, the old, LGBTQ communities, the differently abled. All of these are constantly targeted as dangers from which we need protection. And that's part of the way in which the state in 2019 establishes its legitimacy, as well as a way to bring militarism home.

The second set of connections is between capitalism and environmental catastrophe. Again, these are necessary connections between a capitalist political economy and its consequences. The underlying motive is the need for continuous capital growth and expansion. Competition drives it in a lot of ways that we'll talk about. Unfortunately, however, we are in a finite world. Some of the results include widespread resource depletion, as well as pervasive environmental pollution, including climate change. Many of these consequences occur because of capitalism's dependence on externalizing (that is, putting the burden on others) any costs that detract from the bottom line—the issue of externalities, which we'll talk about in a couple of weeks. Pervasive common sense that underlies this tension is that quality of life, happiness, and satisfaction must be defined by the acquisition of things. That results in rampant and endless consumerism, novelty, obsolescence, and waste, because these are things that capitalism produces.

Finally, there is a set of connections between capitalism, in its neoliberal, financialized, and globalized form, and a set of consequences resulting from that form. I'm just going to go through these very, very quickly, because we are out of time, but we are also going to cover them in a couple of weeks. The underlying motive for capital to have taken on this form is that, at the end of the previous period, which was roughly 1945 to 1970, capital came up against steeply falling rates of profit. Capital needed a new form, new areas for invasion and accumulation.

Capital, under the right circumstances, is free to roam the globe, depending on the nature and extent of your sunk (or fixed) costs. That is, if you have a lot of investment in a place, and plant equipment, you are not so free to roam. But if you are not encumbered by such investment, as a capitalist you can roam around the globe in search of cheaper and/or more submissive labor, newer cheaper resources, new markets, places to dump pollution, and so forth. Other opportunities for renewed accumulation and profit include the privatization of previously public goods and services. This is a form of accumulation by dispossession—an update of primitive accumulation. Finally, extensions of new intellectual property rights, colonization of indigenous and traditional knowledge can all be used as profit sources.

While capital is free to roam around, labor is held in place. If workers could travel freely to areas of higher wages or better working conditions, this would dampen capitalists' power. This is a large part of the reason we have these incredible controversies about so-called immigrants and refugees. Pervasive common sense underlying this neoliberal form is the market or business ontology that I discussed before: markets good, government bad.

Finally, there is a relationship between all of these effects and the resistance and response that the issues generate. There are labor movements, peace movements, environmental movements, social justice and equality movements, civil rights movements, identity politics movements, and on and on. However, they are often disconnected from each other. A crucial point of the lecture, and the course more generally, is to demonstrate that these varied movements should be bound together, because all have the same underlying structural systemic causes. I will stop with that.

Chomsky Lecture, January 24, 2019

I'll start with some good news, or at least not awful news. As maybe you've seen, the Doomsday Clock was set this morning, and contrary to many people's fears, mine included, it was not moved closer to midnight. It's staying at two minutes to midnight, which is as close as it's been to terminal destruction since it was set. The original setting in 1947 was seven minutes to midnight. It reached two minutes to midnight in 1953 when the United States and the Soviet Union set off thermonuclear explosions, informing the world that humans, in their magnificence, had achieved the ability to destroy everything. Since then, the minute hand has oscillated, but it never returned to two minutes to midnight until January 2018 after Trump's first year in office. And that's where it stays today. My personal guess is that the analysts felt that if they moved it closer to midnight, within a year or two we'd reach the limit (goodbye), so they're holding back.

Well, let's turn to our current topic: hegemonic common sense, particularly as shaped and reflected in the intellectual domains, including the political and social sciences. Research in these areas is quite hard, for many reasons. One is that you can't set up controlled experiments the way you can in the hard sciences. But occasionally, history obliges and constructs a pretty good one for us.

Actually, that happened for market fundamentalism, the Friedmanite market fundamentalism that Marv was talking about in our last meeting. It happened in 1973 in Chile, when the Pinochet military coup overthrew the social democratic parliamentary government of Salvador Allende, instituting a vicious dictatorship. That was another chapter in the plague of repression that swept over the hemisphere from the early 1960s that I alluded to before, and that we'll return to later from its interesting origins on.

There is a background to this, which is worth a couple of minutes' reflection. From the late 1950s, the CIA was running one of its major operations in Chile to try to prevent Allende from being elected. It included massive electoral interference and numerous other forms of subversion (rather normal, hence unremarked). There was also large-scale economic support for the effort from the US corporate sector, the US government, the World Bank, all doing everything they could to make sure that this catastrophe didn't take place. It worked until 1970, when Allende was elected.

Note incidentally that the CIA is not a "rogue elephant," as sometimes claimed—a convenient evasion. It is an agency of the executive branch, which regularly follows orders and provides "plausible deniability" to those who issue them in the White House.

Allende's election set off a frenzy in Washington, first for the CIA, whose huge investment had collapsed, but quite generally. The US cut off foreign aid. The president of the World Bank, Robert McNamara, formerly Kennedy-Johnson secretary of defense, banned all World Bank loans, in opposition to the advice of his advisors, who wanted an accommodation with the new government. There was a sharp increase in subversion of all types, including media, which are so far to the right in Chile that you need a strong telescope to find them.

The US government itself set up what it called two tracks, a soft track and a hard track. The soft track was to destroy the economy. The phrase that was used in internal documents was "to make the economy scream," to try to crush the society so that in desperation people would throw out the government. That was the soft track.

The hard track was to prepare a military coup. There are very good sources on this, mainly a book called *The Pinochet Files*, edited by Peter Kornbluh, a Latin America scholar. It's essentially a collection of government documents that describe very carefully, lucidly, what was going on.

The central figure in all of this was Henry Kissinger, Nixon's national security advisor, then also secretary of state. The *Files* contain a report that CIA covert operations led to the assassination of the commander of the armed forces, René Schneider, who was supporting the government. The CIA thought that might be enough to set off an uprising, but it didn't. It failed to stop Allende's inauguration on November 4, 1967.

After the failure, Kissinger lobbied President Nixon to reject the State Department's recommendation that the US seek a *modus vivendi* with Allende. In an eight-page secret briefing paper that provided Kissinger's clearest rationale for regime change in Chile, he emphasized to Nixon that "the election of Allende as president of Chile poses for us one of the most serious challenges ever faced in this hemisphere [and] your decision as to what to do about it may be the most historic and difficult foreign affairs decision you will make this year."

Remember, this was right at the peak of the Vietnam War and many other things, but overthrow of the Allende regime was of transcendent importance.

Kissinger goes on to say that not only were a billion dollars of US investments at stake, but also what he called "the insidious model effect" of Allende's democratic election. There was no way for the US to deny Allende's legitimacy, Kissinger noted, and if he succeeded in peacefully reallocating resources in Chile in a socialist direction, other countries might follow suit. "The example of a successful elected Marxist government in Chile would surely have an impact on—and even precedent value for—other parts of the world, especially in Italy; the imitative spread of similar phenomena elsewhere would in turn significantly affect the world balance and our own position in it."

The "Marxist government" was in reality a social democratic government, but as Dean Acheson had explained much earlier, it's necessary to be "clearer than truth" when seeking to "bludgeon the mass mind of government." As for Italy, Kissinger didn't have to explain. He and Nixon knew why Italy was a problem: there were major left parties and a huge CIA operation had been going on since 1948 to subvert Italian democracy, one of the CIA's major operations. So the Chilean moves toward social change by parliamentary means might well have an effect on Italy and beyond.

A day later, Nixon made it clear to the entire National Security Council that the policy would be to bring Allende down. "Our main concern," he informed them, "is the prospect that he can consolidate himself and the picture projected to the world will be his success."

This "insidious model effect" is actually a leading theme of foreign policy planning rather generally. As Dean Acheson formulated the problem, a rotten apple can spoil the barrel. In Kissinger's version, the Allende government is a "virus" that might "spread contagion." The solution to that dilemma is clear: you kill the virus and you inoculate potential victims, if necessary by violent and repressive military dictatorships.

That's quite conventional thinking. It's often called the domino theory. The US didn't invent it, of course. It's second nature to any imperial power. They just took it over when the US replaced Britain and France, the major international imperial powers prior to the Second World War. The theory had been applied before. One critical case was the revolution that established the first free country of free men in the hemisphere, in Haiti in 1804. The US joined the combined effort by the great powers—France, the imperial power in Haiti, and Britain, the major world power—to crush the Haitian revolution. It was, plausibly, feared that the Haitian revolution would be an insidious model for others, especially for slave states like the United States. Haiti did achieve its freedom, at tremendous cost, but never recovered from the interventions and their aftermath. We'll return to some of the details. Participation in the assault on Haiti was the first example of resorting to the domino theory in US foreign policy.

The domino theory is often ridiculed when the dominoes don't fall, but why don't they fall? Well, because the cure was successful. Policy succeeds, dominoes don't fall, the insidious model is destroyed, the virus is killed, others are protected from infection by military dictatorships or other devices. There are many illustrations of this pattern, including, incidentally, Vietnam. I'll return to this when we discuss imperial policy later on. The Allende example is a striking one.

Though constantly ridiculed, the domino theory is maintained, as it was right through the Cold War. It is quite rational. It makes good sense.

Well, the Pinochet coup set up an almost perfect experiment for market fundamentalism, for Friedmanite policies. There could be no objection to policy decisions. The torture chambers took care of that. To use per capita equivalents, the appropriate measure, the accomplishments of the terror launched on 9/11, 1973, the date of the coup, were as if about 100,000 people were killed in the United States and half a million tortured.

Some food for thought.

I got some sense of the torture when I visited Chile a couple of years ago. I was taken on a visit to the Villa Grimaldi, the main torture chamber. It's been turned into a kind of shrine. I was taken through it by a prominent human rights activist in Chile who was a victim of the torture in the Villa Grimaldi, one of the few who survived. He took me through it step by step. Prisoners were taken through a succession of stages. First, mild torture, then harsher torture, then on and on until, at the last stage, if they'd survived so far, they were thrown into a nearby tower, which few survived. He was one.

He said at each stage there was a doctor present to make sure that the patient didn't die so he could go on to the next and harsher stage. I asked him afterward, "What happened to the doctors after democracy was restored?" He said that they're practicing in Santiago. That's one of the effects of not having a Truth Commission, not having any investigation of crimes of state. I mentioned earlier that that's something that we can think about with regard to ourselves.

In any event, there couldn't be any objections to any of the regime's policies. Furthermore, the dictatorship had huge external support. During the Allende years, as I mentioned, everything was cut off, but as soon as the dictatorship was imposed and the frenzy of murder and torture was underway, the spigot was opened. There was a flood of US aid. The World Bank provided new loans, quite substantial ones. Multinational corporations came in to profit from the grand experiment, and to help maintain the dictatorship. The market model was imposed by students of the doctrines of Friedman and his associates, the so-called "Chicago boys," Chileans who studied economics at the University of Chicago. They were operating with the advice of their neoliberal mentors, Friedman and other leading market economists who visited regularly. And who were much impressed, not just by the economic policies but even by the freedom under the dictatorship. One of the patron saints of neoliberalism and libertarianism, Friedrich Hayek, said, "I have not been able to find a single person even in much maligned Chile who did not agree that personal freedom was much greater under Pinochet than it had been under Allende." Which may tell us something about whom he chose to see.

The Chicago boys and their mentors had the good sense to maintain the highly efficient, nationalized copper producer Codelco, the world's largest. That's, of course, a radical violation of market principles, of neoliberal principles, but worthwhile since the company was the source of much of Chile's export earnings and the basis of the state's fiscal revenues.

In general, it was close to a perfect experiment. It looked like a great success, if you ignored the human costs.

In 1982, Friedman published the second edition of his manifesto, *Capitalism and Freedom*, celebrating the triumph of the cause. The timing was auspicious. In 1982 the Chilean economy crashed and had to be bailed out by state intervention. The state then controlled more of the economy than it had under Allende. Analysts who had their eyes open called it "the Chicago road to socialism." The prominent OECD (Organisation for Economic Co-operation and Development) economist Javier Santiso described the "paradox [that] able economists committed to laissez-faire showed the world yet another road to a de facto socialized banking system" (2006).

Incidentally, the chief economist of the far-right Brazilian government that was voted into office recently, Paulo Guedes, was in Chile during these years working on the miracle and has announced that those are the policies Brazil is going to follow. In his words, "privatize everything," sell off the whole country to investors, most foreign, make some profit in the short term, maybe it can get you elected for a couple years. In the longer term, the country goes down the drain. And maybe Brazil will even achieve the success of the Chilean experiment, even though it lacks the same ideal conditions.

There have been other experiments, not as clear as this one is. It is hard to find something like a controlled experiment in the complex historical world. But there are more complex cases. If we had time, it would be interesting to go through the development of industrial societies, starting with England in the seventeenth century, then the United States, the European countries, Japan, finally the East Asian tigers. There are some striking uniformities. Every single case involved radical violation of market principles. The pattern has not passed unnoticed. Economic historian Paul Bairoch, after an extensive review, concludes that "it is difficult to find another case where the facts so contradict a dominant theory [as the theory] concerning the negative impact of protectionism" (Bairoch), which is only one of the forms of market interference employed by the United States and other developed societies, and far from the most extreme.

There are some societies that did observe market principles, though not by choice: the colonies, where these policies were rammed down their throats. They became the Third World. It's not that they all started off poor. In fact, in the eighteenth century, the most advanced industrial and commercial societies were India and China, and West Africa is described by Africa historians as about at the same stage as Japan at the time of its takeoff in the nineteenth century. India was subjected to what Adam Smith called "the savage injustice of the Europeans." It was deindustrialized. England stole its high technology in the manner that we're now accusing China of doing to us (but by force in England's case). The US did the same thing with England. In fact, appropriating higher technology from others was one of the major forms of development, now barred by World Trade Organization rules—a process economic historians call "kicking away the ladder": first use the ladder to climb up, then kick it away so that others don't do so.

India became India, a deeply impoverished, largely peasant society; England developed. It has continued this way right to the present. That's a large part of the reason for the division between what's called the First and the Third World. There's one interesting exception in the Global South to this process, Japan. It's the one country of the South that developed, and the one country that wasn't colonized. Coincidence? Oddly, no lessons are drawn from it, but you might want to think about it.

Let's go back to Robin Hahnel's criticisms of Friedmanite market theory in the readings for today. He mostly criticized the economic policies, but he also had some comments on Friedman's conception that what he calls economic freedom leads to democracy. Hahnel made the obvious comment that it's a kind of democracy where the number of votes you have depends on the number of dollars in your pocket. You have a million dollars, you have a million votes. If you have no dollars, you have no votes.

Friedman, if he'd bothered, could have put up quite a good defense, namely, that's pretty much the way democracies operate, so what's the problem?

There's very good research on this in mainstream political science. Some is by an outstanding political scientist, Thomas Ferguson, who's done the main studies of the effect of campaign spending on electability and policy formation. The results are quite remarkable. Both for the executive and for Congress, you can predict electability with astonishing precision just by looking at the single variable of campaign spending. Of course, that affects policies.

It's not new, though it takes new and more sophisticated forms. In 1895, there was a famous campaign manager, Mark Hanna, who was celebrated for running successful campaigns. He was asked once what it takes to run a successful campaign, and his answer was, "There are two things that you need. The first one is money, and I've forgotten what the second one is." Ferguson's "investment theory of politics"—the idea that investors form coalitions to control the state—places Hanna's conclusions from practice on firm ground with a rich historical record, up to the present moment.

That's just the bare beginning. Campaign spending is overwhelmed by lobbying, which expanded rapidly from the seventies and through the neoliberal period. An effect of these developments is something like Friedman's concept of democracy: your votes reflect your dollars.

As I discussed earlier, the basic pattern goes back to the first democratic revolution in seventeenth-century England and continues to the second one a century later in the newly liberated colonies, to which we'll return. But we shouldn't overlook the fact that however flawed, these democratic revolutions constituted real progress toward democracy and rights. Establishing parliamentary sovereignty in England in 1689 was no small achievement, and the American Revolution opened a new era in functioning democracy. In fact, simply the phrase, "We the people" was a very radical idea, a revolutionary idea, however flawed it was in formulation and implementation.

From the perspective of the powers of the day, the American Revolution was one of those terrifying dominoes. King George III feared that if successful, the American Revolution might lead to erosion of the British Empire by the domino effect, one reason why the British clamped down harshly on the colonies as revolutionary sentiment was brewing. And after its success, the revolution deeply concerned the reactionary powers of Europe. The czar and Metternich feared that "the pernicious doctrines of republicanism and popular self-rule" spread by "the apostles of sedition" in the colonies that had cast off the British yoke might encourage similar "vicious principles" beyond.

A century after the czar and Metternich warned about the domino effect of republicanism, American leaders were expressing similar fears about Russia. Woodrow Wilson's secretary of state Robert Lansing warned that if the Bolshevik disease were to spread, it would leave the "ignorant and incapable mass of humanity dominant in the earth." The Bolsheviks were appealing "to the proletariat of all countries, to the ignorant and mentally deficient, who by their numbers are urged to become masters, . . . a very real danger in view of the process of social unrest throughout the world" (Gardner). President Wilson thought that it might already be happening. A notorious racist, he was concerned that the establishment of soldiers and workers councils in Germany would inspire dangerous thoughts among "the American negro [soldiers] returning from abroad." Already, he had heard, negro laundresses were demanding more than the going wage, saying that "money is as much mine as it is yours." Among other disasters, Wilson feared that businessmen might have to adjust to having workers on their boards of directors if the Bolshevik virus were not exterminated (Gardner 1987).

The threat of Bolshevik appeals to the "ignorant and mentally deficient" working class was so dire that the US and other Western powers were entirely justified in invading Bolshevik Russia in self-defense against "the Revolution's challenge . . . to the very survival of the capitalist order" (Gaddis 1987). That is the judgment of John Lewis Gaddis, the most highly regarded historian of the Cold War, which actually began in 1917, he argues, with the Bolshevik call for social reform and institutional change and the Western response in defense.

It was no less important to defend the civilized order against the popular enemy at home. Force must be used to prevent "the leaders of Bolshevism and anarchy" from trying to "organize or preach against government in the United States," Lansing explained. The Wilson administration recognized the threat and launched the most severe repression in US history, which successfully undermined democratic politics, unions, freedom of the press, and independent thought, as usual, with the general approval of the media and elites, all in self-defense against the ignorant rabble. Much the same story was reenacted after World War II under the pretext of a communist threat, and a few years later once again as the civil rights movement and other miscreants threatened properly functioning democracy, matters to which we will return.

There's nothing original about the regular resort to the domino theory in US post–World War II planning, in the international arena and at home. Viruses can indeed spread contagion.

I mentioned earlier the second modern democratic revolution, the one that should primarily concern us, particularly the formation of the Constitution. It's worth some elaboration.

During the 1780s, there was an impressive level of activism, discussion, debate, and popular meetings. There was a very lively pamphlet literature, meetings, all kinds of groups and associations. And rebellions, including a major rebellion in Massachusetts, Shays' Rebellion, in 1786 and '87—farmers who were protesting economic injustice at about the time that the Constitutional Convention was meeting. The rebellion enhanced the concerns of the Framers about the dangers of democracy, and was part of the reason for the "Framers' coup" that established the Constitution. The best source on these matters is the scholarly study by Michael Klarman, with that title (2016). It provides a very revealing record of the popular discussions, debates, and interchanges that were going on in the background, and also of what actually transpired at the Constitutional Convention.

The Framers themselves were comparatively wealthy, the elite. Poor farmers couldn't make the long trek to Philadelphia and spend several months there; remember, there was almost no transportation. So fairly wealthy people from the thirteen colonies gathered in Philadelphia to revise the earlier Articles of Confederation, and found themselves, to the surprise of many, constructing a radically new political system with a strong federal structure that many feared and disliked. Almost thirteen; Rhode Island didn't send any delegates, partly because of such concerns.

The discussions and the debates were sophisticated and impressive, fascinating reading. One of the main concerns all the way through was how to suppress popular pressures for liberty and democracy, all somewhat reminiscent of the first democratic revolution in England a century earlier, which established the English constitutional system in 1689, according sovereignty to Parliament.

The most influential of the Framers, James Madison, captured the dominant theme when he instructed the Convention that the government must "protect the minority of the opulent against the majority." He presented an interesting argument, referring to England, which was the model that everybody had in mind not only because they were English but because it was the most democratic society of the day.

Madison observed that "in England at this day, if elections were open to all classes of people, the property of landed proprietors would be insecure. An agrarian law would soon take place"—meaning land reform, undermining the rights of property owners, not a tolerable outcome.

The problem Madison posed was an old one, tracing back to the first classic of political science, Aristotle's *Politics*. Of the variety of systems he surveyed, Aristotle found democracy "the most tolerable," though of course he had in mind a limited democracy of free men, much as Madison did two thousand years later. Aristotle recognized the flaws of democracy, however, among them the one that Madison presented to the Convention. The poor "covet their neighbours' goods" and if wealth is narrowly concentrated, they will use their majority power to redistribute it more equitably, which would be unfair: "In democracies the rich should be spared; not only should their property not be divided, but their incomes too . . . should be protected. . . . Great then is the good fortune of a state in which the citizens have a moderate and sufficient property; for where some possess much, and others nothing, there may arise an extreme democracy" that does not recognize the rights of the rich, perhaps deteriorating to tyranny as democracy might in Aristotle's view—with unpleasant resonances today.

Aristotle and Madison posed essentially the same problem, but drew opposite conclusions. Madison's solution was to restrict democracy; Aristotle's, to reduce inequality by what amounted to welfare state programs. For democracy to function properly, Aristotle argued, "measures therefore should be taken which will give [all people] lasting prosperity [and] the proceeds of the public revenues should be accumulated and distributed among its poor" to enable them to "purchase a little farm, or, at any rate, make a beginning in trade or husbandry," along with other means, such as "common meals" with costs defrayed by "public land."

The issues remain alive, in many ways.

The Madisonian conception of the constitutional structure, which largely prevailed at the Convention, established the Senate as the most powerful branch of government, and the principle that it "ought to come from and represent the wealth of the nation," the "more capable sett [*sic*] of men." The Senate was not directly elected at the time, in fact not until 1913, when there was an amendment to elect senators by popular vote. The Senate was selected by the state legislatures, which it was assumed could be under elite control. Madison proposed other devices to limit democratic aspirations, including very large electoral districts, which would prevent people from assembling at a time when one could not easily travel very far. The public would therefore not have close supervision and control over their elected representatives, who would be free from popular pressures.

In defense of Madison's stand, we should recall that his mentality was precapitalist. He assumed that the people who would run the country, those who had the wealth of the nation, would be "enlightened gentlemen," people who have the good of the society at heart, not their own fortunes. They would be like the mostly mythical Roman noblemen who were an image for the Framers, even providing the names for the pseudonymous pamphlets of the intellectual elite.

Adam Smith had a sharper eye. As I quoted last time, he understood that the "masters of mankind," the merchants and manufacturers, would make sure that their own interests are cared for no matter how grievous the effect on others and would follow their vile maxim: all for ourselves, nothing for anyone else. Madison didn't see things this way at the time of the Convention, though it didn't take long for him to gain a more realistic understanding of the world. Already by 1792 he recognized that the Hamiltonian developmental capitalist state would be a social system "substituting the motive of private interest in place of public duty," leading to "a real domination of the few under an apparent liberty of the many." In a letter to Jefferson he deplored "the daring depravity of the times [as the] stockjobbers will become the pretorian band of the government—at once its tools and its tyrant; bribed by its largesses, and overawing it by clamors and combinations."

Not an unfamiliar picture.

One prominent issue in the debates at the Constitutional Convention was paper money. During the Revolutionary War, the individual states assumed enormous debts. They had to borrow to pay for the Continental Army and to keep their societies running. The debts were owned by rich men, often speculators, who wanted to be paid. The states were creating paper money, which devalued through time. The public favored that. They were the debtors and wanted the value of money to decline. One of the major issues throughout the Constitutional Convention was whether states should be permitted to print money, paper money, instead of gold and silver, the currency of the federal government. It was a major battle, a class issue: the debtors versus the creditors and speculators. The latter won. Article I of the Constitution bans paper money.

It's a complicated story, but in general it is fair to conclude that the Framers did manage to carry out an elite coup against the democratic aspirations of the general population. As Klarman concludes, the Constitution was a "conservative counterrevolution [against] excessive democracy" (2016). That is not a novel interpretation as he points out, though he provides a much more detailed, nuanced, and substantiated account than anything that preceded.

The Framers were quite frank about the coup that they were implementing. The leading figures were Alexander Hamilton and James Madison. Hamilton explained that the Constitution was designed to be a "defense against depredations which the democratic spirit is apt to make on property," which, as was generally agreed, "is certainly the principle object of society." Madison elaborated in rich detail. The Constitution was designed to secure "the permanent interests of the country against innovation," the "permanent interests" being property rights, and innovation any threat to them. It was for that reason that effective power was to be placed in the hands of "the wealth of the nation," the "responsible men" who have sympathy for property and its rights and recognize that government must be "so constituted as to protect the minority of the opulent against the majority."

As explained succinctly by the president of the Continental Congress and first chief justice of the Supreme Court, John Jay, "The people who own the country ought to govern it."

The Convention had to deal with many other issues besides preventing excessive democracy. It had to deal with slavery, which was a huge issue; almost all of the leading figures were slave owners. It had to deal with a developing urban-rural conflict: the urban, mostly the wealthier manufacturing and commercial areas, versus the backcountry, where individual farmers lived. Also, the large states versus the small states, and quite a lot more.

It's an intriguing story. There are plenty of ramifications to the present. One of them is the radically undemocratic structure of the Senate, with inhabitants of small states having far greater voting power than those of the larger ones. That arrangement was a necessity. There was no other way that the small states would ratify the Constitution. A very serious matter today, to which we'll return.

All of our discussion so far has dealt with one aspect of government, political government, though class conflict lurks close to the surface. Political government is usually understood to exhaust the concept of government. But that's a conceptual error. There are also private governments alongside the formal government. An interesting book recently appeared about this topic by political philosopher Elizabeth Anderson, critiquing hegemonic common sense. You might want to take a look at it. It's very readable. Anderson discusses something we are all quite familiar with, but do not "see": the fact that in reality the great majority of the population is governed for most of their waking lives by private governments, more accurately, private tyrannies (2017).

When you rent yourself to some concentration of capital in the private sector—that's what taking a job is—you're giving your life over to a dictatorship, in fact, an extreme form of dictatorship that reaches far beyond political dictatorships. The tyranny to which you are handing yourself over to has almost total control over you. It controls every minute of your working day: what you wear and are allowed to say, when you're allowed to get a bathroom break, how your hands and legs move, whether you smoke cigarettes at home. Just about everything in your life is controlled by this extreme dictatorship, which goes far beyond any totalitarian dictatorship in the degree of control it exercises.

That raises some questions. One is whether a socioeconomic system is legitimate if it subjects people to extreme forms of tyranny for most of their lives. And that leads to the next question, whether the wage labor contract is itself legitimate. The argument in favor of legitimacy is that the contract is freely undertaken—in the sense of Anatole France's remark that the rich and poor are equally free to sleep under the bridge at night. In the real world, the contract is accepted under duress. You accept it or you starve, conditions exacerbated under increasing monopolization, as Marv discussed in our last session. There are very few options.

Even if there are options, questions arise about the legitimacy of a system in which people have to rent themselves to dictatorships to survive. Does such a system violate rights, inalienable rights of human beings, like the right not to be a slave, for example, or the right not to be property: to be a person, not property?

It's worth bearing in mind that the right not to be property was denied to women until quite recently. The founding constitutional system adopted British common law, in Blackstone's formulation, according to which a woman is not a person but property: the property of her father, later handed over to her husband. That lasted quite long, in some respects as late as 1975 when the Supreme Court finally determined that women are peers, not property. They have a right to serve on a federal jury.

Anderson draws an interesting analogy. She points out that in the political sphere, we regard Mussolini as a dictator even though people were free to emigrate, to leave Italy. It's rather like Friedman's concept of freedom: you're free to leave the job, so the enterprise that employs you is not a dictatorship. She also points out that we regarded Kremlin-run Eastern Europe as a dictatorship, even though people were free to go from one country to another. You could take a job in Poland or the Ukraine, very much as you can leave a job at GM and—if you're lucky—find one at Ford. Well, we didn't regard that as freedom.

The analogy to the private economic system is close, which again raises questions about the legitimacy of private governments. Actually, these questions are not new. They were central to the tradition of classical liberalism, which, Anderson argues, regarded wage labor as a violation of inalienable rights. That perspective lasted pretty much through the mid-nineteenth century, when the Industrial Revolution and capitalist hegemony fostered "common sense" of a sharply different kind.

In earlier days, advocacy of free markets was a progressive doctrine. It was upheld by the rascal multitude and the radicals of the English revolution. The idea was that free markets would eliminate hierarchy and subordination to authority. They would free people from autocratic systems, from state, church, landlords. Free markets would enable them to become self-employed, self-ruled. That was the ideal for John Locke, Adam Smith, Thomas Paine, Abraham Lincoln, other classical liberals.

All of that crashed with the Industrial Revolution of the nineteenth century. Everything changed, but it's very important to understand the classical liberal reasoning, which has considerable resonance right to today. Take Adam Smith again. All people have "an equal right to the earth," he held, and it's absurd to claim that land ownership should be restrained by "the fancy of those who died perhaps five hundred years ago." Great estates should be broken up and sold equitably.

Smith also gave an argument for markets. If free, he argued, they would tend toward equality. Commerce, manufacturing, small-scale enterprises, should be run by independent artisans and merchants. His model for efficient division of labor was a pin factory, with a handful of workers, who might participate in some ways in its governance.

Smith, as you know, did value division of labor. You've all heard about the butcher and the baker and so on—all enjoying self-rule. He's famous for that. But he's less famous for his harsh criticism of division of labor when the principle of self-rule is violated. In *Wealth of Nations*, he wrote that a person who keeps to repeated simple operations under division of labor becomes "as stupid and ignorant" as a person can possibly be, but that will be "the fate of the laboring poor" under a regime of division of labor for those who rent themselves to survive. It's a fate he said that must be prevented by government intervention in any civilized society. That's not exactly what you learn about Smith and division of labor in courses and texts.

Actually, in the standard scholarly edition of *Wealth of Nations*, the University of Chicago Bicentennial edition, this passage is not even cited in the index under "division of labor."

There's more to say about how Smith is generally interpreted, but I don't want to run too far over. Just take his most famous phrase, "invisible hand." Everybody's learned about the wonders of the invisible hand, but it's very unlikely you've learned how Smith used the phrase. Actually, he almost never did. He used it twice in any relevant context, once in *Wealth of Nations*, once in his second major book *Moral Sentiments*.

In *Wealth of Nations* he uses the phrase "invisible hand" in what in effect is an argument against neoliberal globalization. He observes that if the merchants and manufacturers of England imported from and invested in foreign countries, they might make more profit but it would be harmful to the people of England. Fortunately, however, they have a "home bias." Their concern about the people of England is such that they won't care about making more profit and will invest and purchase at home. So as if by an invisible hand, the people of England will be spared the ravages of what we now call neoliberal globalization. The other major founder of modern economics, David Ricardo, was even more outspoken about this. He's famous for the theory of comparative advantage, but he wrote that he hoped that the merchants and manufacturers of England wouldn't follow it but would instead be concerned with their own people.

The other example of Smith's use of the phrase "invisible hand" is in an interesting argument in *Moral Sentiments*. England was then, of course, mostly an agrarian society. He considers the possibility that one landowner would obtain almost all the land, a sharp concentration of wealth. Smith argues that it won't matter much. Because of his sympathy with other people (whatever its roots), he would divide his wealth in such a way that as if by an invisible hand, its distribution will be relatively egalitarian.

That's the totality of Smith's relevant use of the phrase.

The idea that wage labor is basically a form of slavery and becomes tolerable only if temporary, lasting only until you become independent, was widely held well into the mid-nineteenth century. Abraham Lincoln, for example, was a strong advocate of that position. In fact, it was a slogan of his Republican Party. Wage labor was regarded as essentially the same as chattel slavery except insofar as it's temporary, a step toward freedom. The ideal is self-rule. Other contributors to the classical liberal canon went much further.

More significant, similar ideas were upheld by working people in the early Industrial Revolution. In the United States in the nineteenth century, in the early days of the Industrial Revolution in eastern Massachusetts, there was a lively labor press written, edited, and produced by the men and women who worked in the factories. Many were women, called "factory girls," young women coming from the farms to work in the mills. Their writings are very interesting. There's good work about them, the first major work on American labor history, by Norman Ware

(1924). The original documents are available in a publication edited by Philip Foner.

The independent labor press condemned what it called "the blasting influence of monarchical principles on democratic soil." Working people recognized that the assault on elementary human rights in the capitalist industrial system, including wage labor, will not be overcome until "they who work in the mills [will] own them" and sovereignty will return to free producers. Then working people will no longer be "menials or the humble subjects of the foreign despot," the absentee owners, "slaves in the strictest sense of the word [who] toil . . . for their masters." Rather, they'll regain their status as "free American citizens." The Knights of Labor, the first major labor organization, had essentially the same ideas.

The capitalist Industrial Revolution instituted a crucial change from price to wage. When the producer sold his product for a price, Ware writes, "he retained his person. But when he came to sell his labor, he sold himself," and lost his dignity as a person as he became a slave—a "wage slave," the term commonly used (1924). Working people in New England implicitly adopted the insight of the great humanist Wilhelm von Humboldt, the founder of the modern research university, that if an artisan produces a beautiful work on command, "we may admire what he did but we despise what he is"—a slave in all but name, not a free human being.

In the late nineteenth century, a populist movement developed. It was nothing like what's now called populism. It was a major popular movement of independent farmers, starting in Texas and spreading to Kansas and most of the Midwest. Farmers wanted to free themselves from the control of Northeastern bankers who lent them money to plant and then gouged them to pay it back. They established and ran their own cooperative enterprises for banking and marketing. For a time, it seemed as if the Knights of Labor and the agrarian populists might unite, bringing about a real radical democratic revolution. But it was not to be. Both the workers' and farmers' movements were beaten down with plenty of state-corporate violence.

The US has an unusually violent labor history, well into the twentieth century. Labor historian David Montgomery writes that "Modern

America had been created over its workers' protests, even though every step in its formation had been influenced by the activities, organizations, and proposals that had sprung from working class life" (1989), not to speak of the hands and brains of those who actually did the work.

Ware reports the thinking of skilled workers in New York 175 years ago, who repeated the common view that a daily wage is a form of slavery but warned that a day might come when wage slaves "will so far forget what is due to manhood as to glory in a system forced on them by their necessity and in opposition to their feelings of independence and self-respect" (1924). They hoped that that day would be "far distant."

It's taken a long time to beat the ideas of workers and farmers out of people's heads, but they do keep breaking through, including recent strikes that we'll come back to. The demand for independence, self-respect, personal dignity, and control of one's own work and life, like Marx's old mole, continues to burrow not far from the surface, ready to reappear when awakened by circumstances and militant activism.

One way in which it's breaking through right now is the idea that workers should have a voice in the governance of enterprises, apparently a very widely held belief according to recent polls. Thanks largely to the remarkable success of the Bernie Sanders campaigns, these ideas are reaching the political arena. Elizabeth Warren introduced legislation requiring that in large corporations, workers should elect 40 percent of the members of the board of directors. Something similar has existed for a long time in Germany, a system called codetermination.

But then the question is why stop there? Why not go back to the belief of American workers in the early days of the Industrial Revolution that those who work in the mills should own and manage them? In fact, that's happening in the old Rust Belt and other places, with very important efforts to develop worker-owned, worker-managed enterprises, cooperatives, and other forms of mutual aid. There's important work on these initiatives particularly by Gar Alperovitz.

There are quite successful models along these lines. The most famous is in the Basque country in Spain, Mondragón, a substantial enterprise that's been flourishing for sixty years, including manufacturing and banks, housing, hospitals—all worker-owned. In the last decade, Mondragon's been linking up with the US Steelworkers Union to try to form worker-owned cooperatives in the United States and Canada. Very important, and not as well known as it should be, is the Landless Workers Movement (MST) in Brazil, arguably the largest popular movement in the world, poor farmers who take over unused lands and have developed an extensive network of self-managed and often flourishing cooperatives. They received some support from the progressive government of Lula da Silva, who is now the most important political prisoner in the world. The likely winner of the 2018 elections, he was blocked by an ongoing right-wing coup that jailed him right before the elections on highly dubious charges and barred him from making any public statements. Under the harsh and repressive far-right government of Jair Bolsonaro, the MST is under severe threat, but it has sunk deep roots.[*]

All of these and many other initiatives are ways to follow the advice of the anarchist pioneer Mikhail Bakunin, who urged that activists should create the germs of a future society within the present one.

---

[*] Lula da Silva was released from prison, pending the outcome of his various legal appeals, in November 2019.

Chapter 3

CAPITALISM AND MILITARISM

Waterstone Lecture, January 29, 2019

Tonight's topic is the set of relationships, multiple and complicated, between capitalism and militarism. I want to think very carefully about some of the essential qualities of capitalism historically and contemporaneously in terms of the way in which it's related to militarism, colonialism, and conquest.

I'm going to start by drawing on some material from Andrew Bard Schmookler's book *The Parable of the Tribes*, which came out in the early 1980s. In the book, he is assessing underlying conditions for either peace or conflict among groups, and it will help us understand some of the dynamics involved in tonight's topic. He begins this assessment by inviting readers to "imagine that there is a group of tribes living within reach of each other. If all choose the way of peace, they all may live in peace. But what if," he asks, "all but one choose peace and that one is ambitious in some ways for expansion and conquest." He's setting this up as a way to think about what are the possible reactions to this situation.

He lays out four possible responses. The first is, if there is sufficient space, the groups that are threatened by the aggressor can simply withdraw.

They can move out of that sphere, if that's possible. Again, it depends on whether or not there's any place to withdraw to. A second possibility is destruction of subordinate groups by the aggressor. This occurs when the subordinate groups, or the weaker groups, have something that the aggressor wants but the aggressor doesn't want those populations, simply wants what they have, so destruction is a possibility.

A third possibility is when the weaker groups have something that the aggressor wants, but when the aggressor also is interested in the population in some way, and so therefore engages in activities that result in some degree of absorption but certainly some degree of subjugation. This is a third possibility. The fourth possibility is the idea of resistance, that is a group can resist the aggression, but as Schmookler makes clear, that resistance is already an acknowledgment of the relationships of power, and has to occur in some form through some kind of emulation or imitation of the aggressor's behavior.

As Schmookler concludes, in every one of these outcomes, the ways of power are spread throughout the system, and this is what he calls the parable of the tribes. Now, you might imagine that there might be other permutations of this, but this is a good heuristic for thinking a little bit about how power operates in the world. So, a few concluding remarks. In the first three outcomes, the ways of power spread when the mighty expand into areas where the weak have been. If one society in the system develops an important competitive advantage, its neighbors lose the option of continuing their prior way of living. They could either adapt to that new innovation and in some way compete, or they can be, as I said, either subjugated or destroyed.

The course of resistance, that is the fourth response, also requires transformation in the ways of power. It requires the imitation of one's more potent foes. The tyranny of power is such that even self-defense becomes a kind of surrender if one is interested only in peace. Again, these are conclusions from Schmookler. Not to resist is to be transformed or destroyed at the hands of the mighty, and to resist requires that one transform oneself into their likeness. This is the argument that Schmookler puts out. This will become relevant as we move forward. But either way, as he concludes, free human choice is prevented. All ways but the ways of power are blocked once power is unleashed in the world. This is the argument that Schmookler is making, and I'll return to this a couple of times as we think about some specific cases, both historical and contemporary.

Clearly, militarism, imperialism, and colonialism predate capitalism. There have been numerous empires throughout history. There was the age of exploration, which might also be thought of, I think quite legitimately, as the age of extermination around the globe. These activities have most often involved a search for resources, for markets of various kinds, and for labor, often slaves. The endeavors have often been aided by, and in turn have stimulated, changes in both transport and communication over time. Military might has historically provided protection for trade and mercantilism. Even before the capitalist era, we have a lot of adventures around the globe.

Let's now think about how we might explain this, particularly as we begin to move into the capitalist mode of production. In the *Communist Manifesto*, Marx and Engels said:

> The need of a constantly expanding market for its products chases the bourgeoisie over the whole surface of the globe. It must nestle everywhere, settle everywhere, establish connections everywhere. All old established national industries have been dislodged by industries that no longer work up indigenous raw material but raw material drawn from the remotest zones. Industries whose products are consumed not only at home but in every quarter of the globe. In place of the old ones satisfied by the productions of the country, we find new ones requiring for their satisfaction. The products of distant lands and climes. (Marx and Engels 1848)

In 1848, this system was hardly underway, really. In that period, Marx and Engels were already foreseeing what we now think about as a kind of globalized capitalism.

According to Lenin (in *Imperialism: The Highest Stage of Capitalism*, 1916–1917), an adequate definition of modern imperialism needs to embrace five essential features. The first is when "the concentration and

production of capital develops to such a high stage that it creates monopolies which play a decisive role in the economic life." We have already
talked a little bit about why monopolies become such a favored form.

The second condition is "the merging of bank capital with industrial
capital and the creation on the basis of this finance capital of a financial
oligarchy" (1916–1917). Remember, Lenin is actually writing at the very
turn of the twentieth century, so this is, again, still quite early on.

The third feature of imperialism is the "export of capital as distinguished from the export of commodities," which becomes extremely
important (1916–1917). I'll talk about this a bit later on. Rather than
simply moving commodities from place to place, capital was looking for
places to realize itself and to valorize itself and, in fact, to foster maximum accumulation.

The fourth condition is when we see the "formation of international
capitalist monopolies, which share the world among themselves." And
finally, "the territorial division of the whole world amongst the greatest
capitalist powers is completed." Again, recall that Lenin was writing this
in 1916 and 1917.

Hannah Arendt, contrary to Lenin, called the imperialism that arose
toward the end of the nineteenth century the first stage in the political
rule of the bourgeoisie rather than the last or highest stage of capitalism.
She saw this as a new set of phenomena basically.

There are three periods in this evolving relationship between capitalism and militarism (in its various forms) that I want to cover. The
first is a period from 1870 roughly. These are not finite, precise dates but
roughly 1870 to 1945, which we can think about as bourgeois imperialism. Second is a period from 1945 to 1970, so immediately post–World
War II, when the US began to consolidate its domination (military and
economic) over the globe.

The final period, 1970 to 2008 and beyond, neoliberal hegemony,
where different forms of domination begin to take center stage. This
entails some shifting of emphasis from overtly or exclusively military
interventions to the use of varying kinds of financial instruments to exert
control over others. But since the threat of military means constantly

lurks just under the surface, we might think about this period as the iron fist in the velvet glove. As we'll discuss in more detail in a couple of weeks, since 2008 the gloves are coming back off.

Some of this explanation is based on the very cogent analysis that David Harvey provides in *The New Imperialism* (2003), a book that I'd recommend highly to people who are interested.

During these periods, the US and the European cases are a bit different. I'll speak about them a bit separately but then bring them back together. Let's think, first of all, about this period, 1870 to 1945, which is called bourgeois imperialism, and let's speak about the European case first.

One of the first major crises of capital overaccumulation, meaning surplus capital with no means to valorize itself—that is, no investment opportunities that were sufficient to entice capitalists—was a European economic collapse from 1846 to 1850. So very early on, capitalists started to experience these kinds of crises. The temporary way out of this crisis was twofold. That is, there were two main venues available for capitalists looking for places to invest, to be able to accumulate surplus value and profit. One of these was internal (i.e., domestic) investments in vast infrastructure projects in transportation, water, and sewage, housing. This is, for example, when Georges-Eugène Haussmann redesigned Paris. There are all these domestic projects where capital could be invested and a return on capital could be developed. Most of these, of course, involved the cooperation of the state.

The second investment opportunity was outward geographic expansion of capital investment focused in large part on the Atlantic trade, with the US playing a very important role in absorbing some surplus capital. We've thought about this a little bit already, in terms of capital flight when possible.

However, the declining ability to absorb excess capital in internal projects (i.e., these kinds of infrastructure projects) and the interruption of the Atlantic trade by the US Civil War limited the capacity of these mechanisms to solve the crisis. This failure, in turn, produced an enormous wave of international financial speculation and geographically expanded trade on the part of European (and also US) capitalists.

Because these kinds of activities need a safe and secure environment, capitalists required that their nation-states develop a geopolitical rationale for aiding them (militarily if necessary) in opening up new areas and for protecting investment. In other words, capital has a logic that is dictated by its need to maximize profit and return, but that's not always matched by the logic of the state. In this situation, capital needed states to develop a geopolitical logic to accompany its own expansionist logic. But this presented a contradiction that needed to be resolved. Nation-states, which had proliferated in Europe from the mid-1600s onward, had been built primarily on the idea of internal solidarity and sovereignty rather than on foreign engagement. In fact, in large measure, that's what a state is. It's a relatively homogeneous inside population, and separated from a differentiated and heterogeneous outside.

The two logics did not really match up. If capital wants or needs to roam the globe looking for investment opportunity, and it requires the protections that states provide, states at that point didn't really have the rationale to justify these foreign engagements. How then, as Harvey and other analysts have put it, could the problem of overaccumulation and the necessity for a global spatiotemporal fix (i.e., new and different areas for investment and profit seeking—what Harvey means by a fix) find an adequate political response through the mechanism of the nation-state?

This is a problem. In other words, how could national solidarity (up to that point, based largely on internal cohesion) justify foreign adventure? Let's put it briefly. The answer was the mobilization (which is now, I would suggest, more resonant than ever) of nationalism, patriotism, jingoism, and racism to justify such foreign adventures and to legitimate what becomes known as accumulation through dispossession (which I talked about last time when I talked about primitive accumulation). This is another framing of it.

This is one of the ways in which these foreign engagements could be justified. Perfectly reasonable, it was argued, to conquer and exploit the barbarians and inferior peoples who could not put their resources to their highest and best uses. This is a paraphrase of a philosophical position from John Locke.

This launched a brutal period of competing racist-based national imperialisms, colonizations, and conquests by the British, French, Dutch, Germans, Belgians, Japanese, and Italians. These adventures were further justified by emerging social Darwinian ideas of the white man's burden. This is the way in which these two logics (capital and state) were brought together.

The underlying contradictions between nationalisms and imperialisms could not be resolved, however, and this resulted in more than fifty years of clashes between nation-states, just as Lenin had predicted. Eventually, all of this devolved into a carving up of the globe into separate spheres of control or influence exemplified, for example, by the grab for Africa. Toward the end of the 1890s, Africa had been only 10 percent colonized. By 1914, it was 90 percent colonized. So just within a couple of decades, we can see the ways in which capital, looking for investment or resources and so forth, began to divide the globe up for itself.

This competition resulted in divisions resulting from the Versailles Treaty after World War I, including arbitrary divisions of the Middle East into newly formed states ruled over largely by Britain and France. We're still living with some of the results of these actions today. That is, many of the countries that constitute the current Middle East were whole-cloth creations that were produced after the Treaty of Versailles, which divided the region up among the reigning powers and often contradicted long-standing historical arrangements.

As violent and racist as all this imperialism and conquest was, it never adequately resolved the problems of surplus capital. This eventually produced the Great Depression of '30s, which was worldwide and underpinned the catastrophe that was World War II. The same clashes keep coming back, and they're still not resolved.

Now, let me speak a bit about the US case, which is somewhat different, but results in very similar kinds of outcomes in some ways. First of all, the US was bourgeois from the outset. That is, there was no need to overthrow older forms of aristocratic or feudal power. The government represented industrial and upper-class interests, and so was opposed from the beginning to any threats to private property rights or profit maximization.

Secondly, the US was already a multiethnic, immigrant population. Appeals to homogeneous nationalism had to be constructed against non-Caucasians. Of course, the concept or category of "whiteness" is itself an ever-evolving category. So non-Caucasian was a moving target, and the unifying animosity eventually had to be directed against outside others. Historian Richard Hofstadter has characterized this ongoing feature of US politics as the paranoid style, the perennial fear of outside others. And this, we will see, comes back repeatedly to haunt the geo-politics of the US.

Finally, the US, unlike Europe, had enormous possibilities for inter-nal geographic expansion once the inconvenient indigenous population was removed. This was, again, something quite different than the Eu-ropean case with its extensive external colonies. Although there were periods of actual overseas geographic expansion, notably at the end of the nineteenth century and then during the so-called Spanish-American War, when the US did acquire a number of overseas territories. Again, we're living with some of the results still.

The US began to cover its expansions and occupations under the notion of "spreading American values." Seen, of course, as noble and universal and eventually being termed globalization. Rather than con-quering territory, as the European nations tended to do, the US was more about spreading democracy, so called.

Now, let's move to this second period, which is 1945 to 1970, so after World War II. In addition to a new phase of imperialism and militarism, this period also produced a number of very significant internal changes to the US and subsequently to the global economy.

The US emerged from World War II as by far the most technolog-ically, economically, and militarily superior nation on earth. The other combatants, whether in the European or Pacific war, were largely dev-astated. The US's nearest competitor, the Soviet Union, had borne the brunt of the fight against Nazi Germany with enormous losses to both its population and to its productive capacity.

The Allies, interestingly enough, toward the end of World War II, delayed opening a second front in Europe to aid the Soviets, who were fighting the Germans on the Eastern front. The Allies didn't really move heavily in that direction. This inaction may have been a deliberate strategy to weaken Stalin. But one consequence of the delay was that it allowed the Soviets to accumulate and then to keep territory in Eastern Europe, and this becomes very, very important in the postwar, and subsequent Cold War, period.

These Soviet territorial gains and competing military power, combined with the Soviet anti-capitalist ideology that had long grated on US elites, bumped up against the US paranoid style to help produce and sustain the Cold War. The animosities were long-standing. In fact, the US invaded Russia in 1919, two years after the revolutions there, to thwart them, but failed to do so. We had no diplomatic relations with the Soviet Union until 1935. And the alliance between the US, the UK, France, and the USSR during World War II was quickly breaking down.

As a side note and example of this breakdown, Winston Churchill, shortly after the end of hostilities in World War II, gave this very famous speech called the "Sinews of Peace." An interesting kind of juxtaposition: "Sinews of Peace." Anyway, Churchill gave this speech in 1946. I'm just going to refer to it briefly because it has some very interesting elements that carry through basically to the present day.

First of all, he calls attention to what he calls the twin dangers of war and tyranny. "We cannot be blind to the fact that the liberties enjoyed by individual citizens throughout the British Empire are not valid in a considerable number of countries, some of which are very powerful." Interesting at that moment when much of the British Empire still consisted of colonies that were thoroughly and completely repressed by British rule.

> In these states, controls enforced upon the common people by various kinds of all-embracing police governments. The power of the state is exercised without restraint either by dictators or by compact oligarchies operating through a privileged party in a political police. . . . It is not our duty at this time when difficulties are so numerous to interfere forcibly in the internal affairs of countries which we have not conquered in war. [That's an interesting exception.] But, we must never cease to proclaim in fearless tones the great principles of

freedom and the rights of man which are the joint inheritance of the English-speaking world and which through Magna Carta, the Bill of Rights, the habeas corpus, trial by jury and the English common law find their most famous expressions in the American Declaration of Independence. (1946)

These are all quotes from this "Sinews of Peace" speech. The speech also contains the first use of the phrase the "Iron Curtain":

From Stetten in the Baltic, to Trieste and the Adriatic, an Iron Curtain has descended across the continent. Behind that line lie all the capitals of the ancient states of Central and Eastern Europe. Warsaw, Berlin, Prague, Vienna, Budapest, Belgrade, Bucharest and Sofia. All these famous cities and the populations around them lie in what I must call the Soviet sphere, and all are subject in one form or another not only to Soviet influence but to a very high, and in many cases increasing, measure of control from Moscow. Athens alone—Greece with its immortal glories—is free to decide its future at an election under British, American and French observation. (1946)

This is an interesting exception at the end here. I would say that the activities went well beyond observation. In fact, the US and the UK rigged and destabilized the elections, and dislodged what was an incipient leftist, mildly leftist, kind of government structure.

But in any event, we'll let Winston continue for a minute. He also, in his speech, evokes a special relationship between the US and the UK and the English-speaking people of the world.

In a great number of countries far from the Russian frontiers and throughout the world, communist fifth columns are established and work in complete unity and absolute obedience to the directions they receive from the communist center. Except in the British Commonwealth and in the United States where communism is in its infancy [which was actually not true; it was in its death throes through deliberate subversion and extinction], the Communist Party's fifth columns constitute a growing challenge and peril to Christian civilization (1946).

Remember, this is one year after Britain was an ally of the Soviet Union, all of that rhetoric. Immediately thereafter, we have this antagonism.

One other very significant matter is related to this evolving East/West antagonism. Somewhat controversial, but now mostly settled by historians. The use of the atomic bombs in Japan have clearly now been shown to have been militarily unnecessary. Japan would have surrendered. In fact, it sued for peace without an invasion or the bombs. The bombs were dropped in the Pacific War before the Soviets could enter it and possibly acquire more territory in Asia as well as to keep Russia from assisting Mao in the civil war in China (which I'll come back to in a moment). Finally, they were dropped to keep the Soviets "more manageable," as President Truman put it at the time.

This anti-Soviet, anti-communism stance translated into the US foreign policy of containment and encirclement of the Soviet Union. I want to turn now to National Security Council (NSC) Memorandum 68. This was sort of the defining blueprint for how to deal with the world geopolitics following World War II. Most importantly, of course, our relationship with the Soviet Union.

It represents the culmination of a kind of battle of philosophies that can be emblematized by these two figures. One, George Kennan, and the other, Paul Nitze. Immediately after World War II or during World War II and its immediate aftermath, George Kennan's views of containment, which were really a quite passive kind of containment, held sway within US foreign policy circles.

Shortly thereafter, Nitze moved into the foreground and was the key author of NSC 68. He had a very different view of things like nuclear issues and the arms race. He thought that rather than simply passive containment, we should be engaged in an actual, very confrontational engagement with the Soviets everywhere and anywhere that we could. That we should in fact engage them because we had so many more resources and so forth in a kind of arms race, which they would ultimately lose and we would, in fact, come out as much more predominant.

Nitze was a master at two kinds of tactics typically. One, the very scary security memo, of which NSC 68 was a key example. The other, which I'll talk about in a second, was the production of very, very supportive committees and lobby committees to get those policies pushed forward.

One of the things that was in the NSC 68 memo was the invocation of the Chinese revolution. Then a bit later, the advent of the Korean War and, particularly, the intervention in that war by the Chinese. These were mobilized as extremely alarming kinds of movements forward of the Communist front.

The memo that circulated and, in fact, was taken up as the guiding policy document of this period, had almost immediate effects. Military spending increased by 458 percent between 1951 and 1952. This is rather enormous. In virtually all other previous wars, we demobilized after the war was over. In this case, this set in motion the idea of a constantly evolving military budget. Military personnel increased from 2.2 to over 5 million, so the memo was extremely effective.

In the name of anti-communism and the spread of freedom (usually meaning free markets and the rights of private property), following the Nitze Doctrine, the US bolstered friendly regimes through military aid, trade arrangements, credit, and so forth and opposed or toppled regimes through military confrontation, covert actions, interference in internal politics, regime change, assassination, trade and financial sanctions, and so on. Often using either UN or other military alliances, for example, NATO, as "coalitions of the willing" to cover otherwise unilateral actions. I need not enumerate all of these, but I'll have a few more words about them in just a minute.

At home in the US, this paranoid style of politics meant virulent anti-communist, anti-socialist, anti-trade union, anti-leftist repression. This is how this translated to the domestic scene. McCarthyism, which was overt repression, FBI infiltration, subversion, and assassinations, though often covert, was legitimated as necessary for national security in the face of the Soviet and international communist threat.

Interestingly enough, those of you who have been following the news in the last few days have seen the reemergence of the name Roy M. Cohn, who was the advisor to Joseph McCarthy but also was the advisor early on and mentor to both Donald Trump and to Roger Stone. These things keep coming back around.

Whenever there was a conflict between democracy and order, defined as the protection of elites in capital accumulation, the US came down on the side of the latter. This 1945–1970 period also gave rise to the military-industrial complex (MIC), and the related speech by Dwight Eisenhower warning of the incipient power of the MIC and its ongoing control and influence of US economic and military policy.

To generate profits in that sector, there must be continual and expanding arms sales and therefore the constant proliferation of enemies. In addition to building the power of the MIC economically and politically, this has contributed to the ongoing and dangerous militarization of the planet, including proliferation of nuclear weapons. We can see this ongoing. I'll say more about this in just a minute.

Brief update from the Stockholm International Peace Research Institute. Total arms sales in 2017, and this is just from the top one hundred arms companies. Nearly $400 billion, and the US share of that is nearly 60 percent. I'll say more about these figures in a minute.

The second stage ended around 1970 for several reasons. The costs to contain communism were higher than had been anticipated. The Vietnam War costs kept escalating in every dimension. Lives lost, blood and treasure. Not too much concern for what happened over there. These military costs clashed with the ability to satisfy growing consumerism; a guns-versus-butter issue. To deal with these problems, the US began printing money, which led to a worldwide inflation and the collapse of the Bretton Woods system, which we'll discuss again in the week after next.

At this point, the Nixon administration abandoned the gold standard, which had been in place prior to this, and this led to a whole number of problems that we'll also think about in detail in a couple weeks.

Here's a little side note to connect a few dots. I had said that one of the things that Paul Nitze was very, very good at, in addition to writing these threat memos, these scare memos, was to produce these groups that would then lobby on behalf of those policies. One of the first of these that he was involved in, he wasn't the only one who organized this, was something called the Committee on the Present Danger, which I'm calling Committee on the Present Danger 1.0, which pushed to adopt

NSC 68 to prevent another Korea. That was their main rationale, that's what they were pushing on Nitze's policies.

In the 1970s, Paul Nitze and a number of other people formed another Committee on the Present Danger. It deliberately took the name of the first one, but I'm calling this 2.0. There's now a 3.0, by the way. This included an enormous cast of neocon characters that eventually populated the Reagan administration.

In the 1980s, this group was responsible for many of the atrocities and crimes in Latin America, including the Iran-Contra scandal and so forth. I just put this up here now because just this last week, this character reemerged, Elliott Abrams. If you've been following his career, you might have thought he was a little less active, but he was involved in Iran-Contra. In fact, he was convicted of lying to Congress. He was then pardoned by George H. W. Bush. I put William Barr's name up here, who is the nominee [now confirmed] for attorney general, who presided over Elliott Abrams and five other Iran-Contra convicts' pardons. This stuff comes back around.

This quite clearly ties to issues that are live this week in terms of what's happening in Venezuela. I'm not going to say very much about it, but I'll say just a word or two about it in a minute. The idea that the same cast of characters using the same kinds of rationales has in fact fomented an enormous amount of chaos and disruption in this hemisphere and elsewhere.

Now, the third period, 1970 to 2008 approximately. The year 2008 with the financial crash moves us into a slightly different phase, again, that we'll talk about in a couple weeks. The US moves to a different form of imperialism, which we can think about as neoliberal hegemony.

Still plenty of military adventures, so all through the period 1970 and on up. We've been at war basically since I would say 1776, roughly without interruption. Even in this most recent period that we're considering, there were still plenty of military adventures, but now the US began more dominantly using financial institutions to achieve similar ends. The IMF, the World Bank, the World Trade Organization, NAFTA, many other multi- and bilateral trade arrangements to force open financial markets around the world and continue to exercise US dominance.

I posted a piece by Joy Powers, "Off Target: How U.S. Sanctions Are Crippling Venezuela," talking about the Venezuela situation and financial and economic terms that I hope you'll take a look at. Setting in motion a set of policies that have literally hamstrung the Venezuelan government. It can barely govern because of the kinds of tight constrictions that have been placed upon it, including the ones that have been put in place just in the last day, the Venezuelan oil company. This is an enormous set of constraints and constrictions and underpins much of the unrest that we see on the streets of Venezuela.

One key factor during this period in terms of militarism was the end of the Cold War accompanying the fall of the Soviet Union, beginning with the Berlin Wall coming down in 1989 (at that point, we were against walls), and the dissolution of the Soviet Union in 1991.

Among other things, that factor meant a need to find a replacement enemy to keep the military-industrial complex in business. Once the Soviet Union fell, this was a little bit of a problem. There was even some talk of something like a peace dividend. Once we didn't really have an enemy, maybe we could start spending these untold millions and billions at home, but that quickly evaporated.

Basically, what we did, we found a new enemy. The global war on terror is the perfect enemy. In fact, it's better than a state-based adversary. It can never really be defeated, but it can (in fact, must) be continually fought.

This period is what Michael Ignatieff in *Prospect Magazine* called "Empire Lite." It's got a nice ring to it. It sounds good. Says Ignatieff, the new US Empire

> is not like the empires of times past, built on colonies, conquest and the white man's burden. We're no longer in the era of the United Fruit Company [another interesting choice given what happened in Guatemala in this period], when American corporations needed the Marines to secure their investment overseas. 21st-century imperium is a new invention in the annals of political science, an Empire Lite. A global hegemony whose grace notes are free markets, human rights and democracy enforced by the most awesome military power the world has ever known. (2003)

"Lite" right until you need something heavier, in other words, "the most awesome military power the world has ever known." In fact, just for the record, and contrary to these claims, Ignatieff's *New York Times* colleague, Thomas Friedman, openly proclaimed in his column, March 28, 1999, at the time of the bombing of Yugoslavia, that it takes the military contractor McDonnell Douglas to ensure the safety of McDonald's around the world. Slightly different view of Empire Lite.

Now, I want to start thinking a little bit about the consequences of all of this kind of imperialism. We'll leave aside for the moment the European case and just concentrate on the US for now, but we'll come back to the European case the week after this.

William Blum, who died in December 2018, was an incredibly interesting activist, analyst, and had some things to say about US interventions, principally in a publication called *Third World Traveler*:

> The engine of American foreign policy has been fueled not by a devotion to any kind of morality but rather by the necessity to serve other imperatives, which can be summarized as follows: Making the world safe for American corporations. Enhancing the financial statements of defense contractors at home who have contributed generously to members of Congress. Preventing the rise of any society that might serve as a successful example of an alternative to the capitalist model. Extending political and economic hegemony over as wide an area as possible as benefits or befits a great power. This in the name of fighting a supposed moral crusade against what Cold warriors convinced themselves and the American people was the existence of an evil international communist conspiracy, which in fact never existed, evil or not. (1999)

Finally, the United States carried out extremely serious interventions into more than seventy nations in this period, and we're still very busy. This captures, I think, Hofstadter's notion of the paranoid style. Although John Ehrlichman under Richard Nixon made the famous comment that even paranoids have real enemies sometimes, that wasn't the case here.

Let's now consider some of the other consequences of US imperialism, for example, lives lost. Estimating these kinds of numbers is extremely difficult. It's difficult partly in terms of the analytics, how to count direct and indirect fatalities, but the source that I'm using (Lucas 2020 [2015]) actually makes an attempt to do this, and it specifies very clearly the methodology that it used, with which you can agree or disagree, but it gives you some interesting kind of outer boundary of this.

In this worst-case scenario, and they described this as a worst-case scenario, the US has killed more than 20 million people in thirty-seven victim nations since World War II. Even if they're off by a factor of 10, an order of magnitude, this is still an enormous number of fatalities. This is a quote from this study:

> The causes of wars are complex. In some instances, nations other than the US may have been responsible for more deaths, but if the involvement of our nation appeared to have been a necessary cause of a war or conflict, it was considered responsible for the deaths in it. In other words, they probably would not have taken place if the US had not used the heavy hand of its power. The military and economic power of the United States was crucial. (Lucas)

Another consequence of US imperialism, the proliferation of US bases. People are just not aware of this. It doesn't get covered very much. The definition of what constitutes a base is also very difficult to pin down, but again, this is the sort of best estimate. This is according to Dave Vine, who was writing in *The Nation* in 2015, but this has just been updated:

> While there are no freestanding form bases permanently located in the United States, there are now around 800 US bases in foreign countries. Seventy years after World War II and 62 years after the Korean War, there are still 174 US "base sites" in Germany, 113 in Japan and 83 in South Korea, according to the Pentagon. Hundreds more dot the planet in around 80 countries. . . . Although few Americans realize that the United States likely has more bases in foreign lands than any other people, nation or empire in history.
>
> Rarely does anyone ask if we need hundreds of bases overseas or if at an estimated annual cost of perhaps $156 billion or more, the United States can afford them. Again, this doesn't really come up very much in conversation, but is an existential fact.
>
> Rarely does anyone wonder how we would feel if China, Russia or Iran built even a single base anywhere near our borders, let alone in the United States. (2015)

The presumption behind these installations is itself very interesting. That the US has a largely undisputed right (as the indispensable nation) to install these anywhere, while the notion of another country doing so is largely unthinkable. Well, there was one interesting counter-case. This was reported in Reuters in 2007:

> Ecuador wants a military base in Miami. In fact, Rafael Correa said Washington must let him open a military base in Miami if the United States wants to keep using an airbase [the Manta base] on Ecuador's Pacific Coast.

Well, have you seen Ecuador's base in Miami? Okay. It didn't really get there, but the Manta base did close. You could see how preposterous this seems that we would even begin to entertain the idea that another country might install a base here. Just not possible.

Finally, the cost of the bases, in addition to the economic costs that I already mentioned, about $156 or $157 billion annually. There's also a human toll exacted by these activities. There's a tremendous strain on military families. There's an enormous amount of sexual violence around US military bases. There is a tremendous amount of environmental damage in the host area from the bases and so forth.

They also become targets of anti-American activity and animosity, just the emplacement of them. For example, the US military presence in Saudi Arabia was an overtly stated motive that Osama bin Laden gave for the 9/11 attacks. There was an installation of the barbarians in the Holy Land.

These emplacements also make foreign wars more thinkable, and thus make the world more dangerous. That is, as we have people positioned in place, we think about a military solution to a particular kind of issue.

Finally, I urge you to look at this report and then an update, a very good update, by Nick Turse, entitled "Bases, Bases, Everywhere...Except in the Pentagon's Report."

In addition to the factors I've just discussed, there are also the extravagant monetary costs of militarism. US military spending is higher now than at any time other than the height of the Iraq War, adjusted for inflation. The 2019 budget is $716 billion. That's just the amount shown on the books.

According to the Stockholm International Peace Research Institute, the US outpaces all other nations in military expenditures. World military spending totaled more than $1.74 trillion in 2017 and was up 1 percent from the previous year. The US accounted for 35 percent of that total.

US military expenditures are roughly the size of the next eight largest military budgets around the world. A recent article on "overmatch" by Michael Klare indicates that we have now diverged from simple containment, which was the policy basically post–World War II, to now being the preeminent power everywhere all the time, and whatever it takes to achieve that in terms of blood and treasure, we will apparently expend. By we, I mean you and I. Remember, this is taxpayer funded.

In terms of the share of world military expenditures, at 35 percent of the total, the US is vastly predominant. I would guess we are overmatching. By contrast, the UN was created after World War II with leading efforts by the United States and key allies, with a commitment to preserving peace through international cooperation and collective security. That is, nonmilitary means to deal with each other, through diplomacy and so forth.

Yet, the UN's entire budget is a fraction of the world's military expenditure. It's approximately 1.8 percent of what we spend on the military, so we can see where the priorities really are. Yet, having that enormous expenditure on the military means that that's where we look first and foremost for solutions to problems. We have the investment there, we might as well use it.

The military budget has increased substantially under the Trump administration. Trump ordered the military in his very first few days in office to prepare for world war. One week into his term, he said, "I'm signing an executive action to begin a great rebuilding of the armed services of the United States."

The military order directed now-departed defense secretary James "Mad Dog" Mattis, who was sworn in at the ceremony, to complete a thirty-day "readiness review" designed to prepare for the destruction of

ISIS in Syria and Iraq, along with "other forms of Islamic terror." The order further instructed Mattis, in the words of the *Washington Post*, "to examine how to carry out operations against unnamed near-peer competitors," a group that US officials typically identify as China and Russia.

This was signaling an enormous policy change. In the previous decade or so, the focus had been on combating global terrorism. Now, all of a sudden, in this document, we start to see the appearance of this phraseology "near-peer competitors." We're reinvoking the Cold War, essentially.

The order unmistakably threatened the use of nuclear weapons. Section 3 called for a nuclear force "to deter the 21st century threats" and menacingly, "to achieve presidential objective should deterrence fail."

He further called for a plan to achieve "readiness objectives" for the use of the nuclear arsenal by 2022. It's a few years from now, so practice your duck-and-cover maneuver. This would include the modernization of the US nuclear force (which was already begun under the previous administration of Obama). It would also include a greatly expanded missile defense system, an increased emphasis in cyber warfare, which aims to cripple the retaliatory capacity of major adversaries by targeting their digital and telecommunication structures prior to an American strike. What could go wrong if forces of our adversaries can't communicate with their military? Nothing really could happen.

The executive action did not put a price tag on new military spending, but media speculation indicated that the figure could approach an additional $100 billion per year, which it has. Combined with a promise of tax cuts at the top, this additional spending will come at the expense of Social Security and Medicare, Medicaid, education, health care, and infrastructure, and so on.

Then just to put this in another context, the military budget now consumes 60 percent of discretionary spending in the US budget. All the kinds of things that we might do otherwise are consumed by this budget.

Here's a little bit of an update. On January 19th of 2018, then secretary of defense Mattis provided a summary of new directions, which are themselves quite troubling. These are quotes from Mattis's summary of the 2018 national defense strategy of the United States:

Again, this is a national defense strategy, but what it really is, ladies and gentlemen . . . This is an American strategy. It belongs to you. You own it. We work for you tirelessly. It's a pleasure to be at a school named for the gentleman that this one is named for. Oh, Paul Nitze. And I bring this up because National Security Council document or report 68 was a guiding light during the Cold War. In this time of change our military is still strong, yet our competitive advantage has eroded in every domain of warfare. Air, land, sea, space and cyberspace and is continuing to erode [given the amount we spent on it, how could this be?]. Though we will continue to prosecute the campaign against terrorists that we are engaged in today, but great power competition, not terrorism, is now the primary focus of US national security. We face growing threats from revisionist powers as different as China and Russia are from each other. Nations that do seek to create a world consistent with their authoritarian models. . . . Rogue regimes like North Korea and Iran persist in taking outlaw actions that threaten regional and even global stability. Oppressing their own people and shredding their own people's dignity and human rights, they push their warped views outward. Ladies and gentlemen, we have no room for complacency and history makes clear that America has no preordained right to victory on the battlefield. Simply, we must be the best if the values that grew out of the Enlightenment are to survive. We're going to build a more lethal force. Investments in space and cyberspace, nuclear deterrent force of missile defense, advanced autonomous systems. Resilient and agile logistics will provide our high quality troops what they need to win. Of course, we never redefine winning. To those who would threaten America's experiment in democracy, they must know if you challenge us it will be your longest and your worst day. Work with our diplomats, you don't want to fight the Department of Defense. (2018)

The bottom line, President Trump's new budget is $716 billion for 2019, an increase of 7 percent over 2018. Finally, interestingly enough, he had criticized the $700 billion budget. He thought it was crazy, so he offered $750 billion. This is the proposed budget for next fiscal year. He previously called for a cut, but now he's been talked out of that.

There are some troubling trends here, including continuing and escalating the global war on terror. This is something that we continue to do. We are also increasing tensions with Russia and China along with North Korea and Iran, Venezuela, Cuba, and so forth.

We are increasing dependence on drone warfare and special operations and targeted assassination. The US public is quite clearly not maintaining a healthy appetite for US casualties, and so we are moving to these other forms of warfare that don't require as much personnel. We are expanding the US basing program but relying on smaller and more numerous bases called lily pads.

There is also the proposed $1 trillion nuclear weapons upgrade to include tactical and low-yield nuclear weapons. These are extremely dangerous. The idea that you have a low-yield nuclear weapon. These are weapons that presumably have the explosive capacity of about five Hiroshima bombs, rather than three hundred Hiroshima bombs per warhead. The idea that you want to somehow make nuclear weapons more thinkably usable is an extremely dangerous idea. We are also at the same time lowering the conditions or the circumstances under which we will contemplate using nuclear weapons, so, for example, in response to a cyber attack. This is an extremely dangerous moment.

Another ongoing feature of continued militarism is the use of racial, religious, xenophobic, nationalistic rhetoric to keep the public in a constant state of fear. This is part of the way in which we maintain and justify this militarism abroad. But another consequence is that this militarism comes home. There's a pervasive common sense, fear of dangerous others. This is the sort of a Hofstadter model, the paranoid politics on steroids, dangerous others. This fear must be constantly reinforced, and we see it all the time in discussions of the border wall or any number of these other characterizations of these caravans of dangerous people coming to invade us.

Some analysts have renamed the welfare state, which obtained basically from about 1945 until in the 1970s, the garrison state. State legitimacy now depends on protection from these threats by targeting of dangerous others. I'll say more about this in two weeks, but just to repeat what I indicated last week, the idea that the globalized form of capitalism means that decisions about the economic security and welfare of citizens are no longer within the hands necessarily of nation-state governors. To preserve their legitimacy as governors, they need to find a new basis for legitimation. Some people are arguing, and I would agree with much of this, that this is the new basis. The protection from dangerous others. We have endless enemies.

Foreign communism morphed into terrorism. We now have a tremendous fear of immigrants and refugees. Witness the recent ban orders, the deportations, the detentions, the demonization of others. We have domestic enemies, people of color, the young, the old, LGBTQ communities, the differently abled, and along with that the militarization of the police and the criminalization of protest, which we'll talk about in the last couple of weeks. Where is all of this headed? The Pentagon has a very bleak view of the future (see "Megacities: Urban Future, the Emerging Complexity: A Pentagon Video"), which views urban areas (both foreign and domestic) as basically breeding grounds for instability, unrest, and chaos. To think about the kind of underlying view of humanity this way I think comes naturally in some sense out of this very long history of militarization. That is, if you think of yourself as military, then everybody outside is an enemy.

This is also what becomes part of the problem of militarizing the police. As the police become increasingly militaristic, the people that they supposedly protect and serve begin to look more and more like the non-police, like the enemy. This is, I think, an extremely dangerous kind of trend that we're seeing.

The forecast that this is the way in which the military will sort of reproduce itself by now being able to respond to these kinds of future threats where the mass of humanity is either an enemy or is in a witting or unwitting cloak for enemies. It's extremely dangerous. One we should think very carefully about, but this is the Pentagon's view largely of what that future looks like, and it is, in fact, urban, militarized, and dangerous. Okay. I'm going to stop with that for now.

Chomsky Lecture, January 31, 2019

I n the last few lectures, among other things, I've been discussing elite attitudes toward democracy. I sketched a line from the first democratic revolution, with its fear and contempt for the rascal multitude who were asking for ridiculous things like universal education, health care, and democratization of law, wanting to be ruled by countrymen like themselves who know the people's sores, not by knights and gentlemen who just oppress them. From there to the second major democratic revolution establishing the US Constitution, which was, as discussed last time, a Framers' Coup, the title of the main scholarly work, a coup by elites that the author describes as a conservative counterrevolution against excessive democracy.

On to the twentieth century and such leading progressive theorists of democracy as Walter Lippmann, Edward Bernays, Harold Lasswell, and Reinhold Niebuhr, and their conception that the public has to be put in its place. They're spectators, not participants. The responsible men, the elite, have to be protected from the trampling and the roar of the bewildered herd, who have to be kept in line with necessary illusions, emotionally potent oversimplifications, and, in general, engineering of consent, which has become a gigantic industry devoted to some aspects of the task, while responsible intellectuals take care of others.

The men of best quality through the ages have to be self-indoctrinated, as Orwell discussed. They must internalize the understanding that there are certain things it just wouldn't do to say. It must be so fully internalized that it becomes as routine as taking a breath. What else could anyone possibly believe?

As long as all of this is in place, the system functions properly, with no crises.

This picture, I think, captures crucial features of thought control in the more free societies, but it is misleading in essential ways. Most importantly, it largely omitted the constant popular struggles to extend the range of democracy, with many successes. Even in the last generation, there have been quite substantial successes. Such successes typically lead to a reaction. Those with power and privilege don't relinquish it easily. The neoliberal period that we're now enduring, long in planning, is such a reaction. We'll come back to details.

It's also misleading because there have been significant elite exceptions to this dominant tendency. During the Constitutional Convention, the most respected of the delegates was Benjamin Franklin, who objected to what was going on. He expressed his "dislike of everything that tended to debase the spirit of the common people" and reminded his colleagues that "some of the greatest rogues he was ever acquainted with were the richest rogues" (Klarman, op. cit.)—rather like some of Adam Smith's reflections.

Franklin was a lone voice at the convention. Thomas Jefferson expressed somewhat similar sentiments, but he wasn't there. He was then ambassador in Paris. In any event, the coup did proceed on course with consequences to the present, though there was plenty of conflict in the country at the time—hence "a coup"—and in the years that followed, to the present.

The twentieth century also had important exceptions in elite opinion. The most prominent was John Dewey, the most respected American social philosopher of the twentieth century. Most of his work—and also activism—was devoted to democracy and education, along lines very much opposed to the doctrines of "manufacture of consent" and marginalization of the "bewildered herd."

By democracy, Dewey meant full-blooded democracy, with active participation of an informed public. His democratic theory was linked closely to his educational philosophy, which was designed to nurture creativity and independence of thought, for one reason as preparation for participation in a democratic society. It worked. I was lucky enough to go to a Deweyite school from about age two to twelve, and it was very impressive.

Dewey was at first a typical responsible intellectual, joining the self-adulation of intellectuals during World War I for their stellar role in directing the stupid masses to wartime enthusiasm. That was, however, not unusual. The capitulation to power of the intellectual classes during those years, on all sides, is astonishing to behold, and of the few who didn't swim with the tide, the best known ended up in jail: Bertrand Russell in England, Eugene Debs in the US, Karl Liebknecht and Rosa Luxemburg in Germany.

Shortly after the war, Dewey changed and became a sharp and incisive social and media critic. Increasingly through the years, he came to regard "politics as the shadow cast on society by big business." Reforms are of limited utility: "The attenuation of the shadow will not change the substance." The substance is that the very institutions of private power undermine democracy and freedom. "Power today," he recognized, "resides in control of the means of production, exchange, publicity, transportation and communication. Whoever owns them rules the life of the country," even if democratic forms remain. In a free and democratic society, workers should be "the masters of their own industrial fate," not tools rented by employers. Industry must therefore be changed "from a feudalistic to a democratic social order," based on control of production by the workers themselves, much as working people demanded in the early days of the Industrial Revolution, flames never extinguished and frequently fanned since, again today.

The system of actual power in the country, Dewey continued, is "business for private profit through private control of banking, land, industry, reinforced by command of the press, press agents and other means of publicity and propaganda." That is the system of actual power, the source of coercion and control, and until it is unraveled, we cannot talk seriously about democracy and freedom. Dewey also condemned the "unfree press" for yielding to commercialism and deplored its impact "upon the judgment of what news is, upon the selection and elimination of matter that is published, upon the treatment of news in both editorials and news columns." He suggested a "cooperative system" controlled "in the interest of all," rather than commitment by the media to "romanticize . . . profit motives" (Westbrook 1993).

This is not the voice of a wild man in the wings, but of one of the most respected and influential of twentieth-century American intellectuals.

In brief, it oversimplifies to speak of elite attitudes without qualification, though the near uniformity is often impressive.

Dewey's condemnation of wage labor is reminiscent of the stand of Abraham Lincoln and other leading figures of classical liberalism, and of working men and women, as we've seen. And his critique of the media should remind us of a progressive feature of the Constitutional Convention that has an instructive history in the years that follow, with important lessons for today. I have in mind the way the Founders interpreted the First Amendment, specifically, freedom of press.

It is a common practice to distinguish negative from positive rights. Negative rights reduce in essence to "Don't tread on me." Positive rights involve enhancement of welfare and opportunities, what economist Amartya Sen calls "capabilities."

The current prevailing interpretation takes the First Amendment to confer negative rights on the media: the state should not interfere with their work. Even that is a fairly recent innovation, dating back to an important 1964 case involving the civil rights movement (*New York Times v. Sullivan*). The negative-rights interpretation is a sharp departure from the perspective of the Founders, who interpreted the First Amendment more liberally, as conferring positive rights, matters discussed in penetrating work by media critics Robert McChesney (2007) and Victor Pickard (2020). The Founders wanted media to be free, vibrant, independent, not the "unfree press" that Dewey condemned for its subordination to owners and advertisers. And varied; the press of the day was often sharp and adversarial. For the Founders, this was not just a rhetorical commitment. They believed that the government should be directly engaged in fostering a truly free press. The method used was, essentially, subsidy. The US Postal Service was designed as a substantial subsidy to independent media, providing widely available distribution at very low rates. The large majority of postal traffic in the early years was newspapers.

As already discussed, the Founders were in crucial ways pre-capitalist in mentality. But the US soon turned into a business-run society, to an unusual extent. Accordingly, hegemonic common sense came to oppose positive rights, which typically infringe on prerogatives of private capital. And over the years, the Founders' liberal interpretation of the First Amendment has been narrowed to the negative-rights interpretation of today. The matter was highly contested through the twentieth century, first with the advent of radio, then television, finally the internet. In the 1930s, there was strong public opposition to the government decision to hand over the public airwaves to private enterprise, with only the most marginal concern for the positive rights of the public to information, free discussion, and public service. In the late 1940s, a similar debate took place over the decision to hand public assets to private enterprise for television rights. The issue arose again in the mid-1990s, when the neoliberal Clinton administration passed the Telecommunication Act of 1996, handing the internet—public property and largely publicly created—to private ownership, furthermore deregulated and soon converging in the usual manner to monopolization, contrary to the predictions of advocates and most economists but as anticipated by critics and a regular feature of the neoliberal call for deregulation and market worship.

As a consequence, the US is alone among formally democratic societies in lacking major public media that are not subject to the pressures of Dewey's "unfree press"—though the neoliberal assault has taken its toll elsewhere, notably on the BBC, quite visibly since Thatcher and her TINA doctrine: There Is No Alternative to neoliberal orthodoxy.

The "common sense" preference for negative over positive rights has broad policy consequences. In social justice measures, the US ranks near the bottom of the thirty-six members of the OECD—the richer countries—alongside of Greece and Turkey. It is also exhibited clearly in elite attitudes on many issues. One notable case is the Universal Declaration of Human Rights (UD), initiated by the US in its more liberal days and adopted by the UN General Assembly in 1948 as "the foundation of freedom, justice and peace in the world." There were eight abstentions: South Africa, Saudi Arabia, Russia, and several of its satellites. Otherwise, unanimous assent, including the United States.

The UD has three components, of equal status: political, socioeconomic, and community rights. The second and third components are basically positive rights. Most of the signers approve in words while disregarding many of their commitments in practice. The US differs: it even disapproves in words. Positive rights are rejected. Community rights are considered too ridiculous even to reject openly, but socioeconomic rights (to health, decent jobs, etc.) are rejected with scorn. Reagan's UN Ambassador and foreign policy adviser Jeane Kirkpatrick dismissed this section of the UD as "a letter to Santa Claus," seconded by Russia's Andrey Vyshinsky.

The same stand was elaborated by Paula Dobriansky, assistant secretary of state for Human Rights and Human Affairs in the Reagan and Bush I administrations. She dispelled such "myths" about human rights as the so-called "economic and social rights" entrenched in the UD, which just obfuscate human rights discourse. The same view was expressed in 1990 by the US representative to the UN Commission on Human Rights, Ambassador Morris Abram, explaining Washington's solitary veto of the UN resolution on the Right to Development, which virtually repeated the socioeconomic provisions of the UD. These spurious claims "seem preposterous," Abrams declared: such ideas are "little more than an empty vessel into which vague hopes and inchoate expectations can be poured," and even a "dangerous incitement."

US practice is unusual in the same way. Other countries ratify General Assembly conventions on human rights, but often ignore them. The US refuses to ratify them, apart from a few that it ratified but with reservations exempting the US. The rejection of international conventions goes beyond the positive socioeconomic rights of the UD, extending even to the International Covenant on Civil and Political Rights, "the leading treaty for the protection" of the subcategory of rights that the US claims to uphold, to quote Human Rights Watch and the American Civil Liberties Union. The Convention finally was ratified after a long delay, but only with provisions to render it inapplicable to the United States.

In interpreting debate over government decisions and public debate over such matters, we can usefully distinguish rationales, pretexts, and reasons. Rationales are what are offered in defense of choices. We regard them as pretexts if they are too absurd to take seriously. Actual reasons are what we seek to discover by analysis of the historical and documentary record, and by attending to the principle of law that predictable consequences are a good indication of motives. Not surprisingly, we commonly find the reasons to be rather different from the rationales.

To take an uncontroversial case, eighty years ago Hitler invaded Poland. The rationale was defense against the "wild terror" of the Poles, instantly assigned to the category of pretexts outside Nazi Germany and its sympathizers. The reasons were to acquire *Lebensraum* for the superior Aryan race and to eliminate the tens of millions of *Untermenschen* who occupied the territories and who were appropriating the resources that properly belonged to their superiors. If analogies come to mind in American history, and elsewhere today, it is not mere accident.

Let's turn to another case that is uncontroversial within mainstream opinion in the US: the US wars in Indochina. The rationale, sampled earlier, is expounded by the most respected voices of the establishment Left: "blundering efforts to do good" (Anthony Lewis), defense against "aggression" by Communist North Vietnam (historian and Kennedy adviser Arthur Schlesinger), defense against "internal aggression" (Kennedy's UN Ambassador and liberal icon Adlai Stevenson, referring to the aggression of South Vietnamese peasant-based guerrillas against the US-imposed dictatorship), and similar pronouncements by numerous others. The wild men in the wings dismissed these as mere pretext, joined by a large majority of the public, who regarded the war as "fundamentally wrong and immoral," not "a mistake," as we have seen; irrelevantly, with no voice in the mainstream.

To discover the reasons, we can investigate the rich internal record from the early days when the basic decisions were made in the late '40s and early '50s. To some of the wild men, the record reveals the usual imperial concern that the "virus" of an independent Vietnam would "spread contagion" throughout Southeast Asia, reaching as far as Japan, and seriously undermining US postwar plans for global control. We'll come back to this later on.

To take another case, consider the major crime of the twentieth century, the US-UK invasion of Iraq, a textbook case of aggression, the "supreme international crime" according to the Nuremberg Tribunal that hanged Nazi war criminals for less, dismissing Nazi pretexts.

In US mainstream opinion, the war was at worst a "strategic blunder" (Obama). The rationale at first was Saddam's nuclear weapons programs. That was "the single question." When it was answered the wrong way, the rationale instantly and effortlessly shifted to "democracy promotion." US media and other commentary quickly adopted the new rationale, though more sober minds warned that the "noble" and "generous" vision may be beyond our reach: it may be too costly, the beneficiaries may be too backward to benefit from our solicitude. Scholarship joined in as well. One of the rare exceptions, Middle East scholar Augustus Richard Norton, observed caustically that "as fantasies about Iraq's weapons of mass destruction were unmasked, the Bush administration increasingly stressed the democratic transformation of Iraq, and scholars jumped on the democratization bandwagon" (2005).

Some regarded these rationales as pretexts, among them Iraqis, who demonstrated their backwardness in a Gallup poll taken just at the time that the new rationale was eloquently proclaimed in a major address by President Bush. Some Iraqis, it is true, did regard the rationale as valid: 1 percent. Another 4 percent thought that the goal was "to assist the Iraqi people." Most of the rest assumed that the goal was to take control of Iraq's resources and to reorganize the Middle East in the interests of the US and Israel—the "conspiracy theory" derided by rational Westerners, who understood that Washington and London would have been just as dedicated to the "liberation of Iraq" if it produced asparagus rather than oil and the center of world petroleum production were in the South Pacific.

As for the reasons, I'll leave it to you.

The rationale-pretext-reasons distinctions have a critical role throughout history and today. Deregulation, as mentioned above, is an instructive case. And more generally, limited government, allegedly a conservative ideal, though, oddly, government tends to grow under their stewardship, as in the Reagan years, serving primarily the rich.

An early exponent of the ideal of limited government was Andrew Jackson. The rationale was negative rights: citizens of our free society should be free from government intrusion. In his words, the federal government should not be permitted to restrict "human liberty" but should be only allowed to "enforce human rights." The meaning of these fine words, and their predictable consequences, are spelled out by historian Greg Grandin in his *End of the Myth*: by "human rights" Jackson meant the right to slaughter Indians without government interference and to own property; crucially for this vicious slave owner, to own human beings as property. The Age of Jackson, Grandin observes, "entailed a radical empowerment of white men [and] an equally radical subjugation of African-Americans," along with brutal massacres and expulsion of the *Untermenschen* who were improperly appropriating to themselves what belonged by right to the superior Anglo-Saxon race.

There are innumerable other examples of the utility of these distinctions in analysis of policy, but let's now turn to one prominent one. A core feature of received common sense is that the United States is committed to promoting democracy and human rights. It's sometimes called "Wilsonian idealism" or "American exceptionalism."

I mentioned in some opening remarks that it's a good rule of thumb to attend to doctrines about complex matters that are reiterated passionately, constantly, but without any evidence. Under such conditions, it's useful to take a closer look and to see if we're facing one of those cases where there are things that it wouldn't do to say, in Orwell's phrase.

American exceptionalism is one of these cases. In the first place, as soon as we look we find that the doctrine has nothing in particular to do with the United States. It seems to be universal. All imperial powers have had the same doctrine of exceptionalism. France, for example, was carrying out its "civilizing mission" in Algeria while the commanding general was giving orders to "exterminate" the population. That would civilize them properly.

France's noble mission extended to much of West Africa, with such success that people are dying in the Mediterranean trying to flee the wreckage. Britain was very much the same. If there were time, I'd review some pretty remarkable examples, including even the most distinguished people, like John Stuart Mill.

The same is true even of the states that are the most brutal. Take Nazi Germany. When Hitler took over the Sudetenland, large parts of Czechoslovakia, he was just brimming with concern for the suffering people of the region. The Germans were going to undertake a humanitarian intervention, to resolve ethnic conflicts, to bring the backward population under the wing of the advanced civilization of Germany. We know where that led.

Moving to Asia, when the Japanese were rampaging in Manchuria and North China, with horrendous atrocities, what they were thinking is accessible to an unusual extent. Since they were defeated in the war, their internal records were taken, including counterinsurgency manuals. I'm not sure whether these were released to the public, but in the 1960s a friend at the Rand Corporation sent them to me: Tony Russo, who worked with Dan Ellsberg in releasing the *Pentagon Papers*. I published some excerpts from them in a memorial volume for the great American pacifist A. J. Muste, reprinted in *American Power and the New Mandarins*.

They're very interesting. They're very much like US counterinsurgency doctrine except that the rhetoric is more elevated. While they were devastating Manchuria and North China, carrying out the Nanjing Massacre and other hideous crimes, this is what they were saying—talking to each other, no pretense. We're going to create an "earthly paradise" for the people of China, for whom we are expending our lives and treasure to protect from "Chinese bandits," namely, those resisting the Japanese humanitarian intervention. We'll protect the people of China and bring them under the wing of the advanced civilization of Japan. Very elevated.

In fact, if we had records from Attila the Hun, I suspect we'd probably find the same thing. It's hard to find an exception in the entire history of imperialism. That aspect of American exceptionalism is not at all exceptional. It's the norm. Everyone's the same who has any power.

The second thing it wouldn't do to say about American exceptionalism is what the facts are, some of which we've been discussing. It's particularly instructive to see how the historical record is dealt with by really serious scholars, the best scholars, people who are not experts in legitimation. Take Hans Morgenthau. He's one of the founders of realist international relations (IR) theory, the dominant tendency in IR theory, which dismisses sentimental talk about Wilsonian idealism. Morgenthau was much too good a scholar to have any of that. He was a hard-headed realist.

In his 1964 book *The Purpose of American Politics* (a phrase worth pondering), Morgenthau writes that America is unlike other countries because it has a "transcendent purpose." Other countries just have national interests. The US has a transcendent purpose: "the establishment of equality in freedom in America," and indeed throughout the world, since "the arena within which the United States must defend and promote its purpose has become world-wide."

An honest and competent scholar, Morgenthau recognized that the historical record is radically inconsistent with America's transcendent purpose. But that should not mislead us. We should not "confound the abuse of reality with reality itself." Reality itself is the unachieved "national purpose" revealed by "the evidence of history as our minds reflect it." The actual historical record is merely the "abuse of reality," hence of only secondary interest. Those who confuse "reality" with "the abuse of reality" are committing "the error of atheism, which denies the validity of religion on similar grounds." Again, a thought worth pondering.

One of the highly admired elements of American exceptionalism is our long-standing commitment to democracy promotion. Here, too, there is good scholarship. The major scholarly study of democracy promotion is by another serious scholar, Thomas Carothers, then director of the Democracy and Rule of Law Project at the Carnegie Endowment.

Carothers was in an unusually favorable position to study this leading rationale for US foreign policy, re-invoked by Bush in Iraq when the search for weapons of mass destruction went sour. Carothers, who describes himself as a neo-Reaganite, had served in the Reagan State Department in the democracy promotion programs in Latin America, so he had an insider's view of what was going on.

Reviewing the record, Carothers concludes that the democracy programs were "sincere," but a failure, in fact, a systematic failure, failure everywhere. Where US influence was least, in the southern cone of Latin

America, progress toward democracy was greatest, despite Reagan's efforts to impede it by "trying to embrace the fading right-wing dictators that Carter had shunned on human rights grounds." Where US influence was strongest, in the regions nearby, progress was least.

There was a reason: Washington sought to maintain "the basic order of what, historically at least, are quite undemocratic societies" and to avoid "populist-based change in Latin America—with all its implications for upsetting economic and political orders and heading off in a leftist direction." Therefore the US would tolerate only "limited, top-down forms of democratic change that did not risk upsetting the traditional structures of power with which the United States has long been allied" (Carothers 1991).

That's what actually happened: "abuse of reality." Reality is that the programs were "sincere." I'll leave to you an analysis in terms of rationale, pretext, and reasons.

These matters pose a painful dilemma for policymakers, lamented at the extreme dovish end of the spectrum by Robert Pastor, Latin American specialist of the Carter administration, which was derided by Reaganites and many others for its excessive devotion to human rights. Defending US policy, Pastor explains that "the United States did not want to control Nicaragua or other nations in the region, but it also did not want to allow developments to get out of control. It wanted Nicaraguans to act independently, *except* when doing so would affect U.S. interests adversely" (Pastor 1987, his emphasis). In short, Nicaragua and other countries should be free—free to do what we want them to do—and should choose their course independently, as long as their choice conforms to our interests. If they use the freedom we accord them unwisely, then, naturally, we are entitled to respond with violence in self-defense.

Carothers and Pastor are discussing Latin America, but the pattern is worldwide. Let's turn to W. Bush and the Bush doctrine (every president has to have a doctrine, to put his stamp on history). The Bush doctrine is defined simply in the most extensive scholarly study of "the roots of the Bush doctrine," by Jonathan Monten in the prestigious journal *International Security*: "The promotion of democracy is central to the George

W. Bush administration's prosecution of both the war on terrorism and its overall grand strategy." The article appeared in 2005, when Iraq was descending into total chaos after the US invasion. The sentiment was unsurprising. By then it had reached the level of ritual. Why just then? Perhaps because just then the official rationale for the war had shifted from what had been the "single question"—Saddam's nuclear weapons programs—to "democracy promotion," Matters already discussed.

Let's turn to another interesting example, Winston Churchill. In our last session, Marv discussed some of Churchill's noble phrases about our common magnificent history and intentions in his famous 1946 Iron Curtain speech. But Churchill was no fool. He had some other things to say about these matters at the same time, in his history of World War II:

> The government of the world must be entrusted to satisfied nations, who wished nothing more from themselves than what they had. If the world-government were in the hands of hungry nations, there would always be danger. But none of us had any reason to seek for anything more. The peace would be kept by peoples who lived in their own way and were not ambitious. Our power placed us above the rest. We were like rich men dwelling at peace within their habitations.

Rather ample habitations.

That's 1945 in his history of World War II (vol. 5). But in fact, that's an old position of Churchill's. Shortly before World War I, he gave a speech in Parliament in which he explained that "we are not a young people with *an innocent record and* a scanty inheritance. We have engrossed to ourselves an *altogether disproportionate* share of the wealth and traffic of the world. We have got all we want in territory, and our claim to be left in the unmolested enjoyment of vast and splendid possessions, *mainly acquired by violence, largely maintained by force*, often seems less reasonable to others than to us" (Ponting 1994).

Churchill didn't allow this to be published at the time. It was published with the italicized phrases omitted. The original was discovered recently. Churchill is unusual only in his honesty: recognizing the facts and willingness to express them. With this background, let's take a look at how the world has been organized from World War II.

As soon as the war began, the State Department and the Council on Foreign Relations (CFR) established a war-peace study group that was to determine what the shape of the postwar world would be; the CFR is the leading nongovernmental institution concerned with foreign relations, mostly people in and out of government and corporations.

The analysts took for granted the United States would emerge victorious. That was not really in question. For several years they assumed that the war would end with two major power blocs, one dominated by the United States, the other dominated by Germany. In the early stages of the war, Germany was achieving remarkable successes.

The area to be dominated by the United States they called the "Grand Area." The Grand Area was to include at a minimum the entire Western Hemisphere, the Far East, and the former British Empire, which the US was taking over, displacing Britain, which had been the leading global power for a long time before. So that's the minimum of US domination. The rest would be the German-dominated world.

By about 1942, 1943, after the battle in Stalingrad and in particular a huge tank battle at Kursk, it was clear that the Russians were going to defeat the Germans. The conception changed; Grand Area expectations were modified in character and scale. Now it would be the Russians, not the Germans, who would be the adversary. The Grand Area would include everything I just described, plus whatever part of Europe and Asia the United States could take over. At the very least, Western Europe, which is the industrial heartland of the European continent. So that's the expanded Grand Area.

It was understood that in the Grand Area the United States would reign supreme. Long before the war, the United States had been by far the richest country in the world, and it gained enormously from the war. Manufacturing practically quadrupled, while other industrial states were severely harmed or almost destroyed. The prominent statesman George Kennan, head of the early postwar State Department Policy Planning Staff, estimated that the US had half of the world's wealth. Very likely an exaggeration; statistics weren't very good at the time. But probably not by much.

Grand Area planners determined that US domination must be firmly established. In their own words, they planned for a world in which the US would "hold unquestioned power," ensuring "the limitation of any exercise of sovereignty" by states that might interfere with its global designs. The planners therefore sought to develop an "integrated policy to achieve military and economic supremacy" for the United States in the Grand Area, which was to expand as much as possible.

When the war ended, these conceptions were formulated in internal planning documents. The plans were then implemented where possible. The general idea was to impose what is commonly called "the US-led liberal economic order"—now under threat by Trump. There were a number of guiding principles.

The basic principle was that the new economic order should be an open system, which means freedom for investors, for movement of capital, for extraction of resources. Not, of course, for movement of people. And it must be a level playing field; everyone is equal. So the United States would be part of the system, Grenada would be part of it, all perfectly fair and equal.

There was nothing novel in this stance. In fact, the US was replaying what Britain had done a century earlier. Britain became a leading industrial power just as Churchill said, by force and violence, and also by stealing higher technology from other countries: India, Ireland, the countries that are now Belgium and Holland. By the mid-nineteenth century, Britain had become far and away the most advanced society, with more than twice the per-capita capitalization of any other country. It was far enough ahead in the competition to begin to toy with the idea of advocating free trade, assuming it would do quite well in the competition. That was 1846.

Free trade, however, had some qualifications. Britain never really agreed to it fully. India, that's all of South Asia then, was under British control. Before the European onslaught, India and China were the richest, most advanced countries in the world. But imperialism took care of that. India was deindustrialized by the British occupation, but it was still a rich prize—closed off despite free trade pretensions, and barred from real development.

Later Britain abandoned the free trade game altogether because it could no longer compete with Japan. It therefore closed off the empire. Holland, which had a substantial empire in East Asia, did the same, the US as well. That's a large part of the background for the Second World War in the Pacific. The Japanese reacted to the closing of the entire region by the imperial powers, blocking their access to essential resources. They began to carry out aggressive acts, which finally led to war.

The US recapitulated the British experience a century later. Until well into the twentieth century, the US was a leader in protectionism. Economic historian Paul Bairoch described the US as the "the mother country and bastion of protectionism," from its origins (Bairoch, *op. cit.*) The US also resorted to other forms of large-scale state intervention in the economy, some truly extreme, like slavery, which was the basis of much of the modern economy. But by 1945, the United States was far ahead of anyone else. So it was a good time for free trade, an open global system.

But just like Britain before it, there were qualifications. One of the US principles for the postwar liberal world order was that regional alliances were to be dismantled. There should be no more imperial preference systems in which the imperial power had special control and could keep others from entering it on equal terms. With one exception. One regional system was to remain. Henry Stimson, one of the leading US statesmen, when discussing the elimination of regional systems, explained that all must be eliminated except for "our little region over here which has never bothered anyone," the Western hemisphere (Kolko 1968).

So the Western hemisphere, rather like India under the British, would be under US control. But the rest would be open to everyone.

The meaning of open global systems is sometimes articulated quite honestly in internal documents. The most important commodity in the world at the time, still today, was oil. The United States, of course, had a petroleum policy. It was spelled out in a 1944 State Department document entitled *The Petroleum Policy of the United States*. The document called for "the preservation of the absolute position presently obtaining [in the Western hemisphere], and therefore vigilant protection of existing concessions in United States hands coupled with insistence upon the

Open Door principle of equal opportunity for United States companies in new areas."

In brief, what we have, we keep, closing the door to others; what we do not yet have, we take, under the principle of the Open Door.

In "our little region over here," it wasn't too difficult to implement this principle. Long before World War II, the US had expelled Britain from Venezuela when major oil reserves were found there, imposing its own rule. The Middle East, where the main resources of easily accessible oil were and still are, was more complex. Prior to World War II, the region was largely under British control. To implement the petroleum policy, the US, relying on its far superior power, compelled Britain "to accept an arrangement that reserved a privileged position for the U.S. domestic oil industry while exposing all of Britain's oil production, which was in other countries, to the competition of the powerful U.S. international oil companies" (oil industry specialist David Painter, 1986). French interests were dismissed even more easily, by declaring France to be an enemy state, under German occupation, hence forfeiting its rights.

The vast energy reserves of the Middle East, included in the Grand Area, were not important for the US itself, which then, and for many years after, was the world's major petroleum producer (as it is becoming again today). But they were important as a means of world control. The industrial centers of the Grand Area were shifting to reliance on oil, under US influence; much Marshall Plan aid for Europe was dedicated to the purchase of oil, hence moving from one US bank to another. Furthermore, US control over this increasingly essential resource provided the US with "veto power" over its allies, George Kennan explained.

Kennan was referring specifically to Japan. At the time, Japan's development to a major industrial power was considered a remote contingency, but still a potential concern, especially if Japan were to seek an independent role in world affairs. In that case, the "veto power" could become an important tool of diplomacy. These conceptions persisted into the post–Cold War years. The influential planner Zbigniew Brzezinski was not enthusiastic about the US invasion of Iraq in 2003, but he recognized that it might have a bright side. He wrote that "America's security role," the conventional euphemism for military domination, if extended over the second-largest oil producer in the region, would provide Washington with "indirect but politically critical leverage on the European and Asian economies that are also dependent on energy exports from the region" (*National Interest*, Winter 2003/4).

Global control requires thoughtful planning.

The Middle East remains of enormous importance. Just open the newspapers. You read about Iraq, Iran, Syria, Saudi Arabia and its war in Yemen (which is destroying the country with US arms and intelligence support), Qatar, Israel. It's a major focus. And the reason isn't obscure. It was explained by the State Department in 1945 when the new world order was being established. The State Department pointed out that Middle East oil is "a stupendous source of strategic power, and one of the greatest material prizes in world history." That's not a small affair. We have to make sure we have substantial control of that.

In Europe the war ended in 1945, with the Russians and Allied (US-UK) forces separated at the Oder-Neisse Line, which was actually a historical fault line. That was where Eastern and Western Europe had begun to divide in about the fifteenth century. Western Europe at that point was beginning to develop. Eastern Europe was falling behind. Historian of Russia Theodore Shanin writes that in the course of this process, "Russia was becoming a semi-colonial possession of European capital" (Shanin 1985). There was some development in Eastern Europe, but it was mostly Western-owned. That changed in 1917. After the Bolshevik Revolution, Russia went on to become a major industrial power, although nowhere near the scale of the West.

After 1945, each side imposed its rule in the areas they had conquered. For the Russians, it was Eastern Europe. That story is familiar—not in Russia, where it was clouded in propaganda, but here we all know about Russian oppression in Eastern Europe. So we won't have to review it.

For US domains, most of the rest of the world, you have to search the documentary and scholarly record to find out what happened. I talked a little about it earlier.

In Europe and also in Japan, the first task was to dismantle the anti-fascist resistance and the social and political structures that it had established. The problem was faced in the first country occupied by allied forces, Italy. There the resistance had driven the Germans out of large areas and had begun to construct a new radical democratic order on their own. It was therefore necessary to dismantle what had been constructed and to restore the traditional order, including leading fascists and fascist collaborators. Italy remained a tough nut. The CIA carried out one of its major operations there from 1948, aimed at subverting Italian democracy, continuing at least into the 1970s. There were similar tasks all over Western Europe and Japan. And interventions all over the Grand Area, too numerous to mention. If there's time we'll return to some of them.

If we look at the period since 1945, comparing rhetoric and actions, we find as usual two different pictures. The rhetoric was that the United States was defending itself and others from Russian aggression all over the world. The United States was in a posture of defense. To underscore that posture, the Defense Department was established in 1947. The US didn't have a Defense Department before that; it had a War Department. That was the pre-Orwell period, so a War Department that was devoted to wars of aggression was called the War Department.

In fact from the founding of the country right up until today, there's hardly been a year when the United States wasn't at war. A rather unusual history. Just think it through. First there were wars against what the Declaration of Independence calls the "merciless Indian savages" who were brutally attacking peaceful English communities. Then we had to defend ourselves against the Indian nations we were dispossessing and "exterminating," as the leadership sometimes described the process. Also conquering half of Mexico, including where we are meeting now. Then expanding over parts of the Pacific. Endless intervention mainly in the Americas. There's no time to go through it. And it continues throughout the Cold War.

Sometimes it's not direct military aggression, just support of military coups. The most recent is Honduras in 2009, one of the reasons there are so many refugees from Honduras, as we already discussed.

That's essentially the picture, including the actual Cold War. If you take a look at the Cold War in terms of actual actions, not rhetoric, it's not primarily a Russian-American confrontation, though that was always in the background. On the ground, each of the two major powers, the grand superpower and the lesser superpower, intervened often forcefully in their own domains. For the Russians, Eastern Europe, for the United States, most of the rest of the world. And each used the pretext of the threat of the other as a justification for intervention. So when the Russians invaded Hungary in 1956, they were defending free Hungary against the fascist forces supported by the West. And whenever the US intervenes anywhere in the world, whatever the facts may be, it's defending itself and the Free World from Russian subversion or aggression. Even if there are no Russians anywhere in sight, it's the Russians or their proxies.

Though the two sides are unequal in scale and scope of their violent actions, they have followed rather similar policies. That's the real structure of the Cold War as long as it lasted, up until the collapse of the Soviet Union. That's if you look at the actions rather than the rhetoric.

The basic structure was established as the Nazis were defeated. Russia established its harsh and repressive rule in the East, all very familiar. The US and its British ally supported the reconstruction of largely independent state capitalist societies, open to the US multinationals that were then taking their modern form and within the US-run NATO alliance— but only after completing the first task of dismantling the anti-fascist resistance and its radical democratic aspirations and structures and restoring something like the traditional order.

The task even extended to the Western hemisphere, our little region over here. A conflict arose between two different conceptions of how the hemisphere ought to be organized and developed. One of them was the conception that was dominant throughout Latin America. The other was the conception in the United States. And they were diametrically opposed. As the State Department described the problem, Latin Americans advocate "the philosophy of the new nationalism [that] embraces policies designed to bring about a broader distribution of wealth and to raise the standard of living of the masses." Latin Americans are convinced that "the first beneficiaries of the development of a country's resources should be the people of that country" (Green 1971). That failure to understand "sound economics" had to be stopped in its tracks.

To deal with the problem, the US summoned the Latin American countries to a hemispheric conference in Mexico in February 1945, where the US put forth an Economic Charter of the Americas that called for an end to "economic nationalism" in all its forms. "Sound economics" entails that the beneficiaries of a country's resources should be US investors and their local associates. Not the people of that country.

Given power relations, the US position prevailed.

As usual with free trade rhetoric, there was an exception: the United States. Economic nationalism must be banned throughout the continent, but not in the state that issued the rules. The US followed a policy of state-led industrial development under the cover of the Pentagon, essentially creating the modern high-tech economy. That's why you have your computers and iPhones and the internet and all the rest, mostly thanks to extensive state intervention in the economy, massive taxpayer funding for decades to create the high-tech economy. But other than that, no economic nationalism.

It was recognized that it might take force to eradicate the philosophy of the new nationalism and the heretical idea that people should be the beneficiaries of their own resources. That was understood. Again, let's go to the dovish end of the planning spectrum, to George Kennan. He warned that we must ensure "the protection of our raw materials." They're ours; they just happen by accident to be located somewhere else. And it might not be easy.

"The final answer might be an unpleasant one," Kennan concluded: "police repression by the local government." We should not hesitate to support "harsh government measures of repression" as long as "the results are on balance favorable to our purposes." In general, "it is better to have a strong regime in power than a liberal government if it is indulgent and relaxed and penetrated by Communists" (LaFeber 1983), a term with broad application. It can refer to priests and nuns organizing peasants, labor organizers, human rights activists, a pretty comprehensive notion. That's the dovish end of the spectrum.

It remained a doctrine of American liberalism, reiterated much later in the Clinton doctrine, which held that the US has the right to resort to "unilateral use of military power" to ensure "uninhibited access to key markets, energy supplies and strategic resources." Not a right accorded to others, needless to say.

In accord with these principles, there's a vicious record of intervention. I won't go through it. Hundreds of thousands of people killed, countries destroyed, huge refugee flow. A crucial year in this record was 1962, during the Kennedy administration, an important date to which I'll return.

Elsewhere, it was also necessary to discipline countries that were tempted to "go berserk with fanatical nationalism" by trying to control their own resources. That's the *New York Times* editors in 1954 (August 6) praising the CIA coup that overthrew the parliamentary government of Iran and installed the rule of the Shah. Repercussions are right on the front pages until today. Incidentally, the *New York Times* appears to have a near 100 percent record of supporting military coups that are backed directly or supported by the US.

All of this goes back to 1945, when the US was at the height of its power, a kind of power that had never existed in world history. US security was overwhelming. The US controlled the Western hemisphere, both oceans, the opposite sides of both oceans. It had almost half the world's wealth at that time, which is astonishing.

There's a lot of talk these days about recent American decline, but it's worth bearing in mind that the decline began immediately after the war. That level of power could not possibly be maintained. There was a serious decline in American power in 1949, when an event occurred called "loss of China"—an interesting phrase; I can lose my watch but not yours. China's independence was a huge blow to Grand Area planning, and had large effects on international policies, to which we'll return later.

It had a large impact on the domestic scene as well. The question of who was responsible for the loss of China provided a major impetus for the severe McCarthyite repression—which actually began some years earlier with Truman, but was carried forward substantially by McCarthy with effects that have not disappeared.

As decolonization took its agonizing course and other industrial powers reconstructed from wartime damage, the US share of global wealth (GDP) continued to decline, to about 25 percent by 1970—still phenomenal but not what it had been at the peak of US power. By now it's declined further, but these measures are becoming misleading as we enter the period of neoliberal globalization in which national accounts mean much less than they did before. There's a different measure of power that is becoming more significant: the percentage of ownership of the world's wealth by US-based corporations. The answer is an absolutely astounding 50 percent. Today, the statistics are good. They reveal that 50 percent of the world's wealth is in the hands of US-based corporations, even though the national account, GDP, is not anywhere near that. These topics have been explored in depth by political economist Sean Starrs, who also found that US-based corporations are first in just about every category—manufacturing, finance, almost everything else (Starrs, forthcoming).

Nevertheless, global hegemony did decline. The loss of China, as I mentioned, was very serious. In fact, the loss of China was the background for the worst crime of the postwar period, the invasion of Vietnam, which began immediately afterward, with strong US support for France's effort to reconquer its former colony. We'll return to the details, but in the context of our topic tonight, it's interesting to consider how the war is interpreted. Close to universally, across the political spectrum, it is described as a failure, a terrible defeat for the US.

There is, of course, some truth to that. The US did not achieve its maximal goal of conquering Vietnam or even sustaining the regime it had established in the south. But there is more to the story.

One of the good things about the United States is that it's a pretty open society, more than any other that I know of. We have good access to internal records, not everything, of course, but there's a reasonably good record of release of documents. In this case we were helped quite a lot by Dan Ellsberg. The *Pentagon Papers* (*PP*) revealed a huge amount of material on the war, soon supplemented by government release of many documents once the dam had been breached. That included quite revealing internal discussions on the reasons for the early intervention in Vietnam in support of France, which set the stage for what followed.

This material has mostly been disregarded. In the *New York Times* edition of the *PP*, all that most people have seen, you don't find any of this material. The focus is on the sixties, the failure. But the early reasoning is interesting and instructive. Essentially, our old friend the domino theory. The argument was that if Vietnam carried out successful independent development, it would be what Kissinger later called a "virus" that would "spread contagion." It would be a model that might be followed by others in the region who had suffered the harsh consequences of imperialism. They might want to follow the same course, and the system of global domination—the Grand Area—might seriously erode.

Planners were concerned that the contagion might spread not just through mainland Southeast Asia, but all the way to Indonesia. Vietnam didn't matter much, but Indonesia did. A big country, very rich resources. If the rot spread as far as Indonesia, it might reach Japan—the "super-domino," in the words of the prominent Asia scholar John Dower. If Southeast and East Asia became independent, what we call communist, Japan would be tempted to "accommodate" this bloc of states and become its technological and industrial center.

There's a name for that system. It was called the New Order in Asia that Japanese fascists were trying to establish. In the early 1950s, the United States was not ready to lose the Pacific phase of World War II, which was fought to prevent Japan from establishing its new order. Obviously, planners weren't going to accept that.

How then do you prevent it? When a virus is spreading contagion, you must destroy the virus and inoculate potential targets. That was achieved. Vietnam was virtually destroyed. It's not a model for anybody, and is by now increasingly integrated into the global system dominated by US-based corporations. In the surrounding countries, harsh, brutal military dictatorships were established, preventing contagion. Indonesia was the most important domino. The contagion was blocked in Indonesia in 1965 by an unusually brutal US-backed military coup that killed hundreds of thousands of people and totally suppressed all dissent. The main political parties were wiped out. The country has yet to recover, even to discover what happened, all effectively concealed.

It was not concealed in the West, which could scarcely contain its euphoria about the "staggering mass slaughter" that was "a gleam of light in Asia" (*New York Times*), a "boiling bloodbath" that provided "new hope" for the region (the news weeklies).

The domino didn't fall, in fact, was incorporated fully within the US-dominated liberal world order, open to exploitation. US support continued right through the brutal repression and major war crimes. In 1975, Henry Kissinger gave the ruling generals a green light to invade East Timor, where they went on to carry out what appears to be the worst slaughter in per capita terms since Hitler's genocide, always with firm and decisive US support. And admiration. When the dictator, General Suharto, was invited to Washington in 2005, the Clinton administration welcomed him as "our kind of guy."

In later years, McGeorge Bundy, former national security advisor under Kennedy and Johnson, reflected that it might have been a good idea to call off the Vietnam War in 1965, when the "gleam of light" shone and the US had achieved its main goals. No pernicious models, no contagion, Indonesia was rescued, Japan was in our pocket.

Was the Vietnam War a failure, a terrible defeat? True, the US didn't achieve its maximal goal of turning Vietnam into something like the Philippines, a kind of neo-colony, but it did achieve the major goal. The dominoes didn't fall. As I mentioned last week, it's standard in commentary on international affairs to ridicule the domino theory because the dominoes didn't fall as feared. In other words, the remedy was successful. The virus was extirpated, the potential victims inoculated. But as I mentioned, though ridiculed, the domino theory is never abandoned. It's quite rational and has substantial empirical support.

The loss of China was also part of the background for NSC 68 in 1950, excerpts posted for reading this week. The document is widely and correctly recognized as a document of great significance, setting an enduring policy framework. Apart from its substance, the rhetoric is highly illuminating. Remember that this is an internal document, not for the public, not even for most of Congress, only declassified many years later.

The rhetoric is like a fairy tale. On one side there is ultimate evil, on the other, absolute perfection. Each of the antagonists has an essential nature that defines it. The document contrasts the "fundamental design of the Kremlin" with the "fundamental purpose" of the US.

"The implacable purpose of the slave state [is] to eliminate the challenge of freedom" (excerpts from NSC 68, 1950) everywhere. The "compulsion" of the Kremlin "demands total power over all men" in the slave state itself and "absolute authority over the rest of the world." The force of evil is "inescapably militant," so that no accommodation or peaceful settlement is even thinkable.

In contrast, the "fundamental purpose of the United States [is] to assure the integrity and vitality of our free society, which is founded upon the dignity and worth of the individual" (excerpts from NSC 68, 1950)—this at a time of rampant racism, even lynching, federal laws imposing segregation in public housing, and laws against miscegenation so extreme that the Nazis—who took US laws as their model—refused to go anywhere near as far as the US.

And right at the peak of McCarthyism and anti-Communist hysteria, our free society is marked by "marvelous diversity," "deep tolerance," "lawfulness," a commitment "to create and maintain an environment in which every individual has the opportunity to realize his creative powers. [It] does not fear, it welcomes, diversity [and] derives its strength from its hospitality even to antipathetic ideas." The "system of values which animates our society [includes] the principles of freedom, tolerance, the importance of the individual and the supremacy of reason over will" (excerpts from NSC 68, 1950).

Fortunately, the perfect society has some advantages in this conflict. "The essential tolerance of our world outlook, our generous and constructive impulses, and the absence of covetousness in our international relations are assets of potentially enormous influence," particularly among those who have been lucky enough to experience these qualities at first hand, as in Latin America, which has benefited from "our long continuing endeavors to create and now develop the Inter-American system" (excerpts from NSC 68, 1950).

Latin Americans might have had some thoughts about this long-standing benevolence.

Of course, there can be no accommodation with absolute evil, so we must "foster the seeds of destruction within the Soviet Union [and] hasten its decay." We must avoid negotiations because any agreements "would reflect present realities and would therefore be unacceptable, if not disastrous, to the United States and the rest of the free world," though after the success of a "roll back strategy" we might "negotiate a settlement with the Soviet Union (or a successor state or states)" (excerpts from NSC 68, 1950). That policy is forced on us by the fundamental design of the slave state and its compulsion for world domination.

In fairness, the document did recognize some flaws in our perfection, and urged that they be remedied. The flaws are "the excesses of a permanently open mind [and] the excess of tolerance." Another flaw is "dissent among us" when there should be conformity. We will have to learn to "distinguish between the necessity for tolerance and the necessity for just suppression," which is a crucial feature of "the democratic way." It is particularly important to insulate our "labor unions, civic enterprises, schools, churches, and all media for influencing opinion" from the "evil work" of the Kremlin, which seeks to subvert them and "make them sources of confusion in our economy, our culture and our body politic" (excerpts from NSC 68, 1950).

Fortunately, Joe McCarthy, the House Un-American Affairs Committee, and other stalwart figures were upholding these stern obligations right at the time.

There are other flaws of our society beyond open-mindedness and failure to understand the necessity of just suppression. Aspirations are too high. Increased taxes are necessary, along with "Reduction of Federal expenditures for purposes other than defense and foreign assistance, if necessary by the deferment of certain desirable programs." These military Keynesian policies, it is suggested, are likely to stimulate the domestic economy as well and they may prevent "a decline in economic activity of serious proportions." In general, "a large measure of sacrifice and discipline will be demanded of the American people," and they also must "give up some of the benefits" they enjoy as we dedicate ourselves to saving humanity from the implacable campaign of the slave state to destroy freedom everywhere (excerpts from NSC 68, 1950).

NSC 68 called for a huge increase in armaments, tripling the military budget, while carefully concealing their findings that the slave state is weaker not only than the United States, but even than Western Europe. Scattered through the document are statistics and data on Western Europe, which, it turns out, was roughly comparable to the Soviet Union in military force, and, of course, far more advanced industrially and other kinds of development. And needless to say the US was far ahead of anyone.

As I mentioned, NSC 68 is recognized to be one of the founding documents of contemporary world order, and is the subject of extensive scholarship. The interesting rhetorical framework is ignored or downplayed, mistakenly, I think. It tells us something about the perceptions of the dominant political class, though the senior statesman Dean Acheson did confess that it was necessary to be "clearer than truth" in order to "bludgeon the mass mind" of government, and "to scare hell out of the American people," as the influential Senator Arthur Vandenberg interpreted the general government message.

Policies quickly shifted to a harder line, with the usual justification: security. Security is a very interesting concept, rather like defense. So what is security? Let's take a quick look.

In 1950, the actual security of the United States was extraordinary, as already discussed. But there was a potential threat, which didn't materialize until some years later, though it was recognized as a severe, indeed existential, potential threat: ICBMs, intercontinental ballistic missiles, which sooner or later would be developed to the point where they could reach the United States and would carry nuclear warheads.

What then do you do about a potential severe security threat? Well, one possibility would be negotiations to ban the development of such weapons, thereby maximizing security. That didn't happen, and it's interesting to see why. There is a standard scholarly history of the strategic weapons system by McGeorge Bundy (1988), who had access to high-level documents, security documents, and so on. He does mention this option. In the course of discussing other topics, he mentions the fact that if there had been a treaty to ban ICBMs, the one potential threat to American security would have been eliminated. He adds that he was unable to find a single document, even a draft paper anywhere, suggesting that maybe it would be worthwhile pursuing a way to protect the population of the United States from the one potential danger they faced, the threat of destruction.

Bundy has a couple of sentences about this curious fact, and then goes on to the next topic. And rather interestingly, all of the scholarship as far as I know ignores the matter. I've never been able to find a reference to it. I think it's one of the most astonishing discoveries in history of scholarship. Think about it.

Well, was there a possibility of a treaty? We can't be sure because it was apparently never considered. But it looks as if there might have been.

In 1952, Stalin made a remarkable offer. He offered to allow unification of Germany. Remember that only a few years earlier, Germany had virtually wiped out Russia. But Stalin was nevertheless willing to accept unification of Germany, though with one condition: that it not join a hostile military alliance, that it not join NATO. So it would be neutral and independent. There was talk about the prospect of elections, which, of course, the communists would lose.

I know of only one American scholar who paid attention to Stalin's offer, the respected analyst James Warburg, in his important book *Germany: Key to Peace*, where he urged that the prospects be pursued. He was ignored or ridiculed. Anyone who ever mentioned it later—there were very few (I, incidentally, was one)—was ridiculed as well. How could Stalin ever have meant anything like this? There was, of course, a way to find out, but it was never considered: take up the offer. If anything had come of it, the world would have been a much better place.

Russian archives have since come out. And it turns out that the offer may have been pretty serious. One of the most respected Cold War historians, Melvyn Leffler, writes in *Foreign Affairs* (July 1996) that scholars who studied released Soviet archives were surprised to discover that "[Lavrenti] Beria—the sinister, brutal head of the secret police—propos[ed] that the Kremlin offer the West a deal on the unification and neutralization of Germany, [agreeing] to sacrifice the East German communist regime to reduce East-West tensions" and improve internal political and economic conditions in Russia—opportunities that were squandered in favor of securing German participation in NATO, of course, a major threat to Russia.

Well, we don't know if it could have happened, but what we do know is that the security of the population of the United States seems not to have been a consideration, even a marginal consideration.

That's called concern for security, and it's pretty typical. I'll have to skip some revealing illustrations because it's getting too late, but the topic is too important to ignore completely.

After Stalin's death, Khrushchev came along. He understood that Russia couldn't compete with the United States economically; it was inconceivable. So he wanted to cut back military spending on both sides. This is the Kennedy years. As to the reception of his offer, I'll quote Kenneth Waltz, one of the leading international relations scholars. The Kennedy administration, he writes in *PS: Political Science and Politics* (December 1991), "undertook the largest strategic and conventional peace-time military build-up the world has yet seen . . . even as Khrushchev was trying at once to carry through a major reduction in the conventional forces and to follow a strategy of minimum deterrence, and we did so even though the balance of strategic weapons greatly favored the United States."

Once again, Kennedy's decision harmed security, but enhanced state power. That's a consistent pattern.

It was soon learned how seriously the security of the population was endangered by Kennedy's reaction to Khrushchev's offer: in October 1962, the month that Kennedy's associate historian Arthur Schlesinger called, rightly, "the most dangerous moment in history," the Cuban missile crisis. The facts are harrowing. The United States raised military preparedness to DEFCON 2. There's a series of stages of military preparedness starting with five up and going to one. This is the only time DEFCON 2 has ever been imposed. DEFCON 1 means send off the missiles, we're all finished. So it was up to DEFCON 2, right before the end.

The Joint Chiefs wanted to invade Cuba. Kennedy contemplated invasion. If there had been an invasion of Cuba, we'd probably all be dead. The US didn't know it, but the Russians had tactical nuclear weapons in Cuba to try to defend against a US invasion. And if there had been an invasion, they would have been used. The US invasion force would have been wiped out, a lot of the southeastern United States would have been wiped out, we would then have bombed Moscow, and it's all over. So it was that close.

In fact, how close it was is just mind-boggling. There was a point at the peak of the crisis when US destroyers were dropping depth charges on Soviet submarines right outside the so-called quarantine area. These were old submarines, designed for the North Atlantic, not the Caribbean. We now have extensive records about what happened. Inside the submarines the temperature was rising to 140 degrees. CO_2 levels were at such a level that crewmen were fainting, falling down, close to death. Depth charges were falling near the submarines. They had no communication with anyone; they didn't know what was going on.

The US didn't know it at the time, but the Russian subs had torpedoes that were nuclear tipped. One of the commanders decided that "look we're at war, a major war is going on. Let's defend our dignity, and instead of just being murdered down here, let's fire the torpedoes." Had he done so, it very likely would have triggered escalation leading to major nuclear war.

In order to fire the torpedoes, he needed the approval of two subordinate officers. One of them approved, the second, Vassily Arkhipov, did not. He decided that it wouldn't have been legal to fire the torpedoes. So he refused. They didn't fire them. That's how close we were to possible terminal destruction. If Arkhipov had been on one of the other submarines, that would have been the end. It's one of the worst cases in the record—and there are all too many others.

We have since learned that President Eisenhower had sub-delegated authority to use nuclear weapons to commanders. That continues with subsequent administrations. You can read about this in a very important book that just came out, Daniel Ellsberg's *Doomsday Machine*. The book provides detailed information about this from the inside.

We've also learned, from memoirs, that American pilots who were in the air, flying the Chrome Dome missions, assumed that they had authority to use nuclear weapons in extreme circumstances. One shudders to think of the consequences.

Why did Khrushchev put missiles in Cuba in the first place? Scholarship is pretty much in agreement that there were two reasons. One was to try to compensate for Soviet backwardness at the military level after Kennedy had rejected Khrushchev's offer of mutual reductions and had instead carried out a huge military buildup though the US was already far ahead. That was one.

The other was a matter of timing. Kennedy was carrying out a serious terrorist war against Cuba. The goal, as Arthur Schlesinger puts it in his biography of Robert Kennedy, was to bring the "terrors of the Earth" to Cuba. The terrorist campaign was the responsibility of Robert Kennedy, his top priority. He informed the CIA that the Cuban problem carries "the top priority in the United States Government—all else is secondary—no time, no effort, or manpower is to be spared" in the effort to overthrow the Castro regime. One component of the effort was a terrorist program called Operation Mongoose. It had a timetable leading to "open revolt and overthrow of the Communist regime." On August 23, President Kennedy issued National Security Memorandum No. 181, a directive to engineer an internal revolt that would be followed by US military intervention, after terrorism and subversion had laid the basis.

October 1962 was when the missiles were sent to Cuba.

Meanwhile, terrorist attacks continued: speed boat attacks on Cuban seaside hotels where Soviet military technicians were congregating, killing many Russians and Cubans; attacks on British and Cuban cargo ships; contamination of sugar shipments. Lots of other atrocities and sabotage. When this brutal campaign is discussed in US commentary, it's almost always dismissed as silly CIA shenanigans, like plans to make Castro's beard fall out. It was far more severe than that.

Dan Ellsberg was then on the inside, close to the center of analysis and planning. He's reviewed the Cuban missile crisis in extensive detail in his recent book. In personal communication, he has said that in his opinion the invasion threat was the primary reason for Khrushchev's sending the missiles. Notice that that's a case where large-scale terror came very close to ending the human experiment. It's worth thinking about. The terror was very serious. The first book that explores the effect on the victims recently appeared. By a Canadian scholar, Keith Bolender, *Voices from the Other Side: An Oral History of Terrorism.*

There is still more, which was suspected but recently became known. Turns out that right at the peak of the missile crisis, late October 1962, the US was carrying out high-altitude nuclear explosions in order to test some ideas about a defense shield. These were, of course, detected by the Russians, who carried out high-altitude tests in response, which were detected by the Americans. Either side could have easily assumed that it's an attack. Luckily, we escaped. By luck. Again, the security of the population is scarcely even a concern.

Well, the crisis did end with Khrushchev backing down. Just how is an important story that I'll skip. But it's all worth close attention.

It's getting late so I won't go through other cases. But, in fact, there's case after case of very near disaster. It's kind of a miracle that we've escaped. And you can't count on miracles to continue.

Let's move quickly to the end of the Cold War. In 1989, when the Soviet Union collapsed, there were two conflicting visions of the post–Cold War global order. One was Mikhail Gorbachev's. He proposed a Eurasian security system in which there would be no military blocs at all. It would be a common security system from Brussels to Vladivostok. That's one idea.

The other was the US position. That's George H. W. Bush, the first Bush, and his secretary of state James Baker. Their position was that the US had won the war and was going to extend its dominance. Bush and Baker wanted Gorbachev to agree to let Germany be unified inside

NATO—a serious threat to Russia if you think about it, particularly in the light of recent history. They told Gorbachev that if he agreed, the US would not move—the phrase was "one inch to the East," which meant to East Germany. No one was even dreaming about anything beyond—at least they weren't talking about it.

But this was never put in writing, and when Gorbachev agreed to unification of Germany, NATO immediately moved to East Berlin. When Gorbachev complained, he was told in effect, if you're dumb enough to trust a gentleman's agreement, it's your problem.

Then Clinton came along and extended NATO far to the East, right to the Russian border. In 2008, there were proposals to bring Ukraine into NATO, that's the Russian geostrategic heartland. There have been lots of provocative acts on both sides. Obama introduced a trillion dollar modernization program of nuclear weapons, some scaled down to battlefield use. That brings us to today.

I mentioned earlier that 1962 was an important year in other respects. In 1962, Kennedy changed the mission of the Latin American military. Of course we can do that. It was changed from "hemispheric defense," which was a holdover from the Second World War, to "internal security." Internal security is a euphemism for war against the population. That was the official change, and it had consequences. These are described vividly by Charles Maechling, who was the head of counterinsurgency in the US through these years, 1961–1966, under Kennedy and Johnson.

Maechling describes Kennedy's 1962 decision as "a shift from toleration of the rapacity and cruelty of the Latin American military [to] direct complicity" in their crimes, to US support for "the methods of Heinrich Himmler's extermination squads" (*Los Angeles Times*, March 18, 1982).

That's the head of US counterinsurgency describing the 1962 decision and its aftermath. Pretty strong, and regrettably not inaccurate—though without tarnishing the Camelot imagery among liberal intellectuals.

What followed was a huge plague of repression. It began with the military dictatorship in Brazil, the most important country in Latin America, in 1964, overthrowing a moderately reformist parliamentary government. The coup seems to have been pretty much set up with the support of the Kennedy administration, though it took place a couple of weeks after Kennedy's assassination. This was the first of the neo-Nazi national security states that spread through South America, bringing with them mass slaughter, bitter repression, torture, "disappearance," and tight ideological controls. Chile, which we discussed, was one such case.

Like the Suharto coup, the Brazilian coup was welcomed in liberal circles. For example, by Kennedy-Johnson ambassador to Brazil Lincoln Gordon, who then went on to become president of Johns Hopkins University. He described the happy event as "the most decisive victory for freedom in the mid-twentieth century," not least because the Brazilian generals, the "democratic forces" now in charge, should "create a greatly improved climate for private investment" (Parker 1979).

The plague then swept through the hemisphere. We won't run through it, merely noting here how little changes over the years. Thus, Gordon's celebration of the destruction of Brazilian democracy by the military dictatorship was echoed by Obama's ambassador to Honduras Hugo Llorens, who praised the elections held under military rule as "a great celebration of democracy," isolating the US once again from Latin America and most of the rest of the world, which, unlike Obama-Clinton, refused to welcome the overthrow of Honduran democracy and the expulsion of the elected president, and to endorse the "elections" that restored the bitter rule of the Honduran oligarchy and military.

The US-backed plague reached Central America in the Reagan years, with massive state terror, hideous torture, every imaginable kind of horror. The US was overwhelmingly the agent of violence. The US was even condemned by the World Court for "unlawful use of force"—aka international terrorism—and ordered to pay substantial reparations to Nicaragua and to call off its terrorist war. Of course, that was disregarded, and the terror was escalated. The World Court was dismissed by the *New York Times* as a "hostile forum," so we don't have to pay any attention to it. A few years earlier the same Court was lauded as a noble institution when it ruled in favor of the US in a case involving Iran. It all continues right to the present. I mentioned one case, Honduras. Well, that's "our little region over here."

As discussed earlier, the decade of the 1980s was framed by the assassination of Archbishop Romero at the beginning of the decade and the assassination of six leading Latin American intellectuals, Jesuit priests, in November 1989—shortly after the fall of the Berlin Wall. In fact, throughout the post-1962 period there were many religious martyrs. That had to do with another significant event of 1962. Pope John XXIII called Vatican II, the second major Vatican conference. Its theme was to return the Catholic Church to the basic message of the Gospels, which had largely been forgotten ever since Roman Emperor Constantine, in the fourth century, adopted Christianity as the state religion and converted Christianity from "the persecuted church" to a "persecuting church," in the words of the distinguished theologian Hans Küng in his history of Christianity. Vatican II, he continued, "ushered in a new era in the history of the Catholic Church," restoring the teachings of the Gospels (Küng 2001).

The message of Vatican II was taken up by Latin American bishops, who adopted the "preferential option for the poor." Priests, nuns, and laypersons brought the radical pacifist message of the Gospels to the poor, helping them organize to ameliorate their bitter fate in the domains of US power, to take affairs into their own hands, and to be ruled by "countrymen like ourselves who know the people's sores." The founding ideas are called liberation theology.

That, of course, is the kind of heresy that has to be stamped out without mercy or delay. The United States and its local clients launched a war against the Church. That's why there are so many religious martyrs. And they're proud of it. There is a famous branch of the Pentagon called the School of the Americas—since renamed, when the exploits of its graduates became too well known. The School of the Americas trained Latin American killers and torturers, including many of the worst ones. It advertises itself differently of course, with "talking points," which are presented to the public to show how wonderful the work of the school is. One of the talking points is that the liberation theology that was initiated at Vatican II was "defeated with the assistance of the US army," which trained those who brought victory in the war against the Church.

Chapter 4

CAPITALISM VERSUS
THE ENVIRONMENT

Waterstone Lecture, February 5, 2019

Before I get into the main topic, which is capitalism versus the environment, I just wanted to say a couple things by way of preface and to respond to some things that I've been seeing both in people coming in, in office hours a little bit, and also the little bit of lurking I've been doing on the discussion boards and a little bit on voice threads, so I just want to say a couple things about that.

First, this issue of why the tie again to capitalism, and I want to repeat this and make it clear what this set of connections is about. As I'd said, a main objective of the course is to identify the common root causes of today's most pressing problems. That's instrumental to something else, and the something else is to demonstrate the ways in which these problems are necessarily related to each other, and then, in order to be able to see the bases for solidarity and unified, rather than divided, political cohesion and action. The usual notion of these issues being siloed and differentiated from each other, I think, can't emphasize enough that they really are connected to each other in very fundamental ways and that this may be the basis for a unified set of political actions.

The second thing I wanted to just say a word about because I've seen some things on this and people have been asking about this, is a word about capitalism and its alternatives. The alternative to late-stage capitalism, which is what we're describing here, sometimes termed really existing capitalism, which, as we've begun to discuss already, often actually means socialism for the rich and brutal or gangster capitalism for the rest. The alternative to this is not a planned economy run by an authoritarian state, which is often portrayed in the obverse sort of mythology as communism or really existing socialism.

For example, in the former USSR or Russia today, North Korea, China, Cuba, Vietnam, and so on, virtually all of those experiments, many of which were Marxist or socialist inspired, were really a state capitalism in a slightly different inflection than the state capitalism we see elsewhere in the world. That's not the alternative.

The alternative that we're thinking about is an economy that's run by the producers, that is the workers themselves, through a democratization of the workplace. We say we value democracy very highly and yet we don't institute it in the places where we spend most of our lives. That is, the workplace is a very authoritarian kind of environment and we don't really question that.

When we go to work, we don't expect to be able to have a bunch of choices about what we're going to do in the day and what we're going to produce and how we're going to produce it and so forth, but if we really value democracy, why not start to institute that in places where we spend a great deal of our time? Why not democratize the decisions over what gets produced (and this ties into what I hope to speak about a bit tonight and we'll speak about a bit more in the coming weeks, ties very closely to how we define quality of life or happiness or satisfaction). What gets produced is not necessarily tied solely to, or even most importantly to, profit maximization. That is, if you go back to a conversation a couple weeks ago, what if things were produced for their use value rather than for their exchange value? That might, in fact, produce a very different set of outcomes.

The way things get produced would also be democratically organized. That is, if the people who had to live with the consequences of the production process were in charge of that production process rather than those being in charge being absentee or distant owners, we might see very different kinds of effects coming out of our production processes and places, and this includes many of the impacts on the environment.

And then finally, what to do with the profits, if any, which gets to questions about income and wealth inequality, and so forth. Again, if these decisions were democratically arrived at, we might see a very different set of impacts, and so this is something that I think we should think about in terms of the issues that we're discussing. If the production process were organized in very different ways, the kinds of things that we are discussing here, the kinds of outcomes and consequences, might have a very, very different look, and so it's worth thinking about that. But this is typically what we're thinking about when we think about an alternative to capitalism.

So now let's turn to the topic for this evening because we're stuck with this system and it's producing some outcomes. I'm going to go through some of the issues. This list is not meant to be exhaustive, but by the end of it, it might be a bit exhausting, that is, you might feel a little wearied by it so, just going to go through it, and just it's useful to know what we're talking about and what we're confronting when we think about environmental impacts.

First are the kind of overt impacts that we were dealing with, beginning to deal with in a substantive way, in the late 1950s, into the 1960s, but these things like air, water, soil pollution, which were at the time quite overt, quite undeniable in many ways, as I'll talk about in a little while, as the problems became so apparent that they simply couldn't be ignored any longer. The problem of indoor air pollution is something that's come a little bit later. Think about around the world, people who use solid fuels for heating and cooking and so forth, clearly indoor air pollution is an issue. In more technologically developed countries, indoor air pollutants are now being recognized as coming from a lot of the building materials that we use, insulation and so forth, but this is becoming a prevalent problem.

Over time, we've seen a changing nature in the pollutants them-selves, from these overt, unavoidable notions of solid waste to industrial waste to toxics, which have mainly gone through a transformation in their visibility, their tangibility. That is, these early problems, as I say, were quite overt, but the later problems of industrial waste and toxins and so forth are largely out of sight and therefore largely out of mind. So we don't see all these things, but they are becoming ubiquitous in the environment.

Plastic pollution is another, and growing, problem. You can find all sorts of interesting statistics about plastics. In this abbreviated form, I'm giving you just one that I found particularly annoying. By 2050, there will be more plastic than fish in the oceans by weight. Okay, so if you're interested in fishing for plastics, it's good news, but otherwise, not so great.

Then there is the issue of antibiotics, which people have been think-ing about a lot in the last couple of decades, leading to the production of these super pathogens, the super bugs, which evolve much more quickly than the pharmaceutical industry evolves to deal with them. So, people who are taking antibiotics either don't take the full course of them, or more prominently, they're given to animals and 30 to 60 percent of them pass through our or animals' digestive systems unchanged, and so they simply enter the environment. They're in the water supplies. We ingest them through the food chain and so forth, and they are producing a con-stellation of these pathogens that are now not susceptible to treatment by these antibiotics. So some of these were miracle drugs when they first came out in the twenties, thirties, and so forth. Penicillin, amoxicillin, a whole number of them, are now becoming ineffective, and we're seeing the results in increasing resistance and morbidity.

Endocrine disruptors, again, things that disrupt our hormonal sys-tems, these, again, are becoming prevalent in the environment. They're in a wide variety of products, polychlorinated biphenyls, DDT, which is an interesting pesticide. Some of you may recall the famous book by Ra-chel Carson, *Silent Spring*, in which she began to document the ubiquity of pesticides in the environment and their effects, in this case, on bird species and bird habitat. DDT has been banned for use in the United

States for many years, but not for production. So, we produce it and then we distribute it around the world and then it comes back to us on various products. But DDT, household cleaners, all of these things, again, are showing up in the environment in increasing concentrations and are producing these very deleterious effects.

Ozone depletion, which a lot of people get mixed up with climate change or climate disruption. But the ozone hole is a different problem. The ozone layer is very important in keeping out UV radiation. If the ozone hole persists and widens, we see an immediate, concomitant rise in skin cancers, melanomas, and so forth. We thought we had a handle on ozone depletion to a great extent in the 1980s with the Montreal Protocol, which actually outlawed some of the products that were affecting the ozone hole like chlorofluorocarbons and other things that were in propellants. Now, we've backtracked from that international agreement a bit. At least we had some sort of model for thinking about how to deal with this kind of international problem, the ozone depletion. I'll come back to this in a little bit.

Nuclear waste is another major issue, which I will talk about to some extent in a few minutes.

There are a number of marine problems associated with increased atmospheric CO_2. These include problems of ocean acidification, coral reef bleaching, and significant impacts on marine life. Again, these things are occurring at an increasing pace. If you're interested in seeing things like the Great Barrier Reef, probably next year would be a good time to go. In a couple or three years down the line, it may not be there for you to see.

Habitat loss and degradation are occurring through all kinds of activities, including mining, logging, urbanization, and deforestation, just to name a few. These effects are largely and closely tied to species extinction and the loss of biodiversity, which is now estimated by the scholarly literature at about a thousand to ten thousand times the background rate. We are losing one to five species a year, and the rate is increasing.

Another ominous sign is insect loss, and all of the functions they provide, most notably, though not exclusively, in plant pollination (and the implications for the food supply): seventy-six percent of flying insects are expected to disappear in less than thirty years in Germany;

monarch butterflies are down by 90 percent since 1996; bee populations dropping significantly worldwide.

Seventy-five percent of genetic diversity of agricultural crops has already been lost, that is, as we move to conglomeration and we move to monocropping, we see increasing loss of genetic diversity. Seventy-five percent of the world's fisheries are now either fully or overexploited. Up to 70 percent of the world's known species risk extinction if global temperatures rise by more than 3.5 degrees centigrade, a trajectory that we are clearly on. We're moving very rapidly in that direction. (All of these are figures that come from the International Union for the Conservation of Nature Red List of Threatened Species.)

Tropical deforestation is a problem in and of itself in terms of habitat and species loss. It's also an enormous problem in terms of the fact that tropical forests are a very, very effective mechanism for removing carbon from the atmosphere. So as we deforest, whether it's tropical or in other regions, our climate change effects are exacerbated. So, tropical deforestation is a big problem, as is resource depletion of all kinds—water, soil, fertility, arable land, and as I've already mentioned, overfishing.

Another recently emerging issue is genetically engineered food. Many of you—in fact, all of you—have eaten it, whether you know it or not. At the moment, over 90 percent of US corn is genetically modified, and corn, as you know, shows up everywhere as high fructose syrups, as additives in various kinds of processed foods. So, if, in fact, you eat anything, you have likely eaten genetically modified corn. About 90 percent of US soy is now genetically modified. About 50 percent of papaya coming from Hawaii is also genetically modified, 10 percent of tomatoes and on and on and on. We get new materials introduced every year, and I don't know when you were given the call about it, whether you want a genetically modified food in your diet, but I never got that call. Maybe I was out, but in any event, it's now becoming quite prevalent. There are a number of spices and herbs that are genetically modified, which, again, show up in all kinds of processed food. The main concern is the uncertainty around the potential health effects of these products. In the US, which uses a risk assessment process to determine potential harm, it is up to the government to prove that the products are unsafe. Elsewhere, for example in Europe, using a precautionary principle, producers must prove that the products are safe. This is why many US agricultural products have been barred from many European countries.

Climate change, which is a very big topic, I'm not going to say very much about. Professor Chomsky is going to speak about it some on Thursday evening. But clearly there are a whole number of effects from climate change (which we should now really be calling climate disruption or climate crisis), including rising sea levels; shifting temperature, precipitation, and growing-season patterns; intensification, as we've seen—very dramatically in the last couple years—intensification of tropical storms and hurricanes; more extreme weather events; and vector-borne disease, as species migrate into new zones.

And then finally, none of these things have very even effects around the globe. That is, all of the issues that I've been listing have very differential effects depending on where you are on the planet and/or on the socioeconomic spectrum. So the idea that we encounter not only these issues but that they bring with them all kinds of matters of environmental injustice. That is, people of color, poor people, bear the cost of these in very disproportionate ways. So, the planet, in some sense, is engaged, or we are engaged because of our socioeconomic system, we're engaged in a kind of genocide around the planet.

Now let's begin to think about the causes of these problems. Thomas Malthus, whose name you might know, writing in the piece I'm going to think about here written at the very end of the eighteenth century, is identified as the author of a certain set of formulations of how environmental problems work, and these are called Malthusian. There is also a variant of these arguments that is called neo-Malthusian, and I'll make the distinction in a minute but let me first give you a couple of pertinent quotes from Malthus. These are from his "Essay on the Principle of Population" written in 1798, and let me say from the outset that this is very much a political argument. Malthus is writing very much in opposition to the poor laws of England, and he's trying to create a rationale for the elimination of the poor laws, the welfare system of the time.

So, he makes this comment, "The laboring poor, to use a vulgar expression, seem always to live from hand to mouth." I've never quite figured out which the vulgar expression refers to, the "laboring poor" or "living hand to mouth," but in any event, he probably meant both. "Their present wants employ their whole attention and they seldom think of the future. Even when they have an opportunity of saving, they seldom exercise it but all that is beyond their present necessities goes, generally speaking, to the ale house. The poor laws of England may therefore be said to diminish both the power and will to save among the common people and thus to weaken one of the strongest incentives to sobriety and industry and consequently to happiness." Providing welfare to the poor only leads them to increase their numbers and then the demands of "a part of society that cannot in general be considered as the most valuable part diminishes the shares that would otherwise belong to more industrious and worthy members." We can see this echoed right down to the present moment when we think about conversations about welfare dependency and all of the rest of it.

Malthus is rather forthright about this and basically is making an argument against consumption of any sort by the poor because it's not very valuable consumption, doesn't contribute to anything, and then argues for conspicuous consumption by the rich. These arguments that Malthus was making, as I say, propagate right to the present day, as we'll explore now.

Malthus frames environment and resource problems as the result of increasing population, which grows at a geometric rate because the poor can't control themselves. They will simply procreate without restraint. And this growth bumps up against scarce resources, which unfortunately, only grow at an arithmetic rate. So Malthus produces this kind of tension between population and resources, and this argument persists as a very prominent notion of environmental and other resource problems.

As an example of this persistence, I'm going to talk about a couple of essays by someone whose name you might know, Garrett Hardin. He wrote a number of other things. Just before he published his very famous essay on "the tragedy of the commons," his prior major contribution had been an essay on eugenics, in which he asks why in the world we should not really control the less desirable segments of the population and foster those that are more contributory. Shortly thereafter, he wrote "The Tragedy of the Commons." The reason I raise this, in part, is because the basic argument is still very prevalent (in fact, in many quarters is still the dominant argument), but also it's one of the most anthologized essays ever written on these topics. It's appeared in some 115 other volumes. So, it's been picked up repeatedly because it's a kind of argument that resonates with a certain kind of mindset. In the essay, Hardin issues this kind of parable that he based on another article that was written in the 1830s. If, in fact, there is a common piece of arable land or a common piece of grazing land, it is in everyone's self-interest to graze as many animals on that as they can. This, thereby, produces what he calls "the tragedy of the commons." That is, if everyone does this, acting in their own self-interest, as he conceives it, the commons will disappear. That's the tragedy of it.

There are many problems with this argument. First of all, what Hardin is talking about is not a commons. He's talking about what we might more properly think of as open-access resources. A commons is in fact an institutional arrangement that is built on respectful cooperation. That is, it's in everyone's interest to maintain the sustainability of a true commons. Elinor Ostrom, whose name some of you may know, actually won a Nobel Prize in economics a few years ago and her whole body of work was on the issue of the commons as really conceived rather than this way. Hardin also wrote an essay a bit later on in which he espoused this notion of the lifeboat ethic. Here, he was not talking about individuals, he was talking actually about countries and he had them organized into a tripartite categorization. At the top were those countries that were really making it, and well developed and so forth. In the middle were sort of triage countries that might make it with a bit of aid, and at the bottom were those countries that definitely couldn't make it. The analogy is that the planet is the lifeboat. Some countries we shouldn't provide any aid to because they're going to sink the whole lifeboat for all of us. So, a really humane guy.

In addition to the misconception of a commons, the idea of the trag-edy of the commons and this whole notion of a Malthusian argument where population inevitably and solely bumps up and creates a stress against resources is also deficient in other ways. These are connected to several other notions that I just want to spend a minute on. First is the notion of overpopulation, which is a very popular way of thinking about where environmental problems come from, there are just too many peo-ple. If there weren't so many people, everything would be fine. But the question of overpopulation is a very problematic formulation. First of all, when we think about who's too many, I'm sure it's not me, and I'm fairly sure you think it's not you. And that only then leaves *them*. Some undefined *them* are the problem; *they*, *them*, those are not *my* pronouns. They, them, that's them, but overpopulation is often characterized as the problem. It's based, again, on a fallacious kind of understanding.

It's based on this notion of carrying capacity, which is an idea that comes from evolutionary biology. It's an idea that is tied to predator/prey relationships, which operate around a kind of homeostatic mean. That is, when the population of the prey goes up, the population of the predators goes up; there's more for them to eat. But as they then begin to consume the prey population, the predator population also goes down. So there's this kind of regression to a mean, and that mean is the average carrying capacity for a particular territory. But this idea that there's a carrying ca-pacity or natural limits for human populations eliminates the whole role of the way we make choices about what we need and how to satisfy those needs. In a predator/prey relationship, there's not a lot of choice going on. That is, this is a purely instinctual set of relationships. For humans, however, that's not the way we necessarily have to define the relationship between how many of us there are and how many resources there might be to satisfy whatever we think we might need.

This Malthusian argument is also tied to the issue of scarcity, which, as I'm hoping we're beginning to illustrate, capitalism inverts. That is, under capitalism, things that ought to be abundant are made artificially scarce. You can think about things like health care. You can think about things like pharmaceuticals, which cost pennies to make, basically, and yet under a capitalist system, those things become scarce and unavailable to many people. While on the other hand, things that ought to be scarce and be preserved, like natural resources and the one planet that we have, are thought of as infinitely abundant. So this is what I mean by capitalism inverts this notion of scarcity.

Okay, as I began to say, this whole formulation, that is, that simply juxtaposes population against resources, is a formulation that leaves out this essential issue of human choice. This way of seeing the problem also gives us too few variables to work with to solve the problems. It only allows us to either lower population or increase resources in one way or another. By the way, that notion of increasing resources is the core of a kind of neo-Malthusian argument. But it leaves out these important issues of human choice, and a better framing of the issues than simply population versus resources is a relational one. Resources, as I said in the lecture a couple weeks ago, are not simply finite things; they are evolving things. Something that may be a resource at one place in time, may not be at another place in time and vice versa. In any event, a resource is a "cultural, technical and economic appraisal of elements and processes in nature that can be applied to fulfill social objectives and goals through specific material practices" (Harvey 1996). It is that latter part, this idea of the social objectives and goals that we have, that gives us a set of choices to make.

How do we define what we need and how do we figure out how to satisfy those needs and wants? In contrast to the Malthusian formulation, asking these kinds of questions gives us a whole set of things to work with in terms of what constitutes resources and how needs and wants can be both defined and satisfied, including accounting for our impacts on the environment both short- and long-term.

So now I'd like to turn to another take on what are the causes of environmental problems, in other words, capitalism as the underlying cause. Now, it's true that there are a number of people around the planet who do not operate directly under a capitalist system. But as I talked about the other day, the acts of militarism and the idea of accumulation through dispossession, or primitive accumulation, force people into a capitalist frame, whether they are directly exploited by it or not. I'll say something more about that in one second. But I'm posing capitalism as the underlying cause of environmental and resource problems. It has a need for constant accumulation and expanded accumulation.

"Driven by competition, decisions do not depend," and this is a quote from Marx, "on the good or ill will of the individual. Free competition brings out the inherent laws of capitalist production in the shape of external coercive laws having power over every individual capitalist" (Marx, *Capital*, Volume 1: 381). That is, as I think I said, Marx doesn't talk in *Capital*, Volume 1, about individuals, he talks about them in the role of either capitalist or worker. It's the compulsion of competition that drives this formulation. The only escape from it, as I mentioned the other day, is if, as a capitalist, one can secure a monopoly position. If your good or service is still desired, you can produce it and deliver it under conditions that you define. But otherwise, under competition, there is this drive for accumulation and expanded accumulation.

Then this is again a quote from Marx:

> Only as personified capital is the capitalist respectable. As such, he shares with the miser the passion for wealth as wealth. But that which in the miser is mere idiosyncrasy is in the capitalist the effect of a social mechanism of which he is but one of the wheels. Moreover, the development of capitalist production makes it constantly necessary to keep increasing the amount of capital laid out in a given industrial undertaking, and competition makes the immanent laws of capital, that is, the laws that arise from within the workings of capital itself, capitalist production, to be felt as external laws. [That is, they arise from the way capital works, but they look like they're coming from the outside.] It compels him to keep constantly expanding his capital in order to preserve it, but extend it he cannot except by means of progressive accumulation. (*Capital*, Volume 1: 739)

That is, capital standing still, not thrown back into the process, is an absurdity. It cannot happen. For Marx, capital is value in motion. That means it's constantly thrown back into circulation. "Accumulate, accumulate. That is the Moses and the prophets. Accumulation for the sake of accumulation, production for the sake of production" (*Capital*, Volume 1: 742). This is what drives this system.

We go back to this formula very briefly: M → C → C' → M' where we have money at the outset, capitalist buys means of production of labor-power, turns that into surplus commodity, surplus product, and if there's a sale, into more money than the capitalist began with. That's the formulation. Reinvestment decisions have to be made, as I talked about the other day. There's a constant expansion of production. There's a need for greater inputs, that is, more resources. Without automation, more labor-power. Expanded production of outputs, and expanded production of waste, partly because the capitalist system also depends upon obsolescence, planned obsolescence. If you had to buy one good and it lasted you a lifetime, the producer of that good would be dependent simply upon increasing population. It's not a good way to go.

But all this expansion takes place in a finite world. This is the basic tension. If capitalists are constantly in need of expanding their production, expanding their resource use, expanding their need for waste absorption, a finite world is not the best place for that to be happening. And so we have capital roaming the globe looking for places that have not yet been occupied. As I said the other day, if they are not bound by fixed capital costs in place, they will engage in a search for new labor, for new resources, for new markets, and eventually they will transcend what biologists call a particular ecosphere, that is, a particular sort of locale where they operate, and pretty soon they are exploiting the entire biosphere.

So every place on the globe becomes buyable, accessible for resources, for labor, for markets, for hospitable regulatory environments, which I'll say something more about in just a little bit. But in any event, we move from a set of impacts in one set of locations, an ecosphere, to impacts now on an increasing spatial scale. We see these extended supply and distribution chains. You know about the five-thousand-mile salad, we know about Walmart utilizing every place on the globe for cheap production and bringing the products back.

Then as I said, we also encounter the issue of accumulation through dispossession. As all of this is going on, producers, workers, peasants, and so forth, are displaced from their own means of production, which is why we see the growth, enormous growth, of slum populations around the world. These are people being thrown off the land. These are people being deprived of their means of subsistence and production. As capital takes over resources, whether those are land resources or other resources, people are displaced. This becomes part of the refugee stream that we see, in addition to conflict and war and so forth. But these processes of accumulation through dispossession are entailing the planet's population in the capitalist sphere, whether they are directly, as I say, exploited by capitalism or not.

C. Wright Mills in his book *The Power Elite* describes a phenomenon that he calls "the higher immorality," in which, he says, "in a civilization so thoroughly business-penetrated as America," money becomes "the one unambiguous marker of success, the sovereign American value" (Mills 1956) You can begin to see how this operates. We become a society, as Mills argues, of organized irresponsibility, where the legal often supplants the moral. We see this in US society and in other places, where litigiousness is a marker of how the society works. Whether something is right or wrong is not nearly as relevant as whether it's legal or illegal, and sometimes illegality doesn't even really matter that much. But the idea that we bump up against—this whole notion of morality versus legality—is derived from, as at least Wright Mills argues, this notion of higher immorality.

This form of capitalism requires the constant production of desire. We now spend in the US somewhere around $200 billion a year on advertising, somewhere around $500 billion a year on marketing, and then around the world you can see those costs just skyrocketing. All of that is to make sure that people's wants are redefined as needs. That's the point of advertising and marketing. That's how it works. That's what it's for. The constant production of desire. I like to invert the old maxim that "necessity is the mother of invention." Under capitalism, unless you already can prognosticate a market, you'd better not be producing that product. So "invention becomes the mother of necessity." You just flip that around and you get the sort of capitalist form.

Every advertisement . . . You can try this out yourself. Go home and take a look at an advertisement on TV or wherever. You'll see these ads take a very particular form. They're like a little parable, every one. They first produce an anxiety in you. Something's wrong with you. You know, you don't look right, you're never going to get the partner of your choice, this and that. They produce a little anxiety. Then they give you the message that the anxiety can be resolved by purchasing something. That step is at two levels. One, purchasing their particular product, good, or service. But the idea also that problems can be very easily defined in these simple terms, and solved by the purchase of a product, a good, or a service. Every advertisement takes this form. It produces an anxiety, it tells you that the problem can be addressed by purchasing, and then it tells you what to purchase. Try this out. Take a look at a number of ads, and see if they don't work that way.

For the last part of the formula to work (i.e., C' → M'), there must be a sale. This means that the desire has to be there, which leads to this sort of rampant consumerism in some places, versus extreme poverty elsewhere. Some people have the wherewithal to satisfy their desires. For other people, the desire is produced, but they have no capacity to buy. This is why we see aspirations around the world for the so-called "American dream." People see these advertisements, they see the products, they see the services. They can't get them necessarily, but they desire them.

This brings us to a formulation where we think about growth versus progress. Are they the same thing? As growth is typically measured, either as GDP or GDP per capita or some form of that arrangement, we begin to equate growth of a certain kind with progress. But we don't really have the opportunity often to think about whether that's the case, whether or not growth in and of itself, defined in the way that I've just described as being necessary for capitalism, is really progress.

I think this is very interestingly encapsulated in the three articles that you had to read for tonight, on growth versus degrowth. Perhaps, as Jason Hickel argues, we shouldn't be thinking so much about more, we should be thinking about enough: degrowth. We're continually conditioned to think that only by continuing growth can we make progress. In fact, any move away from that immediately puts us in a mindset, "Oh, man, we're going back to the caves to sit and starve in the dark." That any move away from the current status quo of what constitutes quality of life, satisfaction, happiness, is a move backward. I think that's something we need to think about very carefully, and we'll do that in the next few weeks.

Another issue that is tied to capitalism, and again, it's part of the underlying causes of the problems that capitalism produces in the environment, is this problem of externalities and third- and fourth-party effects. I alluded to this a couple of weeks ago, but I want to spend a moment making it clear. The basic nature of an exchange is that there are buyers and sellers who are in a voluntary, noncoercive agreement (and now you understand what I mean by those terms; they should be in quotes. You know, if you're in the labor market, it's not exactly a voluntary exchange). But under typical circumstances, an exchange will often be voluntary and noncoercive. Both benefit, otherwise there'd be no exchange. The buyers and sellers are the first and second parties. They both are in the exchange voluntarily, and they both get something out of it. The buyer gets a good or service; the seller gets the money.

But what about others who are affected by the transition but are not beneficiaries of it? These are the third parties. Think about a power plant, a coal-fired power plant, beautiful, clean coal. The people who sell the power get something from it. The people who buy the power get something from it. But what about all the people who are susceptible to the pollution that the plant produces, whether they are in the present or in the future? The future people are fourth parties. The people who are affected by the transaction in the present but not beneficiaries of it are third parties. So these are third-party effects. It's also why these effects are called externalities. They are external to that bargain. They happen in a way that is not confined within the bargain itself.

If we can understand the nature of externalities, and that capitalists, when given the chance, will externalize any costs that decrease profits, we can think about some possible remedies. One remedy is to internalize the externalities. When the costs and benefits of a transaction are shared by a limited number of direct participants, sellers and buyers, at least in theory it's possible to apply a "polluter pays" principle. I'll return to the example of a beautiful coal-fired power plant. If the plant installs a scrubber on the air stacks, and that has some cost attached to it, and that cost is passed along to the rate payers, that's a way to internalize those costs. It prevents the pollution, but the people who benefit from it are the people who are benefiting from the transaction. That's a way to internalize the costs and to re-internalize the externalities.

As I said, if there are a limited number of direct participants, sellers and buyers, in theory it's possible to do this. But in most cases of externalities, it's very difficult to identify the very diffuse, numerous affected parties, and how to identify the actual costs that they're bearing. The theory works when there's a limited, confined situation, but in most practical instances, it is not possible to identify all of the possible externality bearers, or to identify with any precision what the actual costs are. And so it turns out that internalizing externalities is a very difficult process to engage in.

Then it's made even more difficult by how we value future generations' concerns. That is, what are we doing to the planet and what will we leave behind? I've mentioned, I think, before that I've seen on the same gigantic recreational vehicle, or maybe it's on the Hummer that the vehicle's towing, I've seen two bumper stickers. On one side, "We don't own the earth, we borrow it from our grandchildren," and right on the other side it says, "I'm spending my grandchildren's inheritance." So valuing future generations is something we talk about, we have nice rhetoric about it, but we don't really behave as though we're very concerned about these future generations. After all, what have they ever done for us?

Here's a second possibility for remedying some of these problems. This is the idea of valuing and commodifying nature. Foster talks about this in the piece that you read, which raises the question of how might we value nature? A number of economists say that the reason that the environment gets short shrift is that it's not included in our calculations very effectively, so it always gets undervalued. If somehow we could put a price on it, an effective price, we could, in fact, value it properly. One of the ways to do this is to stop thinking about it as just nature. Too amorphous. Think about it in disaggregated terms, in utilitarian terms, and utilitarian mainly for us. What services do ecosystems provide? This

is the current term of art: ecosystem services. A very big, very interesting, complicated, and troubling topic. This would be one way. That is,
we don't think about it as nature, we think about it as an assortment, an
aggregate of services that it provides, and perhaps we can then use some
of the tools that economists have in order to value it.

Two of these that Foster talks about are hedonic pricing and willingness to pay. Hedonic pricing is a mechanism that's used to try to put
a price on something that would otherwise be intangible. I'll give you
an example. How much is a view lot worth in real estate? How would
we figure out how much a scenic view is worth? Well, you could in fact
look at housing prices in a number of places, and you could compare
very similar houses with and without a view, and you could see if there's
a little extra bonus that's on the price of houses with a view, or houses
in or not in a quiet neighborhood. You can do the same sort of thing.
So you've got a mechanism that allows you to add a little bit of a payoff
for this amenity that would otherwise be very difficult to price. Again,
it's not precise, but it gives you some notion. That's hedonic pricing. That
would be one way to do this.

Another way to begin to put a price on nature is to think about willingness to pay. If you can identify the services that nature is providing,
you could ask people what they'd be willing to pay for that service. Well,
you can, and economists do, and they do this all the time, but there's a
problem with willingness to pay. I mean, there are many problems with
it, but one major problem is the question of how the person getting the
question interprets the question. If you love this service, this ecosystem
service, and you think that it might be taken away, you might then over-
value it in response to the question, "What are you willing to pay?" "Well,
I'd be willing to pay almost anything for that." Of course—unless you
really do have to pay.

But if you're just in a survey, a willingness-to-pay survey, and somebody asks you that question, then that's your mindset, that this is a service that might be taken away from me, but I value it, you might give a
response one way. If, however, you think that there's a service that they're
going to raise the price on once you give that answer, then you might un-

dervalue it. So there's a real problem with willingness to pay studies, and it has to do very much with the way in which the respondent hears the question and where they're at. There's another problem with willingness to pay, which I'll talk about in one second, but it has to do with where you are in the economic hierarchy.

The more crucial problem, however, with commodification of nature (no matter how the calculations are made) is the loss of the notion of intrinsic or inherent value or worth. That is, if we start to put everything into dollar terms, we lose something quite essential. This whole notion of valuing nature in the ways that I just described immediately assumes a utilitarian viewpoint, and it assumes an anthropocentric utilitarian viewpoint. That these things have to be useful, and they have to be useful for us. They can't have any value in and of themselves under this set of assumptions, and this is a problem. This is the much bigger problem, in my view.

This is a contest, I think, that some of the large environmental organizations began to lose in the late 1960s and early 1970s as they began to engage with benefit-cost analysis, as it was coming into vogue. They won a few specific battles, but in winning those and capitulating to this discourse of commodification, they lost the bigger war. This is because the contest is also this problem of, as I'm saying, of economic reductionism, that everything has a price. You know this saying about economists, these are people who know the price of everything and the value of nothing, okay?

There's also then the possibility, once you're in this utilitarian mode, or of nature as nothing but a collection of services, of infinite substitutability. That is, if we're really thinking about nature as a set of services, as the environment as a set of ecosystem services, then as long as we can derive those services somehow, that's fine. I put up two examples here. One is this article by Lawrence Tribe in the early 1970s in the *Yale Law Review*, "Ways Not to Think about Plastic Trees: New Foundations for Environmental Law" (Tribe 1974). He started the article off, because he'd seen a piece in the *Los Angeles Times*, that on one of the very major thoroughfares, the iconic palm trees in a street reconfiguration, there wasn't enough soil to support them, and other people were worried about the smog killing them, so perhaps it would be possible to just substitute plastic trees for the real thing.

So LA did, in fact, put in a number of plastic palm trees. Basically, they fulfilled the same purpose. They give the look that you need, they provide a little bit of shade, pigeons can roost in them. But they don't have to be watered. They could just be dusted periodically, and that would be about it. The point Tribe was trying to make here is that much of environmental law and environmental policy was written with that kind of mindset. That is, infinite substitutability, that if you could, in fact, simply derive the services, you wouldn't need to worry about whether nature exists or is valuable in and of itself for other purposes than fulfilling human needs.

The other piece up here, "Do We Really Need the Rockies?" was a notion put forward by Armand Hammer, who was for many years the CEO of Occidental Petroleum (see Armand Hammer, "Oil Shale Down There, Waiting to Be Tapped," *New York Times*, February 19, 1977). Occidental Petroleum, in the beginning of the 1950s, actually, but moving much more heavily into the 1960s, began to be very interested in shale oil. People at Occidental Petroleum had an idea, that they could minimize the costs of oil shale extraction by detonating explosives underground and rubblizing the material in what they called an in situ shale extraction process.

They would set off explosions . . . In fact, at one point, they were considering using very small, I guess you could call them tactical, nuclear weapons. But the idea was to hollow out chambers underground, and then it's much more economical to extract the shale that way than to actually mine it out, and you also don't have to worry about the shale debris. It just stays in place. But the idea, and the reason that it has this title, was that it wouldn't disturb the surface of the Rockies. They'd be hollowed out underneath, but nobody really cares about that. All we really care about is the scenic grandeur and the ability to ski on them, and so forth, so they would perform the function of the Rockies, but at the same time we would've gotten the oil shale out. So this is another example of utilitarian infinite substitutability. The plan, I think, stopped about 1970, partly because the price of oil changed.

Let's move to another set of remedies. If the approaches that I just went through are not working, maybe we need to move to something different. If market-based strategies don't work, we maybe need to move to a different formulation. Let me introduce you to our greatest environmental president: Richard Milhous Nixon. He was our greatest environmental president, not because he was an environmentalist by any means, but because he was forced by circumstances. There were a number of quite dramatic events in the late 1960s: a giant oil spill in the Santa Barbara Channel; the Cuyahoga River caught on fire in Cleveland; Lake Erie was declared dead (fish kills, oxygen depleted, became completely eutrophic). These kinds of events and others forced the federal government (with Nixon at the helm) to take action.

And so as I say, if markets don't work, maybe we need a different way to deal with these environmental problems, that if externalities can't be internalized, if we can't properly evaluate nature, and so forth, if we can't substitute, maybe we need to confront the problems in another way: command and control regulation. I'm going to go through a little bit of an alphabet soup just to talk about some of the things that came out in the Nixon administration. The first thing was the National Environmental Policy Act in 1969, which created the Council on Environmental Quality, which is an advisory board to the executive branch on how to make decisions at the federal level about major projects. This is where we get the mandate for environmental impact statements and environmental impact assessments, many of which have now gone by the wayside, but it's still in place.

The Environmental Protection Agency, established in 1970, demolished in 2017. Occupational Safety and Health Administration was established in 1970 to protect worker health and safety. The Clean Air Act was first passed in 1955, but it was greatly expanded in 1970 to deal with both stationary, that is power plants and factories and so forth, as well as mobile sources of pollution. The Clean Water Act, which was first passed in 1948, but which was completely rewritten in 1972. The

Federal Environmental Pesticide Control Act was first passed very early on, but updated, again in 1972, to deal with pesticides. The Endangered Species Act was passed in 1973. It's been controversial ever since. The Safe Drinking Water Act passed in 1974 covers all public water supplies. By the way, if you buy bottled water, it doesn't cover that. For that, you have to rely upon the very reliable Food and Drug Administration. It also doesn't cover those machines at the grocery store, you know, where you get natural spring water tapped in directly to these natural springs somewhere in the Rockies, or under the Rockies.

The Resource Conservation and Recovery Act, passed in 1976 shortly after Nixon left office, governs solid and hazardous waste in a system of so-called cradle-to-grave monitoring, from production of these materials to the time when they're finally disposed of, if they are. The Toxic Substances Control Act also passed in '76. This is the only one of all of these laws that I'm showing you that took a preventative rather than a remedial approach. All of the others are end-of-the-pipe, end-of-the-stack approaches. Interestingly enough, this is the only one that was never really funded to any significant degree. It would've changed production processes and prevented these toxic substances from entering the environment to begin with, but of course, that was too sane. The Comprehensive Environmental Response Compensation and Liability Act, which is the Superfund law, was passed in 1980 to clean up hazardous waste sites. It's been very problematic over time. It has fallen into endless litigation. There have been a few sites cleaned up, relatively speaking, but most of the time it falls into argumentation over who put the materials there to begin with.

These regulations always get pushback from capital. We're seeing this monumentally now, as I'll talk about in a little bit. The concerted pushback began largely under the Reagan administration, and the introduction of benefit-cost analysis into new laws and regulations. Many of those laws I just put up there were passed with a set of aspirational achievements in them without any regard to cost to achieving those goals. It wasn't until the Reagan administration came in that they began to apply benefit-cost analysis to the implementation of those laws. That changed their nature in very fundamental ways. This assault continues through pressures on the state for deregulation, as we see and as I'll talk about in a second.

There are also companies that utilize the spatial fix or the threat of relocating to generate less stringent environments. They put pressure on cities and states to say, "If you want the jobs, you have to change some of these regulations to make them much less onerous for us. Otherwise, we're going elsewhere." The trade agreements that we have seen over the last twenty-five years or so, beginning with NAFTA and even prior to that, include these incentives to race to the bottom. That is, when firms employ this spatial fix, they're not looking for higher labor costs or more expensive resources or more stringent regulatory environments. They're looking for environments that are less and less strict, and therefore they put pressure on places all over the globe to reduce their environmental regulations, so that we get this kind of race to the bottom. That's also true in wages. It's also true in commodity prices and resources.

But in any event, companies can, in fact, sue under the WTO (World Trade Organization), and before that under the GATT (General Agreement on Tariffs and Trade). They can sue countries, sovereign countries, if they believe that certain regulations impose what are called non-tariff barriers to trade. Those could be environmental regulations, they could be worker safety regulations, they could be protection of union organizing. All of those things can be interpreted as non-tariff barriers to trade. Under the resolution mechanisms that are built into these agreements, these are adjudicated by industry-friendly lawyers, and they're adjudicated in secret. This becomes a real threat, when they utilize these mechanisms. In any event all of the regulations that I described are under constant pressure. More on the specifics in a moment.

Finally, one other possible remedy to environmental (and many other) problems is the technological fix. If regulations also don't work, maybe we can get out of these problems by utilizing some kind of technology. Tech fixes are infinitely appealing. One of the appeals of a technological fix is that it absolves most of us of the responsibility of dealing with the issues. The technologists will take care of it. Somebody else will have the responsibility to deal with it. A tech fix also constantly defers action in the present for salvation sometime in the future. We in fact fail to address problems because we think a tech fix is somewhere on the horizon. It doesn't require us to change the status quo very much, if at all. That is, we will simply get another mechanism to deal with this. A perfect example of this is renewable energy to solve the climate crisis. If we can just find a new fuel, we can go on pretty much as is.

But if technological innovation is driven by profit maximization, it's unlikely to solve environmental problems. I'll just give you one quick example. Here's how Bill Gates aims to clean up the planet: "It's a simple idea: strip CO_2 from the air and use it to produce carbon-neutral fuel. But can it work on an industrial scale?" Gates is involved now not just in education and other philanthropic activities, but he's going to solve the climate problem for us. "It's nothing much to look at. The tangle of pipes, pumps, tanks, reactors, chimneys, and ducts on a messy industrial estate outside the logging town of Squamish in western Canada could just provide the fix to stop the world tipping into runaway climate change, and substitute dwindling supplies of conventional fuel." Who could be against that? The article goes on to say that, of course, the project could make Gates and his collaborators "more money than they could ever dream of" (see John Vidal, "How Bill Gates Aims to Clean Up the Planet," *Guardian*, February 4, 2018). In any event, this is part of the tech fix for climate change that people are working on, direct air capture of carbon and conversion to fuel.

The tech fix often means more efficient ways of doing what we're already doing, for example, automation may be that kind of tech fix, instead of changing what we're doing. And, for example, by using more benign technologies and . . . So renewables. This is where I think this tension in the growth/degrowth argument is focused: doing pretty much the same thing, but just with more benign approaches. Basically, it's an appeal to not really have to change the way we live our lives or the way we organize our society. We simply need a different energy and/or technology mix. One that doesn't have a carbon footprint.

I want to turn now to nuclear power for a bit because it's rearing its head again as a possible tech fix, a remedy, a green fix, for the climate crisis. First of all, nuclear power was never supposed to happen. When Eisenhower put out the Atoms for Peace program, it was largely a PR or propaganda program, largely meant to assuage both the US public and people around the world after the horrors of Hiroshima and Nagasaki. That is that not only were these fearsome, never-to-be-used weapons, but perhaps that power could be turned to peaceful uses. In medicine, in energy production, and so forth, so much more benign. But it was basically a PR program. If you're interested, Barry Commoner has a very good book on part of this called *The Poverty of Power*, where he talks about the PR campaign.

But in any event, the idea that this was going to happen was really not serious. But some people took it seriously. They said, "Yeah, that's really not a bad idea. We can use two thousand degrees to boil water and turn a turbine. Why not? In fact, if we deploy this right, energy will be too cheap to meter. We won't even have to charge people anything for it. It's going to be so efficient and so effective that it would be ridiculous even to meter it, it'll be so cheap." These were the true believers. But I would suggest to you that the whole history of nuclear power has been a series of unanticipated and rather unpleasant surprises. Virtually everything in the now-long history has been a surprise. People have underestimated enormously. Noam talked about this last time with one of the early tests, but virtually every aspect of nuclear power, whether it's for military or so-called peaceful civilian uses, has been an unexpected and unpleasant surprise.

The costs have been nowhere near what people thought they would be. Part of this has been public antipathy, which has protracted the licensing and construction process and so forth, but the other part is that what was necessary to actually make this work was completely unanticipated, in terms of containment structures, in terms of the way in which the whole industry would have to be militarized and organized because of the nature of the fuel itself, which has enormous terrorist and unanticipated military uses, so the whole enterprise has cost way more than anybody ever thought it might.

Secondly, there have been a number of very disturbing accidents and near-accidents. I just mention three here because you will recognize the names. Three Mile Island, Chernobyl, and Fukushima, most recently. But if you look at the history of nuclear power, there have been literally thousands of incidents over time. Near misses . . . I mean, the industry has an entirely interesting vocabulary for how to describe events. Transitory, nontransitory, incidents versus nonincidents. But there have been many, many of them that have come much closer to producing catastrophe than the public is really aware of.

Another interesting surprise—and I'm not putting up everything here, I just want to talk about a few—is this issue of decommissioning the plants. Many of these plants were built with what was an anticipated fifty-year lifespan, but another surprise is that after operating for maybe twenty or thirty years and being constantly bombarded by radiation, the containment structures themselves become much more friable and much more susceptible to cracking and leaking. And so this whole issue of decommissioning has occurred much more quickly than we thought it might. That is, these things were supposed to have a much longer lifespan.

In one of the early articles in the *Bulletin of the Atomic Scientists*, the same people who do the Doomsday Clock, there was a piece written that said decommissioning, when it happens, is going to cost about 10 to 15 percent of what it costs to build the plants. Well, the few that we have decommissioned have been on the order of anywhere from about $100 million for a very small plant at Shippingport, Pennsylvania, to now the estimates are about $500 million per plant. $500 million per plant. That's if we can do anything with them, which I'll talk about in a second.

To date, even though many plants require it, very few have been decommissioned, whether in the US or in plants around the world where nuclear power has been used. Of the plants in the US that have entered the process, only three are categorized as "license terminated," which means that they are completely devoid of spent fuel. All of the others, which are called "decommissioned" in one way or another, either have spent fuel onsite, or they have been what is now called "entombed." The whole structure, the containment structure and so forth, has been encased in what we hope is impervious material. Concrete, for the most part. So the decommissioning problem is looming for us. This is a huge part of the problem with nuclear power.

The biggest part of the problem, however, is that we don't know what to do with these materials when we decommission the plants. We have no place to put it. We have a facility in New Mexico called the Waste Isolation Pilot Plant (WIPP) facility for low-level nuclear waste. These are things that come, for example, from the medical community, from medical industry. But we have no place to put high-level radioactive waste. We have one site that has been under consideration for some twenty-five to thirty years now, Yucca Mountain in Nevada. When the waste repository site law was passed, there was supposed to be a repository in the east and a repository in the west. Well, guess why Nevada has the one site. They have a congressional delegation of three people. They were outvoted. The one potential site, which has already developed all kinds of interesting geologic and other problems, is the only place that's under consideration, and that consideration is currently in abeyance. There's no active sort of move to get that site online.

But in any event, this is a huge problem. What to do with the waste? There wasn't supposed to be any waste. This is another of the many unpleasant surprises. When the nuclear program really began gearing up, the technologists thought that we would be reprocessing all of the spent fuel in a kind of breeder reactor formulation, so that as you produce spent fuel, you reprocess that fuel, and then you use it again and again and again to create power.

Well, interestingly enough, President Carter, who had worked on nuclear submarines and so forth, came to the conclusion that because a lot of the stuff coming out of these reactors was weapons-grade plutonium, maybe it wasn't a good idea to be simply reprocessing this way. That is, that this was very susceptible to theft by terrorists, that if you could get ahold of this, you were that much closer to making a weapon. And so under the Carter administration, the reprocessing program was discontinued. Since then, we have had waste storing up basically in pools at these nuclear power plant sites for, now, some forty years or more. And that's what we're doing with it.

The plutonium waste has a lifespan, a half-life, of 250,000 years, which means that half of its radioactivity is gone in that time. We don't really have the institutional capacity to deal with these timeframes. We don't have the capacity to be certain about geologic stability over such spans, but we also don't even know how to indicate over those time-frames what would be a hazard. The little symbol that we have for radio-activity, how do we know that that will be meaningful in anything close to the time spans where this will be necessary? Alvin Weinberg, one of the early gurus of nuclear energy, said we would actually need a kind of nuclear priesthood to take care of these sites, if we ever get them. But even the symbology of it is difficult to grapple with over the time spans that are necessary.

One serious suggestion about how to deal with waste was to get it off the Earth. Let's not really keep it around here. It's too dangerous. We can load it onto rockets and shoot them toward the sun. Well, when the *Challenger* disaster happened in 1986, that sort of put an end to that discussion, thankfully. I mean, if this had had a nuclear payload on it, as we have had for a couple of satellites, this could've been quite a problem. In any event, we really have nothing to do with the waste. We don't know what to do with it.

All right. But now nuclear power is being promoted, as I said, as a kind of green tech fix for climate change. That is, if we could switch away from fossil fuels to nuclear power, the carbon footprint would be substantially less. But aside from all the other problems that I've just described with nuclear power itself, if the whole chain, from uranium mining through plant construction and operation and decommission-ing and finally to waste and disposal, temporary storage, is considered, nuclear power is not carbon-free, and is really not the solution. That's not the way to go. But you will see in many, many conversations about climate change nuclear power being advocated yet again.

Before concluding, I just want to say a couple of other things about the climate crisis. First is this weird word, agnotology. It's the study of culturally induced ignorance or doubt, particularly the publication of in-accurate or misleading scientific data. The term was coined by Robert

Proctor when he was studying this history of distortion by big tobacco. If you look at the climate change discussion, the public discourse, and you look at the tobacco discourse, there are some very striking parallels. The idea is to simply sow doubt, where there is almost universal scientific consensus, not only on the nature of climate change, but its causal mechanisms as being human activity. There's nearly universal consensus, more consensus than you would get in science on most anything, and yet certain agents have been able to produce doubt, and thereby derail action. The same kind of thing happened with the adverse health effects of tobacco.

Part of this entails the production of the common sense around this issue. Naomi Klein found in one of her studies that where you align yourself on the climate change issue, as well as a number of other issues, has virtually nothing to do with the facts of the case, but has become part of people's identity. If you consider yourself a mainstream Republican, part of your identity has to be climate change denial. If you consider yourself a mainstream Democrat, part of your identity has to be taking seriously the issue of climate change. But in any event, this is now part of the production of common sense.

I just wanted to say a brief thing about the role of Exxon in this enterprise of agnotology (the production of misinformation), because they're emblematic of what's happened in this sphere over time. Exxon's own research confirmed fossil fuel's role in the global warming debate decades ago, back into the 1970s, basically. Exxon believed that if they went deeply into climate change research, it would protect their business. That is, they had a stake, they thought, in actually coming to grips with the issue of climate change. They outfitted their biggest supertanker to measure oceans' absorption of carbon dioxide. They considered this a crown jewel in their research program. They confirmed the global warming consensus in 1982 with in-house climate models. They had a whole scientific team working on this in the late seventies into the early eighties, and had confirmed all of these findings.

But at some point, their business ambition collided with climate change in a way that led them in a different direction. Throughout the

1980s, the company struggled to solve this dilemma. They made a huge gas field discovery, but they knew about the climate change impacts, and so they made a switch. They started to sow doubt about climate science for decades by stressing this issue of uncertainty. They don't really say it's not happening, they just say, "We're not sure. We just don't know enough yet to take action. We don't want to be precipitate. We don't want to act too soon and incur unnecessary costs as either a company or a society." They collaborated with the Bush/Cheney White House, which was filled with people from the oil industry. Exxon turned ordinary scientific uncertainties into weapons of mass confusion.

If you're interested in charting the whole history of this, there's a very good website, insideclimatenews.org. This group has been charting the way in which Exxon has been going about this. When facts don't square with the theory, throw out the facts. That's the Exxon orientation.

A couple of quotes from Naomi Klein, who is reporting from a meeting of the Heartland Institute, a Koch brothers–funded organization, whose business is to sow doubt about climate change. She says:

> When it comes to the real-world consequences of those scientific findings, specifically the kind of deep changes required not just to our energy consumption but to the underlying logic of our economic system, the crowd gathered at the Marriott Hotel [the Heartland Institute people] may be in considerably less denial than a lot of professional environmentalists. The ones who paint a picture of global warming Armageddon then assure us that we can avert catastrophe by buying green products and creating clever markets in pollution. Half of the problem is that progressives, their hands full with soaring unemployment and multiple wars, tend to assume that the big green groups have the climate issue covered. The other half is that many of those big green groups have avoided, with phobic precision, any serious debate on the blindingly obvious roots of the climate crisis: globalization, deregulation, and contemporary capitalism's quest for perpetual growth, the same forces that are responsible for the destruction of the rest of the economy. The result is that those taking on the failures of capitalism and those fighting for climate action remain two solitudes, with the small but valiant climate justice movement drawing the connections between racism, inequality, and environmental vulnerability stringing up a few swaying bridges between them.

Interestingly enough, in Naomi Klein's own book, *This Changes Everything*, she does exactly what she's accusing people here of doing. She doesn't really take on capitalism as the central culprit in the story. And she is not alone in that deficient analysis.

> There are several websites that are keeping a tally of the assaults by the Trump administration on the institutional, legal, and regulatory frameworks that have been put in place to protect the environment (writ large). I'm not going to say much about them except . . . You can draw your own conclusions (see "A Running List of How Trump Is Changing Environmental Policy" and also Popovich et al. "78 Environmental Rules on the Way Out Under Trump").

Okay. So, couple of final thoughts. Capitalism versus the environment, who's going to win? Well, we don't know. But as former faculty member here at the U of A, who then moved to New Mexico, and I think now has moved to Belize, Guy McPhearson, said, "Nature bats last." So, there is a material reality to all this that is beyond the spin and the rhetoric. But, it raises a question that I just want to end on. If nature bats last, what inning are we in? I'm going to stop there.

Chomsky Lecture, February 7, 2019

The State of the Union talk last Tuesday was very well timed for our topic this week. While Marv was discussing the grim effects of the use of fossil fuels, the president declared—I'll quote him—that "we have unleashed a revolution in American energy. The United States is now the number one producer of oil and natural gas anywhere in the world. For the first time in sixty-five years, we are a net exporter of"—the means to destroy organized human life on Earth. The last few words, after the pause, are my paraphrase of his word "energy," regrettably, an accurate one.

There were, of course, fact checkers. All the newspapers went through the speech to list all the lies and misleading statements. The *New York Times* annotated the text with corrections and qualifications. But the remarks I just quoted escaped unscathed. For very good reasons. They are largely correct. Actually, the only qualification is that while the Trump administration has been working overtime to increase the severe threat to organized life, the revolution was actually underway before. Obama had already substantially increased opportunities for fossil fuel extraction. And he wasn't the first.

I'd like to start by taking a look at a couple of the articles that appeared in the press these last few days, which illustrate the dilemmas that we're confronting, the cliff that we're approaching as we imitate the proverbial lemmings, but in this case with eyes wide open, knowing exactly what we're doing. That includes the political and business leadership class.

Let's start with the first one that Marv mentioned Tuesday, about the melting of the Himalayan glaciers. There's a recent scientific study, which appeared in the press a couple of days ago, reporting that at least a third of the huge ice fields in Asia's towering mountain chain are doomed to melt due to climate change, with serious consequences for almost 2 billion people—that's a fair number of people. There are hundreds of millions today, maybe 500 or 600 million in South Asia, who lack drinkable water, and that's going to sharply increase. Agriculture will severely suffer. Much of the region is already unbearably hot for good parts of the year, and that's getting worse. This is a region with some of the worst levels of poverty in the world. There are two nuclear-armed states that will soon have conflicts about access to more limited water. I leave the rest to your imagination.

That's one. We can add to the miseries of South Asia the anticipated sea level rise. Bangladesh is a very low coastal plain. There will probably be tens or even hundreds of millions of refugees from South Asia alone, many more elsewhere. That's the bare beginning. So anyone who thinks there's a refugee problem now is going to be surprised in a few years, if current tendencies persist.

Let's take a second article, a front-page story in today's *New York Times*. It's a report from NASA on global warming. It reports that the last five years are the warmest on record. And of the nineteen warmest years on record, eighteen have been since 2001. So it's near perfect. There's a graphic accompanying it, which is worth looking at. It shows the increase in global warming. There's a very sharp acceleration since 1980. The report quoting the scientific study says that, "what sets recent warming apart in the sweep of geologic time is the relatively sudden rise in temperatures." And its clear correlation with increasing levels of greenhouse gases like carbon dioxide and methane produced by human activity.

That's NASA this morning. So let's go back to yesterday, the *Washington Post*, a report that says that "during the ancient period called the Eemian about 125,000 years ago, the oceans were about as warm as they are today. And last month intriguing new research emerged suggesting that northern hemisphere glaciers have already retreated just as far as they did in the Eemian, driven by dramatic warming in the Arctic regions," which is warming faster than other regions. That period "was one that's quite close to our current climate," the report continues, "but with one major discrepancy—seas at the time were 20 to 30 feet higher."

The discrepancy may be overcome, the article indicates, by the melting of the enormous Western Antarctica ice sheet, which is now well underway. There are scientific explorations there monitoring it. The article quotes a leading Antarctic researcher who says, "There's one important thing to consider—the Eemian occurred without humans emitting lots of greenhouse gases. Atmospheric carbon dioxide was far lower than it is today. The event was instead driven by changes in the Earth's orbit around the sun, leading to more sunlight falling on the northern hemisphere. The big difference, this time around, is that humans are heating things up far faster than what is believed to have happened in the geologic past," and that "makes a key difference. The current pace of climate change is very fast, and the rate of warming might cause glaciers to behave differently than they did in the past."

So actually it might be much worse today than the Eemian when the sea level was 20 to 30 feet higher, quite apart from the warming around the Earth.

We can back this up with an article that just appeared in the science press authored by James Hansen, one of the leading geophysicists who studies climate change (Hansen 2016). He and a couple of dozen others published a paper that concluded that we're now about 1 degree centigrade short of the temperature 125,000 years ago. The sea level they say was then roughly 25 feet higher than today. And crucially they find that the sea level rise, I'm now quoting, "is better approximated as exponential rather than by a more linear response." So that means instead of sea level continuing to rise as it has been doing, it might be doubling every couple of decades. That's the situation we're now in.

The next item is a front-page story a couple of days ago in the *New York Times*, considered so important that they ran a special online section on it. The headline is, "Monster Texas field revives US oil fortunes." The monster field is called the Permian. It's between New Mexico and Texas. It's now bursting with production and exploration. And the biggest concern for them is how to create more capacity to get all that oil to market. Its bounty has also empowered the United States diplomatically, allowing it to impose sanctions on Iran and Venezuela without concern that there might be an effect on oil production. So we're in good shape to attack the rest of the world freely. The Permian generates more oil than any of the 14 members of OPEC except for Saudi Arabia and Iraq. Remember that's just one of our oil fields. Domestic oil production increased by 2 million barrels a day last year for a record of 12 million barrels a day, making the United States once again the world's top producer. As many as fifteen oil and gas pipelines serving the Permian are expected to be completed by the middle of 2020, potentially increasing exports from the Gulf of Mexico fourfold to 8 million barrels a day after 2021.

ExxonMobil became the most active driller in the basin. It projects that it will increase production fivefold by 2025, others as well. Shell's Permian general manager says, "We're not here through one boom and bust. We are here developing a generational resource."

There's one word missing from the report: "climate." Also missing is the fact that the world's top producer is also the top per capita polluter.

And also missing is a rather crucial fact: if this does go on for a generation as the Shell manager predicts, we're doomed.

Not mentioned.

The reporter is Clifford Krauss. He's one of the top senior reporters at the *New York Times*. Highly qualified, highly experienced, very knowledgeable. He knows all about what is missing in the report, what it means. And, of course, so do the editors. That's not unusual. In fact, it's uniform. If you look through the regular and especially the business press, including quite serious journals like the *Financial Times*, you find exactly the same thing, consistently without a break, as far as I've seen. Many euphoric discussions of the great increase in oil production but no mention of the word "climate" or any of the consequences. Sometimes there is mention of environmental damage. So, for example, the *New York Times* had a long front- and inside-page thousand-word story a couple of days ago about how Trump was opening up vast new areas for oil drilling in Wyoming, Nevada, other areas around there. Euphoric.

The article does mention environmental issues. It says there might be problems for ranchers, they might be running out of water because of the fracking. What about human (and other) life on Earth? Not one word. Again, not ignorance, they all know about it. Everything we're talking about and much more, they are well aware of.

All of which continues to raise some interesting questions, which I'll come back to.

One last example. Ryan Zinke, as you probably know, was forced to resign as secretary of the interior because of all kinds of corruption charges, which turns out to be pretty standard. So he left and there's a new guy appointed, David Bernhardt. According to the report, "While Mr. Zinke had been the public face of some of the largest rollbacks of public land protections in the nation's history, Mr. Bernhardt was the one who was quietly pulling the levers to carry them out, opening up millions of acres of land and water to oil, gas, and coal companies" (*New York Times*, February 4, 2019). He's described by allies and opponents alike as having played a crucial role in advancing what Mr. Trump has described as an energy dominance agenda for the country. One expert on environmental law at the University of Colorado Law School says, "Bernhardt has really been running the show directing the policy shop in a very strong way."

Well, Bernhardt is a former lobbyist for the fossil fuel industry. The new appointment for the Environmental Protection Agency, Andrew Wheeler, is a former lobbyist for the coal industry. So both of the two offices that deal with environment are in safe hands. You can sleep easily tonight.

Bernhardt's views on global warming don't seem to have been reported, at least I can't find them, although Wheeler's have. During his Senate confirmation hearing, he was asked by a senator what he thought about global warming. He said that it's probably happening, but it's way down on the list of urgent issues. He'd rank it about maybe eighth or ninth, so we can forget about it.

I could add another media report that just came out that actually has some good news about what we can do to alleviate the crisis. It was reported by the BBC last week. There was "a little ice age" in the seventeenth century; the temperature dropped. Nobody really understood why, it's been a problem for a long time. But the BBC reports a new study—I looked it up, the report is accurate—which suggests that the drop in CO_2 that caused the cooling was partly due to the settlement of the Americas and the resulting collapse of the indigenous population, which allowed the regrowth of natural vegetation. The report estimates that about 60 million people were killed within a century, many more, of course, later. Now, that happens to be about the number of refugees today. So it gives a suggestion on how to mitigate the climate crisis and also the refugee crisis. We could just kill them all off and maybe that'll reduce the temperature slightly.

Well, if any of you have the talents of Jonathan Swift, I don't, you might write this up as a "modest proposal," his satire on the rationality of economics.

It's not just the US government and the energy corporations that are dedicated to rapidly increasing the production of fossil fuels. The same is true across the corporate sector. So take the biggest bank in the country, JPMorgan Chase. It is devoting major investments to fossil fuel extraction, concentrating on the most dangerous and the most polluting of them, Canadian tar sands.

They all know exactly what they're doing, not just the reporters and the editors of the major press, but also the CEOs of the energy and financial corporations. And, of course, also the political leaders. They're not illiterate.

Marv talked a little Tuesday about ExxonMobil, one of the major energy corporations. We can add a little bit to the story. They were in the lead, starting in the sixties and seventies, with lots of scientists working for them, in discovering the nature and severe threat of global warming. They were producing important papers on the threat, which, of course, went to the management.

Something happened in 1988. In 1988 James Hansen made a very important speech, which was publicized, and for the first time gave large-scale public recognition to the severe threat of global warming.

At that point, management changed policy. They began to pour money into denialism. They recognized that global warming was going to become a big issue, which would affect their profits, of course. So they therefore began to fund not so much direct denialism, but as Marv pointed out last time, skepticism, saying, "Well, we really don't know. A lot of uncertainty, not certain what the effect of the cloud cover is . . . There are arguments both ways. So it's really premature to try to do anything about it, to pour a huge amount of money into this." At the same time, right in front of them were the reports from their own scientists, the leading scientists in the field, saying this is a disaster in the offing.

The same is true of the political system. So take Donald Trump. He knows all about global warming and its dangers. Just recently he applied to the government of Ireland for permission to build a wall—he loves walls. This one is to protect his golf course from rising sea levels. In the request he appeals to the threat of global warming. So when there's something really important, like some money in their pockets, then it's perfectly obvious that it's all happening.

What about the rest of them? In the Republican primaries in 2016, as perhaps you recall, almost every candidate denied that global warming is taking place. Surely, they all know it is. There was an interesting exception, John Kasich, who was regarded as the serious guy, the adult in the room. Kasich was the governor of Ohio. He said, "Yes, it's happening," but "we are going to burn [coal] in Ohio and we are not going to apologize for it" (Geman 2012).

He was regarded as the guy with some moral principles, but it's exactly the opposite. He was the one who said, Yeah, it's happening. We're going to cause a catastrophe, but we're not going to apologize for it. We're just going to go ahead and do it. That's considered the adult in the room. Well, of course the others knew, too.

Now, there are some exceptions, some who really do firmly believe that the climate is none of our business. One of them is the senator from Oklahoma, senior senator, who headed the Senate committee on the environment, James Inhofe. He said that God is up there, and there's a reason for this to happen. So it's therefore a kind of sacrilege to interfere with God's will. And I am pretty confident that he meant it. He's a dedicated, committed Christian. He spoke for many Americans.

Comparatively speaking, among developed societies, maybe almost all societies, this an unusually fundamentalist society. It has been all through its history, and it now shows up in all kinds of ways. That's probably one reason why the United States leads the developed world in the denial of what's happening. There was a recent poll of twenty countries, developed countries. People were asked, "Do you agree with the statement: 'The climate change we are currently seeing is largely the result of human activity'?" Fifty-four percent of Americans said yes. That's 10 points lower than the next lowest country on the list. The others are clustered up above. Take a look at Republicans. Half say it's not happening, not at all. Of the other half, little over half say humans may be responsible for some of it. Well, what is the reason for that?

I suppose a major reason is that that's what people see and read and hear. So tens of millions of people listen daily to Rush Limbaugh, who instructs them that there are "four corners of deceit: government, academia, science and media. Those institutions are now corrupt and exist by virtue of deceit. That's how they promulgate themselves; it is how they prosper." Furthermore, climate-change science is "the biggest scam in the history of the world."

So why should we believe people who are dedicated to deceit, like scientists? Actually, that's not necessarily bad news. It means that there is room for educational and activist work, which could make a big difference if it's carried out.

All of this does raise some pretty interesting questions. So think about the mentality of the people who devote themselves to destroying the prospects for organized human life, know very well what they're doing, and are perfectly rational human beings. How do you put all this together?

Take, say, Rex Tillerson, former CEO of ExxonMobil, then moved into the Trump administration, but was soon kicked out because he was considered too rational. As CEO of ExxonMobil, he was responsible for what I was just describing. Or take Jamie Diamond, CEO of JPMorgan Chase. I haven't seen what he has to say about the topic, but he certainly understands all this. He's an intelligent rational person, keeps his finger on the pulse of the world. He has to in order to make money.

So what's going on? Put yourself in their place. What do you do if you're Rex Tillerson or Jamie Diamond? They actually have a couple of choices. One choice is to seek to maximize profits. The other choice is to quit and be replaced by somebody who will seek to maximize profits. So those are your choices.

Does that account for the mentality? I don't think it absolves the individuals from responsibility, but it does indicate that they have little choice. The problem is not just individual, it's institutional. That's what Marv was talking about in our last session. And we see it very clearly in cases like these.

Well, what about Clifford Krauss, the reporter, the journalist. It's the same problem. He has what's called professional responsibility. Global warming was not part of the story that he was covering, so if he were to bring it up in his report, that would be introducing an opinion into an objective news story. It would reveal unacceptable bias that would violate the principle of objectivity, which says if you're a professional, you keep to the assigned task. You may know that what you're saying is, "We're going to destroy the world," but you don't put that into your column because that would be violating professional responsibility.

Actually, there is a concept of objectivity. If you go to journalism schools, you learn about objectivity, which is very much prized. Objectivity means describing accurately and fairly what's going on "within the Beltway"—within the corridors of power. If you do anything else, that's bias, and we don't want to be biased. So maybe we know all these things, but we can't say them.

That's the situation that these people face, institutional problems.

A couple of weeks ago, I brought up a personal anecdote. I hope you don't mind if I use another one. The first one was one that's been haunting me all my life. August 6, 1945.* There was another one about the same time, which I also can't get out of my mind. An article by a great essayist, Dwight Macdonald, right at the end of the war, around 1945. He wrote some very eloquent essays in his own journal, a dissident journal called *Politics*.

I was reading it at the time as a teenager. Some of the essays were on responsibility of peoples and responsibility of intellectuals. They include one of my favorite lines. He says, "It's a great thing to be able to see what's right under your nose, which we usually miss, but it's a nice talent to cultivate."

These essays are pretty remarkable. I recommend that you look at them, they are online. In the one on responsibility of peoples, Macdonald quotes an interview with a death camp paymaster, a Nazi death camp paymaster, who was apprehended as the camps were liberated. He learns that the Russians who liberated the camp are going to execute him. He bursts into tears, and he asks, "Why should they? What have I done?" I didn't kill anyone. I was just fulfilling a position that someone else would have taken if I'd left. I was just trying to survive.

Sound familiar?

Well, going back to those days, 1945, when we were entering the

---

* I was a counselor at a summer camp. The Hiroshima bombing was announced, everyone went off to the next activity. I was so appalled both by the event and lack of reaction that I went off alone to the woods for a few hours. I have felt the same ever since.

nuclear age, it wasn't known at the time, but it's now known that we were entering another age, a new geological epoch. It's now called the Anthropocene. There have been debates about when to mark its beginning. The World Geological Organization a year ago settled on the period right after the Second World War when all sorts of attacks on the environment were escalating, not just global warming, but plastics, which Marv talked about Tuesday, and many others. So that's the Anthropocene, a new geological epoch in which humans are having a major and deleterious impact on the environment.

There's a corollary to the Anthropocene, namely the Sixth Extinction, which we're now in the middle of. Marv also mentioned it in our last session: the very rapid—astonishingly rapid—decline of species, crucially insects, which is lethal for the future.

Actually, if you look at the nuclear age, it is literally a miracle that we survived. We talked a little about the Cuban missile crisis, the most dangerous moment in history, and one of the miracles that saved us from nuclear war: the decision by Vassily Arkhipov not to authorize firing nuclear-tipped missiles. It's not the only time.

Take one other one. In the early 1980s, when the Reagan administration came in, they decided to test Russian defenses at a time when the general situation was very tense. The way they did it was by simulating attacks on Russia—air, land, and sea attacks, including nuclear attacks, just to see how the Russians would respond, and what we could learn about their defenses. CIA analysts assumed that they didn't take it too seriously. After all, how could anyone believe that the US might contemplate an attack? But when the Russian archives came out, it turned out, not too surprisingly, that they took it very seriously. In fact, the intelligence reports that are being written now in the United States point out that "The War Scare Was for Real," it came very close (Fischer 2008; Adamsky 2013). This was at the time of Operation Able Archer, if you want to look it up.

Shortly before, there was a moment when the Russian air defenses registered an incoming US missile attack. Remember that their systems are primitive; they're not like ours, which use satellites and can tell what's happening anywhere. The Russian system, I think even today, but apparently then, was radar-based, which means you can see as far as the horizon, you don't know what's really happening until it's just about on top of you.

So their systems registered an incoming US missile attack. Incidentally, this happens over and over. We have only our own records, dealing with a much more sophisticated system. There have been hundreds of cases where the automated systems registered an incoming missile attack. The information goes to the Joint Chiefs of Staff and then on to the national security advisor, who informs the president, who then has to decide whether to push the button, and if so, we're all done. All within minutes. Sometimes it's come very close. During the Carter years, National Security Advisor Brzezinski was reportedly on the phone ready to call Carter about a Russian missile attack when the information came in that the report was a mistake, some coding error or something like that. As we move into the area of artificial intelligence, I leave it to you to think about what that means. It's been blocked every time by human intervention.

Anyway, that's what happened in Russia in the very tense period just before Able Archer. The protocol in Russia was for the individual who receives the information to transmit it up to the politburo and then to the top command. Which may decide that their only choice is to send off the missiles.

And remember, they have only a few minutes to decide.

Well, the guy who received the information from the automated systems, whose name was Stanislav Petrov, decided it probably wasn't real. He looked at the reports and figured that it's unlikely that the US would be sending a relatively small number of missiles. It didn't make sense. So he had decided not to send the information up to the high command. Another reason why we're alive.

It's been like this over and over, and it's getting worse. I mentioned earlier that the Doomsday Clock was just set, on January 24, at two minutes to midnight, the closest it's been to extinction since it was first set in 1947—apart from 1953, when the US and USSR set off thermonuclear weapons, demonstrating that human intelligence had devised the means to destroy life on earth. The analysts have now again set the clock at two minutes to midnight. They call it "the new abnormal." That's what we're now living with. And it's getting worse.

Well, there are answers to these terrible prospects. That's important to bear in mind. In the case of nuclear weapons, they can be eliminated, a utopian ideal proposed by such noted doves as Henry Kissinger and Reagan's secretary of state George Shultz.

It looks pretty grim, but in every single case, there are answers. In the case of serious overuse of antibiotics, which Marv talked about, there are obvious answers: stop industrial production of meat. That alone would have a huge effect. Overpopulation is a quite serious problem, but there's a very simple answer, and it's known: education of women. Wherever there's been education of women, fertility has declined sharply, rich countries or poor. That, of course, requires family planning. So how are we dealing with it? By cutting out foreign aid for family planning. That's the way to deal with the problem. The argument is that some of the family planning aid might go to abortions. But, in fact, cutting the aid increases the number of abortions, illegal and dangerous abortions. That's what happens when you don't have access to family planning, cutting contraception and so on. There are going to be more abortions, illegal and dangerous ones.

And it continues.

If you think about it, if you look at what's under your nose, to quote Macdonald again, all of this is pretty transparent.

Well, what about nuclear weapons? On that one, we know the answer: they can be eliminated. They can certainly be reduced. There are arms control agreements, which we could ratify, which would significantly mitigate the problem. There are three main arms control agreements. The first one is the Anti-Ballistic Missile Treaty. The phrase "antiballistic missile" sounds defensive, we're protecting ourselves. But strategic analysts on all sides know perfectly well, and often say, that antiballistic missile systems are first-strike weapons.

Everyone knows that it's inconceivable that any imaginable antiballistic missile system would stop a serious first strike. It's barely conceivable that it might stop a retaliatory strike. Therefore, to have one tells the planners that if we launch a first strike, there's a possibility that we might survive. So it encourages first strikes. It has no other function, except maybe marginally. That's one treaty.

The second treaty is the Intermediate-Range Nuclear Forces (INF) Treaty that was signed by Reagan and Gorbachev in 1987. It is quite important. It prevented the installation of very dangerous short-range nuclear missiles in Europe, which could easily have been used to start a war that would have blown up everything. Why did they sign? Well, a major reason is that there was a huge antinuclear movement in the early eighties, a very important popular movement, which created the conditions under which it was going to be pretty hard not do something.

So this was signed and ratified. It's important to keep the background in mind. It's not the only time. Now, that's the second.

The third is the New START treaty, signed and ratified in 2011. It's led to a radical reduction in launchers and missiles. It runs out in 2021. Those are the three treaties.

Well, how do they stand? The Anti-Ballistic Missile Treaty is dead. The US pulled out of it in 2002 under Bush. The INF Treaty, the Trump administration has just said it's pulling out of. The third one, Trump has indicated that he wants to cancel. He says that this is one of those Obama treaties. Therefore, by definition, the worst treaty ever signed, along with everything else done by the hated Obama. We've got to get rid of that. So that takes care of the three treaties, in which case, the doors for production of more destructive and threatening nuclear weapons are wide open.*

Well, there are plenty of things we can do. We could remember the background for the other treaties, the mass popular protests.

---

* In August 2019, shortly before Hiroshima Day, the Trump administration abrogated the INF Treaty, claiming that the Russians had violated it, a claim widely reported and taken to be obviously true, as perhaps it is. Rarely mentioned is that the Russians have long claimed that US ABM installations on the Russian border violate the treaty, a claim taken seriously enough by US scientists so that the authoritative Bulletin of Atomic Scientists devoted a lead article to expounding it. In a sane world, the paired claims would lead to negotiations, investigation by independent experts, and renewal of this crucially important treaty. Not in our world.

There are many other concrete steps that can be taken to mitigate the severe threat of nuclear war. One of them, which is important, is establishing nuclear weapons–free zones around the world. That reduces the possibility of conflict and development of weapons. There are already several of them. Almost. One of them is in the western hemisphere, but of course that one's not complete. It has to leave out the United States and Canada. Another one, which is important, is Africa, but that one can't be implemented because of one problem. There's an island called Diego Garcia. Africa claims it, but Britain, the former colonial master, does too. At the request of the United States, Britain kicked out the entire population so that the United States could construct a huge military base there.

The British claim of sovereignty is backed by the United States and France, not others. The military base is used. It's one of the main military bases for bombing Iraq and Afghanistan. It has been expanded. It seems that under the Obama administration it was expanded to include nuclear weapons facilities, housing for nuclear submarines and placement of nuclear weapons. So therefore that prevents the African treaty from going into effect.

There's another one in the Pacific, the Pacific nuclear weapons–free zone. That one was held up for years because France was carrying out nuclear weapons tests on its island possessions, but they stopped some years ago. However, the United States insists on maintaining nuclear weapons facilities and facilities for nuclear weapons submarines on its Pacific islands, so that one can't go into effect.

The most important one of all would be a nuclear weapons–free zone in the Middle East, a highly volatile area with plenty of nuclear weapons threats. It's a very interesting case—like the others, almost never discussed, as you can confirm.

There is overwhelming global support for establishing a nuclear weapons–free zone in the Middle East. The campaign to establish it was initiated by the Arab states, Egypt and others, back in the nineties. The campaign to institute it in recent years has been led by Iran, acting in the name of G-77, the former nonaligned countries, by now essentially the Global South, including 132 countries. They are strongly calling for establishing a nuclear weapons–free zone in the region. And the rest of the world agrees, with one exception, the usual one. The United States blocks it.

Every five years there's a review meeting of the nonproliferation treaty countries. Every time, the idea is put forth and supported. The United States blocks it, most recently, Obama in 2015.

Everyone knows the reason. If a nuclear weapons–free zone is established in the Middle East, Israel would have to open up its huge nuclear weapons system to inspection. And the United States would have to concede that it exists. Of course, everybody knows that it exists, but it's necessary for the US and Israel to refuse to acknowledge it. There's a good reason. If they concede that it exists, military aid to Israel has to terminate under US law (the Symington Amendment). So therefore we don't know whether it exists and the US must block the regional and international efforts to establish a nuclear weapons–free zone in the Middle East—which incidentally would eliminate any imaginable threat that Iran might pose, if anyone thinks there is a threat, if supplemented with a serious inspection system. And ample experience, verified by US intelligence and the International Atomic Energy Agency, has shown that Iran has been scrupulously adhering to the inspection agreements of the July 2015 Iran nuclear deal (JCPOA) reached by Iran, the US, and the other veto-wielding UN members, and Germany.[*]

The alleged Iranian nuclear weapons threat has been a major topic for years, all over the front pages and TV, with sober debates about whether we should just bomb them now or whether we should keep that option on the table, in violation of the UN Charter and the US Constitution, as already discussed. Try to find a word on the fact that there's an easy solution to these awesome problems: follow the lead of Iran, the Arab states, and the rest of the world by establishing a nuclear weapons–free zone with a credible inspection regime, quite straightforward—except . . .

---

[*] The deal was abrogated by Trump in May 2019 over the strong objections of all other signers, who vowed to carry on with the agreement, but who cannot in the face of overwhelming US power and threats.

It's an instructive exercise, which tells us quite a lot about the iron grip of official doctrine in a deeply conformist intellectual culture.

One will also have to work hard to find any mention within the mainstream of the fact that the US—and UK—have a unique responsibility to devote themselves to establishing a nuclear weapons–free zone in the Middle East. When the two governments were planning their invasion of Iraq, they tried to construct some thin legal cover for the aggression by appealing to UN Security Council resolution 687 (1991), which called on Iraq to terminate its development of weapons of mass destruction. The US-UK claimed, falsely, that Iraq had failed to do so. A look at resolution 687 reveals that it commits its signers to move to establish a nuclear weapons–free zone in the Middle East. So although Iraq had in fact complied with resolution 687, the US continues to violate it, in isolation.

That's no small matter, as we see daily with the extreme dangers posed by the US-Israeli threats against Iran for its alleged intentions with regard to nuclear weapons.

There is a good deal more to say about all of this, but for now let's let it rest with the observation that these are among the things "it wouldn't do to say," borrowing Orwell's explanation of how important matters are suppressed in free societies.

The most important message is, again, that there are things that can be done to avert serious crises. And to return to earlier comments, that's surely true of global warming. The timescale for action is short, the problems are escalating, but the game is by no means over.

More generally, I think that John Dewey, whom I quoted earlier, was quite right to say that until what he called "industrial feudalism," our current system . . . until it's replaced by industrial democracy, meaning democratic control of production, along with democratic control of all aspects of social life, until that happens, as he put it, "politics will be the shadow cast by business over society."

To remove the shadow is an enormous task. It's beyond the timescale for addressing the environmental crisis, though it's well within the range of possibility to lift it at least in part. That can make a huge difference. It can facilitate means to confront the terrible risks we are facing while also moving on to real democracy.

We've been discussing some of the grave problems we face. In the next few weeks, we'll be going on to talk about others. There are some who say that it's hopeless to try to do anything about them. We simply have to recognize that humanity has lost the game, and that we must give up. One of these voices is the US government. One of the reading assignments for this week is a very interesting publication by the Trump administration department responsible for transportation, the National Highway Traffic Safety Administration. It is a five-hundred-page environmental assessment. Evidently, a great deal of work went into it. The conclusion of the report is that there should be no new regulations for automotive emissions. So don't try to make cars and trucks more efficient, don't try to cut back on emissions. And they have a very rational argument; it's a serious bureaucracy, after all. They conclude that by the end of the century the temperature will have risen to 7 degrees Fahrenheit beyond preindustrial levels, a level that the World Bank called "cataclysmic," about twice as high as the scientific world estimates as possible for organized human life to persist in any recognizable form.

In short, the game will soon be over anyway. And since automotive emissions don't really contribute that much more to the total catastrophe, why not just enjoy ourselves? The human experiment is all over anyhow. You may recall Nero who was supposed to have fiddled while Rome burned. The Republican administration is telling us that we should enjoy ourselves while the world burns. These are the instructions of the most powerful government in world history.

Of course, there's an assumption: that everyone else is as criminally insane as they are and will join them in escalating the threats.

This has got to be the most astonishing document that has ever appeared in human history. See if you can think of anything like it. Quite seriously. And take a look at how it's handled. It did receive a report in the *Washington Post*, probably a few other places, and was then effectively deep-sixed. Who cares?

Fortunately, it's not true that everyone is as criminally insane as our leaders are. Things are being done. So for example, in Denmark, about 50 percent of energy needs are going to be supplied by renewables by 2030, and they're planning to reach zero fossil fuel use by 2050. There are many other cases.

And even though the federal government, under Republican rule, is determined to win the laurels as the most criminal organization in world history—devoted to the destruction of organized human life—things are happening here in states and local areas. Just recently in the Pacific Northwest, the city of Portland and several other areas have declared a commitment to eliminate all fossil fuels. The most extraordinary example is China. There's an interesting study of this by Dean Baker, a very fine economist, a couple of days ago (Baker 2019). He points out that China leads the world in developing sustainable energy. Use of electric cars in China is already at the same level as the entire rest of the world combined and increasing fast. Same with wind power, same as the rest of the world combined, and with solar power even more so. Last year, China added more solar capacity than the entire rest of the world combined. We might think about a place like Tucson where the sun is shining almost all the time.

China is a poor country. It has a big economy, but per capita it remains overall a poor country with severe internal problems unknown in the West. The US could surely do better than this. Are we doing it? Well, ask yourself.

There are lots of other things that should be done—like weatherization of homes. It's happening all over Europe to the point where the companies have no more business and are trying to break into the American market, but nobody's much interested. It makes life better, cheaper, happier, reduces impact on the climate, but it doesn't fit the doctrine. Even just using just things like LED lights, if you add it up, has quite an impact.

There are lots of things that can be done, and there are organizations really working on them. One of them in the United States is a group called the Sunrise Movement. They're mostly young people, like most others. A group called Earth Strike just had their first action on January 15. Another one is a group called Extinction Rebellion, based in Britain.

Thousands of protesters in Britain have shut down the London bridges repeatedly in protest against failure to act on global warming. Now they have, they say, about two hundred chapters around the world. There was a big demonstration in Manhattan a couple of days ago, January 28. They're organizing efforts to have an international week of action in April. Many chapters are springing up around the United States. The Sunrise Movement, to which we will return, has already had a quite a significant effect. One of their actions was a sit-in in Nancy Pelosi's office, the Speaker of the House, protesting against lack of action on global warming.

They were joined by Alexandria Ocasio-Cortez and the other young women, progressive women who were just elected to Congress. And they demanded what they called a Green New Deal, a commitment to decarbonize, completely decarbonize, the US economy by 2030 and to provide a green job to anyone who wants one. That has enlisted quite a broad response, placing the idea on the congressional agenda. In fact, there was a resolution introduced today by Ocasio-Cortez and Ed Markey of Massachusetts in the Senate to implement this proposal. That could become real with public pressure, the kind of public pressure that led to the INF treaty, for example. And it's no small matter. Some form of Green New Deal is essential for survival.

Which all raises a further question. Let's go back to Macdonald on the death camp paymaster. We're not death camp paymasters who know what's happening behind the walls but decide to look away, doing their jobs and living their lives.

That's not us. Actually, we're worse. We're watching a terrible story unfold, much more horrendous even than Auschwitz. And we have to ask ourselves the paymaster's question: "What have I done? What have I failed to do?" Future generations, if there are any, will be asking that about us.

I opened up with the report on the melting of the glaciers in the Himalayas, putting hundreds of millions at risk of losing their meager water supplies. And that's not just something very remote from us. Tucson, as most of you know, has a very fragile water system that's being seriously threatened.

Chapter 5

NEOLIBERALISM, GLOBALIZATION, AND FINANCIALIZATION

Waterstone Lecture, February 12, 2019

O kay. I'd like to get started. Before I dive in to the main topic for tonight, I just wanted to provide a very, very brief update for some material that we covered last week, just because in the last couple of days, a couple of really alarming reports have come out that a number of you probably have seen or might have seen. They've gotten a little bit of news coverage.

One was a piece that just came out in *Biological Conservation* that projects that, within a few decades, insect populations could go extinct by as much as 40 percent, and that all insects might, in fact, disappear within one hundred years. The ramifications of that, you can begin to imagine, are rather incredible. In fact, probably not survivable. But in any event, this was one of the reports that came out just in the last couple of days.

The other one that just came out in the last couple of days has to do with the disappearance of glaciers worldwide, but mostly focusing on the

Himalayan glaciers, a number of which will have completely disappeared, with the fate of between one and a half and two billion people who depend on them for water supplies, for drinking water, for agriculture, and so forth. Both of these just came out in the last couple of days, and so the pace with which science is projecting the circumstances of climate disruption . . . I don't think it's appropriate anymore to simply call it climate change. I think climate catastrophe or climate disruption is probably a better description, but in any event, the pace with which science is uncovering the trajectory of these phenomena is, in fact, accelerating really alarmingly.

Tonight's topic, or topics really, are these three related phenomena: neoliberalism, globalization, and financialization. Let me just give you a very brief road map for what I'd like to cover this evening. First, I'm going to give you just a very brief definition of neoliberalism, and I'm going to distinguish it from globalization and financialization. Then, I want to talk about the development of these phenomena in two distinct periods. The first period covers 1945, immediately post–World War II, to up around 1970 or so. These dates are not precise, of course, but they encapsulate certain kinds of changes in the political economic system.

This is a period that's sometimes called regulated capitalism. Sometimes it's called embedded liberalism. Sometimes it's called the Golden Age of Capitalism. Then, the second period from about 1970 to about 2008, which is really the advent period of neoliberalism. And then, following the crash in 2008, I think we've actually moved into a new moment, which a number of analysts, including people like Henry Giroux, have called gangster capitalism. I'll just say a few words about that tonight, but we'll talk about it a little bit more probably on Thursday, and then into next week. And then finally, I want to think about what kinds of effects these changes in the political economy of the globe have produced. What are the major outcomes of moving from the previous period into the neoliberal period?

Neoliberalism is itself the set of ideas and practices, and I'll describe what those are in a second, but neoliberalism is really a philosophical understanding of how the world not only works, but how it ought to work. Globalization is the spread of those ideas and practices over space and from place to place, and then accompanying this has been the rise of financialization, which really characterizes the changing and increasingly dominant role of finance capital vis-à-vis other capital sectors. Not only has the nature of finance changed, but the nature of its relationship with other sectors of capital has changed quite dramatically, and this has had really important effects.

Let's start with neoliberalism. And you will recognize some of this phraseology having read the piece a few weeks ago by Milton Friedman, one of the major proponents of neoliberalism. At its heart, neoliberalism is a theory of political economic practices that proposes that human well-being can best be advanced by liberating individual—not collective, please note—individual entrepreneurial freedoms defined in very particular ways, and skills within an institutional framework characterized by strong private property rights, so-called "free markets," and so-called "free" trade. If I could just have my hands doing air quotes, I'd be doing it continuously, but you can see that in your imagination.

The role of the state under neoliberal philosophy is to create and preserve an institutional framework that's appropriate to these kinds of practices. It must guarantee the quality and integrity of money. Also set up those military defense, police, and legal structures and functions required to secure private property rights, and to guarantee, by force if need be (and we've seen some of this already in the conversation about militarism; we'll see more of it), by force if need be, the proper functioning of markets. That's the role of the state.

If markets do not exist in areas such as land, water, education, health care, social security, or environmental pollution, then they must be created by state action if necessary. You can see these things immediately as either prior public goods or public resources, these are all to be brought under the rubrics of the market through privatization, an essential feature of neoliberalism. Any other actions by the state are deemed then to be illegitimate, but you can tell already that the state has a very significant role to play here, even though proponents of neoliberalism and their rhetoric constantly downplay both the role and the necessity of the state. It should also be quite clear, immediately and despite this rhetoric, that neoliberalism is not really an unencumbered, non-state-mediated enterprise.

I'm going to talk mainly about two periods, and then the post-2008 timeframe as a separate, but related extension of phenomena that precede it. Let's begin with this chart. The x-axis is years from 1949 to 2015. The y-axis is an index relative to 1970 of the relationship, in this case, between productivity and wages of goods-producing workers. In the period post–World War II up until about 1970 and a little bit later, there's a very close correlation, and what this means clearly is that workers were sharing in the results of this increased productivity.

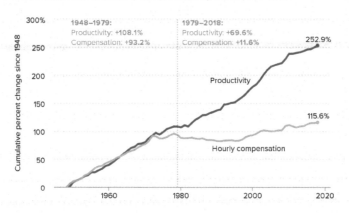

The gap between productivity and a typical worker's compensation has increased dramatically since 1979

Productivity growth and hourly compensation growth, 1948–2018

1948–1979:
Productivity: +108.1%
Compensation: +93.2%

1979–2018:
Productivity: +69.6%
Compensation: +11.6%

252.9%

Productivity

115.6%

Hourly compensation

Notes: Data are for compensation (wages and benefits) of production/nonsupervisory workers in the private sector and net productivity of the total economy. "Net productivity" is the growth of output of goods and services less depreciation per hour worked.

Source: EPI analysis of unpublished Total Economy Productivity data from Bureau of Labor Statistics (BLS) Labor Productivity and Costs program, wage data from the BLS Current Employment Statistics, BLS Employment Cost Trends, BLS Consumer Price Index, and Bureau of Economic Analysis National Income and Product Accounts

Updated from Figure A in *Raising America's Pay: Why It's Our Central Economic Policy Challenge* (Bivens et al. 2014)

Economic Policy Institute

And you see an inflection point in the mid-seventies where these lines begin to diverge quite dramatically, so productivity continues to go up, but in fact, wages remain rather stagnant. I'll talk about that more in a little bit, but in any event, this is the dividing point between these two periods. The first period, 1945–1970, which, as I said before, is sometimes referred to as regulated capitalism, sometimes embedded liberalism, sometimes referred to as the Golden Age of Capitalism, also sometimes referred to as capitalism with a human face.

What's happening in this first period? In the global economy, the Bretton Woods system is established. Shortly before the end of World War II, seven hundred or so delegates meet in New Hampshire in Bretton Woods, and they define, at that point, a monetary system that is going to presumably govern the economic, and therefore the political, relationships among nation-states following the war. It's a framework for international trade and development. It sets up certain institutions. The International Monetary Fund is set up at this time. The predecessors to the World Bank are set up, the General Agreement on Tariffs and Trade, which was succeeded by the World Trade Organization. The OECD, the International Bank of Settlements, so all of these financial institutions that come to really dominate how the world economy works are established, or at least the premises are established at the Bretton Woods conference.

And the central element of this was that countries would, in fact, trade on fixed currency exchange rates. Things would not deviate by more than 1 percent of a fixed rate, that is, fixed to a currency set to gold, so the amount of currency couldn't, in fact, deviate from the amount of gold by more than 1 percent. It was gold backed, and it was also US dollar backed. At the time, the United States controlled about two-thirds of the gold in the world economy, and so the gold became the standard, and the fixation of the US dollar to that gold became the way in which international currency was defined.

It was a moderately open world economy, although there were some tariffs, some protective tariffs, some obstacles to free capital movement. You have to remember, in 1944, as things were emerging out of World War II, the US was, by far, the predominant world economy, so could dictate many of the terms on which these arrangements were made. It allowed for US foreign direct investment, and that included in newly emerging states that were decolonizing, but it had another effect that will come back to be an obstacle. That is, it also opened the US markets to goods from Europe and Japan, and it allowed strong growth in capitalist economies around the world. That didn't seem like very much of a problem at the time of the Bretton Woods conference. That is, that the US was so predominant that this didn't really seem to be much of an issue.

During this period, there was an important role for government in the economy. Primarily, economic and fiscal decisions were governed by a Keynesian set of policies aimed at a low unemployment rate and an acceptable inflation rate. The main feature of a Keynesian economy is demand management. That is, if demand begins to lag, another actor, typically the state, must intervene to stimulate the economy, so this is a set of theories about how the economy works that persisted through this period, and then was overthrown in the next period. It's a demand-based rather than a supply-based economy.

There was government regulation of basic industries. There was government regulation of the financial sector; social regulation, including the rise of environmental, consumer, occupational, safety, and health regulations. All of these begin to be part of the social network of societies. There was strong antitrust enforcement. Reasonably strong, relatively strong. There was also high-level provision of public goods and services, including infrastructure. This is the time when the interstate highway system was developed. The G.I. Bill that we've talked about a little bit.

This is the period when we see the opening up of suburbia, opened up new geographical areas for US development, so there were moves already in this period from the so-called Rust Belt in the upper Midwest, the seat of traditional manufacturing, down to the Sun Belt, with important implications for capital-labor relations. That is, much of the original locus of economic activity was very strongly unionized. The South and the Southwest and the West were not, so this actually makes a very big difference.

I'm not going to say very much about this provision of public goods, but you can think about the way in which the creation of a consumer society depended very much on things like suburbanization and the fracturing, basically, of the population into individual households. Some of the notion of the American Dream that we talked about early really ramps up in this period, and you can see its necessary set of relationships to mass consumption. That is, everybody has to furnish their home, everybody has to have all the kinds of things that are now being converted from wartime production into peacetime production.

We also see the rise of the welfare state during this period, Social Security, Medicare, Medicaid, unemployment insurance. These were part of the New Deal mechanism to save capitalism from capitalists. There was an awful lot of foment during the period of the Depression, and then the war brought the economy out of it, out of the slump, but other factors needed to be ameliorated, and so some of these things, like Social Security, Medicare, and so forth, were meant to save capitalism from capitalists.

Finally, and this is something to note, particularly in light of recent news articles about taxation. During this period there was a very progressive income tax structure. In fact, in 1944, the top marginal tax rate was 94 percent. And all through the fifties and sixties, it remained close to 90 percent. It didn't drop to 70 percent until the 1980s, so the kinds of proposals that are now being made by people like Elizabeth Warren and by Alexandria Ocasio-Cortez are not without historical precedent. And the productivity during this time was the highest we've had, so these are things to keep in mind as you see the arguments circulate around these tax proposals.

There was also, in this period, a very major role for collective bargaining between companies and unions, for reasons that I'll talk about in a second. There was a large proportion of very stable, long-term jobs. People very often would enter a job, a profession, and they would stay with that for life. Not the bounce around that we have now.

The corporate sector itself also had certain interesting features. There were no price wars or all-out competition. Corporate CEOs tended to be promoted from within the corporation rather than headhunted from other firms. Bureaucratic principles rather than economic principles governed many of the relationships inside corporations, so this idea of promotion from within, the idea of seniority, and so forth, those were the more important kinds of relations. Those change in the next period.

Very importantly, in this period, financial institutions mainly provide financing for the nonfinancial businesses and households. That is, the role of finance was to, in fact, grease the skids for the rest of the economy. That is, the idea is you invest. People then go into production, and that produces jobs and output and so forth. That also changes.

Here's a question about this period, 1945–1970: Why did capital agree to this form? Remember, it's called regulated capitalism. Why did capitalists agree to this? First, in the depths of the Great Depression, a major labor upsurge began in the United States and in many other parts of the world. That is, this antipathy to capitalism that came out of the Great Depression was being felt in very, very political ways. People were beginning to organize and organizing on the basis of labor solidarity in large measure. Workers in many industries launched campaigns for union recognition, including in auto, steel, tires, electrical, machinery, trucking, and longshoring. There were fierce and often violent battles that resulted with labor gaining strength over time in some sectors, compelling many giant corporations to recognize and bargain with unions, so this was a typical arrangement.

When the United States entered World War II, the labor leadership accepted a truce agreeing to a no-strike pledge for the duration of the war, in other words, to help the economy during wartime. During the war, with full employment bolstering laborers' bargaining power and the success of the war effort dependent on labor's cooperation, the unions made several further gains, including dues checkoff, grievance procedures, seniority as the basis for promotion and as protection against layoff, and further expansion of union membership. The emerging dynamic is that labor is increasing in its power over this period.

Going into wartime production had taken the US out of the Great Depression. Many feared that, with the war's end, the Depression might return, and with that, the conditions of the Depression, including all of the social and political agitation. In addition to the economic effects, big business feared that such conditions could lead to a spread of socialism and communism, and these were not fears without a basis. Many socialist and communist parties had gained great power in this period, especially, though not only, outside the US. All through Europe, Asia, socialist and communist parties were, in fact, advancing.

Also, much more of the world was governed by communist governments after World War II, a third of the world's population (including, principally, China and the USSR), and this provided at least an alternative imaginary, so concessions were necessary. We've already talked about the difficulty of having this alternative imaginary at play in the world. And I should've put quotes around "communist." They were not communists by any means, for reasons that we talked about, but they claimed rhetorically to be communists, and this allowed a kind of tension to be set up between the West and the rest.

Beginning in the early decades of the twentieth century, but especially after the Russian Revolutions in 1905 and 1917, there was virulent red baiting and repression of communists, socialists, and many other labor leaders. We've already talked about this a bit. This repression increased tremendously in the post–World War II period with McCarthyism and like phenomena. Labor was weakened by legislation.

For example, the passage of the Taft-Hartley Act (which President Truman, interestingly enough, vetoed, but his veto was overridden in 1947), which outlawed, among other things, secondary boycotts, which were a very effective mechanism for unions to use. That is, if one union went on strike, other unions could go out on strike in sympathy. Well, Taft-Hartley prohibited that, among other things.

As the Cold War proceeded, the very conservative Congress of Industrial Organizations, which was still separate from the American Federation of Labor, began to turn against very left-wing leaders, so the AFL-CIO eventually becomes one of the instruments of communist red baiting and witch hunting, and this culminated in the expulsion of several major national unions, led by communists and other leftists, from the CIO in this period from 1949 to 1950.

The year 1949 was very significant, of course, in terms of the so-called "domino effect." Noam talked about this moment when we "lost" China, as though we had had China in some possessive way in 1949. If you recall our discussions of this period and the paranoid style of US politics, the Chinese revolution and the "loss" of China added further fuel to this anti-socialist, anti-communist frenzy. One result was that many left-wing union activists were fired from their jobs by management. Labor unions were quite weakened and de-radicalized, particularly in the United States. What does this have to do with why capital agrees to the bargain?

Under these circumstances (that is, with unions weakened and with their most radical leaders eliminated), bargaining seemed preferable to capital than government intrusion. This was particularly the case if government intrusion meant much more active government management of the economy, for example by nationalization of industries or other kinds of mechanisms. Given these possibilities, capital was more interested in engaging the moderate politics that emerged from union political activity in the United States. By contrast, in most European countries in that period, labor played a much more radical political role, supporting socialist and communist parties that pressed for greater state intervention in business, while proclaiming an ultimate objective of replacing capitalism with socialism. And this conversation, it's hard to imagine now, although it's rebounding a bit, was very prevalent.

A grand bargain, particularly on wages and working conditions, was established between capital and labor. Began during World War II with this kind of agreement by labor not to strike and so forth, not to make excessive demands during wartime, but then it was retained afterward. There was a bigger pie. There was rising productivity and more equitable sharing in that pie. Opposition to the bargain came mainly from small businesses. That is, big business had no trouble paying union wages. They had no trouble acceding to government programs. For example, for worker protection, for environmental protection (internalizing some externalities), and so forth.

But small businesses, which operate on a very small margin (and many of which go out of business in their first year), have a much tougher time adhering to these kinds of arrangements. As a side note, just to suggest to you, sometimes big companies use those kinds of tactics to eliminate smaller competitors while sounding quite high-minded. That is, large companies will agitate for more stringent either labor practices or environmental protections and so forth, knowing that they can easily absorb the cost, while smaller businesses cannot and then will go under. That's a side note, just one of the many, many friendly features of capitalism.

The result of this bargain, as we've talked about, was this equitable sharing of the rise in productivity. During the 1945–1970 period, we see this set of relationships between capital and labor producing a rising set of expectations and a rising set of outcomes. What happens in that moment when things begin to shift? What prompted this change from regulated capitalism to neoliberalism? The short answer was that capital began to experience a falling rate of profit. The much longer answer has to account for why this was so.

First of all, there was a set of conflicts internal to the capitalist form itself. There were conflicts between capital and labor, brought about largely through changing conditions in the production process. Spurred by falling profit rates, capitalists tried to implement new working conditions. There were speedups, unsafe jobs, unequal distribution of profits, and so there was a lot of labor agitation. There was conflict between capital and citizens over the provision of social welfare programs and over complaints about externalities, pollution, unsafe products. We see some of these things reflected in the Powell Memorandum (Powell 1971). When, for example, Lewis Powell goes after Ralph Nader, we can see that that's the beginning of a backlash by capital to the consumer protection movement (and by extension other social welfare movements), and things like auto safety and so forth. These all represented costs to capital that were starting to pile up.

There was also more competition with developing countries, as other economies were on the rise, over resources and rising oil prices. At the very end of this period, we have the formation of the Organization of Petroleum Exporting Countries, OPEC, and a rise in price. There's also competition between US capitalists and capitalists in other developing countries and in developed countries, especially from Western Europe and Japan. We can see that reflected very significantly in the auto industry of the time. That is, this is the first time when Detroit and the big US automakers really start to face very substantial competition from European automakers, and particularly from Japanese automakers. This, as I indicated earlier, is one of the unanticipated (or at least underplayed in 1944) effects of the Bretton Woods arrangement. The opening up of the world economy to US foreign direct investment, but also opening up the US economy to investment here and the interpenetration of US markets.

The result of all of these rising costs to capital was a falling rate of profit, very stagnant productivity growth, rising inflation, increasing unemployment, and the breakdown of the Bretton Woods system. The so-called Nixon Shock when Nixon took the US economy off the gold standard, and therefore all the rest of the economies basically went off the gold standard, went to fiat currency. I know none of you probably will recall, even if you were around at the time. If you looked at US currency, it used to say, "Exchangeable for gold." And then it said, "Exchangeable upon demand." Now it just says, "In God We Trust," so that's a fiat currency. You've got to be aware of that.

All of this produced international monetary and economic chaos, which was part of this destabilization in this period. So there was a need for a new set of arrangements to allow capital accumulation to continue and to expand. That form is neoliberalism. So, beginning in this period and continuing right up to the present (though now with some very significant cracks), how did the neoliberal form of capitalism become the common sense? The ideas around neoliberalism actually began to coalesce most recently in the 1940s. Some of the ideas have been around for as long as capitalism. A small and exclusive group of passionate advocates, mostly academic economists, historians, and philosophers, had gathered together around the renowned political philosopher Friedrich von Hayek to create the Mont Pelerin Society, which was named after the Swiss spa where they first met.

The Mont Pelerin Society, by the way, is still in existence. They first met in 1947. The notables included Hayek, Ludwig von Mises, the economist Milton Friedman, and even for a time, the noted philosopher Karl Popper. The founding statement of the society reads as follows, and you'll see some familiar words now: "The central values of civilization are in danger." Remember, this is immediately post–World War II, so the things that we saw in NSC 68 (1950) are prevalent, the Iron Curtain speech by Churchill (1946), so we already begin to see this antagonism between the East and the West, and then it's re-represented in statements of this sort.

> The central values of civilization are in danger. Over large stretches of the Earth's surface, the essential conditions of human dignity and freedom have already disappeared. In others, they are under constant menace from the development of current tendencies of policy. The position of the individual and the voluntary group are progressively undermined by extensions of arbitrary power. Even that most precious possession of Western man, freedom of thought and expression, is threatened by the spread of creeds, which claiming the privilege of tolerance when in the position of the minority, seek only to establish a position of power in which they can suppress and obliterate all views but their own.

This clearly echoes the language that we see in NSC 68 and so forth, and we will see it come back to haunt us in the Powell Memorandum. The statement continues:

> The group holds that these developments have been fostered by the growth of a view of history which denies all absolute moral standards. And by the growth of theories which question the desirability of the rule of law. It holds further that they had been fostered by decline of belief in private property and the competitive market, for without the diffused power and initiative associated with these institutions, it is difficult to imagine a society in which freedom may be effectively preserved.

I refer you back to the comments that I made earlier about what these kind of groups mean by freedom. It's a very, very narrow definition of economic freedom. Hayek, the author of such key texts as *The Constitution of Liberty*, also *The Road to Serfdom*, argued that the battle for ideas was key. It is crucial to understand that the group at Mont Pelerin was already keenly aware of the way in which common sense must be nurtured and built. And that it would probably take at least a generation for that battle to be won, not only against Marxism, but against socialism, state planning, and Keynesian interventionism, which, remember, was the preceding prevailing common sense. The period, 1945–1970, was dominated by a Keynesian view.

The neoliberal movement remained on the margins of both policy and academic influence until the troubled years of the 1970s, when people were searching around, capitalists particularly, were searching around for a new strategy for increased accumulation. Neoliberal ideas began to move center stage at that time, particularly in the US and Britain, particularly under the Reagan administration here and the Thatcher administration in Britain. Although in the US, the rudiments of the policies began, actually, under the Carter administration.

It was nurtured in various well-financed think tanks, some of them direct offshoots of the Mont Pelerin Society, such as the Institute of Economic Affairs in London, the Heritage Foundation in Washington, and I'll name a few others in a minute. Also, through its growing influence within the academy, particularly at the University of Chicago, where Milton Friedman dominated. I'll say more about him in one second. Neoliberal theory gained an academic respectability by the award of the Nobel Prize in Economics to Hayek in 1974, and Friedman in 1976, along with six other Mont Pelerin affiliated economists, so that seemed to give a lot of cachet to this set of notions.

But you should be aware, of course, that this particular prize, though it's assumed the aura of Nobel, had nothing to do with the other prizes and is basically under the very tight control of the Swedish banking elite. In fact, Peter Nobel, Alfred Nobel's grandson, said that his grandfather would never have wanted a prize awarded for any activity that put profits over people. Hayek himself thought that there shouldn't be a prize in economics, and when he gave his acceptance speech in 1974, he said as much.

Milton Friedman asks in his 1962 preface to *Capitalism and Freedom*,

> What then is the role of books such as this? Twofold, in my opinion. Provide subject matter for bull sessions. Second, and more basic, to keep options open until circumstances make change necessary. There is enormous inertia [this is another way of putting the existing common sense], a tyranny of the status quo in private and especially governmental arrangements. Only a crisis, actual or perceived [or created, which has, in fact, been part of the mode of operation of the neoliberalism system], produces real change. When that crisis occurs, the actions that are taken depend on the ideas that are lying around. (1962)

If anybody's read Naomi Klein's book, *The Shock Doctrine*, she picks up on this idea that it's the ideas that are lying around in a moment of crisis that become predominant. Friedman is saying that these ideas, which neoliberals had been developing since the 1940s, simply awaited a ripe moment to be taken up and become part of the common sense. "That, I believe, is our basic function, to develop alternatives to existing policies, to keep them alive and available until the politically impossible becomes the politically inevitable" (Friedman 1962).

This is Friedman's notion in 1962: "The ideas in our two books are still far from being in the intellectual mainstream, but they are now, at least, respectable in the intellectual community, and very likely almost conventional among the broader public." This is right at the outset, basically, of the Reagan administration, when these ideas, in fact, do begin to have enormous political traction.

Now let's turn to the Powell Memorandum, which is part of the promulgation of neoliberalism as common sense. It's one of the first attempts to organize the business community to actively produce a new common sense, and it really very intentionally attempts to do this. I think you should pay attention, not only to the content of the memo, but to its rhetoric, its rhetorical style. Noam has described it as, and he'll probably say something more about it, but "it sounds like a very spoiled child, who has 99 of 100 marbles, but feels deprived because it doesn't have the 100th."

The memo argued that the free enterprise system, capitalism, was under attack. And he's right. Capitalists hardly ever got a break at this point. "The US Chamber of Commerce," Powell said, "should lead an assault" (1971). And remember, this is a secret memo that was only revealed later. A secret memo from Lewis Powell to the secretary of the US Chamber of Commerce, so he's exhorting the chamber to become politically active in defending the free enterprise system.

"The US Chamber of Commerce should lead an assault upon the major institutions, universities, schools, the media, publishing, the courts, in order to change how individuals think about the corporation, the law, culture, and the individual" (1971). US businesses, Powell suggested, did not lack the resources for such an effort, particularly if they were pooled. The business community could be most effective if people started to think together as a class rather than as individual firms and corporations. The US Chamber of Commerce took up this challenge in a very dramatic way.

The chamber subsequently expanded its base from around sixty thousand firms in 1972 to over a quarter million just ten years later. The basic message was to draw upon the rhetoric of individual freedom, defined very narrowly in economic terms, although they didn't put it that way, to oppose every form of collectivism, including for example, unions and union organizing as major targets. But every form, not only of collectivism, but any notion of the desirability or appropriateness of a public good or public goods. The privatization dimension of neoliberalism is aimed, in both the short and long term, at reducing expectations that there's such a thing as a public good. This, of course, includes limiting so-called "inappropriate interventions" by the state into the economy. But keep in mind the absolute dependence of the neoliberal model on continuing interventions by the state.

Another organization that was developed as a result of the Powell Memorandum was something called the Business Roundtable. This was an organization of CEOs, "committed to the aggressive pursuit of political power for the corporations," and was founded in 1972. So now, this is not only aimed at producing a dominant common sense, but is moving into the political realm. The corporations involved accounted for about one-half of the GNP of the United States during the 1970s. They spent close to $900 million annually, a huge sum at that time, on political matters.

Some of the resources were aimed at developing think tanks (one of the elements that Powell promoted), out of which would emerge the "ideas lying around" as Friedman had advocated. The think tanks would also organize speaker bureaus to spread the ideas around, produce op-ed pieces, and so forth. These included the American Enterprise Institute, which was actually founded in the forties, The Heritage Foundation, which was founded in 1973 by Adolph Coors, and the Center for the Study of American Business. They were all formed with corporate backing at this time.

During the 1970s, business refined its ability to act as a class, just as Powell had suggested. The dominant theme in the political strategy of business became a shared interest in the defeat of bills, such as consumer and environmental protection, labor law reform, and then the enactment of favorable tax, regulatory, and antitrust legislation. They were united and they had a program. There was also a crucial set of Supreme Court decisions beginning in 1976 that are in this long line that went back to a misinterpretation in the late 1870s that gave corporations personhood.

I just want to highlight a few that are relevant to what we're thinking about now. This line of decisions first established the right of a corporation to make unlimited money contributions to political parties and political action committees (PACs), which were basically unknown at the time, but grew enormously. There were eighty-nine of them in 1974. There were nearly 1,500 in 1982. This was protected under the First Amendment, guaranteeing the rights of individuals—in this instance, corporations—to freedom of speech.

One of the key opinions was written by Lewis Powell, whose name you might remember from three minutes ago, who at this point (1978) has become a Nixon-appointed justice on the Supreme Court. The ruling, in the case of *First National Bank of Boston v. Bellotti*, gave this right to corporations. If you're interested, there's a very interesting dissent from the then chief justice William Rehnquist, where he tries to trouble that whole history of precedent about corporations having the same rights as human beings.

Donors gave to PACs of both parties in the 1970s, but then began leaning heavily toward the Republicans. Democrats were more conflicted between support for their working-class base and the need to pursue big money, at least at that time. They don't seem to have the trouble much now. There was a $5,000 cap on donations to PACs at the time, which means that people wanting to motivate change had to come into some sort of class solidarity and pool their money. The political base of the Republican Party began to merge, at this point, with the Christian Right.

Jerry Falwell's Moral Majority was the first politicization, and began a race-based appeal to white working classes, who could be persuaded that they were being left behind and disadvantaged by affirmative action and so forth. Next time, I'll discuss a piece that shows how abortion became one of the central motifs for this alignment, and we'll talk about this a bit when we think about the rise of social movements next week. The political base could be mobilized through very positive mobilizations of things like religion and cultural nationalism, but it could also be mobilized through very negative, though coded (though I would say increasingly less coded if not blatant) racism, homophobia, and anti-feminism. This coalition had a positive valance, but it also had these negative elements that are still prevalent.

The problems that people were facing (and the problems were, and remain, real), as this alliance portrayed it, was not capitalism and the neoliberalization of the political economy. The real problem was liberals, who had used excessive state power to provide for special groups. There's this idea of people cutting in line ahead of you. You've worked hard. You've played by the rules. You're not getting ahead. Well, it's not that the system is stacked against you. It's that "those" people, who are undeserving, are getting more advantages than you get.

The political structure that emerged from all of this was quite simple. The Republican Party could mobilize massive financial resources and mobilize its popular base to vote against its own material interests on cultural or religious grounds. The Democratic Party could not afford to attend to the material needs, for example, for a national health care system, of its traditional popular base because it was afraid of offending its new donor class by reinstituting a truly progressive tax system. Given the asymmetry, the political hegemony of the Republican Party became more sure over this period.

Reagan's election in 1980 was only the first step in the long process of consolidating the political shift necessary to support these neoliberal economic policies, and we've been in this mode ever since, basically, through both Republican and Democratic regimes. Reagan's policies centered on an across-the-board drive to remove the scope and content of federal regulation of industry, the environment, the workplace, health care, and the relationship between buyer and seller. Budget cuts and deregulation and the appointment of anti-regulatory, industry-oriented agency personnel (which may sound familiar) to key positions were the main means.

What are some of the key characteristics of this period of neoliberalism? Going back to what I had said about the previous period, I want to draw some parallels. At the level of the global economy, we see the removal of barriers to the movement of goods, services, capital, and money across national boundaries. But crucially, at the same time, holding labor in place, because if workers could roam around and find the best markets for labor, this would put a kink in the system.

The role of government in the economy is basically just the opposite of the things I put up before: renunciation of aggregate demand, management, that is, a renunciation of a Keynesian approach. Deregulation of basic industries, deregulation of the financial sector, weakening of regulation of all kinds, weakening of antitrust enforcement, privatization and the contracting out of public goods and services, cutbacks in, or elimination of, social welfare programs, and tax cuts for business and the rich.

Marginal taxation rates went from about 90 percent or so in the 1950s for top earners to 28 percent in 1988, and we're still contending with whether that's, in fact, paid at all. Then it rose a little bit, and now it's going to go back down. Corporate tax rates went from 50 percent down to 34 percent. Capital gains went from 30 percent to 15 percent. This is basically the ongoing program of neoliberalism.

In the capital-labor relationship, things also change. There was dramatic marginalization, and, in fact, outright assaults on collective bargaining, which is in fact still the case ongoing. We see a tremendous casualization of jobs, so rather than expecting stable and lifetime employment, people now expect some significant precarity in their job lifetime.

In the corporate sector itself, we witness unrestrained competition, including the move toward monopolization and conglomeration. Corporate CEOs in the neoliberal period more typically now are hired from outside the corporation. That is, you have to go headhunting for CEOs. Market principles penetrate inside companies, so rather than bureaucratic rules dictating what happens, every segment of a firm has to be a profit center, and these compete with each other.

Crucially, financial institutions shift toward new types of activities, and become relatively independent of the nonfinancial sector. This is essential. That is, there starts to be a divorce between finance segments of capital and the so-called real economy, and I'll say more about that in a second.

An important question: How is neoliberalism spread throughout the world? In other words, how does the neoliberal model become globalized, become globalization? We talked about this a little when discussing militarization. I just wanted to reiterate it. Here is a quote I found just the other day, and I thought it was interesting in the current context. This is from Oppenheimer Funds (a major global investment firm). The right way to invest: "Challenge Borders" (see "OppenheimerFunds Invites Investors to 'Challenge Borders' with New Ad Campaign"). You don't see them wanting a lot of walls.

There are three principle methods for spreading these ideas. The first method is, you buy off elites in receptive countries. You find a local strongman, and it's almost entirely men, of course. Examples are legion. Provide economic and military assistance to him and his family and immediate allies, so that they can repress or buy off opposition and amass considerable wealth and power for themselves, and open the country for capitalism's needs. That's one way.

The second way is you replace oppositional leaders and install receptive elites. Again, the examples are legion. Mosaddegh in Iran, 1953; Árbenz in Guatemala in 1954; Allende in Chile in 1973; Zelaya in Honduras, 2009; Maduro in Venezuela in dot dot dot. Then, use step one above. Once you get the right kind of person in, you go back to the old model.

The third method is not to be so direct, but to utilize an array of international financial mechanisms to induce compliance. You induce indebtedness one way or another. Then the IMF, the World Bank, the World Trade Organization come in with what are called structural adjustment programs, which largely consist of countries selling off their public assets, privatizing as much as they can, opening both their financial and commodity markets to foreign investment, eliminating any public welfare systems that might interfere with debt repayment. You have a whole mechanism here that constantly just agitates toward opening countries to the needs of capital.

Here's one exemplary case. This is the case of Paul Bremer, who was the head of the Coalition Provisional Authority. He was essentially the proconsul in Iraq. On September 19, 2003, Bremer promulgated four orders that included: the full privatization of public enterprises; full ownership rights by foreign firms of Iraqi businesses; full repatriation of foreign profits; the opening of Iraq's banks to foreign control; national treatment for foreign companies; and the elimination of nearly all trade barriers.

The orders were to apply to all areas of the economy, including public services, the media, manufacturing, services, transportation, finance, and construction. Only oil was exempt (presumably because of its special status as revenue producer to pay for the war and its geopolitical significance). The labor market, on the other hand, was to be strictly regulated. Strikes were effectively forbidden in key sectors and the right to unionize restricted. What the US evidently sought to impose by main force on Iraq was a state apparatus whose fundamental mission was to facilitate conditions for profitable capital accumulation on the part of both domestic and foreign capital. The freedoms it embodies reflect the interests of private property owners, businesses, multinational corporations, and financial capital. An apt illustration of the spreading of democracy and freedom (which, of course, are synonymous).

What did neoliberalism promise? It promised that all of the gains accruing at the top would eventually be shared by everyone. A rising tide raises all boats. Wealth would trickle down, eventually. That was the promise. But what did it actually produce? I'm going to go through several dimensions of the effects. I'll start with the US and then I'll talk a bit about the global scene. Again, think about the chart above, where we see this disparity starting in 1970, and this turning point has had enormous effects.

One is wealth and income inequality. Where did all the income and wealth gains of that productivity go if they didn't go to wages of working people? These gains went to the wealthy for the most part. The bottom 20 percent barely got anything at all. The next 20 percent did a little better, but at the top, people actually did substantially better. They almost doubled their wealth and income in the period we're examining. Another way to look at it, in terms of total household wealth growth between 1983 and 2010 according to various wealth groups, the top 5 percent of households received 74.2 percent.

Still another way to think about it, this is more contemporary. The four hundred richest Americans now own more than the bottom 150 million. In 1980, the bottom 60 percent had, at a high point, almost 6 percent of the wealth. That went down almost to near zero in 2008–2009, and then bounced back a little to 2 percent. The four hundred richest people, owning about 3.2 percent of the wealth, now have more than the bottom 150 million.

The tax cuts recently enacted are just going to make things worse. They're not doing what they were supposed to be doing. Corporations were supposed to repatriate all of their offshore taxes. That really hasn't happened. Tax returns that are about to come out are going to be a disappointment to a whole lot of people. There's some speculation that the Trump administration actually worked with the IRS and the Department of Treasury to deliberately withhold less from each paycheck for people, so that it would look like the tax cut made an immediate bump. That's going to be a very short-lived kind of political gain, because most people will not remember the few pennies that they got in each paycheck, but they will notice the missing tax refund in April or May, if the IRS is open.

Here's another way to think about wealth and income inequality: average CEO to average worker pay. In 2013, these were the figures: Japan, 11–1; Germany, 12–1; France, 15–1; Canada, 20–1; UK, 22–1; Mexico, 47–1; US, 475–1. JP Morgan, at the turn of the last century, said if this ratio ever got above 10 to one, there would be enormous outpourings of rage on the streets. Don't really see it. See it a little bit in France, yellow vests, but the US population is a little more quiescent.

Let's also look briefly at this picture on the global scale, where globalization was supposed to raise all boats. In 2012, the bottom 99.9 percent of the global population had about 19 percent of the global wealth. Conversely, the top 0.1 percent owned 81 percent, with a full 30 percent owned by the top 0.01 percent. Maybe not that equitable. Another way to think about this, which also just came out recently: the eight richest individuals now own as much wealth as the bottom 50 percent of the world population, so there may be a little unrest at some point.

The World Bank, and a number of other analysts, makes the claim that one of the achievements of capitalism in its neoliberal, globalized form has been to raise enormous numbers of people out of poverty. And in some absolute sense, that is true. It is true that in some absolute sense, more people are out of poverty than, say, in 1800, but it's a very complicated notion. A recent article in the *Economist* describes the reasons why poverty reduction is so very difficult to assess. The statistics are very difficult to collect, and poverty, as a concept, is very difficult to define.

I now want to move on to some other effects of neoliberal globalization. An interesting one that we've talked about a very little bit: life expectancy in the US has now fallen, I think now for the third year in a row. In 1960, Americans had the highest life expectancy, 2.4 years higher than the average for the OECD. But the US started losing ground in the 1980s (right around that inflection point on the graph, interestingly enough). US life expectancy fell below the OECD average in 1998, plateaued in 2012, and is now one and a half years lower than the OECD average. This is unheard of in a developed country. It simply can't happen. In 2015 alone, more than sixty-four thousand Americans died from drug overdoses, exceeding the number of casualties in the Vietnam War. Also exceeding the number of casualties and fatalities from auto accidents. Between 1999 and 2014, the suicide rate rose by 24 percent. These "deaths of despair," as the *British Medical Journal* describes it, and I would also refer you back to the piece that we looked at from the UN, Philip Alston, the UN Commission on Human Rights, are disproportionately affecting white Americans, especially adults age twenty-five to fifty-nine, those with limited education, and women.

The sharpest increases are occurring in rural counties, often in regions with longstanding socioeconomic challenges, some of the places where certain voters are being located. Possible explanations: collapse of industries and the local economies they supported, erosion of social cohesion, and greater social isolation. These are all speculations from the

British Medical Journal based on their data.

Other factors include economic hardship and distress increasing among white workers over losing job security; educational performance weakening; social divides (including some income inequality) widening. Middle-class incomes have stagnated. Poverty rates in the US are now exceeding those of most rich countries. These again are some of the results of the Philip Alston report. Social contract is weaker than in other countries. Those in need have less access to social services, health care, or the prevention and treatment of mental illness and addiction.

Another effect is the commercialization of everything, as we've already talked about, including privatization of all forms of common goods, intellectual property, patents and copyrights, indigenous knowledge, commercialization of governance and politics (i.e., the best democracy money can buy, which has been the title now of several different books). All of which are forms of primitive accumulation or accumulation by dispossession that I talked about earlier.

During the neoliberal period, there have been many episodes of economic instability, exactly what the Keynesian approach was designed to prevent, so there's been rampant financial speculation. We had commodity and asset bubbles of various kinds, the savings and loan scandal of the eighties, the dot-com crash of the nineties, the 2008 financial and housing crisis, only the latest instance. These kinds of cyclical crises are things that the Keynesian approach was meant to dampen down.

The set of effects that I want to talk about a little bit is the idea of surplus and disposable populations, and I'll talk about it more next week. In part, this phenomenon is a result of the dominance of finance capital. That is, that you can produce profits of a certain kind without producing. In fact, the economist Costas Lapavitsas has written a book with that title, *Profiting Without Producing*. Finance capital is increasingly divorced from the real (i.e., the productive) economy. Profits come increasingly from fictitious commodities and rent, either transaction costs or fees or a whole number of other things. It's a form of cheating that Marx tried to avoid in his analysis. That is, you get it from one person, but it's a zero sum. Somebody else loses. There's no additional value produced.

One result is then the production of more and more surplus people. They're not needed as workers because of automation, because of outsourcing, because of profits without production, because of all kinds of other things. If they're not needed as workers, because you're not producing much, you're using the finance system to develop profits, then they're not capable of consumption. What happens to them? They become part of a global reserve army of labor. They do serve some purposes, one of which is to exert downward pressure on wages. Another is to discipline the continuing workforce. That is, if you know there are a bunch of unemployed people out there, you're likely to be quite compliant.

The remaining work is more and more precarious and casual. Many of the new jobs created since the 2008 crash, in which nine million jobs were lost in the US, are low wage, part-time, no benefits. We see the rise of the so-called gig economy, which is now characterized as something that's desirable for people. What to do with the surplus? They're no longer needed as workers, can't use them as consumers, because they don't have any expendable income. Instead of a war on poverty, we now have a war on the poor. One option, you may make money off their bodies through things like mass incarceration. Very lucrative. Prison industrial complex, local, state, federal private prisons. Debtor prisons have come back. You need throughput if you're in this business, so you need prisoners. How do you get them? You invent new crimes.

A prime example, the war on drugs. Anybody who says the war on drugs has been a failure doesn't understand it, doesn't understand what it was for. It's a genocide, basically. It's the removal of young men, particularly young men of color, from the society because they're not productive as either workers or consumers, supposedly. Also, things like detention before deportation, which is tremendously on the rise. And the deportation circuit, which was cruel enough as it was, we now detain people and they become the fodder for these private detention prisons. The companies that run these often profit twice; once for the housing of prisoners in and of itself, the second time, if they can actually use those incarcerated as a very cheap labor force (increasingly the case). Petty fees and fines that many police forces now rely upon for their own sustenance. When these specious fees can't be paid, the debtors are now ending up in jail or prison and feed the cycle.

As I've discussed several times now, because of the present neoliberalized, globalized, financialized nature of capitalism, nation-states can no longer ensure the economic welfare of their citizens, which was a powerful basis of state legitimacy, and therefore hegemonic governance. So now they need a new basis for state legitimacy. That new basis is what the readings by Bauman this week and Henry Giroux are talking about, is a move from a welfare state to a garrison state.

State legitimacy is now increasingly based on protection from dangerous others. The need to maintain a climate of fear becomes an essential part of that. Endless enemies. In the foreign sphere, historically, this enemy has been communism. More recently (especially after the collapse of the USSR) it shifted to terrorism, immigrants and refugees, and so forth. On the domestic scene, people of color, young, old, LGBTQ communities, differently abled. That film that I showed about the Pentagon's view of the populace, which requires a militarized response, that approach has now migrated into domestic policing. And if you have a military outlook, the people you're interested in now look like an enemy. One crucial political and economic effect of all of this is to divide and conquer the population and prevent them from seeing bases for coalition. That is, you keep people distracted from what's producing all of these problems.

In the post-2008 period, which I, along with analysts, am calling the period of gangster capitalism, a number of the trends I've described tonight have ramped up. Some of these we'll discuss in the next couple of weeks, but I just want to enumerate a few things happening on the deregulation front, where current neoliberal warriors have been quite active in the past couple of years. These include:

- Deregulation casualty #1: Workers' health and safety

- Deregulation casualty #2: Workers' wages

- Deregulation casualty #3: Workers' savings

- Deregulation casualty #4: Workers' safety nets

- Deregulation casualty #5: Pay equity

- Deregulation casualty #6: Workers' rights to organize and join a union

- Deregulation casualty #7: Consequences for employers who violate workers' rights

Finally, where to from here? As Marx and Engels declare in *The Communist Manifesto*, class struggles must end in "either a revolutionary constitution of society at large, or the common ruin of the contending classes." Rosa Luxemburg, based on Karl Kautsky's formulation: "As things stand today, capitalist civilization cannot continue. We must either move forward into socialism or fall back into barbarism, neither of which is inevitable." In response to all these things that we've been talking about, there has clearly been a rise of social movements in reaction to neoliberalism, globalization, financialization, the antagonisms between capitalism and the rest of the world, between capitalism and the environment.

One question is, "What are these groups doing?" And the related question, which comes back to this issue of socialism or barbarism is, "What will be the state and elite response? Will elites change and accept, or will they move to further and more brutal repression?" I'll leave it at that.

Chomsky Lecture, February 14, 2019

One recurrent theme through our whole discussion has been hegemonic common sense, how it gets established, how difficult it is to extricate oneself from the spider's web.

One way to explore these issues is simply to take a look at the morning's newspaper and ask yourself what was unsaid—what "it wouldn't do to say," to borrow Orwell's phrase once again. It's a useful exercise. I'll give a couple of examples.

Let's start with today, with the lead story in the *New York Times*, front-page story. It says that US cyberwar attacks are disabling satellite launches in Iran. It also mentions that the Pentagon has determined that a cyberwar attack is an act of war that justifies a military response in retaliation—though no one would say, or think, that the right extends to Iran.

Of course, there is a pretext for the cyberwar attack in this case. The pretext is that the satellite launchers have a dual-use capacity. They could also be adapted to send off missiles, so therefore it is legitimate to carry out an act of war to disable them.

Well, putting aside the credibility of the pretext, let's turn to another example, which is certainly very well known to the writers, editors, readers. The United States has ABM installations on the border of Russia. Russia argues that these have a dual-use capacity, that they can easily be adapted for first-strike missiles, which would have a devastating impact on Russia, vastly beyond anything even imaginable in the Iran case.

The Russian claims are simply dismissed if even mentioned, though not by everyone. For example, not by the *Bulletin of Atomic Scientists*, the leading scientific journal in the United States that deals with military issues. Take a look at their lead story in this month's edition. It is a detailed discussion by a well-known specialist, Theodore Postol of MIT, of how the US ABM systems on Russia's borders can easily be adapted to first-strike weapons.

Suppose that Russia decided to carry out a cyberwar attack disabling US ABM installations on its borders. We don't have to actually speculate on what would happen, because there wouldn't be anybody around to care one way or another.

Well, those are all things that it wouldn't do to say or think when you write the front-page article, or when the editor allows it, or when people read it. You might take a look at comments. I didn't bother, but I doubt that there will be any that bring up these elementary points. A homework exercise.

Let's take another example, from yesterday's *New York Times*, another front-page story, a long and interesting one, worth some thought. The headline is "Congress Poised to Help Veterans Exposed to 'Burn Pits' over Decades of [Iraq] War." The article opens by quoting a veteran who reports that "everywhere he went in Iraq during his yearlong deployment, [he] saw the burning trash pits. Sometimes, like in Ramadi, they were as large as a municipal dump, filled with abandoned or destroyed military vehicles, synthetic piping and discarded combat meals. Sometimes he tossed garbage on them himself. The smell was horrendous."

This has had a toxic effect on US soldiers, who are demanding medical treatment and compensation. The article quotes Senator Amy Klobuchar, Democrat of Minnesota, now running for president. "This is our generation's Agent Orange," she said, adding that she's already got some legislation passed on burn pits and has more on the horizon, "motivated, like many members of Congress, by stories of affected constituents." Representative Tulsi Gabbard, Democrat from Hawaii, helped sponsor legislation to evaluate the exposure of service members to toxic chemicals.

That's all at the progressive end of the political spectrum. Is there something it wouldn't do to say? Can you think of something missing from this account?

Well, yeah, two things. Iraqis and Vietnamese. They are "unworthy victims," to borrow the phrase of an old friend and colleague who passed away recently, Edward Herman. He made a distinction between worthy victims, whose fate matters—victims of enemy states, and unworthy victims, whose fate doesn't matter, our victims. A very useful distinction, with broad range and incisive significance.

Klobuchar made an analogy to Agent Orange, a reference to the Vietnam War. In Vietnam, there was a vast campaign of chemical warfare. It began with John F. Kennedy's escalation of the attack on South Vietnam as soon as he took office. The goal of the chemical warfare was to destroy crops and livestock. Along with the heavy bombing of rural areas, which was intended to drive the population into what were called strategic hamlets, essentially, concentration camps surrounded with barbed wire. The official goal was to "protect" them from the guerrillas whom the US government knew very well they were supporting.

All of this is straight from official government documents and officials, no commie rats or journalists spouting "fake news" in the "failing lamestream media."

Altogether, there were some 20 million gallons of herbicides that saturated much of the country at an intensity that's utterly unimaginable, apart from unworthy victims. Mostly Agent Orange, that's why the reference. Agent Orange has a component, dioxin. It was known by the manufacturers of Agent Orange and by the US government that dioxin is one of the most severe carcinogens. It also has very harmful effects on reproductive and immune systems.

Now, quoting again, "the evidence is overwhelming: Vietnamese soldiers, from both sides, with perfectly healthy children before going to fight, came home and sired offspring with deformities and horrific illnesses; villages repeatedly sprayed have exceptionally high birth-deformity rates; and our own Department of Veterans Affairs now lists 14 illnesses presumed to be related to Agent Orange." A *New York Times* op-ed by the noted Vietnamese-American intellectual Viet Thanh Nguyen and Dick Hughes, a highly respected analyst who lived and worked in Vietnam for many years and still does. And, in fact, hideously deformed fetuses are still appearing in Saigon Hospital in South Vietnam. That's several generations later.

There's alleged to be some concern in the US about protecting fetuses. It somehow seems to be rather selective.

North Vietnam was subjected to massive bombing, with much of the country turned into a moonscape and the major cities heavily bombed as well. I happened to see a little of it firsthand on a brief visit during a bombing pause. But it was spared this particular horror. The chemical warfare attack was only against the South. After extensive campaigns and many court battles, US veterans finally won some recognition from the government that Agent Orange had extremely harmful effects. Many of them were severely harmed. They got some compensation, inadequate but at least some. Vietnamese? They're unworthy victims, peanuts.

Yesterday's article does not ignore the brutal effects of US chemical warfare in South Vietnam. Returning to Klobuchar's comment about "our generation's Agent Orange" and the "stories of affected constituents" in Minnesota, the *Times* article explains that Agent Orange is "an herbicide known to sicken veterans in Vietnam," and after many years of efforts by affected veterans, "has become widely accepted as a cause of illness among veterans of the Vietnam War, [though] there has been a protracted struggle over benefits for those who were sickened after serving off the coast during that conflict."

The suffering of affected veterans was and remains very real—but nothing like the impact of the chemical warfare on the Vietnamese victims. If you want to look into this topic, there are two very good books by Fred Wilcox, one about the effect on American veterans and one on the effect on Vietnamese (see Wilcox, *Waiting for an Army to Die* and *Scorched Earth*, respectively).

There's also no doubt that American vets are suffering from the effects of the burning trash pits littering Iraq. Could there be anyone else in Iraq who is affected by them? A few come to mind, but as unworthy victims, they receive no mention. Maybe thirty or forty years from now, there'll be a retrospective saying, "Too bad something happened to Iraqis."

Well, all of those are things that it wouldn't do to say, right? It might remind you of the death camp paymaster whom I talked about last time. I'll leave it to you to think about.

As an aside, I might mention that US chemical warfare extends beyond Indochina. I happen to have visited poor and remote villages in southern Colombia, along with human rights activists, in the large areas targeted for defoliation under Clinton's Plan Colombia, sharply extended under Bush. The rationale is to destroy coca as part of the US drug war (let's put aside some questions that arise about this). But the defoliation has what are called "unintended consequences"—completely predictable, of course, but "unintended." Peasants plant their crops among the coca plants, and, believe it or not, they and their families are people, even if unworthy. On the ground one can witness the grim effects of intensive use of glyphosate, well beyond levels permitted for worthy people (as Roundup) and modified for Colombia: children with horrible sores and unexplained serious illness, devastated crop land, pathetic stories from poor peasants. You can find scientific papers on the internet using remote sensing in these areas, described as too difficult for direct access. They are judicious and properly cautious, but cannot convey what direct experience provides. As in Dick Hughes's reports from South Vietnam.

Well, let's take a third item. This is a little different, but very instructive. It's close to home, right here, Tucson. Marv posted a story from the *Tucson Sentinel*. Quite a good rag, I should say. It was a few days ago. It's about a closed meeting at a luxurious, gated community south of Tucson. It's worth reading carefully, not only because it's right here but because it tells us quite a lot about our society much more generally, something we surely want to understand.

The meeting featured Steve Bannon, whom you've probably heard of. He's a highly influential figure here and internationally, formerly the leading strategist for Trump. Bannon was joined by Kris Kobach, a leading figure in the Republican Party voter-suppression drive, specializing in tales about voter fraud that collapse on inquiry.

Bannon has been working—quite openly and publicly, nothing hidden—to forge an international "populist" coalition headed by Trump, including such far-right figures as Brazil's Bolsonaro, France's Le Pen, Hungary's Orban, Italy's Salvini, and also including an array of reactionary states: in the Middle East, the Gulf family dictatorships, the Egyptian military dictatorship, and Israel, joined with India's ultranationalist Hindu extremist Modi, and a few others in the wings.

For Europe, a prime goal is to protect its white Christian civilization from the invasion of refugees, who are planning to turn Europe into a Muslim continent, according to the doctrine. A look at figures is instructive. The highest percentage of refugees in any European country is Switzerland, where it's reported to be 1 percent, elsewhere usually a small fraction of 1 percent, but you can't be too careful. They breed like rabbits and keep coming. Here, too, where we are being subjected to an invasion of criminals, rapists, murderers, Muslim terrorists, drug dealers, others who seek genocide of the white race. No question about it. Just listen to the president and his acolytes.

The meeting at the gated community was about organizing private funding for the border wall, in case Congress doesn't meet its responsibilities. Participants appear to advocate the principle of zero tolerance, sending children to concentration camps in the desert and so on, recognizing that it's ugly. But it's necessary. We have to protect ourselves from the hordes invading the country to destroy our white Judeo-Christian civilization and to flood us with drugs.

One of the distinguished figures attending, a former Colorado State representative, suggested that the wall should extend to the Arizona-California border. You know who's going to be coming from there.

And the wall should be outside the nearby Tohono O'odham Reservation, which he knows about because he's been there. He found that "five-year-old kids are walking about loaded. You know it's horrible. Every kid on that reservation, every young kid, has a new truck because they've helped actually transporting the drugs." We obviously have to protect ourselves from that.

The tone of the meeting was captured by an Iraq War veteran, who said, "I refuse to allow our broken political system to leave my family and my country vulnerable to attack." So, in case you didn't know, we're in real danger right here in Tucson, not that far from the border. It wouldn't take long for *them* to get here.

These are pretty common feelings around the country. And Trump, whatever you think of him, has a very keen political nose. That's why he picked the wall as his leading campaign issue. A sure winner. It's just necessary to tar the Democrats with wanting these hordes to invade and destroy us.

The people quoted in the article and the participants in the meeting truly believe in the threats and their severity, I suspect. It sounds very sincere. And many others around the country as well. The concerns, of course, are beyond fantasy. No need to go into that. But the fears are real. All of this tells us something important about our culture, our society, the common sense of a good part of the population. Just as the hideous treatment of refugees in Europe, far worse than here, tells us a lot about Europe's advanced civilization.

A brief look at history may help understand these attitudes. For two hundred years, since the British were out of the way, the United States has probably been the most secure country in the world, maybe in all of history. Also, it's probably the most frightened country and has been for a long time. It's a very striking phenomenon. Why?

It's common these days to deplore the fact that in this century, the US has been engaged in "endless wars." True, but a bit misleading. As discussed earlier, it's hard to come up with another country that has been at war almost without a stop since its founding. Just about every year since 1783. That's quite a record. And being constantly at war engenders a military culture, which has to be justified by fear of terrible enemies, from the "merciless Indian savages" of the Declaration of Independence to the ravings of NSC 68 and the like and on to the hordes attacking us a few miles south of here and to Iran and others plotting our destruction.

One of the reasons for the American Revolution was a Royal Proclamation of King George III in 1763, which banned settlement beyond the Appalachian Mountains. The rest was designated as Indian Country. The colonists were having none of that. They chafed at Britain's barrier against settling what they called at the Constitutional Convention "vacant lands to the west." There were all these vacant lands and the British were barring settlement. That wasn't only the settlers, it was also the land speculators like George Washington, none of whom could tolerate this barrier.

As soon as the barrier was lifted with independence, the newly independent United States went to war against the Indian Nations. George Washington was one of the first, launching a war against the Iroquois Nations. He was known by the Iroquois as the "town destroyer." There could be no problem with this, "the gradual extension of our settlements will as certainly cause the Savage, as the Wolf, to retire; both being beasts of prey tho' they differ in shape" (Washington 1783).

Essentially the same concepts prevailed through the nineteenth century, right to the very end, ending up with virtual genocide in California. Meanwhile, the perpetual wars were punctuated in mid-century by the US conquest of half of Mexico in what General Ulysses S. Grant, later president, called one of the most "wicked wars" in history. The war that put us on this side of the border.

By the end of the nineteenth century, the national territory had been conquered. Wars then extended beyond the Caribbean and Central America, which had already been subjected to half a century of repeated interventions. And on to the far Pacific.

By now, the United States has some eight hundred military bases abroad. We're not the only ones, of course. The former imperial powers, Britain and France, are reported to have about ten each. So, eight hundred, ten, zero, one or two . . . And US military forces are engaged in fighting all over the world.

So, it's a strange history. A unique history. And, as I said at the beginning, just today, this morning, it was announced that the US is engaged in war against Iran (not conceded).

And many of these actions are far from minor. Since World War II, the worst act of aggression is the US war in Vietnam, then expanded to all of Indochina, much of it completely laid waste. In this millennium, the worst crime, a textbook example of the kind of aggression for which Nazi war criminals were hanged, was the invasion of Iraq, joined by the British in this case.

Well, when a country is constantly at war for its entire history, hardly a year without war, it's not too surprising that there's a lot of fear. There's a lot to be frightened about. And if you look at polls, you see some further reasons.

Gallup Poll, the major polling agency, takes international polls regularly, asking many questions. A few years ago, in 2013, one of the questions was: Which is the most dangerous country in the world? The United States was first, nobody even close. Way behind in second place was Pakistan, surely inflated by the Indian vote. Other countries are barely mentioned.

That was the first time Gallup asked that question, and the last. They run the polls every year, but this question hasn't been asked again. Actually, they didn't have to worry too much because although the poll was reported internationally, Americans were protected from the unwanted news. The free press didn't publish it, a database search indicated.

A friend of mine who does extensive database searches said he did find one mention. I didn't see it, so it's secondhand information. He said that the poll was mentioned in a story in a right-wing tabloid, a Murdoch journal, the *New York Post*. The story was about how this shows how totally crazy the world is. But apart from that, it wasn't mentioned. Though the question hasn't been asked again, there's indirect evidence from other polls suggesting that the results would be about the same.

One prime reason for the American Revolution was the imperative of taking over the "vacant lands" to the west. Another was slavery. One of England's leading jurists, Lord Mansfield, in 1772 issued a ruling that slavery was so "odious" that it could not be tolerated within England, understood to include the American colonies. It could be tolerated within England's Caribbean colonies but not in the English-settled American colonies.

The slave owners saw the handwriting on the wall. And remember, just about every leading figure was a slave owner. Of the first dozen or so American presidents, there was only one, John Adams, who wasn't a slave owner. So, that was a second reason for the revolution. Slavery, too, required a military culture, justified by fear, not entirely inauthentic. Right through the eighteenth century, there were slave rebellions in the Caribbean islands, which were then the main slave centers, soon displaced by the US. And there were some slave rebellions in the United States, too. If you look at the demography, in some states, like South Carolina, the slaves outnumbered the overseers, who had a reason to be frightened.

Then came the Haitian rebellion, which had an enormous impact. In 1804, the slave revolt in Haiti established the first free country of free men. It was bitterly resisted. The entire civilized world got together to try to destroy that rebellion. Primarily France, the colonial power—and incidentally, France's slave colony in Haiti was the source of much of France's wealth. Britain joined in, also the US, Canada, just about everyone joined to try to crush this frightening development. The war practically destroyed Haiti, but the revolution succeeded. They were then punished by France for the crime of liberation. This was right after the French Revolution with its impressive rhetoric about liberty, equality, fraternity, and all that nice stuff. France imposed a huge indemnity on Haiti, a huge burden on the society that they never were able to overcome.

In the 1960s, some of the Left in France thought that maybe France should compensate Haiti for its hideous crimes. There was a commission led by Régis Debray, a prominent militant leftist. The commission decided that it wasn't necessary, that France had no need to give any compensation at all. In other words, first we rob and then destroy them, and then when they ask for a little bit of help, we kick them in the face.

The technical term for this is "Western civilization."

Haitian liberation was naturally particularly frightening to the slave state to the north. The US refused to have any formal relations with Haiti. It didn't recognize Haiti until 1862. That was the year of the Emancipation Declaration. These slaves were going to be free so what do we do with them?

That year, the United States recognized Haiti and Liberia for the first time, regarding them as places where the freed slaves could be sent. This was done mostly on humanitarian grounds. Well-meaning people recognized that obviously these inferior people, not authentic humans, wouldn't be able to survive in a civilized society, so we want to rescue them by sending them to some place where they could get along with creatures of a similar kind.

Then came a long series of horror stories. I won't run through it. Haiti's been by some measures the main target of US aggression throughout the last century. Again, this century, with an intervention in 2004 to "rescue" president Aristide—whom the US had barely tolerated ever since he became Haiti's first elected president—in reality to kidnap him and ship him off to Central Africa, also banning him and his party from participating in elections.

In short, there are good historical grounds for fear in the most secure country in the world, even in places like the luxurious gated community near here that is probably about the safest place anywhere, but authentically frightened. *They* are coming after us, just as they have been since they starting attacking us when the first settlers landed and then through the nineteenth century within our national territory, in the slave labor camps that were producing the cheap cotton that was the foundation of the economy, and then on through most of the world, where we defend ourselves with a huge military presence that extends wherever we can reach. Now moving on to space.

The fear is pretty deeply rooted. It's presumably part of the reason for the extraordinary gun culture in the United States. There's nothing comparable anywhere. It's partly just fear. There's actually a lot more to it. If there's time, we might go into it. A very interesting story. But presumably fear is a substantial factor.

This pervasive fear is one reason why it's repeatedly been so easy to terrify the country about both internal and foreign enemies. NSC 68 and Vandenberg's "[scaring] hell out of the country" is a case in point.

In 1950, the same year as NSC 68, the US determined to change its policies in Southeast Asia. The US had followed rather mixed policies toward the various imperial systems. It didn't like them and was generally dubious about the old colonial systems, while recognizing their important function in the reconstruction of the former colonial masters, which relied on their resources and raw materials. In particular, it vacillated about Vietnam, well aware of Ho Chi Minh's conciliatory initiatives. But by 1950, that changed. The US decided to support France in its effort to reconquer its former colony. That led to horrors that I don't have to go into.

Recall that NSC 68 was carefully crafted to obscure the fact that the United States was far more powerful militarily than the Russians. There's an intelligence record since then, and it's quite interesting. Consistently, it greatly overestimates the strength and power of possible enemies, Russians or whoever the next one is. Daniel Ellsberg's book, which you've read one chapter of, is a useful record of this, through the early period into the sixties. But it goes right on to the present. So right now, Iran is the greatest threat to world peace, practically poised to destroy us. The world has a different picture, but what do they know?

Intelligence estimates are necessarily uncertain. One expects errors. But it's striking that consistently they're wrong in the same direction: overestimating—often greatly—the power of those who are going to attack us. That's not conscious deception, I presume, though there may be cases of that, as apparently in NSC 68. Rather, analysts are subject to the same, if you like, common sense as the rest of us. These are features of the dominant culture, exaggerated fear, so that it's natural for state and private power to share the fear to some extent and to exploit it for their own purposes. Speculation of course, but not, I think, without grounds.

That takes us right to the Powell Memorandum, today's reading. A classic example of almost comically exaggerated fear.

In Powell's case, it wasn't the country that was being destroyed, it was the business world. It was the important part of the country that was under attack, in fact, facing destruction. And it was really frightening. The universities were being taken over by Herbert Marcuse—remember him, and his minions, who had essentially taken over the whole university system? Congress was gone. It was under the control of Ralph Nader, who was carrying out a consumer-safety campaign to try to save people from being killed by cars that were poorly made. And, while doing that, he had practically taken over Congress. The media were all bitterly anti-capitalist. You should go back and read them.

It goes on like this. In fact, the rhetoric, which is hysterical, is very similar to NSC 68. Marv pointed out that it has the feel of a three-year-old who has all the toys but his little brother took one away, so he has a tantrum, "How can I live without that one toy? I have to have everything."

Well, all of this is doubtless sincere. That's the important part of it. It's not faked. It's deeply rooted in the culture and the history.

The Powell Memorandum was one of the immediate cultural and intellectual prongs of the neoliberal assault that took off soon after, as Marv discussed last time. The assault was led by the militant business community. The United States is unusual in that respect. And, curiously, its main target, the labor movement, often doesn't seem to grasp the fact. As the neoliberal assault was just beginning to take shape, in 1978, the president of the UAW, United Auto Workers, Doug Fraser, resigned from a labor-management committee that was set up by the Carter administration, expressing his shock that, as he put it, business leaders had "chosen to wage a one-sided class war in this country—a war against working people, the unemployed, the poor, the minorities, the very young and the very old, and even many in the middle class of our society," and had "broken and discarded the fragile, unwritten compact previously existing during a period of growth and progress"—during the period of class collaboration under regimented capitalism (Cowie 2003).

Fraser should have known better than that. That's what business is always doing, constantly. Especially here, where we have a bitterly class-conscious business community. That goes way back. That's why the United States has an unusually violent history of repression of labor at a level that astonished even right-wing observers from Europe.

We talk now about gangster capitalism, and rightly, but elements of it have always been there in bitter repression. As already mentioned, hundreds of American workers were being killed in strike actions well into the twentieth century, at a time when nothing like that was happening in any other comparable country. That's only one of many examples.

Well, the Powell Memorandum is one of the prongs. There's another one, which is quite interesting, maybe more interesting, in my opinion. It's quite similar in content, was produced at the same time, but it was at the opposite end of the spectrum, the political and intellectual spectrum.

This was a document published by the Trilateral Commission, its first publication. The Trilateral Commission was drawn from liberal internationalists in the United States, Europe, and Japan. You get a sense of its complexion by the fact that the Carter administration was drawn almost entirely from its ranks. Same in Europe and Japan, the trilateral partners.

It's a very interesting document. The book is called *The Crisis of Democracy*. The basic message is that the entire society is under threat, not just the business community. The entire society is under threat from the activism of the 1960s.

What happened in the 1960s, it says, is that large parts of the society—what are sometimes called "special interests"—tried to enter the political arena to advance their concerns and demands: young people, old people, women, farmers, workers; in short, the general population.

There's one group that isn't mentioned in these complaints about the special interests: the corporate sector. But that makes sense. They represent the national interest, they're not special interests.

So, all these groups are trying to enter the political arena. That creates the "excessive democracy" that has been such a problem for the "men of best quality" since the first modern democratic revolution. The state cannot handle those pressures. Therefore, the liberal commentators recommend "more moderation in democracy," a return of the general population to passivity and obedience, to their role as "spectators," not "participants." The American rapporteur in the Trilateral study, Harvard political scientist Samuel Huntington, reminisced about the days when President Truman "had been able to govern the country with the cooperation of a relatively small number of Wall Street lawyers and bankers," so that there was no crisis of democracy. But that was before the activism of the sixties threatened to shatter these civilized arrangements.

The Trilateralists were particularly concerned with what they called the institutions responsible for "the indoctrination of the young." Schools, universities, churches. They're failing to control young people. They're failing to indoctrinate them properly. That's why you see them out on the streets protesting against the war, calling for women's rights, all of this disruptive stuff. Therefore, harsher measures are needed in the schools and universities.

They said the same about the media, here agreeing with Powell. The media are out of control. The Trilateral liberals even warned that state intervention might be necessary to get the media back into line.

The general concern, then, is rather like the Powell Memorandum. But these are intellectuals. The rhetoric is more subdued than the Powell Memorandum, though the message is similar. The conclusion across the spectrum, what we call left to right, reflects the cultural and intellectual background of the neoliberal assault.

There's recent scholarly work on the origins of neoliberalism, tracing it back much earlier than has usually been assumed, to the period right after World War I. It brings out very interesting features, which unfortunately there's no time to go into now except very superficially. One interesting revelation, relevant to "gangster capitalism," is the attitude of the founders of the doctrine in post–World War I Vienna to the use of government force to crush the Left. The most respected figure, the guru of the movement, is Ludwig von Mises. He could barely contain his pleasure in 1928 when the Austrian government violently broke up a major strike, undermining the vibrant labor and social democratic movements and setting the stage for Austrian fascism, and thus safeguarding "sound economics" from the disruptive impact of labor unions and of the social reform that sought to soften the harsh edges of market discipline on workers and the poor.

There's a theory behind these characteristic features of neoliberalism back to its earliest days. Labor unions seek rights of workers. That interferes with what these days is called "flexibility of labor"—which means in practice the right of employers to fire workers at will and to determine conditions of work without interference. It interferes with "the optimal use of resources," as determined by markets. Labor unions interfere with these doctrinal verities by their concern for rights of workers, for safety and health, for livable wages, and even—perish the thought—for a say in the plans and operations of the dictatorships in which they spend their working lives. They therefore have to be destroyed.

It is therefore natural that the saints of the movement should have been delighted, as they were, by the crushing of labor unions by the powerful state during the first stages of fascism in Austria and Germany in the late twenties and early thirties. Similarly the attitudes of the great figures of the movement toward the monstrous Pinochet dictatorship come as little surprise.

Another interesting feature of the neoliberal movement from the early days is the close linkage between progressive intellectuals and the neoliberal right wing. More than symbolically, the term "neoliberalism" was adopted by the movement at the Walter Lippmann Colloquium in Paris in 1938. Lippmann, you'll recall, was one of the leading progressive intellectuals in the United States in the twentieth century.

The concept "optimal use of resources" is one we might spend a little time on. It's a very interesting contribution to mysticism when you analyze it closely. But let's put that aside for now.

It's interesting to see how similar themes reverberate through the history of capitalism, even with substantial changes of circumstances.

We've already discussed the continuity from the suppression of the rabble and their demands for democracy and rights in the first democratic revolution in seventeenth-century England, to the Framers' conservative revolution that overcame the popular demand for excessive democracy a century later, to the warnings of progressive twentieth-century intellectuals about succumbing to democratic dogmatisms about the right of the bewildered herd to participate in decisions that affect them, the province of the "intelligent minority." And in another context, the need to suppress the radical democratic currents and their call for independence throughout the world as the postwar global order was being established.

It's not surprising, then, that the same themes should come up again in the early 1970s, when the rascal multitude was getting out of hand again in the activism of the sixties, the "time of troubles" as it's often called. So, you get the same reaction. It was necessary, once again, to counter the threat of the excessive democracy that was arising from sixties activism, which in fact did significantly civilize the country. For the business community, as Powell emphasized in his rather frantic way, it was necessary to protect what Madison had called the "permanent interests of the country," the private enterprise system, which was threatened particularly by the falling rate of profit that was in part a result of the labor militancy that was picking up in the late sixties and early seventies. A lot of it was stimulated by the general activism of young people, including Vietnam veterans. In strikes like Lordstown, which is worth looking into carefully, young workers were not just calling for decent pay but also for dignity in the workplace and for some means to participate in controlling it. Tendencies that are truly ominous and have to be crushed.

Then comes the neoliberal assault, long in preparation, exploiting the economic disorders of the seventies as the opportunity to take control. It has achieved many of its objectives. Discipline was at least partially imposed in the universities, in interesting ways, including the imposition of business models and sharp cutbacks in state funding. You see that here in Arizona very clearly, but it happened all over the country. Another factor was the sharp escalation of tuition, for which there's no authentic economic basis. We'll return to it if there's time.

Crucially, the decline of the rate of profit was reversed. That was really important. Neoliberal policies have led to radical concentration of wealth and new prerogatives for the business sector along with stagnation for the majority of the population. Marv gave some information in our last session. It's striking that real wages for nonsupervisory workers today are lower than they were in 1979, right at the outset of the neoliberal assault. There has been economic growth and increase in productivity, but the results went into very few pockets. That continues after the 2008 crisis, the bursting of the housing bubble and the resulting financial crisis.

No less significantly, there has been erosion of workers' rights, beginning with Reagan's strong attack on unions and rights of workers generally. There are almost no union-organized strikes anymore because it's virtually impossible. Reagan, who was unusual in his bitter anti-labor attitudes, even brought in scabs to break up strikes. That was illegal in every industrial country in the world outside of apartheid South Africa, but Reagan introduced it here. Adopting the Reagan precedent, private corporations adopted the same measures, Caterpillar and others. The attack was carried forward under Clinton by different means, including a particular form of "globalization" geared to the interests of investors, ignoring workers—all serving the august principles of "sound economics."

Meanwhile, liberated by the Reagan revolution from any concern for working people and their rights, the business world resurrected earlier ideas about "scientific methods of strike-breaking" and turned openly to bitter class war—important topics that there's no time to pursue now.

One consequence of all of this has been a severe erosion of democracy, an immediate consequence of sharp concentration of wealth and business power. We've discussed some of the means: virtual purchase of elections, radical escalation of lobbying, undermining of voting rights, all facilitated further by the most reactionary Supreme Court in living memory. There is no longer fear of excessive democracy.

There's a lot of fuss, as you know, about alleged Russian meddling in the elections. It is scarcely detectable, but even if it existed on any substantial scale, it would be invisible in comparison with the interference in elections by extreme wealth and corporate power. But these are more things that it wouldn't do to say. Best to worry about the Russians.

One consequence of all of this, also well established in the academic political science literature, is that a considerable majority of the population, those who are lower on the income-wealth scale, are literally disenfranchised. They may cast votes, but it doesn't much matter. They're disenfranchised in the sense that when you compare their preferences and attitudes with the decisions made by their own representatives, there's virtually no correlation. The legislators are listening to other voices. The donor class.

During the neoliberal period, the past generation, both parties shifted pretty far to the right. The Democrats abandoned the working class. They delivered them to their class enemies, who try to mobilize them on what are called cultural issues: white supremacy, fundamentalist religion, and in other ways to which we'll return. And with the promises of decent jobs, which oddly enough are not fulfilled.

An interesting case right now is the Foxconn affair. The State of Wisconsin provided a handsome gift to Foxconn, the manufacturer of your Apple phones and other such devices. Wisconsin taxpayers provided Foxconn with about $250,000 for each promised job, but the jobs aren't coming. It's the lead story in the current issue of the main business journal this week, *Bloomberg Businessweek*. You can find the details there.

We saw all of this dramatically after the collapse of the housing bubble and the resulting financial crisis in 2008. The crisis itself was the result of predatory, sometimes technically criminal activity by the big banks and financial institutions. They were giving subprime mortgages to people who they knew would never be able to pay, but they were able to use complex financial instruments to divide the loans up so that nobody knew what they were buying. They made tons of profit.

Finally, it crashed. There was bailout legislation under first Bush then Obama. The legislation had two elements. One was to bail out the perpetrators, the banks, who had been responsible for the crisis. The other was to give some aid to the victims, the people who were kicked out of their homes because they were foreclosed. You can guess which part of the legislation was implemented.

If you're interested in details, there's an angry book written by Neil Borofsky, inspector general for the Treasury Department, who was outraged by what happened. This is under Obama.

Some of the things that happened are almost too grotesque to believe. There's a huge insurance company, AIG, that was going under. If they had collapsed, Goldman Sachs would probably have collapsed and a whole bunch of others. That couldn't be permitted. So they were bailed out.

And as soon as they were bailed out with a huge taxpayer gift, they immediately paid big bonuses to the executives who were responsible for the disaster. Well, this was discussed. It seemed a little ugly. But economists explained that it's right. Lawrence Summers, one of the most respected liberal economists, pointed out that a contract is a contract. They were promised bonuses; they had to get them. Didn't matter that they practically destroyed the economy with their chicanery and then were bailed out by the taxpayer.

At the very same time, within weeks, the State of Illinois determined that it was not going to pay pensions to workers because it didn't have the money. Somehow, that contract wasn't that sacred, just the other one.

To make it worse, the CEO of AIG (American International Group) later initiated a suit against the government because AIG wasn't allowed to pay big enough bonuses. You just can't describe it.

Well, people didn't know all the details, but the general picture was pretty clear. In particular, the bailout of the banks and the abandonment of the victims. And it had an immediate effect. In 2008, many working people voted for Obama, believing the nice rhetoric about hope and change and so on. Very quickly they saw what the pretty words meant. And there were effects. Massachusetts is the most liberal state in the country. Ted Kennedy, the "liberal lion," died and had to be replaced. There was an election in 2010 in Massachusetts. An unknown right-wing Republican won the election for Kennedy's seat.

A lot of union workers didn't even bother voting. They were so disillusioned by the sellout that they just figured, "This is not for us." They didn't even participate, or even voted for the right wing. Some of them later gravitated to Trump, although you should bear in mind that the talk about a working-class base for Trump is misleading. As one of the most careful researchers, Anthony DiMaggio, has discussed, the Democrats lost the working class far more than Trump won them. Trump's adoring base is mostly petty bourgeois: storekeepers, salesmen, and so on, mostly relatively affluent, and Christian Evangelicals. There's a good deal of academic research on this.

One very interesting development in the neoliberal period is the rise of ALEC, the American Legislative Exchange Council. This is the major business lobby, which draws from a very wide spectrum of the corporate sector: Silicon Valley, energy corporations, many others. They're doing something very intelligent and insidious. They're working at the state level, targeting state legislators.

Now, there are several good reasons for that. State legislation matters; it affects a lot of things that happen in people's lives. And it's pretty much invisible. Almost no one even knows the name of their state representative. What goes on in the state legislature barely gets reported. Also, the legislators are very vulnerable. Elections are largely bought, but it doesn't take much to buy an election for a state legislator. It's not billions of dollars like a president.

So, it's a very easy target. And the way they're doing it is well designed. The same legislative proposals are being made for every state, almost verbatim. A primary goal of course is to weaken labor unions, to undermine the class enemy.

But also they want to restrict voting, they want to bar the wrong people from voting. They know they'll never gain a majority for their policies in any honest election. They want to facilitate environmental degradation. In their own words, they want to "reduce the regulatory burden" on private enterprise, which means harm for the rest of us. They want to ensure what's called donor privacy. That allows floods of dark money to underwrite elections.

They want to privatize the educational system. Arizona was picked as a prime target to see if they could carry this out. It's a pretty natural target, with very low state educational funding, some of the lowest in the country. We'll see how that works out.

There's a lot more, but one very interesting case, very instructive case, is legislative proposals all through the country to prevent penalty for wage theft, even investigation of the crime. The victims are typically the poor and more vulnerable, easy targets who can't react. Wage theft is a huge robbery every year. Billions of dollars a year are stolen from workers by not paying them for overtime or just not paying them their wages. Billions of dollars. So, ALEC wants to make sure that there are no penalties for this and even no investigation.

That's intriguing. It doesn't amount to much for the wealth of the rich and corporate sector, but it illustrates the extreme savagery of class war. You've got to go after everything. You've got to cut everybody's throat. Even if their wages are being stolen, it can't be investigated.

Adam Smith would nod his head in recognition of the practices of the "masters of mankind."

There's an ALEC stealth campaign going on with far broader consequences, not just robbery of the poor and more vulnerable, but strangling what Thorstein Veblen called "the underlying population" generally. They're aiming for a constitutional amendment for a balanced budget. They've already got almost the required number of states signed up to call for an amendment to the Constitution. What does a balanced budget mean? It means you end all social benefits.

If you have a balanced budget, you don't stop funding the military. You don't stop funding border security to protect us from these hordes attacking us. You just cut back the things that matter to the unworthy people. Those whose real income has stagnated or declined through the neoliberal period. ALEC can't come straight out and say, "Look, we want to kill Social Security and health care." You can't win elections that way, but you can do it indirectly. A balanced budget amendment is one way.

In fact, as you'll recall, that was a major point of the main legislative achievement of the Trump administration, the tax bill of 2017, a huge giveaway to the rich and corporate sector, whose profits are escalating while they fail to invest. An important part of the scam was the subtext, presented to us right away by the architects, Mitch McConnell and Paul Ryan, Republican leaders of the Senate and the House. They explained that that tax cut is creating a huge deficit, so we'll have to cut back on "entitlements" down the road. Can't help it. We'd like you to have food and health care and other superfluities, but what can we do?

A constitutional amendment will drive the last nail into that coffin. All of this is happening very quietly. Doesn't get reported, it's very low level. Same with the packing of the federal judiciary and other measures that are being carried out to ensure that whatever electoral outcomes might turn out to be, policies won't be able to change much because a lot will be fixed.

Even now, states with about a quarter of the population, that's about 15 percent of the vote for the winning party, can dominate the Senate, the most powerful part of Congress thanks to the extremely regressive character of the American democratic system going back to the Framers' coup. These 15 percent are largely rural, white, Christian, often fundamentalist, older, with traditional values.

Notice that this can't be changed by amendment. To change it by amendment, you'd have to enlist three-quarters of the states and you're not going to get that. Small states would never permit it. Actually, right now, about 5 percent of the population could, in principle, block a constitutional amendment. And smaller states will certainly be able to block any effort to change the highly regressive character of the election of the Senate or to tamper with the electoral college.

All of this is going to create a major constitutional crisis in the not-too-distant future, because of the way these tendencies are developing.

The neoliberal policies, though they're achieving the goals of concentrating wealth and power and marginalizing the bewildered herd, are harming the general economy. Growth rates have slowed, productivity growth is low. There's a lot of talk about stagnation, meaning that the economy can't really grow anymore.

One of the interesting things that David Kotz points out in the reading for today is that the very sharp concentration of wealth has led to a situation in which there's simply a lack of options for investment.

There are only so many luxury yachts that you can buy, and there's not much profit to be made in producing what the country desperately needs, such as reconstruction of the crumbling infrastructure or ways to remove carbon from the atmosphere.

So, you've got all this mass of accumulated money but you can't invest it with much profit. So what do you do? Turn to financial manipulations, which are generally much more profitable and have been growing enormously. One of the effects is to cut back on research and development.

Take Apple, the biggest corporation. Take a look at their own budget proposals. They're cutting back on research and development. They have less interest in producing something that would be useful. They're turning to the financial markets, which are much more profitable in the short term. And the same is happening across the board.

As we've discussed, much of the R&D, research and development, that created the high-tech economy, came out of the taxpayer's pocket. The guiding principle, in brief, has been public subsidy, private profit. The taxpayer funds the creative and risky R&D, often over a long period, and if something is produced that can be adapted to the market for profit, it's handed over to private power. These are things "it wouldn't do to say," so various subterfuges are used. The easiest is to appeal to "defense": that can't be questioned. So for a long period, US industrial and educational policy—creating the high-tech economy and research universities—was funneled through the Pentagon, just as Eisenhower's interstate highway project was sold to the public as a Defense Highway System, formally, the National System of Interstate and Defense Highways.

Such matters were discussed in the business press in the early postwar period. There was great concern about a return to the Depression, and wide recognition that government stimulus would be needed to avoid it. Analysts pointed out that social spending has the same stimulative effect as military spending. But the business world had reservations about it, preferring military spending, which can be used as a cover for much else. Social spending has harmful side effects. The public doesn't question military spending, or pay attention to the way it is used, but social spending has direct and visible effects on people's lives. It therefore arouses interest and attention, and might even stimulate subversive ideas about participation in decisions about what kind of society and world we should live in. Excessive democracy again. Military spending doesn't have these negative aspects.

From the perspective of business, the public subsidy/private profit system has been advantageous, but raises other problems. If conducted openly, it might engender the belief that your government can actually do something for you and that maybe it should be a government "by the people." That's another reason to prefer the cover of defense, and to concoct tales of evil enemies about to destroy us.

In the longer term, business itself will be harmed by shifting from R&D to financial manipulations. In earlier days, that might have been a concern. But managerial ethic has shifted from the time when viability of the firm was a serious concern to today's focus on gain tomorrow. The long-term prospects for the firm become lesser considerations—or for human society generally.

Nothing could reveal this shift with more brilliant clarity than a matter already discussed: the virtually reflexive decisions to race toward destruction, with eyes open, if it yields short-term gain. Right now profits are spectacular and CEO salaries have skyrocketed to the stratosphere, dragging other managerial rewards with them, while for the general population, real wages stagnate, social spending is meager, unions and other interferences with "sound economics" are dismantled. The best of all possible worlds. So why care if my firm will go under after I've moved to greener pastures, or for that matter, why care if I leave to my grandchildren a world in which they have some chance for decent survival?

Capitalist mentality gone insane.

There is, of course, the usual problem. The rascal multitude. They're not too happy about the undermining of functioning democracy and basic rights. I should add the same is true in Europe. In fact, even more so. The attack on democracy in Europe is even sharper than here. Significant decisions about society and politics are out of the hands of the population. They're made by unelected bureaucrats in Brussels: the IMF, the Central Bank, the European Commission.

All of this, all over the world, is leading to anger, resentment, and bitterness. You see it right now in the Yellow Vest movement in France, but it's everywhere. In election after election, the centrist parties are collapsing. It's happening here, too. Parties happen to be keeping their names in our rigid two-party system, but the centrist elements are losing their grip.

Popular anger is often attributed to xenophobia, and fear that immigrants are destroying our economies and poisoning our culture; sentiments that are real enough. There's a good bit of research on this. What it shows, I think pretty convincingly, is that the basic problem is economic distress and loss of control—concern over stagnation, insecurity, undermining of social welfare policies, along with the lack of any opportunity to participate as democracy declines. All of that opens the door to pathological symptoms—seeking scapegoats, fear, unfocused anger. And these can be exploited by demagogues, often for quite ugly ends. None of this is at all surprising.

Recently, a now very famous economist, Thomas Piketty, along with his colleagues, pointed out that "an economy that fails to deliver growth for half of its people for an entire generation is bound to generate discontent with the *status quo* and a rejection of establishment policies" (Piketty et al. 2017). Pretty obvious. But discontent can take many forms. It doesn't determine which forces will prevail. It's become common these days to quote Gramsci's observation that the old order is collapsing but a new one has not yet risen, and "in the interregnum a great variety of morbid symptoms appear." And encouraging ones as well. To mention just one, today the Green New Deal, initiated by the Sunrise Movement, has been accepted by virtually the whole House of Representatives, something that seemed unimaginable not long ago.

There's plenty of room for will and choice, for active engagement. One thing we can expect with considerable confidence, just looking at history, is that however we're going to find a way out of this mess, it's going to have to be based substantially on a revived, vital labor movement.

Chapter 6

RESISTANCE AND RESPONSE

Waterstone Lecture, February 19, 2019

elcome to the solutions part of the course. Don't get too
excited. I want to emphasize just as in the title, in fact, that
tonight's topic is both resistance *and* response. I want to
make clear that the kinds of things we examine here are really a set of
contests and struggles. I just want to put that theme out very promptly at
the beginning, that is, to think about the kinds of things that we're going
to think about as a constant back and forth.

I'll remind you of a couple of things that I said in the very first week,
when we were talking about common sense, in just a minute. But the
topic is really both resistance *and* response. And by response, I typically
am going to mean the response of those people who are very much interested in preserving the status quo as it is because they're advantaged
by it.

Let's begin by thinking a bit about social movements in general and
then I'm going to speak about some very specific ones in just a little bit,
but let's think about some of the things that these entail. In a very general sense, these entail collective action to resist or to promote change.

So, some social movements clearly are conservative in the sense that they want to keep things as they are. I don't mean that in a partisan, political way necessarily, but some social movements work to maintain things exactly the way they are. Some work to promote change.

Another way to say that, they either work to maintain or to change the status quo. They either reinforce or subvert the prevailing common sense typically (just to keep this in terms that we've been talking about all semester), for either regressive or progressive purposes. Of course, how one defines those things depends on one's point of view and perspectives.

Social movements vary in their scope, whether they're looking simply to resist change, to reform the system in some incremental way, or in some sense to revolutionize things. We talked a little bit about revolution the last time. We'll talk about it a little bit more tonight and next week.

Such movements also range spatially, as you might expect, from the local to the global and sometimes interacting among those scales quite clearly. Their methods vary, for example from the nonviolent to the violent. These are just two polar ends of a spectrum. There are many other spectrums we could think about in terms of methodology. They vary in terms of the targets. Clearly, some organizations and movements, and their activities, target individuals all the way out to society.

Now, I want to make a couple of ties between social movements and capitalism. One of the readings you have for this week, the pieces by Jim O'Connor, make some very clear ties to social movements growing out of a capitalist system. First, he distinguishes two contradictions within capitalism and he makes some connections between those two basic contradictions and the way in which social movements emerge out of them.

The first contradiction. The most basic contradiction in capitalism, something we talked about very early on, is the exploitative relationship between capital and labor in the production process, that is, capital works only because it extracts surplus value in an exploitive relationship with labor, and this is the basic contradiction, at least O'Connor and others identify it. This leads to what are typically called "old social movements." Old in the sense that they have a kind of historical longevity compared to some others that we'll talk about in a second. This contradiction leads to old social movements regarding the conditions of labor.

As O'Connor argues, the contradictions that exist within a set of capitalist social relations in the production process lead to a fundamental antagonism between capital and labor. That antagonism leads to social movements over things like wages, hours, working conditions, and so forth. This set of social movements is very much centered on the class relationship. So, this is class conflict, class warfare, class antagonism.

But then O'Connor talks about a second contradiction of capitalism in which he's moving away a bit from the labor process per se and talks about the way in which capital has a kind of inevitable tendency to destroy its own conditions of production. We've discussed this earlier, for example, when we looked at the relationships between capitalism and the environment.

But when O'Connor's talking about it, he really talks about these three factors: the natural environment; infrastructure, community, and other public goods; and labor power. When he talks about this, he says these are also sometimes reducible or reduced to the categories of land and labor. But again, he's talking about conditions or factors of production that are not provided to capital through the market. These are elements or conditions of production that capital either has typically been unwilling or unable to provide for itself, and so it seeks these through other means. They're typically not provided through the market, although markets can be created to produce them, but these are typically then supplied by the state. One example tied to some things we were talking about last week, the privatization schemes of neoliberalism, things that have typically been public goods, come into the sphere of capital through the production of artificial markets of one kind or another, or through privatization and commodification.

When you think about the environment or you think about infrastructure and community, when you think about reproduction of the labor force through things like education, these are typically conditions of production that are provided by the state. But as these conditions deteriorate, O'Connor is arguing, social movements build up to protect these conditions or to resist adverse changes.

So, we can think about the way in which these things develop in reaction to this set of contradictions, and these are so-called "new social movements." These include the environmental movement operating around deteriorating conditions of the natural environment, urban and civil rights movements, and so forth, around urban decay, urban deterioration, infrastructure destruction, and so forth. Then there are also movements that arise around conditions concerning the reproduction of the labor force. So, feminist movements, other kinds of identity movements, and so forth. These, O'Connor is saying, are outgrowths of this contradiction, or set of contradictions, that capital always produces.

These new social movements go beyond but remain connected to the class connection. They are movements that are not always centrally tied to class but can be immediately tied back to class in the way that O'Connor does this.

Now I want to make this tie very clear to the idea of social movements and common sense. The struggle over common sense and progressive change is continual. There's rarely a final settlement. The contending forces, each convinced of the rightness of their view, are obliged to push back. That is, if you believe that your view of how the world not only is but ought to be, you have the obligation to push that onto other people. But often the terrain in which the contests are waged is changed irretrievably by previous rounds of struggles. The grounds on which contests are waged shift over time.

I would like to expand on the quote from Stuart Hall that I used in the very first week:

> Why then is common sense so important? Because it is the terrain of conceptions and categories on which the practical consciousness of the masses of the people is actually formed. It is the already formed and taken for granted terrain on which more coherent ideologies and philosophies must contend for mastery; the ground which new conceptions of the world must take into account, contest, and transform if they are to shape the conceptions of the world of the masses and in that way become historically effective. Popular beliefs, the culture of a people, Gramsci argues, are not arenas of struggle, which can be left to look after themselves. They are themselves material forces. (Hall 1986)

Social change must contend with this, whether it's for progressive or regressive purposes. It has to deal with things as they are and with things that are so thoroughly integrated into people's worldview, that they are simply taken for granted. Common sense, as I say, is a field of struggle and contestation, and to have one's view of how the world operates become predominant, that is, for it to become the taken-for-granted common sense is a very potent form of political power. This is the connection between common sense and progressive change or regressive change.

All of this basically also speaks to the ways in which we think about the boundaries of discussion. What are the priorities for policy making? What is the practical? What is the overly idealistic and so forth? Many things contribute to our understanding of how this works. Here's one:

Okay. I know this is funny, but it's the way it is.

All right, here are a few clichés. "The longest journey begins with a single step." "No doubt that a small group of thoughtful, committed citizens can change the world. Indeed, it's the only thing that ever has." Margaret Mead. "First they ignore you, then they laugh at you, then they fight you, then you win," Mahatma Gandhi.

Now I want to turn to some examples of social movements. I want to begin with a few historical examples, and then come up to some more contemporary examples in a little bit. The reason to do this is to think about the fact that progress has been made. Every time we think that things don't change for the better, we should keep in mind that there are historical cases where things, in fact, have changed, sometimes for the better. But I also want to leave you with the impression, which I'm hoping to do, that these are struggles that are not completed. The first is the abolition movement, second is the women's movement, and third is the LGBTQ movement.

Let's begin with the abolition movement. Here are a couple of quotes from Jefferson Davis:

> My own convictions as to negro slavery are strong. It has its evils and abuses. We recognize the negro as God and God's Book and God's Laws, in nature, tell us to recognize him, our inferior, fitted expressly for servitude. You cannot transform the negro into anything one-tenth as useful or as good as what slavery enables them to be.
>
> Slavery was established by decree of Almighty God. It is sanctioned in the Bible in both testaments, from Genesis to Revelation. It has existed in all ages. It's been found among the people of the highest civilization and in the nations of the highest proficiency in the arts.

Slavery was formally eliminated in much of the developed world by the 1860s, some places earlier, some places later. In the US and elsewhere, different forms of bondage followed on almost immediately, from chain gangs to Jim Crow to mass incarceration and forced labor.

Now slavery has returned. Current estimates are that there are as many as 40.3 million people enslaved in about 167 countries worldwide. This includes forced marriage, forced labor, trafficking. As you can imagine, these statistics are very, very difficult to get with precision, so this is very likely an undercount.

But the point is that some things have changed, but the struggle continues. Clearly, slavery is not a thing of the past, but some things are fought on different grounds. One could hardly make the kind of arguments that Jefferson Davis was able to make now with any kind of seriousness. But it doesn't mean the problem is solved.

We can see a similar trajectory in the case of the feminist movement:

We should look upon the female state as it were, a deformity, the one that occurs in the ordinary course of nature. —Aristotle

The souls of women are so small, some believe they have none at all. —John Donne

We must not allow ourselves to be deflected by the feminists who are anxious to force us to regard the two sexes as completely equal in position and worth. —Sigmund Freud (This is the uncle of Edward Bernays, by the way.)

The feminist agenda is not about equal rights for women. It is about a socialist, anti-family political movement that encourages women to leave their husbands, kill their children, practice witchcraft, destroy capitalism and become lesbians. —Pat Robertson (in a fundraising letter in 1992)

Since 1920, the vast increase in welfare beneficiaries and the extension of the franchise to women, two constituencies that are notoriously tough for libertarians, have rendered the notion of capitalist democracy into an oxymoron. —Peter Thiel (the developer of PayPal and a number of other Silicon Valley adventures)

Undoubtedly, some substantial gains have been made for women's equality, but here's one way to think about the fact that this is not yet an accomplished task. There is still a significant disparity between men's and women's earnings. At present, women in the US still earn about 79 percent of what men earn for similar work. Some trends seem to suggest that there will be pay equity by 2059. That's the good news. The bad news is that since 2001, women's pay has flattened out a bit, and now pay equity won't be reached until 2152. Sorry for the bad news.

Another way to think about this, other elements of feminism are still under tremendous assault, for example women's control over their own

THE CONSEQUENCES OF CAPITALISM

bodies. Between 2011 and 2016, 334 abortion restrictions were passed by state legislatures in the US. This accounted for fully 30 percent of all abortion restrictions passed since *Roe v. Wade* in 1973.

Again, the point is there are now new forms of feminist struggle, but the contest continues. Again, this is not a battle that's over, even though, on some grounds, we cannot use the same vocabulary that we've used historically, at least not in polite company.

Finally, we can see a similar pattern in LGBTQ+ rights:

> Don't misunderstand. I'm not here bashing people who are homosexuals, who are lesbians, who are bisexual, who are transgender. We need a profound compassion for people who are dealing with the very real issue of sexual dysfunction in their life and sexual identity disorders.
> —Former Minnesota senator then congresswoman then candidate for president, Michelle Bachmann, speaking about homosexuality as a mental disorder in 2004

Undoubtedly, again, substantial gains have been made. Same-sex marriage is now legally recognized nationwide, or in significant parts, in about twenty-six countries. Clearly, some things have changed. The discourse has changed very substantially. But same-sex sexual activity, let alone the protection of relationships, is still illegal in many countries. It's down, from 2006 to 2017, from ninety-two countries to seventy-three. That's a significant change. But still, in many countries, there are very severe punishments up to and including the death penalty. Again, things have changed, but the struggle goes on.

Now I want to turn to a few more contemporary examples, not that those struggles are not, as I say, continuing. But I want to look at a few that are more recent: The Arab Spring, which provided a lot of hope for people in its early stages; the Occupy movement (and I'll draw in some of the work that Kate Crehan did and for which we had a reading tonight; the Black Lives Matter movement; and finally, I just want to say a couple of words about what were the J20 protests, which were protests that took place on the inauguration day of the current president.

The Arab Spring. I'm going to go through this reasonably quickly and highlight some of the principal events and a rough timeline. It began on

December 17, 2010, with a street trader in Tunisia, who set himself on fire in protest against police harassment. About a month later (January 14, 2011), people took to the streets en masse after President Ben Ali's government collapsed. He stepped down and fled the country, which opened the way for Tunisians to elect a new president and adopt a new constitution.

A little bit later in that month (January 25, 2011), in Egypt, the January 25 Revolution mass protest began, centered around Tahrir Square. Some 840 protesters were killed and more than six thousand injured by Egyptian security forces and the thugs who were assisting them.

In Yemen mass protest erupted (February 3, 2011), and months of political turmoil followed, during which the government forces killed hundreds of protesters.

In Egypt, people celebrated in Tahrir Square (February 11, 2011) after Hosni Mubarak stepped down and handed over control to the armed forces.

In Bahrain (which is very important strategically to the US; part of the US Naval Fleet is stationed there) mass protests broke out (February 14, 2011) demanding reform, met by a very heavy-handed clampdown.

In Libya, an uprising against Muammar Gaddafi began (February 17, 2011) at the eastern city of Benghazi; internal conflict followed. Gaddafi is killed in October 2011.

In Syria, mass protests broke out (March 15, 2011), which were brutally suppressed by the government of Assad. Since then, more than 250,000 people have been killed, more than 12 million forced from their homes.

On March 18, 2011, Yemeni protests take to the streets. Fifty people are killed, hundreds injured. The day becomes known as Friday of Dignity.

What has happened since the so-called Arab Spring? Eight years later, human rights are under attack across the region. Hundreds of thousands of people, many of them children, have been killed during armed conflicts that continue to rage in Syria, Libya, and Yemen. The Syrian conflict has created the largest refugee crisis of the twenty-first century, humanitarian crisis.

Tunisia is the only relative success story. It has a new constitution, some justice for past crimes, but human rights are still under attack.

In Egypt, peaceful activists, critics of the government, and many others remain in jail. Torture and other ill treatment are rife. Hundreds have been sentenced to death and tens of thousands put behind bars for protesting or for their alleged links to political opposition. However, we saw that the current president was just authorized to stay in power until 2034.

In Bahrain, the authorities are silencing dissent.

Libya has turned into chaos. There are many armed conflicts all across the country, and all sides have committed war crimes and serious human rights abuses.

In Syria, the region's bloodiest armed conflict emerged in response to the brutal suppression of mass protests by the government. Atrocious crimes are being committed on a massive scale. Half the population has been displaced.

Yemen is an ongoing tragedy, with a Saudi Arabia–led coalition (principally with the United Arab Emirates), but with the US supplying arms, providing refueling and intelligence, and so forth. Here's an interesting Tucson connection. The Emirates just bought $1.6 billion of arms from Raytheon, so the Tucson economy stays strong. The Saudi Arabia–led coalition air strikes and shelling by Houthi forces have killed more than ten thousand civilians, forty thousand wounded. Ten million are now in jeopardy of famine and disease. Some of the attacks amount to war crimes.

The Arab Spring, which started out as an enormously hopeful movement for progressive change, has now largely been subjected to brutal repression and pushback from the forces of the status quo ante. It represents a poignant and tragic example of social struggle.

The next thing I just wanted to say a few things about is the Occupy Wall Street (OWS) movement. I'm also going to say a bit about the Tea Party patriots, a word or two about the Yellow Vest movement in France, and make a few comments about right-wing populism because there's an awful lot of intersection here. Some of the analysis of the OWS movement draws directly on the material we've read in Crehan's book (2016).

The Occupy Wall Street movement might seem a very different movement from the Tea Party, but it too can be seen as having, at its heart, a reconfiguration of certain strands of American common sense. A good example is the "It's Morning in America" rhetoric of Reagan's first presidential campaign. Drawing on a very imagined idyllic past, this emotionally persuasive rhetoric conjured up a vision of unfettered capitalism and a new coming of that lost golden land in which all prospered. I'll leave it to you to make the leap to "Make America Great Again." It's a very tiny leap. It's not even a chasm.

In content, the story of Occupy Wall Street is very different from that of the Tea Party, but it too can be seen as a response to the widespread feeling that America has taken a wrong turn somewhere. This is also true, I would suggest, of many of the movements that are occurring in Europe, in Latin America, and elsewhere, that is, there's a sense that the center is not holding and not serving people very well. This neoliberal period that we talked about last week has produced enormous dislocation for many, many people, and there are very different ways of interpreting how that has come about.

Millions of Americans share the sense that they're losing control of their lives. This is one of the bases on which I think it's fair to make a comparison between the Sanders campaign and the Trump campaign. That is, they had very different diagnoses of the problems, and certainly very different remedies. But the problems that they were raising and addressing stem from very similar kinds of dislocation of the population.

As Crehan articulates, it is "much easier to refurbish an old capitalist narrative so it speaks to the fears and resentments of 21st century Americans than it is to develop a new narrative" (2016). This refers to the Tea Party, which was able to resuscitate this capitalist narrative, and Occupy, which is up against this, which is something quite different.

The racialized Tea Party (and I would suggest these right-wing "populist" movements, "populism," of course, in quotes, these populist movements around the globe) narrative is a country run by a profligate government that is slipping away from those with rightful claims and into the hands of freeloaders happy to depend on welfare handouts. This is the interpretation that the Tea Party makes, and I would say it's the interpretation that the Trump administration makes to a very large extent.

This is what's gone wrong with the country. People have cut in line in front of the deserving citizenry.

On the other hand, the Occupy Wall Street (and I would say the Yellow Vest movement, which has been largely misinterpreted; I'll say a little bit more about that probably next time) critique is that the decline of the middle class is not due to government handouts to undeserving moochers, but to the wealthiest taking more than their fair share.

One of the achievements of OWS was to create a space where these alternative strands of common sense were able to emerge with a new potency, a new power. "The task of progressives is made all the harder," again this is part of Crehan's comparison between Tea Party and OWS, "when those who would question the existing hegemony lack the roving billionaire advocates and right-wing media purveyors that propelled the rise of the Tea Party" (2016). The Tea Party, for those of you who are familiar with its origins and development, was mostly bankrolled by very, very wealthy backers, so people like Dick Armey, the Koch brothers, a whole number of people, produced it as what looked like a grassroots organization, but it was largely an AstroTurf organization.

"What does Occupy Wall Street look like if it's approached as one aspect of a cultural battle to transform the popular mentality," that is, the popular common sense? "It did succeed, and there seems to be very widespread agreement on this, in forcing inequality to the forefront of the political debate in the United States" (Crehan 2016). Prior to Occupy Wall Street, even in the wake of the 2008 financial crash, there was very little attention to the stark issue of inequality.

"The Occupy Wall Street slogan, 'We are the 99%', seemed to do no more than express an obvious truth. There was something profoundly wrong with the ever-growing gulf between the rich, 1%, and the rest of Americans, the 99%. This gulf is evidence that something has gone terribly wrong with the American system itself. The slogan seemed to encompass the many different ways that profound inequality manifests itself in the contemporary United States. The elephant in the room had been named" (Crehan 2016). Or, as somebody I heard at a conference once say, this opened up a whole new box of Pandoras.

We could say, as many commentators have observed, that Occupy Wall Street changed the conversation. Approached from this perspective, OWS can be seen as a particular aspect of the long war of position Gramsci saw as an essential element in any struggle for transformation, that is, you have get these issues at least on the agenda so people would begin to think about them.

For example, in a December 2011 speech, and I highlight that because I'm going to come back to this date in a minute, Obama stated, "I believe, this country succeeds when everyone gets a fair shot, when everyone does their fair share, and when everyone plays by the same rules. Those aren't Democratic or Republican values; 1% values or 99% values. They're American values, and we have to reclaim them."

Now he does something interesting here rhetorically, which Crehan points out, which is that, "one cannot but admire the skillful way Obama here simultaneously embraces, 'We are the 99%,' and defangs its recognition of a fundamental opposition between the 1% and the 99%" (2016). When he says these are not 1% values or 99%, they're everybody, but they're really not everybody's. They are also, emphatically, not everybody's rules. There is, in fact, an enormous gulf between the 99% and the 1%, which was OWS's main point.

"Political narratives that resonate with the common sense," this is something we've talked about all along, "are a crucial part of any effective oppositional political movement. The occupation of Zuccotti Park and the hundreds of other occupations across the country may have lacked political coherence, which was quite deliberate, and may, for all their energy and enthusiasm, *have soon flamed out*" (Crehan 2016). I'm highlighting that because I'm going to come back to this passive construction in a minute. It (OWS) just disappeared under its own incoherence.

> But maybe they, nonetheless, represent the genuine beginning of such narrative, that is starting a new conversation. Any political narrative that runs against the grain of the prevailing hegemony [which OWS certainly did] faces the problem that hegemony does not just refer to a set of ideas, it is woven into the very fabric of the institutions and practices of everyday life. This is what a change in the common sense is always up against. It is hard for an embryonic conception of the world

that genuinely challenges the existing hegemony to find the space to develop. (Crehan 2016)

Then I would just refer you back to that quote by Stuart Hall. This is what's always in play.

"In the aftermath, we can say that while OWS *did not threaten capitalism in any serious way*," and again I'm highlighting this because I'm going to come back and tear that apart, "it did perhaps, as Republican pollster Frank Luntz feared, have 'an impact on what American people think of capitalism'" (Crehan 2016). That, of course, is not a discussion that can be opened up.

I want to think a bit now about what kind of impact OWS actually did have. If it did not threaten capitalism in any way, what were the reactions to it? Let's take a look at a few of these in a chronological series.

First is a November 22, 2011, story headlined "The FBI Claims It Does Not Have Any Documents on Occupy Wall Street." This is the non-threat, remember? This is the thing that did not threaten capitalism.

Next there's this smirky little article in *Forbes* on November 26, 2011, by Erik Kain, "No, the Crackdown Against Occupy Wall Street is Not the Work of the Shadowy Elite." Subhead: "Police action against Occupy Wall Street protesters has been over the top, but that doesn't mean the government and economic elites are coordinating the crackdown."

Then, about one year later, the Partnership for Civil Justice obtained redacted documents showing that FBI offices and agents around the country were in high gear conducting surveillance against the movement, even as early as August 2011. You should note that this is several months before Obama made his statements, saying we're all in this together. He probably didn't know what the FBI was doing. I'm pretty sure that's the case. Also, this a month prior to the establishment of the OWS encampment in Zuccotti Park and other Occupy actions around the country. This was before things even happened. I'll come back to that in a minute.

"This production, which we believe is just the tip of the iceberg, is a window into the nationwide scope of the FBI's surveillance, monitoring, and reporting on peaceful protests organizing within the Occupy movement." This is from the Partnership for Civil Justice report. "These documents show that the FBI and the Department of Homeland Security are treating protests against the corporate and banking structure of America as potential criminal and terrorist activity." The word "terrorism" or "terrorist" keeps coming up again and again in ways that I will describe. "These documents also show these federal agencies were functioning as a de facto intelligence arm of Wall Street and Corporate America" (see "FBI Documents Reveal Secret Nationwide Occupy Monitoring").

Then we learn a bit more from this article, about a year later, June 27, 2013, by Todd Gitlin in *Mother Jones*, "What the Occupy Wall Street Crackdown Can Teach Us About NSA Spying." The original location for the protests was not going to be Zuccotti Park. But when the Occupy Wall Street people arrived at their intended location, it was already blocked off. What Gitlin is talking about in this article is two things. One is the surveillance, which these documents demonstrated was beginning to occur as early as July or August of 2011, months before the occupation, but also the infiltration of the Occupy movement. These are activities with which the FBI and other elements of the security state have a very long and nefarious history. The most notorious of these was the COINTELPRO program, which we've talked about a little bit, which infiltrated the civil rights movement and antiwar movements. Again, those are tactics that are still being used by the FBI and instigated a number of problems that will come up in just a minute.

Let me turn now to the Black Lives Matter (BLM) movement, which is clearly an ongoing struggle to reconfigure the so-called criminal justice system. Much as the OWS movement opened up some areas for dialogue that have really not been on the agenda, so has BLM. Black Lives Matter started with the killing of Michael Brown in August of 2014. But there have been an enormous number of well-publicized (not to mention non-publicized) murders of African American men since then.

It is quite clear that this is an ongoing set of issues, as the list grows continuously. But I'm very interested in the way in which the state and elites have responded to this movement. One of the responses, the state response, the elite response, is that the FBI now has a new category of concern: black identity extremists. It was first described in a document dated August 3, 2017, entitled "Black Identity Extremists, Likely Motivated to Target Law Enforcement Officers." The cover also indicates that the document is unclassified, for official use only, and is law enforcement–sensitive information. It is clearly aimed at criminalizing what should be protected behavior. These are some key quotes from the report. Keep in mind that this is elite response to popular resistance.

"The FBI assesses it is very likely black identity extremist perception of police brutality against African Americans spurred an increase in premeditated, retaliatory lethal violence against law enforcement"—there's no evidence for this, by the way, whatsoever; the statistics do not support an increase in police-directed violence—"and will very likely serve as justification for such violence."

"The FBI assesses it is very likely incidents of alleged police abuse against African Americans since then have continued to feed the resurgence in ideologically motivated, violent criminal activity within the BIE [Black identity extremist] movement." There is a category that was just invented. It's already a movement. I mean this is extraordinarily quick, even for the FBI.

Even though the report mentions in a footnote that "political activism and strong rhetoric by themselves don't amount to extremism and may be constitutionally protected" (and I emphasize here the use of the phrase "may be"), "it identifies anger with police or anti-white rhetoric as indicators of a potential violent threat." You can imagine how this kind of rhetoric is mobilized in law enforcement. It doesn't take much imagination.

"The FBI says there are nine persistent extremist movements in the United States at present. These include white supremacy, black identities, militia, sovereign citizens, anarchists, abortion, animal rights, environmental rights, and Puerto Rican Nationalism." These are the things that the FBI thinks of as constituting terrorist threats.

I want to turn now to the J20 protests (named in reference to the January 20, 2017, date of Trump's inauguration), because these are also extremely interesting and troubling indicators of how elites are responding to legitimate resistance through tactics of criminalization and intimidation.

This narrative should frighten anyone who's concerned about the future of both free assembly and dissent in the US. In this activity, police swept up over two hundred protesters, journalists, legal observers. Police used the tactic of kettling, in which they use some kind of confining material like netting to force people into confined areas and then arrest them en masse. That's what happened here.

The charges included felony rioting, inciting or urging others to riot, conspiracy to riot, and property destruction. Allegedly, about $100,000 of property damage occurred during this set of events. The charges all stem from the same mass arrest. What made the charges all the more troubling was that prosecutors then failed to allege that the bulk of defendants did anything specifically unlawful. This is what becomes particularly troubling about this case. Rather, merely being at the protest itself was a crime, that is they didn't find specific evidence of anybody particularly doing anything, but just being there now has turned into a crime.

Felony rioting carries a penalty of up to ten years in prison and a $25,000 fine. These were not insignificant charges. Prosecutors very quickly did what prosecutors are now being accused of in many, many instances. They're overcharging. They just pile charges on. As a side note, but very significant, prosecutors have the most discretion of anyone in the entire criminal justice system. They can determine whether someone should be arrested, charged, what they should be charged with, whether to go to court, whether to plead it out, and so on. Prosecutors have enormous discretion. In this case, as in many others, they started piling charges on.

The grand jury, secret grand jury, returned a superseding indictment that added inciting or urging to riot and conspiracy to riot to the list of crimes, turning what would, in many cases, have been misdemeanors into potential felonies. The new charges brought the number of felony counts up from one to eight for each person, and the amount of time defendants faced from ten years to more than seventy years in prison.

The Department of Justice requested that the web host provider DreamHost share all of the information associated with its customers who utilized the disruptj20.org website. To comply, this would have meant that they needed to turn over the 1.3 million IP addresses of those who visited the disruptj20.org site, a move that would have amounted essentially to a list of individuals potentially politically opposed to Trump. The DOJ subsequently modified this request. They didn't withdraw it, but they modified it. Similarly, the DOJ issued a warrant, subsequently dropped, against Facebook that would have required the company to turn over the names of all six thousand people who liked the disruptj20.org page.

All of these things finally worked their way into court. In December 2017, the first six defendants were found not guilty. This made the prosecution rethink the case a bit, but not drop it. Finally, in January 2018, the DOJ dropped charges against 129 defendants. Fifty-nine defendants still, at that point, faced charges. Twenty-one of them eventually did accept plea deals and pled to misdemeanors. In July of 2018, the DOJ dropped the charges against the remaining thirty-eight defendants.

In essence, the prosecutors were unable to get any convictions when anyone went before a jury. Eventually, the Department of Justice realized that they had overreached and withdrew the case. Though DOJ lost on many of the specifics, the chilling effects of these prosecutions cannot be overstated.

The DOJ prosecutors also learned a few lessons from this case. One of the most recent manifestations of those lessons is a bill, H.R. 6054, "The Unmasking Antifa Act of 2018" that was introduced in the last Congress. You can tell by the title it has a fairly specific intent, quite literally unmasking Antifa (that is, the antifascist group). The act now makes it a crime, and includes a prison sentence of up to fifteen years, for anyone who injures, oppresses, threatens, or intimidates any person while wearing a mask or disguise, a bill that telegraphs the government's future attempts to prosecute the masked protesters they failed to criminalize in the J20 trial.

The tie to the J20 prosecution is that this was one of the grounds for acquittals that the jury used. When they were presented with the case, they couldn't identify specific people because many of them, in fact, were masked. This will unmask those people and make them available for prosecution.

Let me use that example to continue a discussion about the future of protest, which is, in fact, being criminalized. This is the resistance part and the response part. Resistance is rising all over the place. If you are elites and want to preserve the advantages that the status quo provides, how do you deal with that? Well, one way is to make that resistance illegal.

As of January 19, 2017, Republican lawmakers in five states had proposed bills to criminalize peaceful protest. Just four days later, that number increased to ten states. Our old friend ALEC (the American Legislative Exchange Council) is behind many of these bills. They have model legislation on how to criminalize protests, including many laws that involve so-called critical infrastructure, by which they typically mean oil and gas pipelines.

At this point ten states have enacted anti-protest legislation, and thirty-five additional states have considered it. Some bills have been defeated and some are pending. But, typically, this is the way ALEC operates. They bring legislators in for workshop/conference sessions, they send them home with model bills that they've already voted on, the legislators bring these back to their own legislature, and this begins to sweep the country.

In some states, nonviolent demonstrating may soon carry increased legal risks, including punishing fines and significant prison terms. Sometimes these are simply put on the books as chilling measures. If people know they're facing horrific kinds of penalties, the likelihood that they may come out for a protest, even a very peaceful and legal protest, is enormously discouraged, so the new legislation often includes punishing fines, significant prison terms for people who participate in protests involving civil disobedience.

The proposals, which strengthen or supplement existing laws addressing blocking or obstructing traffic, come in response to a string of high-profile highway closures and other actions that have been led by groups like Black Lives Matter and opponents of the Dakota Access Pipeline. In North Dakota, for instance, Republicans introduced a bill in 2017 that would allow motorists to run over and kill any protester obstructing a highway as long as a driver did it accidentally. It didn't pass, but it will come back. A Minnesota bill introduced by Republicans in 2018 seeks to dramatically stiffen fines for freeway protests. It would allow prosecutors to seek a full year of jail time for protesters blocking the highway. You can imagine as these penalties are rolled out, the effect on even legal and peaceful protest is severely dampened.

Republicans in Washington State have proposed a plan to reclassify as a felony civil disobedience protests that are deemed economic "terrorism." As you might imagine, this is a very flexible term. These kinds of charges have been lodged against animal rights activists, environmental activists, and so forth. This is part of what's going on.

North Dakota now, in February of 2019, seeks to restrict access to public records after Standing Rock reporting exposed law enforcement abuses. Through Freedom of Information Act requests, people got access to law enforcement records that demonstrated the ways in which the police, the National Guard, military, Homeland Security, were mobilized to very strenuously and significantly repress these protests even when they were legal and justified. This is, again, another way to cut off the possibility of protesting in this case by simply restricting access to information.

This set of activities is not just happening in the US. We see a similar reaction to the Yellow Vest movement in France. I think this movement has been largely misinterpreted. It arose as a reaction to a tax on gasoline. It was immediately portrayed as a protest against taking any action on climate change, which is not at all what the protesters were about, and their slogan actually demonstrates this. "Rich people are worried about the end of the world. We're basically worried about the end of the month." These are people, working-class people, who really are having a very difficult time making ends meet, and are protesting either the delinquent actions of the government or the positive actions of the government that are repressing them further.

But in reaction, just as in the US, the reaction is not to remedy the situation, or even to open up the avenues for dissent, but rather to close them down. This is building on an already declared state of emergency that now has gone on for quite a long time in France; the Yellow Vest protests are in about their third month. But now police prefects will be able to ban any individual from attending a public protest for a month. All that's required is that the government believes serious reasons exist to think that their behavior constitutes a particularly grave threat to public order. Anyone banned in that way will be added to a government watch list, of course.

Interior and justice ministers will be authorized to put in place "automated monitoring of personal information in order to ensure surveillance." These are people who are rather arbitrarily designated as a threat to public order. They become listed and surveilled. Police officers will be powered on the say-so of the state prosecutor to search bags and cars of anyone at a protest or its immediate surroundings. This codifies into law an existing practice.

It will now be an offense to conceal (and this is back to the Antifa unmasking law) voluntarily, totally or partially, one's face in order not to be identified in such circumstances as would provide fears of a threat to public order. Wearing a mask at a protest was already punishable with a €1,500 fine, but its upper limit will now be increased to a €15,000 fine and a year in prison. Again, you can see the chilling effect this might produce.

In conclusion, let me draw a few lessons from these cases. As the response from the state and elites moves more to the coercion end of the spectrum, I would suggest this is a sign of failing legitimacy. Remember, we talked about this continuum from coercion to hegemony, where hegemony is really consent of the governed. This move to the coercive is, I think, an indication that legitimacy is failing. Once it slips away, the governed may be inclined to withdraw their consent, that is they may not be so happy with the governance structure, which may, in turn, lead to ever-greater resistance.

The question then is the one that I ended up with last Tuesday, will this resistance lead to a responsive change or to greater brutality? If, as we have been arguing, capitalism is at the root of many of these problems, will we move toward socialism, or something like it, or move away even more deeply into the current system, toward a more brutal barbarism?

Many people will recall the incident in November 2011 from UC Davis that went viral. This was a very peaceful Occupy Wall Street protest at UC Davis. A UC Davis police officer just went along the line of seated protesters continually spraying them with pepper spray. It was very traumatic, I mean really traumatic, especially for Officer Pike, who got a $38,000 settlement for emotional distress. The students eventually received a collective million-dollar settlement, about $30,000 per student. But you can see in this incident, not only the ability, but the willingness to use this extreme kind of coercion under the right circumstances when elites and their representatives in the state feel threatened.

I'm just going to stop with this and then talk about this more next time. But it is clear that elites are starting to feel some pressure from below. The bumbling herd, as Noam has talked about it, are starting to assert themselves a little too much.

Chomsky Lecture, February 21, 2019

Our topic this week is resistance and the reaction to resistance. Marv mentioned a long list of examples of resistance activities. I'd like to take a look at several of them a little more closely. It's instructive to see what works, what fails, what the reasons are, what we can learn from these experiences.

In the sixties there was a major revival of activism. That was after a quiescent period through the fifties. Activism was then at a very low level. That was in part because of the Cold War hysteria that demonized any form of protest, but in part it was just because, as we discussed earlier, it was a period of substantial economic growth within the framework of "regulated capitalism." Economists often call it the "Golden Age." In Europe, the same period, the period of recovery from wartime damage and then proceeding beyond, is called the *trentes glorieuses*, the "thirty glorious [years]." Growth was high and was egalitarian; the lowest and highest quintiles had about the same growth rates. There were prospects for a better life after the Great Depression and the war. So there was a sense of relief that we can go on with our lives and put the problems of the world aside. For a while at least.

Activism revived in the early sixties, building on earlier foundations, taking new and innovative forms. A fair question is what it achieved. The general elite assessment is largely negative. The sixties was the "time of troubles," caused in part by failures of the institutions responsible for the "indoctrination of the young." One way to evaluate this judgment—and more significantly, to evaluate the actual impact of the activism that took off in the sixties and then expanded—is to look at what the country was like in the sixties and how it has changed. Not thanks to gifts from enlightened leaders but from popular struggle.

As late as the 1960s, as noted earlier, the United States had severe anti-miscegenation laws. When the Nazis were looking for a model for their racist Nuremberg laws, the only one they could find was the American one. But they couldn't fully accept the American laws because they were too harsh. The American laws were based on the principle of "One Drop of Blood." So if any remote ancestor was black, you're black. That was too extreme for Hitler and Goebbels. These laws lasted in the US until the 1960s.

So did vicious racism. One case that became known thanks to the courage of the victim's mother is the brutal murder of Emmett Till in 1955. He was a fourteen-year-old boy from Chicago who was visiting relatives in the South. He was accused of having spoken the wrong way to a white woman. She later recanted and said it wasn't true. A few days after this alleged event, he was picked up by a couple of relatives of the woman's and viciously tortured, his eyes gouged out. Then murdered. His body was so mutilated that they could barely identify him. When the murderers, who were at once identified, were put on trial, they were quickly released on the grounds that the body couldn't be identified. An all-white jury of course. Well, this case became known only because his mother didn't drop it—an act of unusual courage under the circumstances—and a black newspaper picked it up. Finally, it became known. Which was unusual.

The racism was backed by law. That's important to remember. Under New Deal legislation, during the 1950s pleasant suburban communities were developed with public funding, the Levittowns and others. By law they were restricted to "the Caucasian race." That went on until the late 1960s. Even liberals supported the racist legislation, for very good reasons. There was no other way to get public housing passed. Congress would not pass the laws unless the funding was restricted to whites. The reason was that the Democratic Party was a strange coalition of Southern Democrats and northern working class and professionals. The Southern Democrats had enormous power because they were elected over and over, and with their seniority were able to control committees. To get New Deal legislation passed in the 1930s, it had to be racist. So, for example, Social Security was designed to exclude the professions in which the workers were mostly black or Hispanic. Agricultural work and domestic employment were excluded. There was no other way to get Social Security passed. Same with public housing.

All of that had a lasting impact. In the 1950s, almost for the first time since slaves were brought to the colonies, there were substantial opportunities for black people to get decent jobs. Black men could get a job in an auto plant, make a little money, buy a house, and so on. But they couldn't get houses under the federal system because that was blocked. That's important. In the United States, the main source of wealth is housing. So they were blocked from building up some limited wealth. By the seventies, after the racist laws were overturned, it was possible for African Americans to move into Levittowns and other middle-class housing. It was, however. too late. That's when the neoliberal regime was imposed. Jobs declined, stagnation set in. There's a lasting effect of the deeply rooted racism that traces back to the hideous crimes of slavery. One consequence is that the total wealth of black families averages around $5,000, virtually nothing. It's a fraction of the wealth of white families. So these segregated housing laws, and their much deeper roots, had long-term effects.

Well, take another category, women. As discussed earlier, when the country was established, it took over British law, under which women were property. That persisted for a long time, until 1975, when the Supreme Court determined that women were peers with a legal right to serve on federal juries.

In the sixties, the fate of Native Americans was barely recognized. Even leading anthropologists vastly underestimated not only the scale of the pre-contact population but also the nature of their rich and complex civilizations—though the colonists knew better from direct experience. That changed a great deal thanks to the activism of the sixties and its aftermath. Not enough, but the civilizing impact of activism was again substantial.

Another crucial fact was that aggression and subversion were not only acceptable but admirable. We've discussed a number of cases, which were not exceptions but rather the norm, and which reverberate to the present: the CIA overthrow of the parliamentary regimes in Iran and Guatemala in the early fifties, among others.

A very crucial example from the early postwar years is the US intervention in Vietnam. As discussed earlier, the US was, in general, opposed to allowing imperial preference systems in the liberal international order it sought to establish. In the early postwar years, it was ambivalent about how to deal with these systems. In principle, they were to be dismantled, but in the short term the reconstruction of the industrial systems of Western Europe within the US global system required access to the resources and raw materials of the colonies. Another question for policymakers was how the colonies might act after independence. Would they become "viruses" that might "spread contagion," or would they be easily incorporated within the US global system? Policies varied depending on assessment of these factors.

Vietnam was one of the cases of ambivalence. The Ho Chi Minh government sought friendly relations with the US. Its constitution was modeled on the US Constitution. The ambivalence ended in 1949 with "the loss of China." The US at once decided to support the French effort to reconquer their former colony so that nothing else would be "lost." There were powerful motives, discussed earlier.

The US intervention was substantial. Eighty percent of French arms were coming from the United States. Finally, France capitulated. There was an international conference at Geneva in 1954, which arranged a settlement. As we now know from internal documents, the

US government regarded that as a "disaster" and intervened directly to block it.

In violation of the Geneva Accords, the US imposed the Diem government in the South and refused to allow the planned elections to unify the country, which Washington took for granted that Ho would easily win. The Diem dictatorship instituted harsh repression, killing perhaps sixty to seventy thousand people through the fifties, finally eliciting resistance. North Vietnam at first discouraged resistance, still hoping to maintain the political settlement and to reconstruct from the French-US war. The program of the southern resistance, the National Liberation Front (in US propaganda, the Viet Cong), called for neutralization of South Vietnam, Laos, and Cambodia. Resistance became strong enough so that the Diem regime couldn't control it. When Kennedy came into office, he immediately escalated the war in ways we discussed. There was scarcely any reporting about any of this, even the direct bombing of South Vietnam by the US Air Force—under South Vietnamese markings, but that fooled no one. I recall learning about this from a brief item on an inside page of the *New York Times*. But the resistance was resilient and in fact seemed poised to take over the South. President Johnson came into office and sharply escalated the war.

There is a widespread belief that Kennedy was planning to withdraw US troops and that Johnson abandoned the plans in favor of escalation. There's no time to go into the matter here—I have done so in detail elsewhere—but it is a myth, based on misreading of internal documents and misunderstanding of the facts on the ground. To his last days, Kennedy was at the hawkish end of the spectrum, insisting that US troops could only be withdrawn "after victory."

By the early sixties, some protest began. It was very scattered. I was giving talks literally in someone's living room or in a church with half a dozen people. And there were some broader protests, but it was not easy.

Just to illustrate what the attitude was like, well into the sixties, take Boston, where I was living, maybe the most liberal city in the country. An international day of protest was scheduled for October 1965. The local antiwar groups participated with a march from Harvard Square to the Boston Common, the usual place for demonstrations and protest. I was supposed to be one of the speakers. The meeting was broken up by protesters, many of them students. Speakers were protected by state police, who may have hated us but didn't want to see bloodshed on the Boston Common. The events were major front-page news the next day in the *Boston Globe*, a serious newspaper then, perhaps the most liberal in the country. The news reports and opinion pieces were outraged—at the protesters, not the patriotic actions to prevent any protest.

That was the first international day of protest.

There was a second international day of protest in March 1966. We realized that it wouldn't be possible to have a public meeting, so we decided to meet in a church, the Arlington Street Church. The church was attacked, lots of police to prevent a break-in to the church, but tomatoes, cans, and so on. That was early 1966.

Right about then the respected military historian and Vietnam specialist Bernard Fall—no dove, highly respected even by the Pentagon—forecast that "Vietnam as a cultural and historic entity . . . is threatened with extinction . . . [as] . . . the countryside literally dies under the blows of the largest military machine ever unleashed on an area of this size" (Fall 1967).

A little after that, a mass movement did finally develop and reached an impressive scale, moving from protest to resistance, including courageous refusal of young men to serve in a criminal war.

In January 1968, there was a huge uprising in South Vietnam, one of the most amazing in history. The country was saturated with over half a million American troops. The Saigon army added another seven to eight hundred thousand. There were informers everywhere. Every village was penetrated. Nevertheless, Washington and the Saigon government were taken completely by surprise. What that indicates is that the degree of support for the South Vietnamese resistance must have been pretty remarkable. Elite circles drew a different lesson: that the promise that victory was in sight was not going to be fulfilled.

President Johnson considered sending several hundred thousand more troops to South Vietnam, but the top military command objected.

They said that if the war was escalated further, they would need the troops for civil disorder control in the United States. Young people, women, others would be protesting in the streets. The impact of the popular movement against the war was quite serious. One of the revelations of the *Pentagon Papers*.

By then, mass movements had taken off in many areas: the civil rights movement, the antiwar movement, the germs of others, like the feminist and environmental movements that truly took off in later years.

Let's take a look at the first of the sixties movements, the civil rights movement, which of course has a long and brutal history that goes back to the slaves who were brought four hundred years ago with the first settlers. What followed is a hideous story, some of it just coming to light in recent scholarship by Edward Baptist, Sven Beckert, and others, who have also brought out the enormous contribution of the slave labor camps in the South to the wealth and development of the United States and also England. Cotton was rather like oil today, it was the fuel of the first industrial revolution: manufacturing, finance, commerce, retail, right through the nineteenth century.

Slavery formally ended in the 1860s. The Civil War was followed by the decade of Reconstruction, in which black people actually had an opportunity to enter into mainstream American life, to work and get elected to office and so on.

The Freedman's Bureau, established by President Lincoln as a branch of the War Department shortly before his assassination, sent thousands of agents to the South to protect the newly freed slaves and also to ensure their welfare, with quite extensive programs. The great African American scholar and activist W. E. B. Du Bois described it as the "most extraordinary and far-reaching institution of social uplift that America has ever attempted." But not for long. Vicious atrocities against freed slaves continued, becoming a shameful plague after federal troops were withdrawn, and the Bureau was closed in the 1877 North-South compromise to settle the presidential election. Southerners were then free to do whatever they wanted—in effect, to restore slavery. One of the major books on the topic, by Douglas Blackmon—*Wall Street Journal*

Atlanta bureau chief—is simply called *Slavery by Another Name*. Black life was effectively criminalized. If a black man was standing on a corner, he could be accused of vagrancy and fined. Since of course he couldn't pay it, he'd go to jail and then be lost in the criminal justice system. If he was charged with looking at a white woman, he could be accused of attempted rape and then be in real trouble. Meanwhile, the savagery of the slave system reappeared in other forms.

Soon the whole system was pretty much back to where it was, restoring slavery. And providing a perfect workforce for private enterprise: no rights, no protests, harsh conditions, and no need to waste money on maintaining the workforce. The state took care of that. The part that's familiar is what was visible, the chain gangs. But in reality, this convenient system provided a large part of the workforce for the second Industrial Revolution from the late nineteenth century, with a residue almost to World War II.

The South was the scene of horrible atrocities: massacres, torture, lynchings that went on into the 1950s. There was constant courageous resistance by the victims, but it was crushed, brutally.

There were some gains over the years, sometimes by working-class struggle that brought about interracial solidarity. But the record remained awful.

By the 1950s there were some steps forward, but it was pretty shocking to see how they were achieved. Many of you may remember the picture of federal troops sent to accompany a little girl who was walking to a formerly segregated school, facing jeering, furious crowds screaming at her, eager to kill her. That was 1950s America.

There were several turning points. One was in 1960, in Greensboro, North Carolina. Four black students decided to sit-in at the segregated lunch counter in Woolworth's. They were arrested for the crime, which could have ended it, except that others came back. Pretty soon it spread to other colleges. Shortly after that, SNCC, the Student Nonviolent Coordinating Committee, was formed, becoming the spearhead of the civil rights movement on the ground. Young people, mostly black, but they were joined by some whites. They became "freedom riders," traveling to rural areas to encourage black farmers to be willing to vote—which was extremely dangerous and hazardous in the culture of barbarous racism. Hazardous to the activists, as well. A number of them were murdered.

One place that became a center of the civil rights movement was Spelman College in Atlanta, a college for black girls, who were also taught to be ladies. They were taught decorum, the way to act and what clothes to wear and so on. I should add that these practices were not restricted to black colleges. At the Ivy League university I attended in the 1940s, there were obligatory "orientation courses" for freshmen girls where they learned how to serve tea properly and other such necessities of civilized life, and the elite universities had similar ways of socializing young gentlemen (women were barred). Another feature of American life that was swept away by sixties activism.

At Spelman, a problem arose. Some of the students began to become active in the growing civil rights movement. Worse, they had some (very limited) faculty support, notably a guy named Howard Zinn who was teaching there. Zinn (an old friend) supported the students, including some who became quite prominent in later years, like Alice Walker and Marian Wright Edelman.

He was duly fired in 1963 on faked charges. Staughton Lynd, a radical historian who was also teaching there, resigned in protest. But it was too late to stop the wave. By then it had really developed, under the leadership of Martin Luther King, a truly historic figure. In 1963 King led an enormous demonstration in Washington, a major step toward the Civil Rights Act of 1964 enacted under the vigorous leadership of President Johnson. That was the main official achievement of the civil rights movement. Official achievement; no less significant was its impact on the general culture. A few years later came the termination of the racist laws I mentioned before. But racist brutality persisted, and still does.

After the 1964 Civil Rights Act, protests and demonstrations continued. One of the major ones was in Jackson, Mississippi. A quick look at the situation then and now tells us something more about the impact of popular struggles.

Howard Zinn and I went down to take part in the demonstration and also to provide some support for the mostly young black and white demonstrators. When you wear a tie and jacket and you're white, you have some extra space—though often not too much. State police were brutally beating demonstrators. There were federal marshals sent to observe and in principle to enforce the law. According to credible reports by demonstrators, they were standing on the steps of the federal building and if demonstrators tried to flee from the police to the federal building, the marshals would throw them back into the crowd.

When the demonstrations wound down, Howard and I were able to visit a jail—anointing ourselves a delegation of New England professors. The police chief took us through the jail. By the standards of jails—I've seen quite a few—it wasn't that bad. The prisoners were all black. As we were walking down one hall, passing a cell with about fifty or sixty black men, a little kid, maybe ten years old, tapped on the bars. I walked over and he asked me if I could get him a cup of water. I asked the police chief, who said OK, and I was able to do it. When we got back to the chief's office afterward, we asked what that little kid was doing in the cell with all those men. He asked a secretary to look it up. It turned out that they'd found him in the streets and they didn't know who he was. So they put him in jail, to spend the rest of his life there. Nobody knows how many people there are like that. A slice of life after the main achievement of the civil rights movement.

Well, the movement didn't end. By now, Jackson has a black mayor, Chokwe Lumumba, a longtime activist in Jackson. He won very easily on a platform of, in his words, "turning Jackson into the most radical city on the planet." He's well on his way to doing that. Not the Jackson of 1964.

There are real victories, it takes a long time, a lot of bitterness and pain, but sometimes committed struggle yields real successes.

Not always of course. The history of Martin Luther King is illustrative, and worth looking into more closely.

King is greatly honored, rightly. On MLK Day, he is praised as a great figure. The praise usually ends with his inspiring "I Have a Dream" speech from 1963. It would be hard to find mention of another remarkable speech of his, his eloquent "I've Been to the Mountaintop" speech. This was in Memphis, Tennessee, on April 3, 1968, the day before he was assassinated.

By that time, he had lost the liberal support that had remained strong as long as his targets were racist sheriffs in Alabama.

After the Civil Rights Act of 1964, King moved on. He began to criticize the Vietnam War, sharply. He shifted his organizing activities to the North, to racism in the North—not quite the right thing to do. Worse still, he was bringing up class issues. He was organizing a poor people's campaign, black and white. He was in Memphis to support a strike of sanitation workers, considered the lowest of the low. On April 4, the day after his "I've Been to the Mountaintop," he was assassinated. He seems to have had a premonition. His speech comes to its climax with the words, "And He's allowed me to go up to the mountain. And I've looked over. And I've seen the Promised Land. I may not get there with you. But I want you to know tonight, that we, as a people, will get to the Promised Land!"

His plan was to lead a march from Memphis through the cities in the South where the great demonstrations had taken place and then on to Washington. After his death, the march took place, led by his wife, Coretta King. When they got to Washington, they set up a tent city called Resurrection City, appealing to Congress—controlled by liberal Democrats—to do something about poverty in general. They didn't get anywhere. As soon as the permit ran out, they were evicted. That ended the poor people's movement.

Struggle for rights is a work in progress, and the trajectory is not steady. We are now in the fortieth year of a period of regression. I've been talking about the successes of the activism of the past years. It hasn't come to an end. There may be more committed young activists today, in many areas, than in "the time of troubles." Still, it's useful to look back and see how far we've regressed, alongside many successes.

You've probably noticed that a couple of days ago Elizabeth Warren initiated child care legislation, a bill calling for universal high-quality child care, as in other developed countries, even some others. Here it is considered highly controversial.

It's interesting to compare it with legislation that was introduced in 1971, passed by large majorities in Congress. It was called the Comprehensive Child Development Act. You can find it on the internet. It went well beyond what Warren is proposing today. It was introduced by Senators Walter Mondale and John Brademas, two progressive senators. And vetoed by President Nixon because it was endorsing a "communal approach to child-rearing," harming families and opening the door to communism. Another illustration of American exceptionalism.

Struggle is a long work in progress. Lacking the participation of engaged activist movements, a very long struggle, with uncertain outcomes.

I've been talking about activism and resistance and their consequences. Let's look more closely at these.

Perhaps the most interesting case is the aftermath of the Vietnam War. The popular movement did have a significant effect on bringing the war finally to an end. It took a long time. By 1968, after the Tet Offensive, the US began to deescalate, to move to negotiations. But the war went on. Some of the worst atrocities took place afterward. One is famous, the My Lai massacre, which was actually a footnote to much worse crimes. There was a Quaker Center for refugees and health care right nearby. They knew right away about the My Lai massacre, but barely reacted. A friend was working at the center, Claire Culhane, a Canadian nurse. She told me that they paid little attention because similar atrocities were going on all the time, everywhere. The official Peers Commission, which investigated the My Lai massacre, by accident came across a similar one at the village of My Khe a few kilometers away, which gives some sense of the density.

But these massacres on the ground were minor as compared with the intensive bombing of heavily populated areas causing huge casualties, investigated in depth by *Newsweek* bureau chief Kevin Buckley. When the journal published only limited excerpts, Buckley provided me with much additional information that Edward Herman and I published in our 1979 book *Political Economy of Human Rights*. My Lai pales into insignificance in comparison. But outrage focused on the criminal acts of half-crazed GIs in the field, who didn't know who was going to shoot at them next. Not on the gentlemen in air-conditioned offices who were orchestrating mass slaughter of miserable civilians by intensive bombing of heavily populated areas.

Despite the continuing, even escalating massacres, military policies were changing. One reason was that the army was falling apart and the top brass wanted it to be withdrawn. Soldiers were killing officers and dropping out on drugs. They didn't want to fight this horrible war anymore. Organized opposition from within the military also developed, in this case with close relations with the antiwar movement at home: Vietnam Veterans Against the War, which carried out protests and conducted war crimes trials where soldiers testified about their experiences, to great effect.

The military command learned a lesson, one that other imperial powers had known about for a long time. You can't fight a brutal colonial war with a civilian army, people you just pick up off the streets. They are not trained to slaughter civilians. That's why the British relied on Gurkhas and the French on their Foreign Legion. Post-Vietnam, the US has moved in the same direction, relying on "contractors"—professional killers—and special forces. And on murder from a distance, the drone warfare perfected by Obama to assassinate people who are thought to be planning to harm Americans (and whatever unfortunates are nearby).

We might incidentally ask ourselves what the reaction would be if, say, Iran had a major program to assassinate people who are not just thought to be harming Iran but are in fact doing so on a major scale.

The popular movement against the war had a lasting impact on the general culture. The government no longer had the free rein it once did for Vietnam-style wars of aggression. That became clear very soon. In 1981, Reagan took office, planning for intervention in Central America. His administration tried to duplicate almost point by point what Kennedy had done in the early 1960s. First came an official white paper providing the rationale for defense against communist aggression. Then a major propaganda campaign about the terrible threat of international terrorism directed by Russia and Cuba. Next would come intervention of US forces to counter the threat—which was portrayed as serious indeed. At one point Reagan even declared a national emergency because of the threat to our existence posed by the government of Nicaragua, warning that its troops were only two days' marching time from Harlingen, Texas. Like the hordes invading us today.

It didn't work. As soon as the campaign was launched, there was a strong reaction from church groups, antiwar organizations, and much of the public. The *Wall Street Journal* published a devastating critique of the white paper; in the Kennedy years, that was done by the great independent journalist I. F. Stone in his *Weekly*, and dismissed. Not in the eighties. Soon the Reaganites backed off. What happened was awful enough, but the US wars in Central America were nothing like Vietnam.

Twenty years later, the US and UK invaded Iraq. For the first time in the history of imperial wars, there was enormous protest even before the war was officially launched. Again, what happened was horrible enough. We're still seeing the terrible effects. But it was nothing like Vietnam. There were some restraints, which I think can fairly be attributed to popular attitudes—what the prominent Reaganite intellectual Norman Podhoretz called "the sickly inhibition against the use of military force" (Podhoretz 1985), the dreaded "Vietnam syndrome."

Well, there's a lot more to say about protest and resistance, and I'll return to it. But let's turn to government reactions.

The most significant one I know of is discussed in the paper on domestic terrorism that Marv posted, a paper of mine that is primarily concerned with the government program called COINTELPRO—counterintelligence program, a program of the FBI, the national political police—discussing also earlier and much more severe state repression at the time the FBI was established.

COINTELPRO started around 1960. It was exposed finally in 1973, right at about the time of Watergate. The revelations of COINTELPRO and of Watergate, and the reaction to them, provide a graphic example of the comparisons that we've been discussing throughout, and what they teach us about the intellectual culture, about prevailing common sense.

Watergate was considered an extraordinary crisis, the worst constitutional crisis in the history of the country. But it was overcome. The famous liberal historian Henry Steele Commager wrote in the *New York*

Times that the attack on the foundations of the Republic was overcome in "a stunning vindication of our constitutional system."

Recall that this was at the same time that the COINTELPRO revelations were starting to leak out. In fact, Watergate was a tea party in comparison to COINTELPRO, a far more serious attack on the constitutional system—which was hardly vindicated by the marginal reaction.

There was a crucial distinction between Watergate and COINTELPRO. Watergate, carried out by a bunch of minor thugs that Nixon recruited, was targeting people who matter, the Democratic Party, half of the political power in the country. COINTELPRO was an operation of the national political police, targeting all of the popular movements that developed in the sixties, and in far more extreme ways than anything contemplated in the Watergate operations.

COINTELPRO started, of course, by aiming at the Communist Party, or what was left of it. By then probably three-quarters of the Communist Party were FBI infiltrators, whose dues were keeping the party alive. But there was still something around.

Then it went after the Puerto Rican liberation movement and the American Indian movement. It continued to broaden its scope, finally targeting the entire New Left, quite a considerable part of the population by the late sixties. Martin Luther King was a particular target. Also the antiwar movement, of course, and then beyond. It was an extensive program of terror and disruption, intimidation, and FBI instigation of violence. It was initiated and pursued under the most liberal democratic administrations, then carried forward under Nixon. It reached the level of outright political assassination, the Fred Hampton case, to which I'll return.

FBI agents incited and sometimes carried out arson and other violent acts, attacked college officials, including college presidents on the stage, all blamed on student activists. The FBI went so far as to form actual paramilitary organizations, which carried out violence, mainly in San Diego, seeking to blame the acts on the Left.

Something that you might bear in mind today.

By the late sixties, movement groups came to realize that they were very likely infiltrated by police or FBI agents. They learned to try to identify the likely infiltrators, the ones who would show up as government witnesses in trials. That turned out not to be very difficult. If someone looked like a hippie from central casting, he was probably an infiltrator. Same if someone was shouting "Off the cops" or "Let's blow things up." I was deeply involved in resistance activities and groups supporting resistance. We all knew that if you wanted to do anything serious, say something that involved a person's life, you did it with affinity groups, people you knew personally. Never even in a staff meeting of a resistance organization because you just couldn't trust all of those present, too many infiltrators around.

The prime target of COINTELPRO, as you might guess, was black activist movements. There were many black criminal gangs, but they were of little interest to the FBI. What concerned official Washington was groups trying to organize communities, a real problem. Much like the "viruses" in the international arena. The main such group was the Black Panthers. We now have a lot of released documents about the FBI campaign against the Panthers, some quoted in the posted article. The Panthers were portrayed as a major threat to the country—the usual pattern of concocting terrifying enemies that we've been discussing.

The FBI estimated that this frightening organization had about eight hundred members. It was decimated.

The particular targets of COINTELPRO were organizers and activists carrying out service to the community: free breakfasts, things like that. Fred Hampton, who was assassinated, was recognized to be one of the most successful organizers and most promising leaders of the Panthers. The FBI ran a major program to get rid of this dangerous figure. This was in Chicago. There was a black criminal gang called the Blackstone Rangers. The FBI fabricated letters they sent to the Rangers. The letters pretended to be from a simple black guy from the ghetto, written in fake dialect, who had picked up evidence that the Panthers were planning to kill Jeff Fort, the leader of the Rangers. The idea was to incite the Rangers to kill Hampton.

None of that worked. The black groups were in contact, and easily saw through the pretense. So something else had to be done.

The FBI managed to infiltrate an agent to be Fred Hampton's body-guard, who was with him all the time. They then provided the Chicago police with fabricated documents claiming that the Panthers were stashing guns in Hampton's apartment. That was enough for the police to carry out an early morning raid on the apartment and to murder Hampton and another Panther activist, Mark Clark, who was also there, both asleep—with some suspicion that they might have been drugged.

Perhaps we can be frank and describe this as a Gestapo-style assassination.

The police department claimed that officers were responding to fire from inside the apartment. The story was investigated by a young reporter, John Kifner, who later became one of the best investigative reporters for the *New York Times*. Kifner was able to establish that the bullet holes were from outside the apartment, from the police raiders.

Nothing could be done through the legal system, but like Emmett Till's mother, Fred Hampton's family refused to drop the matter. They were joined by some very good young lawyers from a small law firm in Chicago, really admirable people. There's a good book about what happened by one of the lawyers, Jeffrey Haas. It's called *The Assassination of Fred Hampton*. After many years, they were able to get some compensation in a civil suit, but for the actual perpetrators, all the way up to Washington, nothing ever happened. Maybe some taps on the wrist. It's all unknown, like the assassination of the Jesuit intellectuals in 1989. Unknown outside the black community, that is (and some activist groups). This murder and the broader attack on the Panthers have had a long-term impact on black communities, inducing fear and hopelessness, a sense there's nothing you can do.

The Hampton assassination alone easily outweighs the Watergate charges.

It's always enlightening to adopt a broader perspective. Hampton was not the only promising black leader who might have carried his community forward, but was assassinated to avert that threat. Another one at about the same time, in this case with far broader consequences, was Patrice Lumumba in the former Belgian Congo—a region with extremely rich resources and potential, which should be one of the most prosperous countries in the world, carrying black Africa along with it. It was devastated by Belgian colonialism, perhaps the most horrendous of the European criminal operations in Africa—a pretty high bar to reach.

The horrors of Belgian colonialism came to end in 1960, when Congo declared independence. Its leading figure was the young charismatic leader Patrice Lumumba, who might have extricated Congo from the misery of colonialism, perhaps leading Africa out of the darkness. But that was not to be. President Eisenhower assigned to the CIA the task of murdering him, an effort carried further under Kennedy. But the Belgians got there first, and together with the US and other liberal democracies plunged Congo back to terror and destruction under the leadership of their favorite, the murderous kleptomaniac Mobutu, who ensured that the riches of the Congo would flow in the right direction. Fast forwarding to today, those of you who enjoy smart phones and other technical delights benefit from the rich minerals of eastern Congo, handed over to the multinationals hovering nearby by vicious militias and marauders from US-backed Rwanda, while the death toll mounts to many millions.

An African Hampton, one might say.

An interesting question is how typical COINTELPRO was of FBI concerns in those years. Light is cast on this question by a very significant resistance action initiated by a physics professor at Haverford, Bill Davidon, a Quaker (and personal acquaintance from resistance days). He organized a group that managed to break into the offices of the FBI in Media, a small town in Pennsylvania, which was the main storage place for FBI documents on operations in the eastern Pennsylvania region. They stole lots of documents, which they released to the press. And they managed to get away. Years later they identified themselves. The documents they released, which were published, are highly informative. Most were about protest activities. I think 1 percent were about organized crime. Some were on bank robberies. Some were administrative. But the bulk of the documents were about how to repress popular activism. We don't know whether that's representative of FBI activities in general at the time. There has been some investigation but not much. It's probably a fair sample.

Well, let's turn to what the future's likely to be. Marv talked a bit about the prospects for repression and violence. When we think about that, we should remember what recent history was like. It'll have to be pretty violent to go beyond what was the norm not long ago.

COINTELPRO was called off under court orders in the 1970s and as far as we know, hasn't been reinstituted. My own guess is that we're likely to see softer measures in the near future, for the same reasons why you can't carry out a Vietnam-style intervention any longer. There's just too much popular opposition. The country became too civilized, at least large parts of it. So I suspect that what we'll see is more along the lines of Shoshana Zuboff's article ("Once We Searched Google. Now It Searches Us," 2019), which was excerpted from a very interesting book of hers, a five-hundred-page inquiry into what she calls "surveillance capitalism" (Zuboff 2019).

The basic idea is that methods are being devised to keep everyone under total surveillance. Everything you do is recorded and the data goes back to Google and tech companies who use it for commercial purposes. For example, providing the behavioral data they compile for advertisers. Personal profiles, a huge mass of data, that can be sent to advertisers who can gear their public relations activities to your particular interests and vulnerabilities and also try to control what you do. So for example, if you drive a car, there's a ton of data being picked up by the car manufacturers. They haven't known what to do with it until recently, but now they are figuring out how they can sell the data to advertisers. You can be offered some gimmick by the car dealer and in return, you agree to have the panel in front of the driver show ads. So if you're driving along Campbell Avenue and the personal data says you like Japanese restaurants, there will be an ad saying there's a Japanese restaurant in a half a mile. Things like that. With smart whatevers, smart phones or smart anything else, all the data goes to a central store accumulating massive material about you.

What's called the internet of things is a big exciting development. This should make it possible to have almost everything around, your refrigerator or your toothbrush, anything will have a surveillance device which will collect information about what you're doing. Zuboff comments plausibly that this is a new stage in capitalism. So in capitalism, as Marv's been discussing, everything has to be turned into a commodity of some kind. First human life was turned into labor to be bought and sold. Nature was turned by enclosures and other devices into land, privately owned land, that can be bought and sold. Ordinary exchange among people is turned into money. Now we have the new stage: experience, human experience can be turned into behavioral data, to quote Zuboff, "ready for fabrication into predictions that are bought and sold."

The new stage of capitalism recognizes that serving the genuine needs of people can be less lucrative than selling predictions of their behavior. We therefore have a new model of capitalism in which devices aren't developed for your use but so that business can use the data that's collected about you, which can also be used to control. It can modify behavior to get maximum profitability. The analysis of behavior can trigger punishments in real time. Suppose you're driving a car and the insurance company sees that you didn't stop at a red light. They can warn you instantly that they're going to raise your rates, or even go as far as engine lockdowns. And they can provide rate discounts, coupons, gold stars for good behavior.

It's not discussed in that article, but as you can imagine, this is being used even more intensively to control lives in the private dictatorships in which people spend most of their lives, what we call having a job. Surveillance in industry began with a supervisor who would sit somewhere and try to see what everybody's doing. That was extended with Taylorism, controlling detailed operations. Henry Ford introduced the assembly line, which was efficient but also a highly controlling device. There was a problem with the assembly line. It's so onerous that people dropped out. They couldn't stand it. They had to hire almost a thousand workers to see if they could get one hundred to stay on. That seems to be the prime reason why Henry Ford instituted the five-dollar wage, which is usually called an act of benevolence but was apparently a way to induce workers to stay on. The Ford company carried out extensive surveillance of workers not only on the line, but even in their homes. Agents would go into their homes to make sure that their personal lives were being dealt with properly. Ford himself believed you had to have a healthy and moral life. Workers were subjected to close monitoring at work and at home. The new surveillance capitalism goes well beyond. Now every instant of your life can be monitored, obviously in the workplace as well.

For example, in the Amazon warehouses, where work is very rough, management has worked out the shortest distances between two positions. If a worker racing from one place to another happens to go a little bit somewhere else, he gets a warning. If you get too many warnings, you're fired. Spend a little too much time in a bathroom, you're fired. Talk to the wrong people for too long, no good. Stop to look at your email for a minute or talk to somebody, and you get a demerit. It's a terrific technique of control. The delivery systems like UPS have also instituted these practices. So if the driver, say, backs up or drives too fast or stops for a cup of coffee somewhere, he'll immediately get a warning: you'd better shape up or else. Some studies indicate that this does improve productivity. UPS has been able to extend deliveries with fewer drivers, a softer version of the old slave systems where a whip and a pistol could increase productivity significantly.

Now it's being used for business, for advertising and control of the workforce. But one can be fairly confident that the same information is, or soon will be, going to the government to be stored and used if needed.

The ideal, I think, is probably China, which has carried these methods very far forward. China has instituted what they call a social credit system. You're given one thousand points and you get black marks or credit depending on how you behave. There are a few cities where it's been started experimentally. It'll presumably extend to the whole country. Surveillance cameras everywhere, face recognition. If you jaywalk, you get a black mark. If you help an old lady across the street, you might get a gold star. Over time all of this gets internalized. Pretty soon you're monitoring your own behavior because so much depends on it. It's internalized discipline. You're already seeing it in factories, and we'll pretty soon see it with the internet of things. Did you sleep too long or eat too much? You'll get a reaction, maybe a reward or punishment. It is to become internalized as a technique of control. I suspect that we'll be seeing techniques like these as a way of ensuring preferred behavior. It also separates people from one another. It's highly individualized. That's another important technique of control, used in many contexts. We've discussed a few.

If we're going to be saved from some nightmare like this, as I think I mentioned before, it will be with a vibrant and dynamic organized labor movement. That's been what's spearheaded progress throughout modern history. The labor movement in the United States has been subjected to unusual violence and repression, more so than in similar countries. But it has continually revived. Now it's in a period of regression. It may revive again, and I think that's where we can expect one major source of hope, not the only one, but a major one.

Chapter 7

SOCIAL CHANGE

Waterstone Lecture, February 26, 2019

Tonight's topic, social change, is going to tie clearly to material from last week on social movements. But I'm also going to use this opportunity to tie together a whole number of things from the course and bring them to a kind of closure, hopefully. All right. So, social change. A few quotes to begin:

> Once social change begins it cannot be reversed, you cannot un-educate the person who has learned to read, you cannot humiliate the person who feels pride, you cannot oppress the people who are not afraid anymore. —Cesar Chavez

> The new scientific truth does not triumph by convincing its opponents and making them see the light, but rather because its opponents eventually die and a new generation grows up that is familiar with it. This is not pointed at anyone. —Max Planck

> Without a revolutionary theory there cannot be a revolutionary movement. Social change and critical pedagogy, I think involve a couple of tasks. —Vladimir Lenin

For social change to occur, the first task that's necessary is to open a space for *oppositional* critique, not just any critique, but *oppositional* critique, which relies upon a recognition of the difference between what is and what ought to be, or what might be. Clearing the way toward this oppositional space is one function of critical pedagogy and critical thinking, as argued by Henry Giroux (2004). "Is" and "ought" or "might" are not at all necessarily the same thing, though a dominant common sense that seeks to maintain the status quo endeavors to equate them. That is, to make the way things *are* the equivalent of the way things *ought to be*, and thereby closing down any sort of alternative imaginary.

The second task, beyond opening up a space for oppositional critique, is to examine and begin to dismantle the common sense in the wide variety of areas where social change is sought. Under such circumstances, the taken for granted should never be taken for granted. For our purposes tonight, I want to discuss the prevailing common sense in three areas, and they'll be familiar to you from what we've discussed previously: first, the common sense underlying imperialism and militarism; second, the common sense that underlies environmental and resource degradation; and third, a set of common sense ideas that underlie neoliberalism, globalization, and fictionalization.

Let us return just for a moment to our familiar formula: M $\longleftrightarrow$ C $\longleftrightarrow$ C' $\longleftrightarrow$ M', where, as you will recall, M is money, C is input commodity, C' is the output of one cycle of production, M' is more money, which is the point of the endeavor. Also, remember, this is buying in order to sell to emerge with more money at the end of each cycle. In the model, what capitalists buy as inputs are means of production (raw materials, plant materials, plant equipment, tools, etc.) and labor power.

I now want to take this formula and put it into the context of the things we want to talk about this evening. So that formula is now in the middle here, and expanded, and it's going to tie a number of things into the discussion.

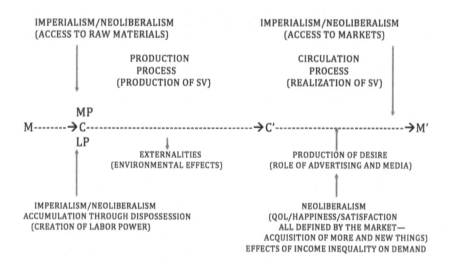

Let's look at just the left side first, which is the point where capitalists spend money, and they buy a couple of things, they buy labor power at the bottom, they buy means of production.

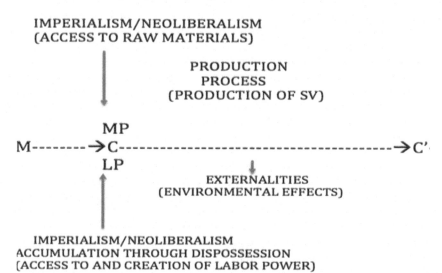

And, the relationship between imperialism and neoliberalism, as we've talked about, includes a whole number of particular dimensions.

At the bottom imperialism and neoliberalism have been utilized, both historically and contemporaneously, to gain access to labor pools and to create labor power through the mechanisms of primitive accumulation or accumulation through dispossession in which people are dispossessed of their own means of subsistence, and therefore become available as having only their skins to sell. Militarism in its various guises (colonialism, neocolonialism, imperialism), has been an enormous part of that project over time.

At the top, imperialism (or other forms of militarism) and neoliberalism clearly have provided access to raw materials, and we're seeing this being played out at the moment in the Venezuela case. Very overtly, (then national security advisor) John Bolton has said, "It would be very good if American companies could develop Venezuelan oil and all options, of course, are on the table" (see "John Bolton Admits US-Backed Coup in Venezuela Is about Oil Not Democracy").

So here we can see rather clearly the ways in which imperialism and neoliberalism are tied to this capitalist model, but what kind of taken-for-granted, common sense understanding of the world underlies these activities? What allows this to continue? Why do we continue to support this kind of interventionism around the planet?

What I would suggest is that the problematic common sense underlying this is *fear*. I'm going to talk about this in a number of ways. It underlies and justifies the linkages between capitalism and militarism, and imperialism in its many forms, whether these are colonialism, neocolonialism, latter-day imperialism, economic imperialism, and so forth. But one of the things that underlies and justifies these linkages is fear. The question for us, in terms of social change, is how do we dismantle this underlying common sense of pervasive fear? How do we begin to break this down? First we must ask the question of how we became, or were induced to become, so fearful?

Why are we so afraid as Americans? One point, we talked about this earlier, is Hofstadter's notion of the paranoid style of American politics, which goes back, it underpins the Cold War, it underpins the US position in the world in many ways, it endorses this Manichaean worldview of good versus evil: "You're either with us, or you're with the terrorists." There are lots of ways that this gets expressed, but this is part of the American psyche. I want to tell a little bit of a story here to put this in a useful context. So let's look at September 11, 2001, and its aftermath, which is ongoing. What happened on September 11, 2001? Well, there are two stories, with very different interpretations and very different implications. One of these stories served and furthered the interest of the status quo, the other did not.

Here's the first 9/11 story. Nineteen men—by the way, fifteen were from Saudi Arabia, two from the United Arab Emirates, one from Egypt, one from Lebanon. Notice any two countries in particular that are not in the list? Afghanistan perhaps and Iraq? They were armed with box cutters, which were legal at the time to bring onto planes. They boarded the planes with legally purchased tickets, a few of them purchased with credit cards. They hijacked the planes, they crashed two into the World Trade Center towers, one into the Pentagon, one into the ground in Pennsylvania.

So what did this take? What was required for this to happen? Some money, clearly they had to buy the airplane tickets, pay for some flight training. They got a discount because they didn't have to learn how to land. It clearly took some coordination so they could board the planes at approximately the same time and coordinate these impacts. It also required nineteen men willing to die for a cause and some people who directed them.

Did it take a great deal of sophistication? Vast resources? A global network? Not really, so this clearly couldn't be the dominant story. This is a story. This is one story, one interpretation of what happened.

Here's the second story. A widespread network of insane terrorists, coordinated by an evil mastermind, Osama bin Laden. Vast resources. They hate our freedoms, that's why they did it. This is part of their insanity; they had no ulterior motives of any kind. They just hate our freedoms. This vast, well-funded, and coordinated network must be fought everywhere and forever. It's like a new *Pearl Harbor* and I highlight that event because I'm going to come back to that formulation in just a minute. But clearly the 9/11 attacks represented a new and existential threat to the homeland.

This terminology of "homeland," which has a very disreputable history and past, became synonymous with the US in the aftermath of 9/11 (very shortly after the event, we see the creation, for example of the Department of Homeland Security). But, in any case, this was represented as an existential threat to the homeland. So, was this the dominant story? Absolutely, this is the story that has persisted. Here are a couple of excerpts from a report that John Pilger (a very good investigative journalist and videographer/filmmaker) wrote in the *New Statesman* (December 16, 2002) after the 9/11 attacks.

> The threat posed by US terrorism to the security of nations and individuals was outlined in prophetic detail, in a document written more than two years ago [actually at the end of 1999], and disclosed only recently. What was needed for America to dominate much of humanity and the world's resources was quote "Some catastrophic and catalyzing event, like a new *Pearl Harbor*, described as "the opportunity of ages."
>
> Time and again 11 September is described as an opportunity. In last April's *New Yorker*, the investigative reporter Nicolas Leman wrote that "Bush's most senior advisor Condoleezza Rice told him she had called together senior members of the National Security Council and asked them to "to think about how do you capitalize on these opportunities?" Which she compared with those of "1945 to 1947," the start of the cold war.

So clearly people were thinking about how to get an event of this sort and if you recall, one of the comments from Milton Friedman when he was talking about the advent of neoliberalism, was that "in moments of crisis whether naturally occurring or created, the important thing is to have your ideas lying around as the ones to be picked up in the moment of crisis and its aftermath." So here's a moment where crisis, in fact, created enormous opportunity.

Once again from Pilger's report: "The extremists who have since exploited 11 September come from the era of Ronald Reagan. When far right groups and 'think-tanks' were established to avenge the American [so-called] 'defeat' in Vietnam" (2002). There was something called Vietnam syndrome, you may recall, that after the "defeat" in Southeast Asia, the US would never recover its pride.

Also, in the 1990s there was a need to justify the denial of a peace dividend, following the Cold War, you wouldn't want that to happen. Once the Soviet Union fell, and our ostensible principal enemy was no longer capable of sustaining a kind of adversarial relationship, there was the possibility that peace might break out. This was the notion of a possible peace dividend, that it might have been possible to divert funds from the MIC to other societal needs. The war machine clearly wanted to avoid that outcome, so this was the added agenda: we had to find a way to deny the opportunity of a peace dividend following the end of the Cold War.

Back to Pilger's report:

> The project for the new American century was formed [the group that wrote this report that Pilger is referring to] along with the American Enterprise Institute, the Hudson Institute, and others that have since merged the ambitions of the Reagan administration with those of the current Bush regime [remember, Pilger is writing in 2002]. . . . One of George W. Bush's thinkers is Richard Perle. I interviewed Perle when he was advising Reagan and when he spoke about total war, I mistakenly dismissed him as mad. He recently used the term again in describing America's war on terror [remember, this was the new coinage]. "No stages," he said. "This is total war. We are fighting a variety of enemies, there are lots of them out there. All this talk about, first we are going to do Afghanistan, then we will do Iraq, this is entirely the wrong way to go about it. If we just let our vision of the world go forth and we embrace it entirely, we don't try to piece together clever diplomacy, but just wage a total war, our children will sing great songs about us years from now.

If there are any children left at all, that is. This is still very predominant in the thinking and rhetoric from our leaders. We now have the global war on terror, this is part of the aftermath of 9/11 clearly. Global war on terror, even though it's now been renamed any number of times. I characterize it as the Doritos model of terrorist production. What does that mean? It means: "Don't worry, we'll make more." This has been one of the principal effects of the global war on terror.

First we have the attack on Afghanistan, who you remember was notably absent from the list of perpetrators of 9/11, although it was argued that they were harboring the terrorists. Then, the completely unprovoked attack on Iraq, how was that justified? Constant amplification of fear. You recall WMDs, weapons of mass destruction, as well as the ostensible link or links between Iraq and the events on 9/11. Saddam Hussein constantly portrayed as the equivalent of Hitler; he gassed his own people. We have some evidence for that charge because we have the receipts for the gas that we sold him. There were no Al-Qaeda elements in Iraq prior to the attack, but since the invasion there has been proliferation everywhere with constant new forms: ISIS, Boko Haram, Al-Qaeda in the Arabian Peninsula, and on and on and on. So this is now one of the results.

So what has this by now taken-for-granted common sensical fear enabled? What's been part of the consequence? Attacks on civil rights and liberties, the Patriot Act, which came out immediately after 9/11, so you know that it had been written prior to that. We've been trading freedom for security and I needn't remind you of Benjamin Franklin's comment on that. The expansion of the police state and militarization of policing. We've talked about increases in the military budget, as we've also talked about cuts in the social safety net. Deregulation everywhere, cuts to the State Department, that is the diplomatic approach to problems rather than the militaristic approach to problems. Cuts in foreign aid, which was never a very big part of the budget to begin with, and expansion of military bases everywhere as we mentioned (more than eight hundred now).

The pervasive fear has also been used to justify military extensions that are often a rather thin cover for the acquisition of raw materials and the opening of markets (other essential connections to a capitalist political economy). AFRICOM, the African Command, one of the newest divisions of the military, again cover for mineral extraction. Just recently, the announcement of Space COM and a resuscitated interest in a Space Force, with space as the next battleground. So endless fear resulting in cycles of endless war, producing more enemies, producing yet more endless war. The Axis of Evil recently, and rather seamlessly, morphed into the Troika of Tyranny. The Axis of Evil, when we were concentrating on the Middle East; now we're concentrating on Latin America, John Bolton has come up with a new epithet, the Troika of Tyranny (Cuba, Nicaragua, Venezuela).

Other outcomes include the forty-three thousand allied troops and police killed in Iraq and Afghanistan, not to mention in the other conflicts that have ensued in Syria, Yemen, and so forth. Hundreds of thousands of contractor and civilian casualties, additional hundreds of thousands wounded. The US has spent over $5.9 trillion on homeland security and multiple wars since 9/11. It's also useful, though somewhat dispiriting, to think about the opportunity costs here, in other words, where else all these resources might have gone.

We know the story since then. One questions, how does it possibly continue to play? Why, eighteen years after September 11, 2001, are we still living with this fear and these consequences this way? What's the actual threat? Is it invasion? I mean do people really believe, as the president keeps telling us, that people are going to be coming in from the southern border to take us over? The establishment everywhere of Sharia Law? Are we the land of the free? The home of the brave? So we need to see through this myth and break down the fear. That is, if there's going to be a change to this common sense that has taken hold, and we need to be able to break through it.

I'll give you a very brief case that might help us break down some of this fear. It's very hard to prove a negative typically, but I came up with a way in this case. Some of you may remember that during the 2013 New Orleans Super Bowl, there were thirty-four minutes of a power outage. Well, my theory here was that if there really were any kind of terrorist networks, they could have at least stepped up and taken credit for the blackout. Wouldn't have taken anything more than a tweet. And they could have said, "Yeah, we blacked out the Super Bowl." Well, they didn't do it, so here's the proof of the negative, they don't really exist in the kind of sophisticated, far-flung way that we think they do.

But the fear clearly persists, and we need to understand what is it that actually sets it off and sustains it? As one example, a short video produced by Newsy in 2016, titled "American Fear Climbs Despite Drop in Violence," details the ways in which politicians, and quite cynically, exploit and heighten this fear to pursue their own electoral and policy decisions (Newsy 2016).

As another example to amplify this point, there's been an enormous amount of coverage in the last week or so of the declaration of an emergency, to justify building a wall on the southern US border.

Here's another emergency declaration with a similar intent of furthering and reinforcing fear of others:

> Pursuant to the international emergency economic powers act . . . I hereby report that I have issued an executive order, the order declaring a national emergency with respect to the unusual and extraordinary threat to the national security and foreign policy of the United States posed by the situation in Venezuela. The order does not target the people of Venezuela but rather is aimed at persons involved in or responsible for the erosion of human rights guarantees, persecution of political opponents. (Obama, Declaration of a National Emergency with Respect to Venezuela, March 9, 2015)

You can see where this may go, especially in light of the inclusion of Venezuela in Bolton's Troika of Tyranny. Except, this was, in fact, a declaration of emergency, by the previous, Obama, administration, issued in 2015. We see the same kind of hysteria. But when Obama did this, it didn't produce the same kind of reaction as the ones issued by Trump. And this declaration was very much embedded in the whole sanctions regime that had begun prior to the Obama administration, but was used to justify making those sanctions even more stringent. So this promulgation of fear of dangerous others is clearly not confined to one party or another, but is the constantly reinforced, pervasive common sense.

Let's go back to this diagram:

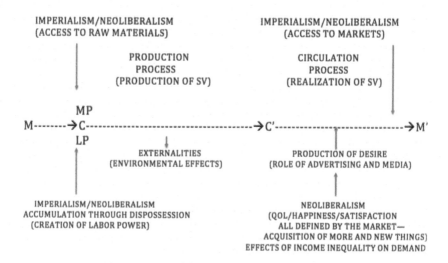

But now I want to look at the right side of the process and make some ties between imperialism (and militarism) and neoliberalism and things like the circulation process, access to markets.

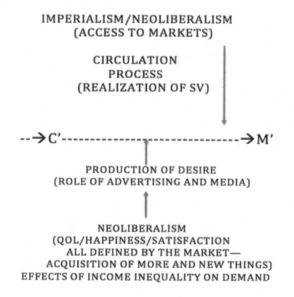

Remember, once a good or service is produced, it has to be sold. So we will also focus on the bottom section, where we will want to think about issues of quality of life, happiness, satisfaction, as defined by the market. The acquisition of more and more things, the effects of income inequality on demand. So again, ties between the capitalist mode of production, and the ways in which we're thinking about some of these effects and outcomes.

On this side, one of the things we're concerned about is the quest for infinite growth (an unavoidable feature of capitalism) on a finite planet. With that imperative, the biosphere is now subsumed under the economy. This has to be reversed. That is, the biosphere is now seen in strictly utilitarian terms to be simply a storehouse of resources, and/or a receptacle for waste.

Also under capitalist compulsion, people now serve the economy, rather than the other way around. Development should be about people, not about objects. Development, often seen as synonymous with progress, is equated with growth, measured as GNP or GDP, sometimes per capita. This must be challenged, and we need differential criteria and different metrics for what constitutes development and progress. Right now these are equated. Development doesn't necessarily require growth, development has no limits, growth has limits or should. And this is clearly referring back to the growth/de-growth debate that we read about.

All of this is underlain by issues of what constitutes happiness, satisfaction, and quality of life. What do these actually essential elements of life actually depend on? At the moment, under our current capitalist system, and its associated common sense, these aspects are measured by the acquisition of more and more things. But we don't go readily into this mindset, we have to actually be induced or seduced.

Global advertising spending in 2014 was $488.48 billion and is projected to grow to $757.44 billion by 2021. So, think about the enormous effort, the enormous, strenuous, and continuous effort to persuade people that things that they merely want are really things that they must have, that they need. And this is the business of marketing and advertising. And as Noam pointed out previously, this completely distorts the notion of the so-called free market in which rational people make rational choices based on real needs.

What is all this advertising trying to sell us? I'll just name a couple of things that, even though they were introduced rather recently, they are now so thoroughly, and common sensibly, a part of our world that we cannot live without them.

Computers, quite clearly, are now completely necessary. The first personal computer appeared in 1977, the Apple 2, and has become ever-more ubiquitous since then. The cell phone, an unadulterated success, no downsides to the cell phone. First call on a mobile phone was made in 1973. The first iPhone was introduced in 2007, just twelve years ago, and it (or its competitor clones) has now become completely indispensable to billions of people.

Social media, another good or service without which life would not be worth living. Google (which, of course, is now also a verb) was registered in 1997, Facebook became available in 2004, but available to the public only in 2006, the same year that gave us the many benefits of Twitter. But again, I'm naming these just to demonstrate the recency of their development, and the degree to which they've actually taken over our mindset about how the world both does and should operate. The perfect exemplar of taken-for-granted common sense.

So a critical question that arises out of this: might it be possible to define happiness, satisfaction, quality of life differently than we are defining them now? Perhaps not based on the acquisition of more and more things; that is, commodities, which is what the capitalist system is equipped to deliver. The common sense response to that question is that any move away from the present standards of living, measured in numbers of things, constitutes a giant step backward. We're going to be living in the caves in the dark, if we abandon any of these essentials. But in a recent poll that was conducted, actually, by American Express, "Americans are increasingly placing greater priority on living a fulfilling life, in which being wealthy is not the most significant factor." In fact out of some twenty-two items that people could choose from, being wealthy was number twenty from most of the respondents. So clearly people are thinking about, trying to think about things somewhat differently. But given the figures I shared with you about advertising and marketing, imagining other possibilities is not easy.

Chilean economist Manfred Max-Neef developed a notion of how we might think about what constitutes our needs and wants in a different way than simply through commodification. Only one of his categories requires some kind of goods, and I should point out that this category refers to the physical satisfaction of what people need to subsist, that is, basic caloric intake, clothing, shelter, if you're in particular geographic settings. Beyond those subsistence factors, however, there is very little agreement about what these "needs" might actually mean. But his intention with this exercise was simply to open up a whole set of possibilities for deriving human satisfaction and happiness, without an automatic resort to commodities. Again this is a way to break through some of this prevailing common sense.

Now I want to turn to the third area requiring social change, which is neoliberalism and the problematic common sense underlying neoliberalism, which is that markets know best. I've already talked about some of the problematic effects of neoliberalism, globalization, fictionalization. One is rapidly widening wealth and income inequality. US wealth increased by eight and a half trillion dollars in 2017, with the richest 2 percent getting about $1.15 trillion. That figure is more than the total cost of Medicaid and the complete safety net, both mandatory and discretionary. The 2017 tax reform will greatly exacerbate this inequality. The big banks did very well in the tax cut; they received $28 billion in extra profits. There are numerous uncertainties for other taxpayers. Many, many tax filers this year are going to get unpleasant surprises. People who are either expecting a large refund or expecting not to pay, may find something quite different.

Another effect of this form of capitalism is the commodification and privatization of everything, including what had been public or common goods and services, nature, governance and politics, all of this has come under the commodity form.

The large-scale production of surplus and disposable populations, which I've talked about previously, in large part, due to the dominance of finance capital. That is, this whole idea of being able to derive profits without producing, so you don't need workers. And if you're not a worker, you can't be a consumer, so therefore you're not really very valuable to the capital system.

Another outcome has been continuing economic instability. One example is the 2008–2009 crash; the total of the bank bailout has now been estimated at $29 trillion. That's not the typical numbers that you see, but some very reputable economists had done these kinds of calculations. Twenty-nine trillion dollars for the bailout. The UN Food and Agricultural Organization estimates that to wipe out global hunger would cost $30 to $60 billion per year, so if we had not spent this on bailing out the banks, we could have eliminated hunger for over five hundred years. It's always useful to think about the opportunity costs, the things that we might have spent money on that we didn't.

The neoliberal model, we've argued, is failing billions of people around the planet who are wising up. So think about social movements that we talked about last time and the response to them. The material conditions are producing radical shifts in consciousness on both the Left and the Right. We've talked about this as well, so the rise of so-called populist alt-right movements, when people are in this kind of precarity, they're susceptible to demagoguery, and they're susceptible to saviors who are going to come along and help them out.

Because of these effects, the logic of the market is under assault. Many surveys show the rising appeal, especially to younger people, of socialism (in some form) over capitalism. It's also clear, however, that while market fundamentalism, neoliberalism, and globalization are under assault, they are also being heavily guarded. One place we can see this is within the emerging contours of the 2020 US presidential campaign. This is going to be an unrelenting assault, primarily by Republicans, but also by elite Democrats, on candidates and ideas on the Left. The boundaries of debate are being set.

I want to conclude with a few lessons from thinking about social change. First a counter-hegemony, that is, a new common sense, can be mounted and effective, even when the forces of the status quo undertake massive maintenance activities. Despite the asymmetry of material resources available to the contending parties, the opponents of an existing hegemony may prevail by drawing upon resources of representation and ideology. In the ongoing wars of position, counter-hegemonies may finally gain the upper hand by manipulating powerful discourses in ways that resonate with their position rather than their opponents', and that draw out the kernel of good sense from within the shared common sense available to all sides.

A second lesson: a counter-hegemony is itself never completely unassailable. The new status quo requires constant reinforcement and maintenance as well if it is to be naturalized and eventually internalized as the new common sense.

Third, to achieve even a limited new common sense may take several decades. This is a critical lesson for those seeking change, but again sustaining such efforts and avoiding demoralization and burnout can be greatly bolstered by a focus on the fact that change is both possible and realistic.

Fourth, the ways in which shifts in common sense occurred in particular situations are analytically tractable, that is we can understand them. The tactics, strategies, and lessons from one case might be amenable, with appropriate and specific modification, to many others, in both a diagnostic and a prescriptive sense. In addition as we as scholars and activists begin to build up a catalog of these examples, they will serve as an effective counter to the pervasive conception that the status quo is necessary, stable, and unchangeable.

Finally, and perhaps most importantly, even in the face of a seemingly unassailable hegemony, discourses and practices can be shifted through conscious effort. Understanding that this is possible, and providing concrete, grounded examples of instances when such shifts have taken place, is a key starting point for progressive change. The struggles that are most certain to be lost are those that are never taken up. The battles that are sure to be lost are the ones that are never taken up. So belief that struggle is futile and that change is impossible is itself paralyzing and debilitating. This is one of the most potent elements in the naturalized common sense. That is, it rules everything in opposition to it as nonsense, quite literally. Demonstrating the fragility of this claim is the first step to change, I would say. Okay, I'm going to stop there.

Chomsky Lecture, February 28, 2019

Well, this is my last opportunity to "indoctrinate the young"—and the not so young—in this captive audience, so I'll try to run through a series of matters that seem to be important, much too briefly. There's a lot more to say about each one of them, but at least I'll have time for a few words. I'll also be reviewing briefly some of what we've been discussing and filling in gaps from a somewhat different perspective from before: resistance and repression.

Let's start by supposing that you're contracting a malignant cancer. There are two ways to handle it. One way is to put it aside, don't disrupt your life, let it grow, and at some later point treat it, maybe using brutal methods because that's the only option. The second alternative would be to prevent it from growing, obviously much more cost-effective.

The choice is arising right now in connection with one of the existential crises that pose serious questions of survival: global warming. Among those who agree that it is a growing cancer, two views have emerged, the two just mentioned. The overwhelming consensus of scientists strongly favors the second alternative: prevent it from growing, and quickly, or we are doomed. The first alternative has been advanced by some groups of economists (among them a conference of economists organized by Danish environmentalist Bjørn Lomborg, author of a best-selling work promoting this view): let the cancer grow, devote resources to more immediate problems, continue to use fossil fuels to grow the economy, leaving it to a richer future society to deal with the global warming issue more effectively. After all, there has been growth for a long time producing a richer society, so why shouldn't it continue?

The logic is that of a man falling from a skyscraper who waves to a friend on the fiftieth floor and says it's all fine, just look how many floors I've passed with no problems.

In a different context, the one we have been discussing in the last few sessions, the same choices constantly face those whom Adam Smith called the "masters of mankind." The cancer is the constant struggle of the rabble for more rights and for what dominant elites call "excessive democracy." We've run through several examples, beginning with the first modern democratic revolution in mid-seventeenth-century England, when the men of best quality were scandalized by the desire of the rascal multitude to be ruled by countrymen like themselves who know the people's sores, not by their betters. A conflict that persists in later years, taking many forms.

The problem is rising again. A generation of neoliberal policies has aroused anger, bitterness, resentment, and contempt for established institutions over much of the world. The masters have the usual two choices as to how to deal with the cancer. One is force; the other is prevention. Force would include, for example, the kinds of measures that were shown in the Pentagon film that Marv played a little while ago, or maybe something like a COINTELPRO approach, as we discussed last time.

We should recall that the reigning neoliberal doctrines easily tolerate state violence when it protects "sound economics." We saw such tolerance—in fact, enthusiasm—in the reaction of the founding father of neoliberalism, Ludwig von Mises, to the violent repression of labor and social democracy by the Austrian state and to early fascism generally, and again in the willing acceptance of the Pinochet dictatorship by the leading figures of the movement.

If I can again interpolate a personal experience, I learned about neoliberalism from none other than von Mises when I was a grad student and attended a visiting lecture of his, in which he explained why unemployment is the fault of the government. The gist of the argument is simple. Someone who is faced with either starvation or a hazardous job for ten cents an hour will pick the latter—but is prevented from doing so by evil socialists who control the government and infringe on the liberty of this poor soul by barring such work arrangements. The same argument demonstrates the illegitimacy of efforts to bar child labor, to impose health and safety regulations, and other government infringements on liberty.

The ideas trace back to the Mises seminar in Vienna in the 1920s, which attracted the leading lights of what became the neoliberal movement, Friedrich Hayek, Wilhelm Röpke, and others. They also established close links with progressive American intellectuals, like Walter Lippmann. I think I may have mentioned that the term "neoliberalism" was adopted as the slogan of the movement in 1938 at the Lippmann colloquium in Paris, indicating how some ideas pretty much extend across the spectrum.

In general, as we have discussed, neoliberal doctrine easily tolerates state violence when it protects "sound economics" from illegitimate interferences. Some of the most extreme interferences are the initiatives of labor unions, which have always been a prime enemy. That's understandable. Unions protect rights of workers, such as the right not to be fired capriciously without notice, or the right to have safe work conditions. Such interferences with the market undermine optimal use of resources. Furthermore, they interfere with the liberty of the employer to maximize profit. Liberty, along with "sound economics," is one of the sacred principles of neoliberalism and what's called in the US "libertarianism," a departure from traditional usage. Liberty in this sense means the liberty of market actors—the liberty of Jeff Bezos and of the people who are racing around his warehouse, trying to survive. They all should have liberty, and they have no right to interfere with the liberty of others who are adhering to market principles.

Optimal use of resources translates into something like this: suppose I have a billion dollars and each of you has one dollar. Then optimal use of resources means that the unhampered market will be producing luxury yachts for me and maybe a small package of french fries for you. And if you organize to try to get something more, like a little ketchup for the fries, maybe even forming a union to do it, then you're undermining markets and interfering with liberty and "sound economics."

Therefore, the use of violence to prevent these crimes is entirely legitimate, even praiseworthy, and, in fact, principled if you think it through, like the argument against state intervention to create unemployment.

There are, of course, diametrically opposed views. For example, the view that "I have no use for those—regardless of their political party— who hold some foolish dream of spinning the clock back to days when unorganized labor was a huddled, almost helpless mass. . . . Only a handful of unreconstructed reactionaries harbor the ugly thought of breaking unions. Only a fool would try to deprive working men and women of the right to join the union of their choice..."

The wild men in the wings again. In this case President Dwight Eisenhower.

That was conservatism in the 1950s.

By the 1980s under Reagan, conservatism had reversed quite radically, not just harboring "the ugly thought of breaking unions" but proceeding to do it, vigorously, from Reagan's first days, as we've already discussed. Clintonite globalization carried the process further. Clinton's NAFTA, passed over strong labor objection (joined by most of the public), provided employers with such options as blocking efforts to organize by threatening to "transfer" to Mexico. The options are widely used, as shown in an important (and ignored) study by labor historian Kate Bronfenbrenner undertaken under NAFTA rules (Bronfenbrenner 1997).

The tactics are illegal, but when laws are not enforced, that's a mere technicality.

The effects of the new economy on working people were described by Fed chair Alan Greenspan in Senate testimony in 1997. He reported on an "extraordinary state of affairs": "heightened job insecurity" among working people, which "explains a significant part of the restraint on (wages), and the consequent muted price inflation." Greenspan told the Senate Budget Committee that workers' insecurity about layoffs had nearly doubled in the last five years. Despite rising employment, workers are too intimidated to press for decent wages and benefits.

Greenspan's remarks "cheered markets," CNN Money reported, very pleased with the "healthy labor market" he described. Greenspan was celebrated as "St. Alan" because of his management of the flourishing economy during the "great moderation"—until the economy crashed in 2008, leading Greenspan to confess that there were some flaws in his understanding of markets. To his credit. Most of those who were euphoric about the wonderful economy, confidently predicting that the triumph of economic theory would last forever, remained silent.

After the perpetrators were bailed out by the public, all went back to normal, with a sharp increase in wealth for the wealthy but not others, intensified by public policy, such as Trump's one major legislative achievement, the tax scam of 2017.

Unions are not the only enemy of liberty and optimal use of resources. The same is true for all social programs, by the same impeccable logic. You may recall that during the war, Roosevelt issued his Four Freedoms, the values that we were fighting for. One of them was freedom from want. That was bitterly denounced right away by the prominent neoliberal intellectual Wilhelm Röpke, whom I mentioned before, a man who was revered here by leading conservatives—William Buckley and Russell Kirk, among others. Röpke ridiculed the outlandish idea of freedom from want. As he put it, "It is unlikely that the true liberal will be caught by such glib phrases as the 'Freedom from want' by which the essence of liberty is surrendered to collectivism"—the ultimate sin. The New Deal measures to improve people's lives—Social Security, workers' rights, and so on—were despised for the same reasons.

The attitudes are quite general in principled neoliberal/libertarian circles, and they do adhere to principles—of a sort.

The general principles are so broadly accepted, at least at some level, that it's barely even noticed. A good example is the attitude toward the Universal Declaration of Human Rights, discussed earlier.

Despite the broad acceptance, it's important to make sure that nothing goes wrong. While state violence is an entirely appropriate means under neoliberal principles, prevention is a far better way to treat an incipient cancer. At the end last time I discussed some of the newly developed soft methods of control, "surveillance capitalism." There's more to say about that.

Marv posted an interesting article on how workplace discipline is being imposed, not just here but in Europe. It's an article in *Monthly Review*, the one major Marxist journal in the country, which reports that

one of the most recent developments is the practice of "microchipping" employees—placing rice grain–sized radio-frequency identification (RFID) implants under the skin—a technology developed by the Swedish enterprise Epicenter, most of whose employees now have these microchips implanted. Another company, Three Square Market, which is based in Wisconsin, also recently microchipped half of its employees at a "chip party" organized for this purpose. The key advantage of the implant, according to the chief executive of Epicenter, is that it "replaces a lot of things you have, other communication devices, whether it be credit cards or keys" as it allows individuals to operate printers, open electronic locks, and purchase snacks from company vending machines, to name a few examples. Because of the device's convenience, Three Square Market representatives believe that "everyone will soon be doing it." At the same time, it is acknowledged that these chips enable management to track employees' every move, from the number and duration of toilet breaks to the purchase of drinks and food from company vending machines. (Manokha 2019)

The whole article is worth reading, alongside of Zuboff's, for those who want to have a sense of the working environment being planned by the masters—and more generally what is being designed to prevent the cancer of excessive democracy from growing.

The major technique of prevention is a much more ancient one, with no high tech, available to every power group. It's diversion: try to divert attention away from what's happening, away from the sources of your distress on fundamental issues with an institutional base, like the fact that "today's real average wage," Pew Research reports, "has about the same purchasing power it did 40 years ago. And what wage gains there have been have mostly flowed to the highest-paid tier of workers." Or the fact that the bottom half of Americans combined have a negative net worth, debts greater than assets, while 0.1 percent have over 20 percent of the wealth. Better to turn attention to scapegoats, people even more vulnerable than you are, right now immigrants, or black Americans, or whoever's down below you on the totem pole. Make them responsible for your fate.

All of this became a very significant matter with the shift in the early seventies from the regimented capitalism of the previous period, which tolerated such subversive ideas as those of Eisenhower, to the "sound economics" of neoliberalism. The shift causes a problem—more accurately sharpens a persistent problem: it's necessary to figure out ways to keep people from understanding what's happening to them. They see it, of course, in their lives. They can see that there's no growth of wages, that they're losing benefits, that they're intimidated with insecurity. They can see all that, but it's necessary to divert their attention to other matters. If not scapegoats, then to what are called "cultural issues." It's revealing to see how this is done. Will return to it.

How are these matters handled within the political system? An intriguing matter. The political party system in the US has been restructured in recent years. As I discussed earlier, the Democrats had been an uneasy coalition between Southern Democrat white supremacists and Northern workers and liberals, two sectors that differed sharply on many central issues, a tricky coalition with plenty of effects. One quite serious effect was that the New Deal measures of the 1930s had to accept significant compromises. They had to be designed to keep out African Americans in order to placate the Southern Democrats, who had a very powerful position. They would regularly be reelected, so they had tenure and headed important committees, giving them plenty of power.

So for example, Social Security was designed to omit the professions that are mostly African American and Hispanic, agricultural and domestic workers. I talked before about federal housing. In New Deal measures, federal housing was designed to impose segregation. There was no federal funding for public housing unless it was officially segregated, right up to the late sixties. These deliberately racist measures gained the votes of staunch liberals, William Douglas and others, who hated the idea but knew that there was no other way to get any funding for public housing.

That was the coalition. It broke apart during the civil rights movement. The Northern Democrats supported Lyndon Johnson's civil rights legislation, which meant that they lost the Southern vote. That was recognized by Richard Nixon, who developed his Southern Strategy: to capture the South for the Republican Party on the basis of racism and white supremacy. All of this is particularly important for understanding the character of the Republican Party, not the party of Eisenhower or Abraham Lincoln, but the modern Republican Party.

The Republicans for some time had been the more business oriented of the two business parties. In the US we only have business-run parties.

There are two of them, one a little more extreme than the other, more dedicated to protecting the minority of the opulent against the majority, in Madison's words.

But that orientation of both parties raises problems. If your policies are designed to harm the majority of the population for the benefit of a privileged group, you have a problem. You have to find some way of mobilizing a voting base. The problem has become quite serious during the neoliberal period, as both parties shifted to the right. By the 1970s the Democrats had pretty much abandoned the working class. I guess the last gasp was in 1978, the Humphrey-Hawkins Full Employment Act, which was watered down by Carter to have no teeth. That was the end. After that, there were hardly more than gestures to supporting working people, and under Clinton, policies to harm them.

That's left an opening for the Republicans. It's a little tricky because they're the class enemy of the working class, so they have to figure out a way to divert their attention from the actual policies and somehow mobilize them as voters. The party's committed to undermining workers' rights. It's interesting to compare Trumpian rhetoric about loving working people with the policies reported almost daily to harm them. It's imperative to divert attention to prevent awareness of what's happening, to keep the cancer in remission.

Some of the means, which we've already discussed, are pretty obvious, like the traditional tactic of inspiring fear (the Russians are coming, the Nicaraguan army is two days' marching time from Texas, Grenada is going to become a major Russian military base, rapists and murderers are pouring over the border, etc.). And creating scapegoats, like Reagan's rich black women driving in limousines to the welfare offices to steal your hard-earned money, or Muslims imposing Sharia rule on all of us— but not here in Arizona fortunately; the state legislature protected us by passing a law barring the imminent threat, joining many other states that are awake to the peril.

But less transparent means are also needed, and they've been devised.

In the 1970s, the leading Republican strategist Paul Weyrich had a brilliant idea for the party platform: pretend to be opposed to abortion.

That would attract Northern Catholic workers, a big bloc, and it would also attract evangelicals, a huge part of the population that had not been politically mobilized. Now that's a flag you can wave to tell them to vote for us. Don't vote for those baby killers, vote for us, because we're opposed to abortion. It was a brilliant success. You see it almost every day in the news in one form or other.

In the sixties and early seventies, before Weyrich came up with his idea, the Republicans had been committed to reproductive choice. Reagan, when he was governor of California in the sixties, signed one of the most liberal abortion laws in the country, and the same was true in other Republican states. Here, for example, Arizona's Barry Goldwater. Also Richard Nixon, Gerald Ford, George H. W. Bush, the first Bush, all strongly pro-choice. That's not the term that was used then, that's anachronistic.

In 1972, a Gallup poll found that 68 percent of Republicans believed abortion to be a private matter between a woman and her doctor. The government should not be involved. That was the Republican Party up until the mid-seventies. The party leadership flipped on a dime as soon as the potential for gaining votes and diverting the population was perceived. For Reagan, Trump, and the like it's no big problem. They scarcely pretended to have principles anyway. It may be a little surprising for the first Bush, H. W. Bush, who was reputed to have had some principles, but apparently they didn't reach very far.

This is one of the great illustrations of utter cynicism in modern political history, all totally independent of what you believe about abortion. We posted a very good article about it (see Halpern, "How Republicans Became Anti-Choice," 2018). Pure cynicism, and worked brilliantly. By now, for the Republican Party it's a litmus test for appointment to the courts, and in public, party leaders have to passionately proclaim this belief. It's proven to be a marvelous technique to drive class issues into the shadows. The people you're shafting at every turn will vote for you because you're pretending to be in favor of banning abortion.

Interestingly, the pretended dedication to end abortion is so extreme that the leadership doesn't even care, and commentators rarely point out, that their policies are dedicated to increasing abortion—furthermore, illegal abortion, the dangerous kind. That follows at once when you cut family planning aid to Planned Parenthood, or much more seriously than that, family planning aid programs in Africa. When you cancel them, what's the effect going to be? It doesn't take a genius to figure it out.

So we pretend to be opposed to abortion, but we pursue policies that increase abortions—illegal dangerous abortions. We win the world championship for the "baby killing" that we scream about. Meanwhile, we get votes and efface class issues, suppressing the fact that we're undermining the working class and the poor.

It's a pretty neat trick, one has to give them credit.

Let's take another example, gun rights. A live issue here in Arizona, and throughout the country. The history of the gun culture is quite interesting. I'll come back to it directly. Gun rights now are kind of holy writ. To be more accurate, a certain version of gun rights is sacred, the one that was established by the Supreme Court in 2008. The right-wing Roberts Court reversed long-standing precedent and revised the interpretation of the Second Amendment to provide an individual the right to bear arms unrelated to militias. You perhaps remember the wording of the Second Amendment. It's a little ambiguous, so I'll read it: "A well regulated Militia, being necessary to the security of a free State, the right of the people to keep and bear Arms, shall not be infringed."

The interpretation up to 2008 was that people have a right to bear arms because of the right of states to establish militias. That was switched in 2008, now it's a sacred right to have a closet full of assault rifles and so on. All of this is, again, now a litmus test for the Republican Party, for election, for appointment, anything, much like abortion.

The history of the gun culture is quite interesting, well studied by Pamela Haag in a recent work (2016). As she shows, the gun culture is a twentieth-century phenomenon. There was no gun culture in the nineteenth century. It was then mostly a country of farmers. They had guns, but they were like shovels, a tool. Nothing special about it. But that created a problem. After the Civil War, the big gun manufacturers, Winchester and Remington and the rest, came to realize that they no longer had much of a market. During the Civil War they could produce endlessly and the government would buy it. What happens at the end of the Civil War?

Well, farmers still wanted guns, but they didn't want the fancy guns that were being produced by the big gun manufacturers. They just wanted another shovel, the simple gun that they had. So what do you do? The answer was the first great triumph of the public relations industry, now a huge industry. Working for the gun manufacturers, these pioneers of "engineering consent" undertook a publicity campaign to try to create a domestic market for guns. The techniques were later copied by the tobacco industry and many others. The principle, as it was described back in the nineteenth century by the great political economist Thorstein Veblen, was to fabricate wants. If people don't want things, we'll fabricate wants. That'll create a market; we'll trap them.

So the PR specialists for the gun companies concocted tales of a Wild West with brave cowboys and sheriffs fast on the draw and all that exciting stuff. I remember as a kid we all believed the tales. And then, with it comes the ad campaign saying your son has to have a Winchester rifle or he's not a real man, and your daughter has to have a pink pistol or she's not protected, and so on. And again, it worked very well, soon followed by the tobacco companies, the Marlboro man and the rest. The invention of the Wild West became a major part of our lives, creating a gun culture—and a great market for sophisticated guns. It was later enhanced by further PR achievements. It was the first great triumph of what became a huge and flourishing industry that now underpins the economy, which relies crucially on consumer spending, much of it for fabricated wants.

We might take off for a moment to mention a curious aspect of the enormous PR industry that doesn't receive enough attention. It is radically anti-capitalist. As you learned if you took an introductory economics course, markets are based on informed consumers making rational choices. Then you walk into the streets or turn on the TV and immediately see that you are utterly immersed in efforts to create uninformed consumers who will make irrational choices. That's, after all, the point of the sign advertising something for $2.99, not $3.00. Or an ad on TV showing a car with a famous athlete or fashionable model looking on in wonder as it performs some amazing feat. In a market economy, the ad would simply present the car's characteristics along with a column from *Consumer Reports* discussing its positive features and flaws.

The picture generalizes to virtually every moment of our lives. Still, we're supposed to worship markets based on informed consumers making rational choices, and to adopt the economic policies based on this theory of how the economy works. That's just common sense. There's no alternative, as Margaret Thatcher famously proclaimed.

Let's return to the gun culture and the Second Amendment, and the 2008 Court decision (*DC v. Heller*) that changed its interpretation, conferring an individual the right to bear arms. The decision was written by Justice Antonin Scalia, a highly respected libertarian scholar and the dean of originalism, the doctrine that we should adhere strictly to the texts and what they mean—which of course means what they mean to *someone*. Who? Surely the understanding of the Constitution by its authors. We must avoid any liberal revisionism about changing the law to fit the current times and its problems and understanding—a curious doctrine, incidentally. Does it really make sense to be bound by the customs and perceptions of the eighteenth century? But put that aside.

Justice Scalia's decision is not that long. Worth reading. You can pick it up on the internet. It does show great scholarship, as we would expect, citing all sorts of obscure documents from the seventeenth century and so on. There is, however, a curious omission: every reason why the Founders included the Second Amendment in the Bill of Rights.

Their reasons are not obscure. Let's go back to the 1790s. There were some serious problems. One was that the Brits were out there. The British were the great threat. They had a formidable army and a world-dominant navy. The new Republic had almost no army. So suppose the British came again, as, in fact, they did not many years later. Well, you'd better have a well-regulated militia that could be quickly mobilized, which means that people have to have arms, like the minutemen. That was one reason for the Second Amendment.

A second reason was to guard against tyranny. As we saw earlier, there was a real split when the Constitution was established between the Federalists, who wanted a pretty strong central government, and the anti-Federalists, who were probably the majority of the population and who were afraid it would take away their liberty. They're the ones who wanted what the Framers called "excessive democracy." They wanted to be able to defend themselves against another King George III. It wasn't a completely idle concern. Thus, Alexander Hamilton, one of the main Framers, regarded the British system as the optimal one and thought the US should imitate it, including the House of Lords and a strong executive. Well-regulated state militias would be a defense against such a threat to liberty. That was a second reason for the Second Amendment.

There are two further reasons, more fundamental I think. They have to do with why the American Revolution took place. Of course taxation without representation and all that, but there were much more serious reasons, which we have already discussed.

One reason was the Royal Proclamation of 1763, which banned expansion of the colonies to Indian Country, intolerable to the colonists, who understood, as their most revered figure George Washington explained, that their inhabitants differed from wolves only in shape and are bound to "retire" elsewhere as they are replaced by a superior race. To clear those areas of the native scourge, militias would be necessary, though later on the federal army took over the job.

The fourth reason was Britain's clear moves toward banning slavery, declared explicitly in Lord Manfield's 1772 decision that slavery was so "odious" that it could not be tolerated in England. That included the American colonies, where practically all of the leading figures were slave owners. With Britain expelled, the threat that slavery might be barred was overcome, but slaves themselves were a truly serious threat. There were slave rebellions going on all over the Caribbean, which was the main center of slavery until the American South replaced it. In some places, like South Carolina, slaves outnumbered the owners, and as slavery became more vicious, surpassing by far its historical precedents, the danger that slaves might not tolerate it became more pressing. That means you really needed guns and militias.

These are the essential reasons for the Second Amendment, from the perspective of the Founders. All are completely ignored in Scalia's decision. And, interestingly, they appear to be ignored in the substantial legal literature debating his reversal of precedent, which keeps to the issue of individual or collective right to have arms.

So much for vaunted originalism.

It's also of interest that none of these reasons for the Second Amendment applies by the twentieth century, or today. The "vacant lands" have been conquered and the wolves and Indians expelled, apart from territories reserved for them by the conquerors. Slavery was formally ended 150 years ago, though its bitter consequences remain. The British were under control by the late nineteenth century, and since World War II have become a "junior partner" of the US, in the rueful words of the British Foreign Office—and are likely to become a client state if Brexit goes through. That leaves only the idea that guns could be a defense against government tyranny, such sheer fantasy that the only reason for mentioning it is there are sectors of the population that believe it and are heavily arming to protect themselves. That's not an insignificant phenomenon in the age of Trump. But it plainly has nothing to do with defense against tyranny, whatever the beliefs of the men with assault rifles strapped on their backs and others stored away. More like the opposite.

In brief, none of the reasons of the Founders for the Second Amendment holds today, or has for a long time. Though basically irrelevant to modern life, it's become the 11th Commandment, buttressed by a passionate gun culture fabricated by the public relations industry. And it has become a core principle of the Republican Party, a prime mechanism for diverting attention from its assault on the "underlying population," recalling Veblen's term.

That's quite an achievement.

Opposition to abortion and support for the divine right to have an arsenal of assault weapons are two basic planks of the contemporary Republican Party, with an interesting history. They have a plausible rationale as part of the need to maintain a voting base while concealing the fact that policies are designed to undermine those you are seeking to mobilize—a problem that arises for the other business party as well, though in a less extreme form.

There is a third plank in the party platform that doesn't have this rationale, at least not transparently, as in the former two cases. But it merits serious attention primarily because of its importance, but also because it provides further insight into the role of high principle in our political life, along with the devotion to originalism and the passionate opposition to the crime of abortion. This plank is far more serious than the other two, and might even turn out to be a death knell for organized human life. I'm referring to the outright denial of climate change, as in the case of the figure who virtually owns the party by now, or marginalization of the issue, as is standard across the board in party circles, seeping down to the voting constituency. We've discussed the facts of the matter.

It was not always so, and it is instructive to see how this plank in the program was added to the virtual catechism. A decade ago, Republicans came close to supporting a market-based cap-and-trade plan for greenhouse gas emissions. John McCain ran for president on the Republican ticket in 2008, warning about climate change.

Highly influential figures among the "masters of mankind" were deeply concerned by this serious threat to right-thinking and their treasured policies, most prominently the Koch brothers, in particular David Koch, who had "worked tirelessly, over decades, to jettison from office any moderate Republicans who proposed to regulate greenhouse gases," as recounted by Christopher Leonard, author of a major in-depth study of the Koch empire and corporate America (Leonard, "David Koch Was the Ultimate Climate Change Denier," 2019; Leonard, "Kochland," 2019). Much like liberation theology and other heresies, this one could not be permitted to flourish. The Koch empire went into high gear to cut it off before it could begin its evil work, the proper way to deal with incipient cancer.

Leonard describes David Koch as the "ultimate denier," whose rejection of anthropogenic global warming was deep and sincere. Let us suspend disbelief about whether his holding them has something to do with the huge profits at stake. Let's accept that the convictions were entirely sincere.

That's not impossible. It's not a novel insight that it is easy to come to believe, with utter sincerity, what happens to be convenient to believe. There are many striking historical examples. John Calhoun, the grand ideologist of slavery, was no doubt sincere in believing that the horrifying slave labor camps of the South were the necessary foundation for the higher civilization that the planters had created. I presume that Hitler sincerely believed in the right of a superior race to eliminate the *Untermenschen* and take over their lands, and to cleanse their territories of Jews, Roma, and other undesirables. And it is all too easy to find other examples.

The Koch brothers' denialism, however, did not limit itself to just holding these sincere beliefs. They sought to ensure that these convictions would rule the world. In their dedicated pursuit of this goal, they did not limit themselves to employing "the very essence of the democratic process, the freedom to persuade and suggest" (Bernays 1947). They launched huge campaigns to ensure that nothing would be done that might impede the exploitation of the fossil fuels on which their fortune rests. They launched a true juggernaut to derail the mild efforts to deal with global warming. With the help of current vice president Mike Pence and others like him, they were able to cleanse the party of deviants who might not fully toe the line on denialism while twisting the arms of those who remained with public vilification, defunding, and other punishments.

The Koch network, Leonard explained, "has tried to build a Republican Party in its image: one that not only refuses to consider action on climate change but continues to deny that the problem is real." To safeguard this commitment, no stone was left unturned: organization of networks of rich donors, founding of think tanks to shift the discourse, establishment of one of the largest lobbying groups in the country, creation of fake grassroots organizations to ring doorbells, effectively shaping the Tea Party. The party leadership quickly capitulated, and had no problem with the other goals pursued by the Koch juggernaut along with denialism, such as undermining labor rights, destroying unions, and blocking government policies that might help people—what's called "libertarianism" in US usage.

David Koch's campaign to excise the cancer before it could grow achieved great success. It added another crucial plank to the Republican Party platform. For the time being at least, the effort seems to mobilize the popular voting base, just as the others do. As noted, the achievement reveals again the devotion to high principle in the political life of the country. And in light of the consequences, which I need not review, it counts as one of the gravest crimes of history—another small fact that seems to pass under the radar.

A very important question is how long can the scam persist? Can the cancer of seeking authentic freedom and rights be contained by the kinds of means just briefly reviewed, or will it metastasize? Will working people—a very broad category—come to realize that their elected representatives are listening to other voices, not theirs?

In the past, the organized working class has been at the forefront of social struggles, a long and interesting history that I'm sorry there's no time to talk about. It's been beaten down many times, often by violence, but it may well rise again, as in the past. This is not an idle dream. In the 1920s, the vigorous and militant US labor movement had been virtually destroyed by state corporate repression, often violence. A few years later it rose in new forms and spearheaded the New Deal reforms.

To take a more recent precedent, in the early 1970s there was a significant rise in labor militancy, mostly repressed but not entirely. Tony Mazzocchi and his Oil, Chemical, and Atomic Workers International (OCAW)—who are right on the frontline, facing destruction of the environment every day at work—were the driving force behind the establishment of the Occupational Safety and Health Act (OSHA), protecting workers on the job. And they went on from there. Mazzocchi was a harsh critic of capitalism as well as a committed environmentalist. He held that workers should "control the plant environment" while also taking the lead in combating industrial pollution. As the Democrats abandoned working people, Mazzocchi began to advocate for a union-based Labor Party, an initiative that made considerable progress in the 1990s but couldn't survive the decline of the labor movement under severe business-government attack, reminiscent of the 1920s (see Dudzic, "What Happened to the Labor Party?" 2017).

There are in fact some indications of revival, like the teachers' strikes that we discussed earlier. Another is a very important popular campaign for a living wage, which has had some resonance. A related but somewhat more narrow issue has to do with the minimum wage. If you remember Marv's charts a couple of weeks ago, through the period of regimented capitalism the minimum wage tracked productivity. As productivity increased, the minimum wage increased with it. That stops in the mid-seventies. While productivity continued to increase, the minimum wage leveled off. If it had continued to track productivity, by now it would be more than $20 an hour.

There are efforts to at least partially compensate for this neoliberal achievement. By now many states have some minimum wage legislation, quite an important matter. There's a deeper question than the minimum wage, or the living wage. A topic we're already discussed, along with a look at its history. What about wage labor altogether? Is it legitimate? It's generally accepted that if you sign a contract to submit yourself to slavery, the contract is not legitimate. Then why is a contract to submit yourself to totalitarian rule legitimate? That's what a wage contract is. It says that for most of my waking life I'm going to live under totalitarian rule, in fact rules that no totalitarian state ever comes close to achieving if you consider the degree of control of a person in the workplace, even without the microchipping and all that. That's what wage contract is.

Well, going back to Marv's opening comments, that idea dramatically violates common sense today, but that wasn't always true. You may have noticed that our president modestly describes himself as the greatest president in history, but he did grudgingly concede that maybe Abraham Lincoln, the founder of the Republican Party, was of some merit, so we might return to him. As we discussed earlier, Lincoln did have a position on wage labor. He regarded it as the same as slavery except that it was temporary, or supposed to be until the worker could escape it and become a free person again. And recall that that was the position of the Republican Party at the time, and more significantly, of the working class, expressed eloquently in their lively and independent press. The right of "self-rule" was the common sense of the day.

The idea that productive enterprise should be owned by the workforce was pretty common in the nineteenth century, not just by Karl Marx and the Left, but also by classical liberals. So here's John Stuart Mill, the most prominent classical liberal figure of the day, one of the great modern intellectuals. He held that "the form of association, . . . which if mankind continue to improve, must be expected to predominate is . . . the association of the labourers themselves on terms of equality, collectively owning the capital with which they carry on their operations, and working under managers electable and removable by themselves."

The concept has solid roots in insights that animated classical liberal thought from its earliest days—John Locke, Adam Smith, and others. It is a short step to link it to control of other institutions and of communities within a framework of free association and federal organization, in the general style of a range of thought that includes much of the anarchist tradition and left anti-Bolshevik Marxism, and also current activist work of the kind we discussed earlier as people seek to gain control over their lives and fate in worker-owned enterprises and cooperatives.

We may recall Karl Marx's old mole, who continues to burrow under the ground, not far from the surface, and then breaks through when the proper situation arises through activism and engagement. The hope of the future, I think.

CAPITALISM AND COVID-19

A Concluding Coda

A s we were wrapping up our most recent offering of the "What is Politics?" course in the first week of March 2020, the contours of the novel coronavirus or Covid-19 (known more technically as SARS-CoV-2) were just becoming more widely known. As we are writing now at the end of April 2020, the extent and implications are considerably clearer and quite alarming. Though even at this point there is still great uncertainty about the ultimate effects, duration, or aftermath of the pandemic.

In this brief postscript we want to demonstrate that the Covid-19 pandemic currently ravaging the health and economic status of large swaths of the global population emerged predictably (indeed, almost inevitably) out of the kinds of conditions we describe in the rest of the book. Both in terms of the etiology and spread of the pandemic, and in the very uneven response to it, we can see the inexorable workings of the cruel logics of neoliberal, late-stage, globalized capitalism. While much more detail could be included, here we are concerned to highlight those defects in the capitalist political economy that have been most glaringly revealed by the current pandemic.

ETIOLOGY AND SPREAD—AN ABBREVIATED
TIMELINE OF COVID-19

Health professionals and research scientists have been issuing warnings about the likelihood of new and dangerous pandemics for quite some time hearkening back, for example, to the 1918 Spanish flu (which actually originated in Kansas in the US), but especially since the advent of more recent outbreaks such as HIV/AIDS, SARS, MERS, and Ebola.

Recognition and identification of the new virus actually dates from December of 2019, when doctors in China noticed emerging cases of an unusual pneumonia in Wuhan (a city in Hubei Province). Scientists in China sequenced the virus's genome and made it available on January 10, just a month after the December 8 report of the first case of pneumonia-like symptoms from an unknown virus in Wuhan. In contrast, after the SARS outbreak began in late 2002, it took scientists much longer to sequence that coronavirus. It peaked in February 2003—and the complete genome of 29,727 nucleotides wasn't sequenced until that April.

Chinese medical teams reported preliminary findings to the World Health Organization (WHO) on December 31, 2019. The WHO indicated on January 4, 2020, that China had notified it of these unusual cases. The WHO first made a public announcement of the virus on January 5; three weeks later, after more knowledge was gathered about the virus and after its spread matched the institutional definition of a public health emergency, the WHO made the appropriate announcement. Further cases were identified in China, Thailand, Japan, and South Korea by January 20, 2020. The actuality of human-to-human transmission was also recognized on January 20, 2020. Wuhan City was shut down by Chinese authorities on January 23, 2020.

A WHO committee issued the following advice on January 22, 2020, to countries around the world: "It is expected that further international exportation of cases may appear in any country. Thus, all countries should be prepared for containment, including active surveillance, early detection, isolation and case management, contact tracing and prevention of onward spread of 2019-nCoV infection, and to share full data with WHO." The WHO declared a global pandemic on March 11, 2020.

Numerous sources have falsely reported that the Chinese government withheld crucial information for six days from January 14 to 20; in fact (and as the above timeline shows), the Chinese government provided crucial information to the US, the Centers for Disease Control (CDC), and the WHO on January 3, and made multiple public statements of what they knew thereafter. It is clear that this information was emerging even as the epidemic was raging and no one knew precisely what was happening. Doctors were working feverishly to contain it and figure out what it was and what to do. A more accurate portrayal of events, even though it was buried in a typical "China withheld information" story from the Associate Press on April 14, 2020, is: "It's uncertain whether it was local officials who failed to report cases or national officials who failed to record them. It's also not clear exactly what officials knew at the time in Wuhan, which only opened back up last week with restrictions after its quarantine."

Despite early approbation of Chinese efforts, President Trump, utilizing these numerous dishonest claims, and in an attempt to scapegoat the organization and shift blame from his own mishandling of the crisis, announced his plan to withdraw US support for the WHO on April 14, 2020. In fact, as the *Washington Post* reports, Trump wants to destroy the WHO, with dire implications far beyond the current pandemic for unknown numbers of people around the globe who rely on the organization for health services for a wide range of diseases.

As of late April 2020, the coronavirus has infected more than 2.8 million people worldwide, with more than 200,000 fatalities. Both figures, due to very uneven testing and case reporting, include substantial uncertainties, but are undoubtedly serious underestimates. The eventual toll is impossible to predict. And although statistics in the US are even less reliable than in other major countries (and therefore, per capita death rates are difficult to calculate), what is clear at this point is that with approximately 4.5 percent of the world's population, the US has over 25 percent of the world's fatalities.

THE RESPONSE THUS FAR

Beginning in January 2020, after the WHO advisory, countries have adopted varying approaches to dealing with the pandemic. Those who have been most successful (e.g., China, Taiwan, South Korea, Singapore, Vietnam, Germany, Australia, and New Zealand) began comprehensive testing, contact tracing, quarantines, and shutdowns very early. These measures, when combined with adequate economic and social support, have managed to slow the spread of cases in these countries to the point where medical capacities have not been overwhelmed and lower per capita fatality rates have been achieved. In many other countries, including the US, response has been much slower and haphazard, with consequently much higher rates of infection and death.

Capitalist Common Sense and Covid-19

"Moments are the elements of profit"—Karl Marx, *Capital*, Volume 1, p. 352 [see chapter 2, "Additional Chapter References"]

To begin, it is crucial to note that much more effective prevention, preparedness, and coping measures have been available or could have been developed in advance of the present pandemic. Because of capitalist logics, and the governance structures they command that prioritize profits over people, such measures have remained out of reach. A recent article in the *New York Times* magazine, for example, quotes zoologist and disease ecologist Peter Daszak: "The problem isn't that prevention was impossible. . . . It was very possible. But we didn't do it. Governments thought it was too expensive. Pharmaceutical companies operate for profit." The same article goes on to make clear that contemporary science already has the necessary tools for developing panvirals (which might provide safeguards against a variety of pathogens) or vaccines, but then quotes microbiologist Vincent Racaniello: "The real obstacle to making panviral drugs or vaccines has been that no one was willing to pay for their development. For pharmaceutical companies . . . panviral vaccines are simply a terrible business proposition: Companies have to spend hundreds of millions of dollars to develop a shot that people will get once a year at most—and not at all in years when no particular disease is ascendant. Panviral drug treatments are unprofitable for similar reasons. For one, the course of treatment is short, usually just a few weeks; for chronic diseases (diabetes, high blood pressure), patients take regimens of pills daily, often for years." This same profits *über alles* logic, as Racaniello continues, applies to testing: it's "a chicken-and-egg situation: No one is developing drugs for these viruses because there's no way to test for them. And no one is developing tests, because there aren't any drugs to prescribe."

It is also then possible to employ this ethos to explain many other elements of the current response. Though there is variation in terms of worldwide reaction, we concentrate here on the US case, as the most extreme version of neoliberal capitalism. It is critical to note, however, that at the moment we are writing the pandemic has yet to manifest its full ferocity on the most vulnerable segments of the planet's population, especially in Africa and Latin America, areas where lack of preparedness in terms of health care professionals and medical supplies is more pronounced and dire than even in the US. It should also be evident that these problems will be drastically exacerbated if the campaign to destroy the WHO succeeds.

Over the past forty years, the US health care "system" (along with most other public goods and services) has been under continuous assault. Following Ronald Reagan's dictum that "government is the problem" (except for coddling those at the top of the private sector, about which more in a moment), massive neoliberal efforts to defund, deregulate, and privatize have produced the most expensive, complicated, and patchworked health care apparatus in the developed world; one that still leaves 40 million citizens uninsured and an additional 40 million underinsured. It is also an arrangement that, despite its exorbitant costs, produces some of the poorest health outcomes among advanced countries. For many of those "lucky" enough to participate in this scheme, health coverage is tied to employment, a precarity now highlighted vividly by the advent of the pandemic.

Driven by the same insatiable desire for profit, capital has roamed the globe searching for cheaper labor or raw materials, more lucrative markets, or more desirable (i.e., more lax) regulatory environments. When combined with other neoliberal tenets, such as privatization and "just in time" production regimes (i.e., no more inventory on hand than absolutely necessary), these thousand-mile commodity chains go a long way in explaining the woefully inadequate supplies of masks, test kits, ventilators, hospital beds, and the myriad additional elements necessary for an effective response.

Finally, this logic also elucidates the nature and content of the US "recovery" packages, and the extreme urgency of "reopening the economy," no matter the risks to the population. The brief epigram from Marx that opens this section was meant to make clear that sunk costs in means of production (raw materials, tools, buildings, etc.) cannot sit idle for a moment. Any such disruption is not only profit foregone, but also an actual loss. Thus the desperate need for (some) people to get back to work, and to get the gears of the profit machine back up to speed as quickly as possible. Here it is also worth thinking about the very uneven landscape of governmental prescriptions. While all levels (federal, state, and local), though to varying extent, have issued stay-at-home guidelines or mandates for "non-essential" workers, and closures for "non-essential" businesses (most typically small enterprises), there have been no such shut-down orders issued for financial institutions, large landlords, insurance companies, and the like. Likewise, in the rush to "reopen" the economy, we have yet to see government mandates (at any level) requiring employers to provide verifiably safe working conditions for their returning employees. Rather, workers are being asked, as before the pandemic, to risk their own health and safety for the sake of a return to profit making for those above them.

The lopsided recovery legislation passed thus far (with *overwhelming bipartisan support*, it must be noted) provides enormous relief for those at the top, and mere crumbs to the public. The first CARES bill allocated $500 billion to large corporations, banks, and other financial institutions, although when leveraged with other resources from the Federal Reserve really amounted to $4.5 trillion at a minimum, and with virtually no oversight or accountability. By contrast workers were promised a one-time payment of $1,200, plus $500 per child. As Treasury Secretary Mnuchin indicated, this payment should provide "bridge liquidity" (terminology always familiar to working men and women!) for ten weeks, which actually works out to $17/day; plenty to get by on. The legislation also expanded eligibility for unemployment insurance, as well as increasing weekly unemployment payments by $600. Of course, all of that assumes that the new 26 million claimants can access those benefits. Thus far, state and local agencies have been overwhelmed by demand. These problems will only worsen as resources for those government sectors dry up, and as the federal response to such resource needs remains anemic. Finally, the legislation has included the Paycheck Protection Program (PPP) to benefit small businesses (those with fewer than five hundred employees!) to be administered by the Small Business Administration. The PPP was initially funded with $350 billion for forgivable loans (depleted almost immediately, with large chunks going to much-larger businesses and chains), and was augmented by an additional $350 billion on April 24, 2020. One final aspect of the PPP is critical: rather than resources going directly to workers, these funds go to employers, who then retain the discretion of whether to keep workers on the payroll, at what levels of employment, and at what rates of pay. This leaves all power in the hands of capitalists, and makes clear that whatever benefits workers might derive in society (including, at this fraught moment, health care) must come through a relationship of waged labor, if at all.

Militarism and Covid-19

The connections between militarism, capitalism, and the pandemic are extensive. The most obvious and immediate are the opportunity costs connected with the bloated US military budget, now topping $750 billion per year (outspending the next ten national "competitors" combined). Current expenditures on the National Institutes of Health and the National Science Foundation combined are under $50 billion, approximately 6 percent of the military budget. As disease ecologist and zoologist Peter Daszak has put it: "We don't think twice about the cost of protecting against terrorism. We go out there, we listen to the whispers, we send out the drones—we have a whole array of approaches. We need to start thinking about pandemics the same way."

Another important link between militarism and the pandemic works through neo-imperialism and globalized neoliberalism. The US utilizes military means to secure access to strategic and necessary resources, and to deny that access to economic, near-peer competitors (to use the military argot), as well as to open markets and provide protection for US firms operating internationally. A concomitant consequence of this far-flung, globalized system is the spread of infection from country to country through traveler contact. In fact, one of the characteristics that distinguishes Covid-19 from its most recent predecessors (SARS, MERS, and Ebola) is just that rapid and extensive geographic spread.

Environmental Catastrophe and Covid-19

Again, the connections here are numerous, but we highlight only two. The first pertains to the increasing likelihood of pandemics like Covid-19 occurring as mounting appetites for resources push development further and further into previously wild lands. As experts like Daszak have warned, "as populations and global travel continued to grow and development increasingly pushed into wild areas, it was almost inevitable that once-containable local outbreaks, like SARS or Ebola, could become global disasters." Here Daszak is pointing to the potential calamities awaiting humanity through zoonotic vectors of animal-to-human infection. More frequent and extensive contact between people and wild animals (and the myriad viruses they carry), which has also been put in motion as global warming and the climate crisis put animal populations on the move, set the stage for yet more Covid-19s.

The second connection comes through the neoliberal waves of environmental deregulation that have made air, water, and land much more toxic, and have thereby significantly increased susceptibility to effects of coronavirus infections by inducing debilitating preexisting conditions. These effects (as well as correlated socioeconomic characteristics), of course, are distributed very unevenly through the population; a fact which helps to explain the substantial and disproportionate rates of infection and fatality in US communities of color.

Social Movements (Regressive and Progressive) and Covid-19

Finally, we want to note some of the important linkages between the pandemic and social reactions. On the right, predictably, we see numerous examples of authoritarian regimes around the globe utilizing the pandemic as a cover for repression, added surveillance, and curtailing of civil liberties. In the US, as we write, those most anxious to open up the country and get back to *business* as usual are stirring up combinations of financial insecurity, boredom, impatience, and distrust of government to provoke flouting of stay-at-home orders, thereby putting the protesters themselves and others at increased risk. Politicians in several US states are both responding to these demands and encouraging them, and are either contemplating or actually opening their states back up prematurely before necessary conditions and safeguards are in place.

On the other hand, some very significant social movements, both established and emerging are working toward positive change. On an international scale, it is possible to identify a number of country-to-country assistance programs (some occurring even in defiance of heavy US sanction regimes). Most notably, Cuba, as has happened many times during past crises, has been sending medical teams and equipment to places that have been hardest hit. China, despite all of the usual US scapegoating and blaming the "yellow peril," got a relatively early handle on its own outbreak (as we note above), and has now been assisting others with personnel and materials, and most crucially, with knowledge gained from its own experience with the pandemic. Similar mutual aid activities are rising spontaneously at smaller scales planet wide.

Additionally, and hopefully of lasting significance beyond the immediate crisis, we see previously powerless segments of the population, now recognized as essential heroes (and perhaps taking those epithets more seriously than those who deploy them), rising up to demand rights and benefits commensurate with that putative status. Whether from frontline medical workers, people who keep the lights on, the water flowing, the grocery shelves stocked, the buses running, and the garbage collected, demands are emerging for decent pay, safe working conditions, health care, sick and parental leave, and debt relief (for mortgages or rent, utilities, credit cards, etc.). Whether and how these demands register in the political system will help shape the post-pandemic landscape.

Covid-19 has revealed glaring failures and monstrous brutalities in the current capitalist system. It represents both a crisis and an opportunity. Contests for controlling the narratives around the meaning of this pandemic will be the terrain of struggle for either a new, more humane common sense and society or a return to the status quo ante. The outcome of those contests is uncertain; everything depends on the actions that people take into their own hands.

FURTHER RESOURCES

Chapter 1

COURSE READINGS

Becker, Elizabeth. *New York Times*, May 27, 2004.

Bernays, Edward. "The Engineering of Consent." *Annals of the American Academy of Political and Social Science* 250, no. 1 (1947): 113–20.

Besar, Elena. "Hundreds of Journalists Jailed Globally Becomes the New Normal." Committee to Protect Journalists, December 13, 2018. https://cpj.org/reports/2018/12/journalists-jailed-imprisoned-turkey -china-egypt-saudi-arabia/.

Carter, Jacob, et al. *Science under Siege at the Department of the Interior.* PDF file. Union of Concerned Scientists, December 2018. https://www .ucsusa.org/sites/default/files/attach/2018/12/science-under-siege-at -department-of-interior-full-report.pdf.

Chomsky, Noam. *Deterring Democracy.* Chapter 12. New York: Hill & Wang, 1992. First published 1991 by Verso (London and New York).

Crehan, Kate. *Gramsci's Common Sense: Inequality and Its Narratives.* Preface and chapter 3. Durham and London: Duke University Press, 2016.

Hedges, Chris. "Banishing Truth." Truthdig, December 24, 2018. https://www.truthdig.com/articles/banishing-truth/.

———. "The Permanent Lie." Truthdig, December 17, 2017. https://www.truthdig.com/articles/permanent-lie-deadliest-threat/.

Reporters Without Borders. *Worldwide Roundup of Journalists Killed, Detained, Held Hostage, or Missing in 2018.* PDF file. December 2018. https://rsf .org/sites/default/files/worldwilde_round-up.pdf.

ADDITIONAL CHAPTER REFERENCES

Associated Press. "Grassley Answers Reactions to His 'Booze or Women or Movies' Remark on Estate Tax." *Des Moines Register*, December 4, 2017. https://www.desmoinesregister.com/story/news/politics/2017/12/04 /grassley-answers-reactions-his-booze-women-movies-remark-estate -tax/919542001/.

Baker, Dean. "The Green New Deal Is Happening in China." Truthout, January 14, 2019. https://truthout.org/articles/the-green-new-deal-is -happening-in-china/.

Bernays, Edward. *Propaganda*. New York: H. Liveright, 1928.

Chomsky, Noam. *Towards a New Cold War*. New York: New Press, 2003. First published 1982 by Pantheon (New York).

———. *Deterring Democracy*. New York: Hill & Wang, 1992. First published 1991 by Verso (London and New York).

Geman, Ben. "Ohio Gov. Kasich Concerned by Climate Change, but Won't 'Apologize' for Coal." *The Hill*, May 2, 2012. https://thehill.com/policy /energy-environment/225073-kasich-touts-climate-belief-but-wont -apologize-for-coal.

Giddens, Anthony. *The Constitution of Society: Outline of the Theory of Structuration*. Berkeley: University of California Press, 1984.

Gramsci, Antonio. *Selections from Cultural Writings*. Edited by David Forgacs and Geoffrey Nowell-Smith. Cambridge: Harvard University Press, 1985.

Hall, Stuart. "Gramsci's Relevance for the Study of Race and Ethnicity." *Journal of Communication Inquiry* 10, no. 2 (1986): 5–27.

Hansen, James, et al. "Ice Melt, Sea Level Rise and Superstorms: Evidence from Paleoclimate Data, Climate Modeling, and Modern Observations that 2°C Global Warming Could Be Dangerous," *Atmospheric Chemistry and Physics*, 16, 3761–3812, https://doi.org/10.5194/acp-16-3761-2016, 2016.

Lucas, John. "US Has Killed More Than 20 Million People in 37 'Victim Nations' since World War II." Global Research, May 28, 2020 (originally published November 27, 2015). http://www.globalresearch.ca/us-has -killed-more-than-20-million-people-in-37-victim-nations-since-world -war-ii/5492051.

"Megacities: Urban Future, the Emerging Complexity: A Pentagon Video." YouTube video, 4:55. October 14, 2016. https://www.youtube.com /watch?v=gEPdOZbyzbw&t=17s.

Popovich, Nadja, Livia Albeck-Ripka, and Kendra Pierre-Louis. "78 Environmental Rules on the Way Out Under Trump." *New York Times*, October 5, 2017. https://www.nytimes.com/interactive/2017/10/05/climate

/trump-environment-rules-reversed.html.

Rielly, John, ed. *American Public Opinion and U.S. Foreign Policy.* Chicago Council on Foreign Relations, 1987.

"A Running List of How Trump Is Changing Environmental Policy." *National Geographic*, March 31, 2017. https://news.nationalgeographic.com /2017/03/how-trump-is-changing-science-environment/.

Savage, Charles. "Trump Says He Alone Can Do It. His Attorney General Nominee Usually Agrees." *New York Times*, January 14, 2019. https://www .nytimes.com/2019/01/14/us/politics/william-barr-executive-power.html.

Smith, Adam. *The Wealth of Nations.* Chicago: Chicago University Press, 1977.

ACTIVIST/PRACTITIONER INSIGHTS

Angelo Carusone, President, Media Matters for America.

> Alerted the class to the emergence of a new form of "fake news" consisting of completely fabricated news stories masquerading as real news, including in the near future fake or synthetic video.

Janine Jackson, Program Director, Fairness and Accuracy in Reporting.

> Drew out for the class the implications of having made a historical choice to fund news gathering and journalism as a private commercially driven enterprise in the US; clarified that journalism is (or ought to be) a public service, but media is a business.

Chapter 2

COURSE READINGS

Alperovitz, Gar. "Principles of a Pluralist Economy: Introduction." The Next System Project, May 15, 2017. https://thenextsystem.org/principles -introduction.

Alston, Philip. "Report of the Special Rapporteur on Extreme Poverty and Human Rights on His Mission to the United States of America." May 4, 2018. Report available at Rosa Furneau, "United States Gets an F for Failing to Help Its Neediest." *Mother Jones*, June 22, 2018. https://www

.motherjones.com/politics/2018/06/united-nations-human-rights
-council-report-america-gets-f-poverty/.

Bivens, Josh, and Heidi Shierholz. "What Labor Market Changes Have
Generated Inequality and Wage Suppression?" PDF file. Economic Policy
Institute, December 12, 2018. https://files.epi.org/pdf/148880.pdf.

Fisher, Mark. *Capitalist Realism: Is There No Alternative?* Chapters 1–3.
Winchester, UK: Zero Books, 2009.

Friedman, Milton. *Capitalism and Freedom.* Prefaces (2002, 1982, 1962),
introduction, and chapter 1. Chicago: University of Chicago Press, 1962.

Hahnel, Robin. "Why the Market Subverts Democracy." *American Behavioral
Scientist* 52, no. 7 (2009): 1006–22.

ADDITIONAL CHAPTER REFERENCES

Anderson, Elizabeth. *Private Government: How Employers Rule Our Lives (and
Why We Don't Talk about It).* Princeton, NJ, and Oxford, UK: Princeton
University Press, 2017.

Bairoch, Paul. *Economics and World History.* Chicago: Chicago University Press,
1993.

Chomsky, Noam. "Consent without Consent: Reflections on the Theory and
Practice of Democracy." *Cleveland State Law Review* 44, no. 4 (1996). This
essay also available in Noam Chomsky, *Masters of Mankind: Essays and
Lectures, 1969–2013* (Chicago: Haymarket Books, 2014).

Gaddis, John Lewis. *The Long Peace: Inquiries into the History of the Cold War.*
New York: Oxford University Press, 1987.

Gardner, Lloyd. *Safe for Democracy.* Oxford, UK: Oxford University Press,
1987.

Klarman, Michael J. *The Framers' Coup: The Making of the United States
Constitution.* New York: Oxford University Press, 2016.

Marx, Karl. *Capital: A Critique of Political Economy,* Volume 1. New York:
Penguin Classics, 1976/1990.

Montgomery, David. *The Fall of the House of Labor: the Workplace, the State, and
American Labor Activism, 1865–1925.* Cambridge: Cambridge University
Press, 1989.

Santiso, Javier. *Latin America's Political Economy of the Possible.* Cambridge:
MIT Press, 2006.

Ware, Norman. *The Industrial Worker, 1840–1860.* Boston: Houghton Mifflin,
1924.

ACTIVIST/PRACTIONER INSIGHTS

Eduardo Garcia, Coordinator, AFGJ's Prison Imperialism Project, Alliance for Global Justice.

> Described the work of AFGJ to find new ways to put some light on US intervention in Latin America, and the focus of the organization on economic and environmental justice, the creation of authentic democratic institutions, and opposition to US militarism.

John Duda, Director of Communications, The Democracy Collaborative.

> Presented the class with some concrete examples of alternatives to our present economic arrangements, drawing on the real-world experiments in worker ownership and control that make up the heart of The Next System Project (one of the chief activities of The Democracy Collaborative).

Chapter 3

COURSE READINGS

Chomsky, Noam. "'The Most Dangerous Moment,' 50 Years Later." TomsDispatch.com, October 15, 2012. http://www.tomdispatch.com/blog/175605/.

Crawford, Neta C. "Human Cost of the Post-9/11 Wars: Lethality and the Need for Transparency." PDF file. Brown University Costs of War Project. November 2018. https://watson.brown.edu/costsofwar/files/cow/imce/papers/2018/Human%20Costs%2C%20Nov%208%202018%20CoW.pdf.

Engelhardt, Tom. "Mapping a World from Hell: 76 Countries Are Now Involved in Washington's War on Terror." Counterpunch, January 5, 2018. https://www.counterpunch.org/2018/01/05/mapping-a-world-from-hell-76-countries-are-now-involved-in-washingtons-war-on-terror/.

Excerpts from *NSC 68, A Report to the National Security Council, 1950.* PDF file. http://www.trumanlibrary.org/whistlestop/study_collections/coldwar/documents/pdf/10-1.pdf.

"Global Arms Industry: US Companies Dominate the Top 100; Russian Arms Industry Moves to Second Place." Stockholm International Peace Research Institute, December 10, 2018. https://www.sipri.org/media

/press-release/2018/global-arms-industry-us-companies-dominate-top
-100-russian-arms-industry-moves-second-place.

Hartung, William. "The Doctrine of Armed Exceptionalism: The Urge
to Splurge: Why Is It So Hard to Reduce the Pentagon Budget?"
CommonDreams.org, October 25, 2016. http://www.tomdispatch.com
/post/176202/tomgram%3A_william_hartung%2C_the_doctrine_of
_armed_exceptionalism/.

Klare, Michael. "Why 'Overmatch' Is Overkill." *The Nation*, December 20,
2018. https://www.thenation.com/article/archive/overmatch-pentagon
-military-budget-strategy/.

Lindorff, Dave. "Exclusive: The Pentagon's Massive Accounting Fraud
Exposed." PDF file. *The Nation*, November 27, 2018.

Schivone, Gabriel, and John Lindsay-Poland. "Opinion: Mexico's Gun Violence
a 'Moral Crisis of Complicity' for U.S. Border States." Special to the
Arizona Daily Star, December 17, 2018. https://tucson.com/opinion
/local/opinion-mexico-s-gun-violence-a-moral-crisis-of-complicity/article
_2292df4f-b0f9-54bd-924d-66b5d2470573.html.

Shultz, George P., William J. Perry, Henry A. Kissinger, and Sam Nunn. "A
World Free of Nuclear Weapons," Nuclear Security Project, January 4,
2007. https://www.hoover.org/research/world-free-nuclear-weapons-0.

Stern, Jeffrey E. "From Arizona to Yemen: The Journey of an American Bomb."
New York Times Magazine, December 11, 2018. https://www.nytimes
.com/2018/12/11/magazine/war-yemen-american-bomb-strike.html.

William J. Perry Project. https://www.wjperryproject.org/about.

ADDITIONAL CHAPTER REFERENCES

Bach, J. R. Borosage, M. Honey, and T. Barry, eds. *Global Focus*. New York: St.
Martins, 2000.

Carothers, Thomas. *In the Name of Democracy*. Berkeley: University of
California Press, 1991.

Carothers, Thomas. In Abraham Lowenthal, ed., *Exporting Democracy*.
Baltimore: Johns Hopkins, 1991.

Chomsky, Noam. *For Reasons of State*. New York: New Press, 2003. First
published in 1973 by Pantheon (New York).

———. *Failed States*. Chapter 4. New York: Metropolitan Books, 2006.

———. *Deterring Democracy*. Chapter 11. New York: Hill & Wang, 1992.
First published 1991 by Verso (London and New York).

Chomsky, Noam, and Howard Zinn, eds. *Pentagon Papers*. Gravel edition, volume 5. Boston: Beacon Press, 1972.

Green, David. *The Containment of Latin America*. Chicago: Quadrangle Books, 1971.

Harvey, David. *The New Imperialism*. Oxford, UK: Oxford University Press, 2003.

Küng, Hans. *The Catholic Church*. New York: Modern Library, 2001.

LaFeber, Walter. *Inevitable Revolutions*. New York: Norton, 1983.

Lenin, Vladimir I. *Imperialism, The Highest Stage of Capitalism*. 1916. Marxists. org. https://www.marxists.org/archive/lenin/works/1916/imp-hsc.

Marx, Karl, and F. Engels. *The Communist Manifesto*. 1848. Marxists.org. https://www.marxists.org/archive/marx/works/1848/communist -manifesto/index.htm.

McChesney, Robert. *Communication Revolution: Critical Junctures and the Future of Media*. New York: New Press, 2007.

Pickard, Victor. *Democracy without Journalism?: Confronting the Misinformation Society*. Oxford, UK: Oxford University Press, 2020.

Ponting, Clive. *Churchill*. London: Sinclair-Stevenson, 1994.

Schmookler, Andrew Bard. *The Parable of the Tribes: The Problem of Power in Social Evolution*. Berkeley: University of California Press, 1984 (hardback); (paperback, Houghton Mifflin, 1986).

Shoup, Laurence H., and William Minter. *Imperial Brain Trust: The Council on Foreign Relations and United States Foreign Policy*. New York: Monthly Review Press, 1977.

Starrs, Sean K. *American Power Globalized: Rethinking National Power in the Age of Globalization* (forthcoming).

Westbrook, Robert B. *John Dewey and American Democracy*. Ithaca, NY: Cornell University Press, 1991.

ACTIVIST/PRACTITIONER INSIGHTS

Sterling Vinson, Member, Veterans for Peace, Tucson Chapter.

Laid out the principle goals and activities of Veterans for Peace as consisting of efforts to increase public awareness of the causes and costs of war; to restrain our governments from intervening overtly and covertly in the internal affairs of other nations; to end the arms race and to reduce and eventually eliminate nuclear weapons; to seek justice for veterans and victims of war; and to abolish war as an instrument of national policy.

Devora Gonzalez, Field Organizer, School of the Americas Watch.

Took the class through a brief history of the School of the Americas (now renamed Western Hemisphere Institute for Security Cooperation, WHINSEC), its involvement in the training and arming of repressive police and military forces throughout Latin America, and the efforts of SOAW to shut them down.

Chapter 4

COURSE READINGS

Baker, Dean. "Saving the Environment: Is Degrowthing the Answer?" *Counterpunch*, November 28, 2018. https://www.counterpunch.org /2018/11/28/saving-the-environment-is-degrowthing-the-answer/.

Bellamy, John Foster. *Ecology against Capitalism.* Preface and chapter 2. New York: Monthly Review Press, 2002.

Bledsoe, Paul. "Going Nowhere Fast on Climate Change." *New York Times*, December 29, 2018. https://www.nytimes.com/2018/12/29/opinion /climate-change-global-warming-history.html.

Eilperin, Julie, et al. "Trump Administration Sees a 7 Degree Rise in Global Temperatures by 2100." *Washington Post*, September 27, 2018.

Hickel, Jason. "Why Growth Can't Be Green." *Foreign Policy*, Fall 2018. https://foreignpolicy.com/2018/09/12/why-growth-cant-be-green/.

Lipton, Eric, et al. "The Real-Life Effects of Trump's Environmental Rollbacks: 5 Takeaways from Our Investigation." *New York Times*, December 26, 2018. https://www.nytimes.com/2018/12/26/us/trump -environment-regulation-rollbacks.html.

Pollin, Robert. "Degrowth vs. a Green New Deal." PDF file. *New Left Review*, July/August 2018. https://newleftreview.org/issues/II112/articles/robert -pollin-de-growth-vs-a-green-new-deal.pdf.

Polychroniou, C. J. "Global Warming and the Future of Humanity: An Interview with Noam Chomsky and Graciela Chichilnisky." Truthout.org, September 17, 2016. https://truthout.org/articles/global-warming-and -the-future-of-humanity-an-interview-with-noam-chomsky-and -graciela-chichilnisky/.

Waterstone, Marv. "Adrift on a Sea of Platitudes: Why We Will Not Solve the Greenhouse Issue." *Environmental Management* 17, no. 2 (1993): 141–52.

ADDITIONAL CHAPTER REFERENCES

Hansen, James, et al. "Ice Melt, Sea Level Rise and Superstorms: Evidence from Paleoclimate Data, Climate Modeling, and Modern Observations that 2°C Global Warming Could Be Dangerous." *Atmospheric Chemistry and Physics*, 16, 3761–3812. https://doi.org/10.5194/acp-16-3761-2016, 2016.

Harvey, David. *Justice, Nature and the Geography of Difference*. Oxford, UK: Blackwell Publishing, 1996.

Klein, Naomi. *Capitalism vs. the Climate. The Nation*. November 9, 2011. https://www.thenation.com/article/archive/capitalism-vs-climate/.

ACTIVIST/PRACTITIONER INSIGHTS

Carolyn Shafer, Member, Board of Directors, Patagonia Area Resource Alliance (PARA).

Presented, as a case study of environmental conflict, the work of PARA, a watchdog organization that monitors the activities of mining companies, as well as ensures government agencies' due diligence, to make sure their actions have long-term, sustainable benefits to our public lands, our water, and the town of Patagonia, Arizona.

Chapter 5

COURSE READINGS

Bauman, Zygmunt. *Wasted Lives: Modernity and Its Outcasts*. Introduction and chapter 3. Cambridge, UK: Polity Press, 2004.

Brown, Wendy. *Undoing the Demos: Neoliberalism's Stealth Revolution*. Chapter 1. New York: Zone Books, 2015.

Giroux, Henry. "Culture of Cruelty: The Age of Neoliberal Authoritarianism." Counterpunch, October 23, 2015. https://www.counterpunch.org/2015/10/23/culture-of-cruelty-the-age-of-neoliberal-authoritarianism/.

Kotz, David M. "End of the Neoliberal Era? Crisis and Restructuring in American Capitalism." *New Left Review* 113 (2018): 29–55.

McCoy, Alfred W. "It's Not Just Trump: A Toxic Right-Wing Nationalism Is

Rising across the Planet." AlterNet, April 2, 2017. https://www.alternet
.org/2017/04/its-not-just-trump-toxic-right-wing-nationalism-rising
-across-planet/.

O'Toole, Fintan. "Trial Runs for Fascism are in Full Flow." *Irish Times*, June
24, 2018. https://www.irishtimes.com/opinion/fintan-o-toole-trial-runs
-for-fascism-are-in-full-flow-1.3543375.

Powell, Lewis F. Jr. "The Powell Memorandum/Manifesto." PDF file. August
23, 1971. https://rmokhiber.wpengine.com/wp-content/uploads/2012/09
/Lewis-Powell-Memo.pdf.

ADDITIONAL CHAPTER REFERENCES

Adamsky, Dmitry Dima. "The 1983 Nuclear Crisis—Lessons for Deterrence
Theory and Practice." *Journal of Strategic Studies*, 2013.

Baker, Dean. "The Green New Deal Is Happening in China." January 14,
2019. Truthout, January 14, 2019. https://truthout.org/articles/the-green-
new-deal-is-happening-in-china/.

Cardoso, Pedro, Philip S. Barton, Klaus Birkhofer, Filipe Chichorro, Charl
Deacon, Thomas Fartmann, Caroline S. Fukushima, et al. "Scientists'
Warning to Humanity on Insect Extinctions." *Biological Conservation* 242
(February 2020): 108246.

Cowie, Jefferson. "Notes and Documents: 'A One-Sided Class War':
Rethinking Doug Fraser's 1978 Resignation from the Labor-Management
Group." Researchgate, August 1, 2003. https://www.researchgate
.net/publication/263724727_Notes_and_Documents_A_One-Sided
_Class_War_Rethinking_Doug_Fraser%27s_1978_Resignation_from
_the_Labor-Management_Group.

DiMaggio, Anthony. "The 'Trump Recovery': Behind Right-Wing Populism's
Radical Transformation." *Counterpunch*, August 9, 2019. https://www
.counterpunch.org/2019/08/09/the-trump-recovery-behind-right-wing
-populisms-radical-transformation/.

Fischer, Benjamin B. "A Cold War Conundrum: The 1983 Soviet War Scare."
Summary. https://www.cia.gov/library/center-for-the-study-of
-intelligence/csi-publications/books-and-monographs/a-cold
-war conundrum/source.htm.

Friedman, Milton. *Capitalism and Freedom*. Preface. Chicago: University of
Chicago Press, 1962.

"From George Washington to James Duane, September 7, 1783." *Founders
Online*, National Archives. https://founders.archives.gov/documents

/Washington/99-01-02-11798.

"Global Pay Ratio: CEO vs. Average Worker." https://onsizzle.com/i/global
-pay-vs-average-worker-c-e-0-country-ratio-of-pay-15406559.

Harvey, David. *The New Imperialism*. Oxford, UK: Oxford University Press, 2003.

Ho, Jessica Y., and Arun S. Hendi. "Recent Trends in Life Expectancy across
High Income Countries: Retrospective Observational Study." *BMJ* 362
(2018). https://doi.org/10.1136/bmj.k2562.

Lafer, Gordon. *The One Percent Solution: How Corporations are Remaking
America One State at a Time*. Ithaca, NY: Cornell University Press, 2017.

McNichols, Celine, Heidi Shierholz, and Marni von Wilpert. "Workers'
Health, Safety, and Pay Are Among the Casualties of Trump's War on
Regulations." Economic Policy Institute, January 29, 2018. http://www
.epi.org/publication/deregulation-year-in-review/#epi-toc-4.

"Mont Pelerin Society Statement of Aims." https://www.montpelerin.org
/statement-of-aims/.

Nguyen, Viet Thanh, and R. Hughes. "The Forgotten Victims of Agent
Orange." *New York Times* op-ed, September 15, 2017.

"OppenheimerFunds Invites Investors to 'Challenge Borders' with New Ad
Campaign." PR Newswire, June 6, 2018. https://www.prnewswire.com
/news-releases/oppenheimerfunds-invites-investors-to-challenge-borders
-with-new-ad-campaign-300660726.html.

Piketty, Thomas, Emmanuel Saez, and Gabriel Zucman. "Economic Growth
in the US: A Tale of Two Countries." VoxEU, March 29, 2017. https://
voxeu.org/article/economic-growth-us-tale-two-countries.

Postol, T. "Russia May Have Violated the INF Treaty. Here's How the United
States Appears to Have Done the Same." *Bulletin of Atomic Scientists*,
February 14, 2019.

Slobodian, Quinn. *Globalists: The End of Empire and the Birth of Neoliberalism*.
Cambridge: Harvard University Press, 2018.

Wester, Philippus, Arabinda Mishra, Aditi Mukherji, and Arun Bhakta
Shrestha, eds. *The Hindu Kush Himalaya Assessment*. Cham, Switzerland:
Springer Nature, 2019. https://link.springer.com/book/10.1007%2F978
-3-319-92288-1.

Wilcox, Fred A. *Scorched Earth*. New York: Seven Stories Press, 2011.

———. *Waiting for an Army to Die*. 2nd ed. New York: Seven Stories Press, 2011.

ACTIVIST/PRACTITIONER INSIGHTS

Lisa Graves, Cofounder, Documented Investigations.

> Described the work of Documented Investigations, which is a watchdog group that investigates how corporations manipulate public policy, harming our environment, communities, and democracy. The presentation focused, extensively and usefully, on the activities of the American Legislative Exchange Council (ALEC) and its activities in furthering the neoliberal agenda.

Chapter 6

COURSE READINGS

Crehan, Kate. *Gramsci's Common Sense: Inequality and Its Narratives.* Chapter 7. Durham and London: Duke University Press, 2016.

Draft for a Select Committee on Green New Deal. https://www.congress.gov /bill/116th-congress/house-resolution/109/text.

Jackson, Janine. "They're Going to Pen You In and Charge You for It." *CounterSpin* interview, October 24, 2018. https://fair.org/home/theyre -going-to-pen-you-in-and-charge-you-for-it/.

O'Connor, James. *Natural Causes: Essays in Ecological Marxism.* Pages 255–65 and chapters 15 and 19. New York: Guilford Press, 1998.

Queally, John. "For Next Weapon in Anti-Protest Arsenal, US Military Building Plasma Gun Capable of Vaporizing Human Flesh." Common Dreams, October 18, 2018. https://www.commondreams.org /news/2018/10/18/next-weapon-anti-protest-arsenal-us-military -building-plasma-gun-capable-vaporizing.

Sunrise Movement (youth organizing to fight climate change). "Statement of Principles." https://www.sunrisemovement.org/principles.

ADDITIONAL CHAPTER REFERENCES

"FBI Documents Reveal Secret Nationwide Occupy Monitoring." Partnership for Civil Justice Fund. http://www.justiceonline.org/fbi_files_ows.

Hall, Stuart. "Gramsci's Relevance for the Study of Race and Ethnicity." *Journal of Communication Inquiry* 10, no. 2 (1986): 5–27.

Newsy. "American Fear Climbs Despite Drop in Violence." YouTube video, 3:14. September 13, 2016. https://www.youtube.com/watch?v =DSwVxl6ABuc.

Rothstein, Richard. *The Color of Law: A Forgotten History of How Our Government Segregated America.* New York: Liveright, 2017.

Zuboff, Shoshana. *The Age of Surveillance Capitalism: The Fight for a Human Future at the New Frontier of Power.* New York: Hachette, 2019.

———. "Once We Searched Google. Now It Searches Us." *Le Monde diplomatique*, January 2019. https://mondediplo.com/2019/01/06google.

ACTIVIST/PRACTITIONER INSIGHTS

Justine Orlovsky-Schnitzler, Media Coordinator, No More Deaths.
Jeff Reinhardt, Volunteer, No More Deaths.

> Presented a history of border militarization, the US government policy of "prevention through deterrence" to brutalize all efforts to cross the US–Mexican border, and the consequences of these actions in terms of enormous numbers of migrant deaths in the desert regions of the Southwest. Described the efforts of No More Deaths (a Tucson-based volunteer organization) to provide humanitarian aid to help mitigate these effects.

Joe Thomas, President, Arizona Education Association.

> Gave an overview of the set of recent strikes across the US by educators, parents, and students to provide adequate funding and working/learning conditions, and placed the Arizona Red for Ed movement into this context.

Chapter 7

COURSE READINGS

Chomsky, Noam. *What Kind of Creatures Are We?* Chapter 3. New York: Columbia University Press, 2015.

Giroux, Henry. "Cultural Studies, Public Pedagogy, and the Responsibility of Intellectuals." PDF file. *Communication and Critical/Cultural Studies* 1 no. 1 (2004): 59–79. https://www.tandfonline.com/doi/abs/10.1080 /1479142042000180926.

Waterstone, Marv. "Smoke and Mirrors: Inverting the Discourse on Tobacco." *Antipode* 42, no. 4 (2010): 875–96.

ADDITIONAL CHAPTER REFERENCES

Bronfenbrenner, Kate. "Organizing in the NAFTA Environment: How Companies Use 'Free Trade' to Stop Unions." Cornell University ILR School, 1997. https://digitalcommons.ilr.cornell.edu/articles/826/.

Dudzic, Mark. "What Happened to the Labor Party?" *Jacobin*, October 11, 2015. https://www.jacobinmag.com/2015/10/tony-mazzochi-mark -dudzic-us-labor-party-wto-nafta-globalization-democrats-union/.

Haag, Pamela. *The Gunning of America: Business and the Making of American Gun Culture*. New York: Basic Books, 2016.

Halpern, Sue. "How Republicans Became Anti-Choice." *New York Review of Books*, November 8, 2018. https://www.nybooks.com/articles/2018/11/08 /how-republicans-became-anti-choice/.

"John Bolton Admits US-Backed Coup in Venezuela Is about Oil, Not Democracy." Telesur, January 30, 2019. https://www.telesurenglish.net /news/John-Bolton-Admits-US-backed-Coup-in-Venezuela-Is-About -Oil-Not-Democracy-20190130-0020.html.

Kilpatrick, Connor. "Victory Over the Sun." *Jacobin*, August 31, 2017. https://jacobinmag.com/2017/08/victory-over-the-sun.

Leonard, Christopher. "David Koch Was the Ultimate Climate Change Denier." *New York Times*, August 23, 2019. https://www.nytimes.com /2019/08/23/opinion/sunday/david-koch-climate-change.html.

———. "Kochland: How David Koch Helped Build an Empire to Shape U.S. Politics and Thwart Climate Action." Interview with Amy Goodman. *Democracy Now!*, August 27, 2019. https://www.democracynow.org /2019/8/27/christopher_leonard_kochland_koch_brother.

Manokha, Ivan. "New Means of Workplace Surveillance: From the Gaze of the Supervisor to the Digitalization of Employees." *Monthly Review*, February 1, 2019. https://monthlyreview.org/2019/02/01/new-means -of-workplace-surveillance/.

Pilger, John. December 16, 2002. http://johnpilger.com/articles/two-years-ago -a-project-set-up-by-the-men-who-now-surround-george-w-bush-said -what-america-needed-was-a-new-pearl-harbor-its-published-aims-have -come-alarmingly-true.

ACTIVIST/PRACTITIONER INSIGHTS

Rudy Balles, Director, Southern Colorado American Indian Movement.

> Presented a very personal and moving account of protest actions in the face of the development of the Dakota Access Pipeline, and described vividly for the class what it means to be on the front lines of nonviolent civil disobedience.

Rodrigo Cornejo, Volunteer, Wikipolitica; Youth political organizer, Jalisco, Mexico.

> Described several political campaigns organized in Mexico to develop an alternative to the established party systems, and presented the class with a useful overview of the successes and failures of the efforts, including a number of quite concrete strategic and tactical insights.

INDEX

ABOUT HAYMARKET BOOKS

Haymarket Books is a radical, independent, nonprofit book publisher based in Chicago. Our mission is to publish books that contribute to struggles for social and economic justice. We strive to make our books a vibrant and organic part of social movements and the education and development of a critical, engaged, international left.

We take inspiration and courage from our namesakes, the Haymarket martyrs, who gave their lives fighting for a better world. Their 1886 struggle for the eight-hour day—which gave us May Day, the international workers' holiday—reminds workers around the world that ordinary people can organize and struggle for their own liberation. These struggles continue today across the globe—struggles against oppression, exploitation, poverty, and war.

Since our founding in 2001, Haymarket Books has published more than five hundred titles. Radically independent, we seek to drive a wedge into the risk-averse world of corporate book publishing. Our authors include Noam Chomsky, Arundhati Roy, Rebecca Solnit, Angela Y. Davis, Howard Zinn, Amy Goodman, Wallace Shawn, Mike Davis, Winona LaDuke, Ilan Pappé, Richard Wolff, Dave Zirin, Keeanga-Yamahtta Taylor, Nick Turse, Dahr Jamail, David Barsamian, Elizabeth Laird, Amira Hass, Mark Steel, Avi Lewis, Naomi Klein, and Neil Davidson. We are also the trade publishers of the acclaimed Historical Materialism Book Series and of Dispatch Books.

ALSO AVAILABLE FROM HAYMARKET BOOKS

Azadi: Freedom. Fascism. Fiction.
Arundhati Roy

Can't Pay, Won't Pay
The Case for Economic Disobedience and Debt Abolition
Debt Collective, foreword by Astra Taylor

Change Everything: Racial Capitalism and the Case for Abolition
Ruth Wilson Gilmore, edited by Naomi Murakawa

Masters of Mankind: Essays and Lectures, 1969-2013
Noam Chomsky, foreword by Marcus Raskin

Night Thoughts: An Essay
Wallace Shawn

Optimism over Despair: On Capitalism, Empire, and Social Change
Noam Chomsky and C. J. Polychroniou

A People's Guide to Capitalism: An Introduction to Marxist Economics
Hadas Thier

The Precipice
Neoliberalism, the Pandemic, and the Urgent Need for Radical Change
Noam Chomsky and C. J. Polychroniou

We Still Here: Pandemic, Policing, Protest, and Possibility
Marc Lamont Hill, edited by Frank Barat
Foreword by Keeanga-Yamahtta Taylor

ABOUT THE AUTHORS

Noam Chomsky is institute professor (emeritus) in the department of linguistics and philosophy at the Massachusetts Institute of Technology and Laureate Professor of Linguistics and Agnese Nelms Haury Chair in the Program in Environment and Social Justice at the University of Arizona. He is the author of numerous bestselling political works, which have been translated into scores of languages worldwide. Among his books are *Who Rules the World?*, *Requiem for the American Dream*, and *What Kind of Creatures Are We?* Haymarket has published twelve of his classic works with new introductions, as well as his books *Masters of Mankind, Hopes and Prospects, Intervenciones, On Palestine, Gaza in Crisis*, and *Optimism over Despair*.

Marv Waterstone is professor emeritus in the School of Geography, Development & Environment at the University of Arizona, where he has been a faculty member for more than thirty years. He is the former director of the University of Arizona Graduate Interdisciplinary Program in Comparative Cultural and Literary Studies. His research and teaching focus on the Gramscian notions of hegemony and common sense, and their connections to social justice and progressive social change. His most recent books are *Wageless Life: A Manifesto for a Future beyond Capitalism* (University of Minnesota Press, coauthored with Ian Shaw) and *Geographic Thought: A Praxis Perspective* (Routledge, coedited with George Henderson).